AJ   Hall   820 9355
bn/h

D1740401

BRITISH TRAVEL WRITERS IN EUROPE 1750–1800

British Travel Writers in
Europe 1750–1800

Authorship, gender and national identity

Katherine Turner

Studies in European Cultural Transition

Volume 10

General Editors: Martin Stannard and Greg Walker

Ashgate

Aldershot • Burlington USA • Singapore • Sydney

Published by
Ashgate Publishing Limited
Gower House
Croft Road
Aldershot
Hants GU11 3HR
England

Ashgate Publishing Company
131 Main Street
Burlington, VT 05401–5600 USA

Ashgate website: http://www.ashgate.com

British Library Cataloguing-in-Publication Data

Turner, Katherine
  British travel writers in Europe, 1750–1800: authorship, gender and national
    identity. (Studies in European Cultural Transition)
1. Travel writing   2. English prose literature – 18th century   3. Europe –
Description and travel – Early works to 1800 I. Title
820. 9'355

Library of Congress Cataloging-in-Publication Data

Turner, Katherine
  British travel writers in Europe, 1750–1800: authorship, gender and national
identity / Katherine Turner
    p. cm. – (Studies in European Cultural Transition; 10)
Includes bibliographical references (p.) and index
1. Travellers' writings, English – history and criticism. 2. English prose literature
– 18th century – History and criticism. 3. British – Travel – Europe – History –
18th century. 4. Europe – History –18th century – Historiography. 5. Travellers –
Europe – History – 18th century. 6. Europe – Description and travel – History. 7.
National characteristics in literature. 8. Sex role in literature. I. Title. II. Series

PR756.T72. T87 2001
828'.60809355–dc21   2001022831

ISBN 0 7546 0242 7

Printed on acid-free paper by MPG Books Ltd, Bodmin, Cornwall

Contents

General Editors' Preface

The European dimension of research in the humanities has come into sharp focus over recent years, producing scholarship which ranges across disciplines and national boundaries. This new series provides a major channel for this work and unites the fields of cultural studies and traditional scholarship. It will publish in the areas of European history and literature, art history, archaeology, language and translation studies, political, cultural and gay studies, music, psychology, sociology and philosophy. The emphasis is explicitly European and interdisciplinary, concentrating attention on the relativity of cultural perspectives, with a particular interest in issues of cultural transition.

Martin Stannard
Greg Walker

University of Leicester

Acknowledgements

I would like to thank the staff of the Bodleian Library, Oxford (especially the long-suffering administrators of the Upper Reading Room) for efficient help over the past few years. Balliol and Wolfson Colleges, Oxford, sustained me during the research on which this book is based, and St Peter's College, Oxford has provided a congenial and supportive atmosphere during the closing stages of writing.

A number of friends and colleagues have contributed in various ways to the emergence of this study. I am enormously grateful to Professor Roger Lonsdale for supervising with characteristic rigour and patience the doctoral dissertation which has gradually developed into the present book. Others to whom I owe thanks for their time, advice and encouragement are Marilyn Butler, Steve Clark, David Fairer, Julia Griffin, Nick Groom, Rohini Jayatilaka, Sian Lewis, Clare Morgan, Francis O'Gorman, David Omissi, Isabel Rivers, Corinne Saunders, Nicola Warrick, and Blair Worden. My anonymous reader for Ashgate made a number of extremely helpful suggestions at an important stage. All errors, of course, I acknowledge as my own. However, my family – travellers all – must share some of the blame for fostering an interest in eighteenth-century travel writing. Finally, Roland Kozlowski has made possible the writing of this book in countless ways.

A version of the section on Montagu and Craven in Chapter 4 has previously appeared in *Travel Writing and Empire: Postcolonial Theory in Transit*, ed. Steve Clark (1999). I am grateful to the editor for permission to reuse this material.

Introduction

This book offers an archaeology of a genre which, although culturally pre-eminent in its day, has fallen victim to the vagaries of canon-building. While most people with a working knowledge of the eighteenth century are familiar with, say, Sterne's *A Sentimental Journey*, Smollett's *Travels through France and Italy*, the Scottish tours of Johnson and Boswell, and (especially in recent years) Mary Wollstonecraft's *Letters Written during a Short Residence in Sweden, Norway and Denmark*, the hundreds of European travelogues produced by less famous, less 'literary' British travellers between 1750 and 1800 remain out of sight in most libraries, and have generally been out of print since the eighteenth century. This neglect is due partly to the ambivalent status of the genre (is it really 'literature'?), and partly to the 'occasional' nature of much of the writing: many important travelogues from the period are by writers active on the fringes of literary culture, or indeed represent the author's only foray into print.

It is, however, puzzling that eighteenth-century travel writing and its lively critical reception is still underappreciated, given recent scholarly interest in issues such as the public/private sphere debate, the emergence of national identity, and the complicated relationship *within* the nation of divisive factors such as gender, class, and region. These are not only topics on which travel writers frequently pass direct comment: more pervasively, they represent areas of cultural and ideological controversy upon which the discourse of travel exercised a significant and widely felt influence, an influence further extended through the energetic reviewing arena of the day. Hence, the following study aims to recreate the world of eighteenth-century travel writing in order to illuminate its central role in shaping Britain's emerging sense of national identity – an identity, moreover, which proves to be more complex and less homogeneous than some recent cultural and historical studies would suggest.

The concept of 'authorship' is important to my investigation: at a time when the practical and financial resources of the book trade were making it increasingly easy and rewarding for both amateur and professional writers to publish, the term 'author' – whether denoting a permanent occupation or an occasional alias – conferred upon a diverse body of men and women the status of authoritative cultural and social commentator, even if only for one print run and a couple of reviews. Travel writing – a genre peculiarly congenial to occasional writers – thus provided a public 'voice' for many otherwise silent citizens.

The lively proliferation of 'authors' during this period relates to the increasing value attached to the notion of British individuality, character, or 'eccentricity'. The reviewing arena in particular celebrates the populous variety of the authorial world throughout these years, even while it attempts to police and discipline its perceived excesses. The developing discourse of national character is inevitably bound up with questions of gender: national and authorial virtue are increasingly projected in terms of appropriately gendered behaviour, for male and female travel writers alike. In turn, gender frequently intersects with class, most obviously in the increasing tendency to denigrate aristocratic travellers as effeminate and celebrate the more manly activities of the middle-class traveller.

These, then – national identity, authorship, and gender – are the central preoccupations of the ensuing study. The remainder of this Introduction will address these interlinked themes in more detail, with reference to recent scholarship which has provided crucial contexts for the present investigation. Of particular relevance are developments such as the rise of middle-class tourism and commercial authorship as mutually enabling factors, and the role of print culture within the formulation of national identity. Later sections of the Introduction will also address the curious absence of much significant travel *poetry* during this time, arguing that between Goldsmith's *The Traveller* in 1759 and the composition of Wordsworth's *Prelude* in 1805, the most powerful literary rendering of travel is to be found in the prose travelogues of the period, which offer a wealth of insights into British identity and its discontents during the formative years with which this study is concerned.

'The English are beyond all doubt the greatest travellers in the world', announces the *Monthly Review* in 1766, 'for in all places on the continent, which are frequented by strangers, we find the number of Englishmen greatly to exceed that of all other nations taken together'.[1] Thirty years later, the *Critical Review* – with the *Monthly*, one of the most powerful cultural arbiters of the later eighteenth century – confirms that 'This may be called the age of peregrination; for we have reason to believe, that the desire of seeing foreign countries never before so diffusively operated'.[2] Consequently, the *Critical* finds itself 'abundantly supplied with narratives of tours', which its reviewers (and those working for its rival publications) diligently appraise and summarize – often with lengthy excerpts – for the benefit of a reading public whose appetite for travelogues was enormous. Particularly after the 1763 Peace of Paris, by which time the physical machinery of travel (road surfaces, vehicle technology, accommodation) had also been dramatically improved, the British began in earnest the process of recreational travel which was to culminate in the mass tourism of the later nineteenth century under the auspices of Baedeker and Thomas Cook.

---

[1] *Monthly Review (MR)*, 34 (1766), 420.
[2] *Critical Review (CR)*, NS 19 (1797), 361.

Not so much the 'Grand Tour' as a variety of shorter, humbler tours offered themselves to the leisured middle classes, for whom the consumption of culture abroad as well as at home was becoming increasingly fashionable. Almost as fashionable was the transcription of one's journey into a publishable narrative, hundreds of which had appeared by 1800. Only a handful of these works were produced by aristocratic Grand Tourists (by whom publication was deemed a vulgar enterprise): the overwhelming majority were by travellers from the ranks of the middle classes, or 'middling sort', ranging from professional writers like Tobias Smollett and Ann Radcliffe, to pseudonymous clergymen like 'Cornelius Cayley' from Leeds, and a host of anonymous 'Gentlemen'. The genre's relaxed formal requirements no doubt contributed to its popularity amongst amateurs. By 1792, the *Critical Review* could pronounce that

> Travels are a species of writing which, besides being particularly easy in point of composition, prove highly gratifying to curiosity. The narratives which have been published of the fashionable Tour of Europe are therefore now become extremely numerous ...[3]

Malcolm Andrews has documented the expanding range of journal-keeping equipment available to the eighteenth-century tourist, including (by the 1780s) notebooks with blank pages divided into columns for dates, place-names, and 'observations'.[4] Virtually all eighteenth-century travelogues took the form of letters or a journal, and could therefore be 'worked up' for publication with minimal effort, especially since the genre's evolving conventions came to associate apparent artlessness with authenticity.

Writers of travels were doubtless motivated by the financial benefits of publication in an increasingly lucrative market, but seem also to have been activated by the opportunity which publication provided for a voice in the discussion of national affairs. Thus, British accounts of Europe and their 'congeneric' forms, or related discourses – literary reviews, philosophy, polemic, fiction, and poetry – afford fascinating and important insights into eighteenth-century culture and its legacy to the Romantic period.[5] But although

---

[3]   *CR*, NS 5 (1792), 294.

[4]   Malcolm Andrews, *The Search for the Picturesque: Landscape Aesthetics and Tourism in Britain, 1760–1800* (1989; repr. Aldershot, 1990), 73–6.

[5]   The term 'congeneric forms' is Peter Hulme's, and has proved particularly congenial to the discourse of travel; see, for example, Sara Mills, *Discourses of Difference: an Analysis of Women's Travel Writing and Colonialism* (1991), 99. Congeneric texts are those which, appearing around the same time as each other, 'cast light by virtue of their deeper similarities, independently of any putative influence' (Peter Hulme, *Colonial Encounters: Europe and the Native Caribbean 1492–1797* [1986], 93). Similarly, Dennis Porter, in *Haunted Journeys: Desire and Transgression in European Travel Writing* (Princeton, 1991) has questioned the usefulness of trying to 'isolate "literary" travel from other kinds', and has instead attempted to recuperate a pre-Victorian sense

a handful of travelogues have entered the canon of eighteenth-century and Romantic literature, we lack a coherent picture of their context, and a proper sense of how representative or innovative they really are. The tendency to focus on a few texts (generally selected because their authors are distinguished in other, more 'literary' forms such as fiction or biography) means not only that many 'minor' texts are almost completely unknown to modern readers, despite their great popularity and influence in their own time: but also that significant exploitations (or subversions) of generic expectations within those travelogues which *have* entered the canon (*A Sentimental Journey* and Wollstonecraft's *Letters* from Scandinavia, for instance) frequently go unnoticed. As Steve Clark has recently argued, the force of travel writing in any given period actually works *against* the critical tendencies of canon-building, since its significance is 'collective and incremental rather than singular and aesthetic'.[6] This study therefore proposes to relate well-known travel writings to their lesser-known textual relatives, to the influential voices of the literary reviews of the day, and to other relevant texts and contexts. Given the paucity of data from lending libraries at this time, and the general difficulty of constructing an empirical reception history, the substantial body of evidence provided by the reviews and the intertextual dialogues between travel writers and reviewers (as well as *amongst* travel writers) offers one of the most effective means of reconstructing the world of eighteenth-century travel writing and its readers.[7] The need for such an investigation comes into sharper focus if we turn briefly to examine critical approaches, to date, towards eighteenth-century travel writing.

The textual records of travel within the British Isles at one extreme, and of exotic and colonial travel narrative at the other, have been well served by recent critical analysis. Malcolm Andrews's *The Search for the Picturesque: Landscape Aesthetics and Tourism in Britain, 1760–1800* (1989) is a wide-ranging and impressive account of the rise of recreational travel within Britain, which Andrews relates not only to practical contingencies such as the difficulty of foreign travel abroad during times of war, but also to powerful cultural factors such as the rise of middle-class leisure and consumerism, and a burgeoning interest in Britain's own historic attractions and picturesque resources: for many Britons after 1760, travelling around their own nation presented a cheaper alternative to foreign travel and a patriotic challenge to the

---

of 'culture criticism', a broader and more fluid exploration of texts and contexts which is free from hierarchies of value (19–20).

[6] Steve Clark ed., *Travel Writing and Empire: Postcolonial Theory in Transit* (1999), 2.

[7] On library borrowing, see Paul Kaufman, *Libraries and their Users: Collected Papers in Library History* (1969), and *Borrowings from the Bristol Library 1773–1784* (Charlottesville, VA, 1960) which suggests that travel books were some of the most frequently borrowed, in Bristol at least.

attractions of Europe. Focusing more on the dynamics of class within the development of British domestic tourism, Carole Fabricant has charted the complex process whereby the growing middle-class practice of visiting the seats of the hard-up aristocracy provided potent imaginary access to prestige and property.[8] She has also demonstrated in some detail how the availability of aesthetic discourse to all 'men' of 'a Polite Imagination' (Addison's influential formulation), enabled the middle classes rhetorically to appropriate great chunks of landscape which were technically the property of the landed classes. Thus, 'the aesthetics of landscape fulfilled important ideological functions, serving to conceal as well as to reveal existing historical realities, and indirectly illuminating certain contradictions inherent in eighteenth-century society'.[9] Likewise shedding light on the class politics of domestic tourism, Anne Wallace, Robin Jarvis and Celeste Langan have explored the increasing popularity during the Romantic period of 'pedestrian' travel within the British Isles, which relates to the growing interest not only in native landscape, but in the social realities of life for the poor and dispossessed.[10]

At the other end of the geographical spectrum, recent years have witnessed an explosion of literary and historical interest in distant voyage and exploration narratives, and the literature of colonialism.[11] However, the post-colonial

---

[8]   Carole Fabricant, 'The Literature of Domestic Tourism and the Public Consumption of Private Property', in Laura Brown and Felicity Nussbaum eds, *The New Eighteenth Century: Theory, Politics, English Literature* (New York, 1987), 254–75.

[9]   Carole Fabricant, 'The Aesthetics and Politics of Landscape in the Eighteenth Century', in Ralph Cohen ed., *Studies in Eighteenth-Century British Art and Aesthetics* (Berkeley and Los Angeles, 1985), 49–81; 53.

[10]   Anne D. Wallace, *Walking, Literature, and English Culture: the Origins and Uses of Peripatetic in the Nineteenth Century* (Oxford, 1993); Robin Jarvis, *Romantic Writing and Pedestrian Travel* (1997); Celeste Langan, *Romantic Vagrancy: Wordsworth and the Simulation of Freedom* (Cambridge, 1995).

[11]   On the opening up of the Pacific world, see J. C. Beaglehole, *The Exploration of the Pacific* (1934; repr. Stanford, 1968); Alan Moorehead, *The Fatal Impact: an Account of the Invasion of the South Pacific, 1767–1840* (1966); Lynne Withey, *Voyages of Discovery: Captain Cook and the Exploration of the Pacific* (1987); *The South Pacific in the Eighteenth Century: Narratives and Myths*, special issue of *Eighteenth-Century Studies*, NS 18 (1994); Rod Edmond, *Representing the South Pacific: Colonial Discourse from Cook to Gauguin* (Cambridge, 1997); Neil Rennie, *Far-Fetched Facts: the Literature of Travel and the Idea of the South Seas* (Oxford, 1995). On the impact of exploration and discovery more generally, see P. J. Marshall and Glyndwr Williams, *The Great Map of Mankind: British Perceptions of the World in the Age of Enlightenment* (1982); Roy Porter and G. S. Rousseau eds, *Exoticism in the Enlightenment* (Manchester, 1990); Douglas Chambers, *The Reinvention of the World: English Writers 1650–1750* (1996). On travel writing and colonialism in the eighteenth century, see Peter Hulme, *Colonial Encounters: Europe and the Native Caribbean 1492–1797* (1986); Mary Louise Pratt, *Imperial Eyes: Travel Writing and Transculturation* (1992). On travel writing and orientalism, with some reference to eighteenth-century beginnings, see Edward Said, *Orientalism* (1978); also Rana Kabbani, *Imperial Fictions: Europe's Myths of Orient* (1986; rev. edn 1994) and Billie Melman, *Women's Orients: English Women and the Middle East, 1718–1918* (1991).

approach has tended, with a few notable exceptions, to mine travel writing for racist and imperialist statements, rather than fully analyse the contexts and strategies of the genre, which actually open up spaces for the articulation of rather more divergent perspectives (related to class, gender, and religion, for example) than the monolithic model of the imperial nation would concede. Recent correctives to this tendency include the collection of essays on *Travel Writing and Empire* (edited by Steve Clark, 1999), some of which owe a theoretical debt to Mary Louise Pratt's ground-breaking study, *Imperial Eyes: Travel Writing and Transculturation* (1992). Pratt influentially showed how the colonial 'fringe' played a central role in the production of metropolitan culture, and *Imperial Eyes* has provided an adaptable model for analysing how 'travel books by Europeans about non-European parts of the world went (and go) about creating the 'domestic subject' of Euroimperialism' (4). This model, invaluable as it has proved in the analysis of race and colonialism, presents, however, too homogeneous a picture of 'Europe' for the purposes of describing the literature of inter-European tourism.

Perhaps surprisingly, Pratt's template for understanding how the 'domestic subject' is constructed through accounts of abroad has not been widely adapted (from a literary perspective) to the contexts proposed here. (Furthermore, Pratt's evidence for reception derives from a limited range of sources, rather than the detailed textual world which this study aims to recreate.) Historians before and after Pratt have, admittedly, made anecdotal use of evidence from travel literature in examining the rise of British nationalism during the eighteenth century, in order to argue, as Linda Colley puts it, that the British 'came to define themselves as a single people not because of any political or cultural consensus at home, but rather in reaction to the Other beyond their shores'.[12] Both Colley and Gerald Newman acknowledge the prime importance of the European 'other', especially the untrustworthy and decadent French and the Catholic bugbear represented by both France and Italy, in this process.[13] And Margaret Hunt has emphasized the role of published material, pointing out that 'print helped order and define eighteenth-century literate people's view of

---

Finally, Inderpal Grewal's study of colonialism and travel within British and Indian culture, *Home and Harem: Nation, Gender, Empire, and the Cultures of Travel* (Durham, NC, 1996), is sensitive to continuity and change between the eighteenth and nineteenth centuries.

[12] Linda Colley, *Britons: Forging the Nation 1707–1837* (1992). See also Raphael Samuel ed., *Patriotism: the Making and Unmaking of British National Identity* (3 vols, 1989) and Jeremy Black, *Natural and Necessary Enemies: Anglo-French Relations in the Eighteenth Century* (1986).

[13] Gerald Newman, *The Rise of English Nationalism: a Cultural History, 1740–1830* (1987). The demonizing of the French has an ancient pedigree, although it had been given fresh impetus by the religious upheavals of the seventeenth century and the Caroline associations with France.

the world and England's place in it'.[14] Such formulations, however, assume a homogeneity which in practice did not exist: for although one might expect eighteenth-century travel literature thus to play a prominent part in shaping British identity, much of it actually resists such a role. The possibilities offered by the genre for the articulation of views shaped as much by specificities of gender, class, profession, religion, and region as by national consensus present more unexpected perspectives on 'abroad', and frequently provide a critique of the illusory domestic coherence which the mythical evils of the 'Other' served to create.[15] Put another way, the example of travel writing provides an important insight into the intermediary factors involved in the production of a national cultural identity, which thus emerges as a more complex entity than some post-colonial formulations of the Euro-imperial subject would acknowledge.[16] In this respect, modern analytical models reproduce (albeit in a less celebratory manner) the tendency of Enlightenment philosophers and historians to downplay national differences in favour of European cosmopolitanism. Gibbon, for instance, announces that it is 'the duty of the patriot to prefer and promote the exclusive interest and glory of his native country: but a philosopher may be permitted to enlarge his views, and to consider Europe as one great republic, whose various inhabitants have attained almost the same level of politeness and cultivation'.[17]

An analytical framework which does accommodate the non-consensual nature of the genre is suggested by Sara Mills's recent study. *Discourses of Difference: an Analysis of Women's Travel Writing and Colonialism*, which appeared just a year before *Imperial Eyes*, in 1991, focuses on nineteenth-century travel narratives, and illuminates the close relationship in imperial discourse between the construction of national and of masculine identity.[18]

---

[14] Margaret Hunt, *The Middling Sort: Commerce, Gender, and the Family in England, 1680–1780* (Berkeley and Los Angeles, 1996), 173. Newman goes further, claiming that English nationalism as it emerged between 1740 and 1789 was largely *created* by writers, especially the disaffected intelligentsia: 'Nationalism is, at the outset, a creation of writers' (87).

[15] See John Brewer's review of Linda Colley's *Britons* in *Times Literary Supplement*, 4672, 16 October 1992, 5–6, 'The Binding of the Free: Creating Great Britain and its Other'.

[16] Tim Youngs, in *Travellers in Africa: British Travelogues, 1850–1900* (Manchester, 1994), 6, observes that 'Studies which assume an undifferentiated imperial centre ... are guilty of creating the very monolith they purport to condemn'.

[17] Edward Gibbon, *The History of the Decline and Fall of the Roman Empire* (6 vols, 1776–88), iii. 633–4).

[18] Nineteenth-century women travel writers, especially within a colonial context, have been well served by scholars in recent years. See Alison Blunt, *Travel, Gender and Imperialism: Mary Kingsley in West Africa* (New York, 1993); Shirley Foster, *Across New Worlds: Nineteenth-Century Women Travellers and their Writings* (Hemel

Mills shows how women writers (both pro- and anti-imperial) struggle to accommodate the conflicting discourses of imperialism and gender, and in doing so expose the unsteady foundations of both. Mills's model can be usefully applied to British accounts of Europe during the eighteenth century, where, as this study will show, class as well as gender destabilizes the discursive structures of British cultural and political superiority.

Elizabeth Bohls's investigation into *Women Travel Writers and the Language of Aesthetics 1716–1818* (Cambridge, 1995) to some extent carries on Mills's exploration of discourse and difference, with reference this time to an earlier period and, generally, a more European arena. Bohls shows with great subtlety and precision how women during the eighteenth century adopted, adapted and interrogated the prevailingly masculine discourse of aesthetic response, in order to expose the harsh ideological foundations of that discourse (which required ruined landscapes, picturesque peasants, and vulnerable females as its objects of contemplation), and to assert alternative modes of perception and social relationship. Brilliantly attuned to the discourse of aesthetics in eighteenth-century writing, Bohls is, however, less interested in the genre and discourses of travel writing, showing, for example, little interest in travel writing between Sterne and Wollstonecraft beyond observing that 'the main current of travel writing still tended toward impersonality' (159), and referring at one point to her core group of travelogues *and* novels as 'eighteenth-century women's aesthetic writing' (10). Her critique is an illuminating one, but does not furnish a satisfactory account of travel writing as a cultural and political force. The same can be said of the various studies of travel literature's influence on other literary forms, predominantly the novel, which have appeared in recent (and not-so-recent) decades, and which effectively relegate travel literature to the status of slave to the master discourse of imaginative prose – a procedure curiously at odds with eighteenth-century reading and critical practices.[19]

An early and notable exception to this critical tendency is Charles Batten's *Pleasurable Instruction: Form and Convention in Eighteenth-Century Travel Literature* (1978).[20] Batten's careful exposition of trends within the genre (such as the increasing tendency to describe manners and customs rather than classical sites) is still a useful guide, and one of the few works to address

---

Hempstead, 1990); Sara Suleri, *The Rhetoric of English India* (Chicago, 1992); Melman, *Women's Orients*; and Grewal, *Home and Harem*.

[19] See Percy Adams, *Travel Literature and the Evolution of the Novel* (Lexington, KY, 1983); Chambers, *The Reinvention of the World*; Michael McKeon, *The Origins of the English Novel, 1600–1740* (Baltimore, 1987); Ian Watt, *The Rise of the Novel* (Berkeley and Los Angeles, 1957).

[20] Charles L. Batten, *Pleasurable Instruction: Form and Convention in Eighteenth-Century Travel Literature* (Berkeley and Los Angeles, 1978).

eighteenth-century travel writing – on Europe as well as further afield – as a distinct literary form. But Batten's valuable formalist analysis of the genre's evolution by definition excludes consideration of the wider social and political issues which, twenty years on, make travel literature so fruitful a territory for critical investigation. A more recent formalist contribution to the field is Chloe Chard's *Pleasure and Guilt on the Grand Tour* (1999), which adds a psychoanalytic dimension to the analysis of eighteenth-century travel.[21] Elegantly executed, Chard's account on its own admission frankly excludes consideration of broader contexts, despite the fact that since *Pleasurable Instruction* appeared eighteenth-century studies have undergone enormous changes. The rediscovery of work by women and other marginalized writers has enabled a significant reorientation of the canon; research into the commodification of culture and the emergent world of print has highlighted the importance of market forces and of cultural fashions; and the active role of literature (both 'high' and 'popular') in helping to construct 'imagined communities' of gender, class and nation has been firmly established.[22] Furthermore, the rapid growth of the public sphere – ' a social space for rational and critical debate' – during the eighteenth century has been credited with powerfully encouraging the emergence of national consciousness.[23] As Benedict Anderson has observed, the expansion of print-capitalism 'made it possible for rapidly growing numbers of people to think about themselves, and to relate themselves to others, in profoundly new ways'.[24] John Moore, author

---

[21] Chloe Chard, *Pleasure and Guilt on the Grand Tour: Travel Writing and Imaginative Geography 1600–1830* (Manchester, 1999).

[22] This is not the place for a full account of works germane to the revising of the eighteenth-century canon. A selective list of works which have played a key role in illuminating the nature of eighteenth-century print and commodity culture may more feasibly be itemized: Alvin Kernan, *Samuel Johnson and the Impact of Print* (Princeton, NJ, 1989); John Brewer, *The Pleasures of Imagination: English Culture in the Eighteenth Century* (1997); Ann Bermingham and John Brewer eds, *The Consumption of Culture 1600–1800: Image, Object, Text* (1995); Margaret Hunt, *The Middling Sort: Commerce, Gender, and the Family in England, 1680–1780* (Berkeley and Los Angeles, 1996). The term 'imagined communities' was coined by Benedict Anderson, *Imagined Communities: Reflections on the Origin and Spread of Nationalism* (1983: rev. edn 1991).

[23] On the now rather disputed notion of the bourgeois public sphere (embodied in coffee houses, salons, newspapers, libraries, book-clubs, popular literature, and so on), see Bermingham and Brewer, *The Consumption of Culture*, 10. Dena Goodman, 'Public Sphere and Private Life: toward a Synthesis of Current Historiographical Approaches to the Old Regime', *History and Theory*, 31 (1992), 2–20 provides a useful overview of recent controversies, essentially arguing that Habermas's bourgeois public sphere still represents a useful analytic category, provided one recognizes that the boundaries between private and public realms remained fluid and were frequently contested. See also Jurgen Habermas, *The Structural Transformation of the Bourgeois Sphere: an Inquiry into a Category of Bourgeois Society*, trans. Thomas Burger (Cambridge, MA, 1989).

[24] Anderson, *Imagined Communities*, 36.

of several accomplished travelogues during the later part of the century, observes in 1779 that the 'unrestrained productions' of the press have 'conveyed to every corner of Great Britain, along with much impertinence and scurrility, such a regard for the constitution, such a sense of the rights of the subject, and such a degree of general knowledge, as never were so universally diffused over any other nation'.[25] Travel writing – the most consistently popular genre of the eighteenth century – likewise played a central role in developing formulations of national identity and comparative constitutional awareness.[26] Kathleen Wilson has recently shown how the newspaper and periodical press, in conjunction with travel literature, were 'instrumental in disseminating a broader consciousness of the significance of Britain's imperial project among an avid public at home'; she has also related the emerging and competitive imperial consciousness to public perceptions of the European 'other' as barbarous or effeminate, and thus as unfit for imperial rule.[27] It is no coincidence that the rise of British nationalism corresponded to the great age of published peregrinations.

And yet European travelogues published by Britons during this period are by no means straightforwardly nationalistic, or consistent in their attitudes to 'abroad'. Indeed, many of them are not even straightforwardly *about* 'abroad', as observations on foreign manners and customs are overlaid with comparative discussions of affairs at home. Although few if any travel narratives fail, in the final analysis, to prefer Britain to the Continent, many nevertheless exploit the genre's potential for social and political critique (whether covert or not). Thus, whilst it is difficult to contest Benedict Anderson's influential assertion that 'regardless of the actual inequality and exploitation that may prevail in each, the nation is always conceived as a deep, horizontal comradeship', I will argue that travel writing often presents a challenge to the discourse of national

---

[25] John Moore, *A View of Society and Manners in France* (2 vols, 1779), i. 399–400. Similarly, the *Critical Review* in 1793 cites the anonymous author of *A Comparative Sketch of England and Italy, with Disquisitions on National Advantages* (2 vols, 1793), who praises the 'extensive circulation of newspapers and other periodical writings which stimulate curiosity, and encourage reading and a spirit of enquiry through all ranks of the people', and which is nowhere more evident than in England. See *CR*, NS 9 (1793), 44.

[26] It has become a commonplace in critical work on eighteenth-century travel writing and fiction to observe that the travelogue was the most consistently popular genre of the century, second only to religious literature in 1700 and only to fiction by 1800. See Batten, *Pleasurable Instruction*, 1. See also Kaufman, *Libraries and their Users* and *Borrowings from the Bristol Library 1773–1784*, for evidence (from library borrowing figures) that travel literature may have been twice as popular as other genres.

[27] Kathleen Wilson, 'Empire of Virtue: the Imperial Project and Hanoverian Culture *c.*1720–1785', in Lawrence Stone ed., *An Imperial State at War: Britain from 1689 to 1815* (1994), 128–64; 136–7.

unity.[28] In a sense, the uneasy relationship between consensus and dissidence becomes a shaping dialectic of the genre, as we shall see.

Scrutinizing another eighteenth-century genre, Markman Ellis has recently demonstrated how sentimental fiction 'consciously participated in some of the most keenly contested public controversies of the late eighteenth century', both through direct reference to particular political and social issues, and through the gradual moulding of readers' political and emotional responses.[29] Ellis argues that the sentimental novel envisaged a readership (largely female and non-property-owning) who were excluded from direct participation in public affairs, but whose increasing engagement with contemporary controversies through the agency of fiction made them an increasingly potent force in the life of public opinion, and especially in the various reform movements (for example, anti-slavery) which came to occupy a central position in politics and culture. The sentimental novel thus 'effectively created a new political role for literature' (3), Ellis claims, a role which empowered the technically disenfranchised.[30] Arguably an over-optimistic view in political terms, this reassessment of the potency of sentimental fiction is nevertheless an important corrective to the prevailing tendency in recent decades to view the genre as little more than the indulgence of middle-class neurosis and economic guilt.[31] However, Ellis perhaps overstates his case when he claims that the sentimental novel was 'the dominant literary form of the late eighteenth century' (2). For travel writing (which shares many formal features and idioms with the sentimental fiction of the period) was a close rival for this position even during the closing decades of the century, and during the 1760s and 1770s it was not only more numerous and popular a genre than fiction, but also provided a paradigm for the model which Ellis outlines, whereby popular literature creates for itself a newly political role.

Furthermore, the influential attention which the review journals devoted to travel literature far exceeded their interest in fiction. While novels received comparatively brief coverage, travel writing was extensively reviewed by the *Monthly* (established in 1749), the *Critical* (founded in 1756), and, after 1788, the *Analytical Review*. Baretti's *Journey from London to Genoa* in 1770

---

[28] Anderson, *Imagined Communities*, 7.
[29] Markman Ellis, *The Politics of Sensibility: Race, Gender and Commerce in the Sentimental Novel* (Cambridge, 1996), 8.
[30] See also Kathleen Wilson, *The Sense of the People: Politics, Culture and Imperialism in England, 1715–1785* (1995; repr. Cambridge, 1998): Wilson looks more broadly at the various forms of 'extra-institutional political culture' which 'created an alternative idiom of political discourse that could be used by a wide range of groups to claim a stake in national affairs' (4).
[31] See, for example, Robert Markley, 'Sentimentality as Performance: Shaftesbury, Sterne, and the Theatrics of Virtue', in Brown and Nussbaum eds, *The New Eighteenth Century*, 210–30.

receives almost thirty pages of coverage in the *Monthly Review* (spread over three months), and almost forty in the *Critical*. As so often with reviews of travelogues, appraisal of and excerpts from Baretti's text rub shoulders with more digressive critical speculations on topics such as national identity, prejudice, and travel's usefulness: the journals came to play an actively prescriptive rather than simply a mediating role in the genre's evolution. Arguably, the anonymity of all book reviews added an aura of objective authority to the journals' pronouncements.[32] Certainly, the generous amount of space which the Reviews devoted to excerpts as well as to appraisal ensured that the developing canon of travel writing reached a far wider readership than would otherwise have been possible: perhaps as much as one-sixth of the reading public had access to one or more review journals on a regular basis.[33]

The notion of a *reading* public is of course central to a study of this nature, and the continuing invisibility of non-literate travellers must here be conceded. The handful of pirate narratives put together from the oral accounts of illiterate sailors, and the case of John Macdonald the footman, are rare records of lower-class travel, which serve really to highlight the difficulty of recuperating such experiences.[34] Macdonald, the son of a Jacobite cattle dealer killed at Culloden, became a postilion and then a footman at a precocious age, and (most unusually) was taught to read by his enlightened Edinburgh employers. In 1790 he published a lively account of his travels in the service of assorted gentlemen around Europe and India, which prompted even the liberal *Analytical Review* to fret that Macdonald's example would 'increase the assurance of footmen'.[35]

---

[32] See Peter Earle, review of James Raven's *Judging New Wealth*, in *Times Literary Supplement*, 4659, 17 July 1992, 22. Earle observes that authors stood 'in awe of reviewers and so were likely to try to write such books as would receive praise. Publishers, too, encouraged authors to write to a formula acceptable to reviewers.'

[33] On the influence of the reviews, see John Brewer, *Party Ideology and Popular Politics at the Accession of George III* (Cambridge, 1976), 154–5; Antonia Forster, *Index to Book Reviews in England, 1749–1774* (Carbondale, 1990) and 'From "Tasters to the Public" to "Beadles of Parnassus": Reviewers, Authors, and the Reading Public, 1749–1774' (PhD diss., University of Melbourne, 1986); Derek Roper, *Reviewing before the Edinburgh, 1788–1802* (1978), especially 19–48; and James G. Basker, *Tobias Smollett, Critic and Journalist* (Newark, 1988). Basker points to a further extension of the reviews' influence through the unsystematic yet widespread network of newspaper piracy of their reviews and excerpts.

[34] See B. R. Burg, *Sodomy and the Pirate Tradition: English Sea Rovers in the Seventeenth Century Caribbean* (1984), 193–209, 'Bibliographical Essay'. See also K. A. Reimann, '"Great as he is in his own good opinion": the Bounty Mutiny and Lieutenant Bligh's Construction of Self', in Alvaro Ribeiro and James G. Basker eds, *Tradition in Transition: Women Writers, Marginal Texts, and the Eighteenth-Century Canon* (Oxford, 1996), 198–218.

[35] *Analytical Review* (*AR*), 8 (1790), 63. See John Macdonald, *Travels in various Parts of Europe, Asia, and Africa* (1790); and my entry on Macdonald, in *New Dictionary of National Biography* (forthcoming, Oxford, 2004).

Eighteenth-century travel writing, then, remains predominantly a middle-class form. However, it was authored by and addressed to a wide range of social groupings, from the élite to the marginalized, and not infrequently articulated the interests or grievances of those who had no direct voice in the public arena.

The reader might be struck by the absence of poetry from the discussion so far. Surely, one might suppose, eighteenth-century travel poetry warrants analysis alongside the prose travelogues which are the main object of enquiry here. In fact, there is quite simply very little of it. The exception which proves the rule is Goldsmith's poem, *The Traveller*. Published in December 1764, it saw four editions before the end of 1765, and six more within Goldsmith's lifetime. It clearly returned an echo to many a traveller's bosom in the following decades; countless prose travel writers, overtly or implicitly, cite from and allude to the poem. Yet Goldsmith seems to have inspired few if any significant or widely popular poetic accounts of Continental Europe in the second half of the century, especially in comparison to the amount of topographical or picturesque verse describing the British Isles at this time.[36] Furthermore, the vigorous and copious cultivation of prose travel narrative as a genre by the main literary reviews does not have a comparable parallel for the verse of the period.

Before Goldsmith, the primary poetic models for European travel had been Addison's *A Letter from Italy* (1703) and Lord Lyttelton's Addisonian verse epistles from abroad (written 1728–30; published 1748).[37] Addison's lament for the decline of the classical world is echoed by many prose narratives of the eighteenth century (though fewer and fewer as the century progresses), and also by a handful of verse responses, such as George Keate's *Ancient and Modern Rome* (1755), which optimistically envisages 'the curious Traveller, who burns / With strong Impatience, by the classic Page / Excited' (ll. 24–6). More influential than Addison's classicism is the Whiggish celebration of British liberty which closes *A Letter from Italy*. This is to become a commonplace of travel writing; but in prose accounts it comes under increasing scrutiny, whereas verse responses to Continental travel more often adhere to the simplistic Addisonian model (which also, of course, finds its way into the so-called 'progress poem', of which Thomson's *Liberty*, Gray's 'The Progress of Poesy', and Collins's 'Liberty: an Ode' are perhaps the best-known mid-century examples). Addison's alliance of classical Roman and British virtue, in opposition to modern Continental despotism, is reiterated in George Keate's

---

[36] See Robert Arnold Aubin, *Topographical Poetry in XVIII-Century England* (New York, 1936).

[37] For Addison, see A. C. Guthkelch ed., *The Miscellaneous Works of Joseph Addison* (2 vols, 1914), i. 48–61. Lyttelton's epistles, *To the Rev. Dr Ayscough* (1728), *Epistle to Mr Pope* (1730) and *To My Lord Hervey* (1730) were first published in Dodsley's *Collection of Poems, by Several Hands* (4 vols, 1748–9).

Ancient and Modern Rome (1755), Eyles Irwin's *Eastern Eclogues* (1780) and his *Occasional Epistles* addressed to William Hayley (1783), some anonymous 'Verses On a Journey from Rome to Leghorn' printed in the *Universal Magazine* (1793), and (albeit transferred to a different location) 'Verses supposed to have been written in the Isle of Cyprus, by the Rev J. Banister' (1793), which laments the Islamic corruption of the ancient island, where once 'Britannia's glorious standards wav'd'.[38]

Goldsmith provided for travellers not only a survey of European landscapes and national characters which encapsulated many previous formulations, but also – and in tension with this expansive and confident analysis of national difference – a more subjective dramatization of the traveller as melancholic exile, the 'houseless stranger' for whom national differences are irrelevant. The poem is addressed to Goldsmith's brother and opens with a description of the reluctant traveller's extensive European wanderings, emphasizing that 'Where'er I roam, whatever realms to see, / My heart untravelled fondly turns to thee' (ll. 7–8). The brother's firmly domestic location ('all the ruddy family around', l. 18) is contrasted with the speaker's 'unceasing' pursuit across Europe, Rasselas-like, of a chimerical 'fleeting good' (ll. 25–6). This mysterious compulsion coexists within the poem with the literally loftier motive of surveying, from an Alpine peak, the vanity of human life, in a spirit of Enlightened observation. The benefits and disadvantages of each part of the globe are summarized in order to illustrate the claim that 'Such is the patriot's boast, where'er we roam, / His first, best country ever is at home' (ll. 73–4). This posture of enlightened cosmopolitanism is, however, undermined by the succeeding sequence of national characterizations: Italy is the land of 'sensual bliss' (l. 124) and decadence, Switzerland of primitive valour but also moral backwardness, and France the 'gay sprightly land of mirth and social ease' (l. 241). Goldsmith's stereotypes echo and are in turn echoed by countless prose travel writers. Especially from the 1760s onwards, however, Goldsmith's evocation of a mysterious solitary wanderer dominates the allusive uses made of the poem, particularly by travel writers of dissident inclinations. Travel writers increasingly tend to stress their isolation, even when their journeys were actually undertaken in company. John Moore and Joseph Baretti, for example, both travelled as tutors to young gentlemen, but neither mentions this in his narrative. Samuel Jackson Pratt in the 1790s describes himself as a 'solitary wanderer' and informs his reader that he always travels with an edition of Goldsmith, 'one of the earliest friends of my youth', in his pocket.[39] Helen Maria Williams reiterates *The Traveller*'s snippets of national stereotyping in her 1786 poem, 'An Epistle to Dr. Moore' (referring to the 'ever-jocund'

[38] *Universal Magazine*, 93 (1793), 68; *GM*, 63 (1793), 358–9.
[39] Samuel Jackson Pratt, *Gleanings through Wales, Holland and Westphalia* (3 vols, 1795), ii. 112; iii. 275.

French and the 'phlegmatic ease' of the Dutch); in her 1798 *Tour of Switzerland*, however, she cultivates instead the pose of the wandering exile at odds with the domestic political culture.[40]

Williams's growing ideological discomfort is adumbrated within Goldsmith's poem, within which tonal and political complexities highlight the problems faced by travellers as they negotiate the relationship between personal and national identity. Quite apart from the self-conscious isolation of the poem's speaker, the structure of Goldsmith's poem is disorientating. The survey of European nations which occupies the central sections of the poem might be expected to make way for a climactic celebration of English liberty – as indeed is the case in Goldsmith's own, earlier essay, *A Comparative View of Races and Nations*.[41] But such a celebration is conspicuous by its absence. This is no doubt due to the dubious resonances of the very term 'liberty' in the later 1760s, indeed its associations with precisely the type of political (specifically, pro-Wilkes) extremism which Goldsmith explicitly repudiates, both in the poem's dedication, and in the lines which lament the decline in British public life:

> That independence Britons prize too high,
> Keeps man from man and breaks the social tie ...
> Ferments arise, imprisoned factions roar,
> Repressed ambition struggles round her shore,
> Till over-wrought, the general system feels
> Its motions stopped or frenzy fire the wheels. (ll. 339–48)

English individualism has had catastrophic results in the political sphere: moreover, the corruption of political life and language has made it impossible for Goldsmith to celebrate British political virtue at the close of his poem, which advocates instead 'That bliss which only centres in the mind' (l. 424), and, in Johnson's words (he supplied the closing lines to *The Traveller*), 'the smooth current of domestic joy' (l. 434). Intense political feeling, paradoxically, has prompted the apparently apolitical, quietist 'subjectivity' which characterizes the poem. However, this very attempt to repudiate the political is ironically impossible: as Richard C. Taylor has recently noted, with reference to Goldsmith's journalism of the 1760s: 'Even the posture of nonpartisanship ... might be interpreted politically: the "extinction of party"

---

[40] 'An Epistle to Dr Moore, Author of a View of Society and Manners in France, Switzerland, and Germany', in *Poems* (1786), 8; 12 (lines unnumbered).
[41] Published in *The Royal Magazine* for June, July and September, 1760. See Arthur Friedman ed., *The Collected Works of Oliver Goldsmith* (5 vols, Oxford, 1966), iii. 66–86.

was one of the stated goals of Bute and the court of George III'[42]. *The Traveller* thus provides a poetic shorthand for a number of tensions which are then worked out with much greater complexity within the prose travel writing of the period: between individual and national identity, patriotism and dissidence, travel and domestic yearning.[43] It is not until Wordsworth's *Prelude* that poetry ventures again into this problematic territory.

Goldsmith's pedestrian wanderer, with his nostalgia for hearth and home, is resolutely non-aristocratic: in this respect again, *The Traveller* functions as a touchstone for prose travelogue. It might surprise some readers to discover how few published travel narratives from the eighteenth century are actually products of the aristocratic Grand Tour. This cultural phenomenon continues to exert a strange fascination, fuelled by lavishly illustrated coffee-table books, historical studies, and art exhibitions, such as the sumptuous display of 'The Lure of Italy' in 1996–7 at London's Tate Gallery. Edward Chaney's recent high-cultural survey of *The Evolution of the Grand Tour: Anglo-Italian Cultural Relations since the Renaissance* (1998) asserts in a slightly cavalier tone that 'There can surely be few topics more worthy of study than the history of how contact with Italy (almost?) civilized Britain and much of its empire, including America' (xi). However, as Ian Christie has pointed out, the Grand Tour was 'an experience undergone by only a small minority, and it was becoming less fashionable after the accession of George III'.[44] Although the numerous letters and diaries from such expeditions which survive in manuscript are a valuable quarry for historians and biographers interested in the English upper-class response to Europe, it is important to register how few Grand Tourists (pitied by Yorick in *A Sentimental Journey* as 'young gentlemen transported by the cruelty of parents and guardians') actually published accounts of their travels.[45] Lord Chesterfield, writing to his son at Rome, remarks that 'Your studies, the respectable remains of antiquity, and your evenings' amusements, cannot, and indeed ought not to, leave you much

---

[42]   Richard C. Taylor, 'The Politics of Goldsmith's Journalism', *Philological Quarterly*, 69 (1990), 71–89. See also Donald Davie, 'Notes on Goldsmith's Politics', in Andrew Swarbrick ed., *The Art of Oliver Goldsmith* (1984), 79–89, who asserts that '*The Traveller* is a fervent apologia for the monarchical form of government' (84).

[43]   On the interplay of cosmopolitanism and 'local attachment' in *The Traveller* and in eighteenth-century thought more generally, see Alan D. McKillop, 'Local Attachment and Cosmopolitanism – the Eighteenth-Century Pattern', in Frederick W. Hilles and Harold Bloom eds, *From Sensibility to Romanticism: Essays presented to Frederick A. Pottle* (Oxford, 1965), 191–218.

[44]   Ian Christie, review of Gerald Newman, *The Rise of English Nationalism*, in *English Historical Review*, 104 (1989), 134–6; 135.

[45]   Laurence Sterne, *A Sentimental Journey through France and Italy by Mr. Yorick* (1768), ed. Gardner D. Stout, Jr (Berkeley and Los Angeles, 1967), 79.

time to write'[46]. Bruce Redford has observed that 'sartorial and linguistic performance', and ostentatious portraits of themselves, were most Grand Tourists' chosen methods of publicizing their travels.[47] In 1766, the *Monthly Review* observes that there are 'but few books of this kind, in proportion to the number of travellers', and explains that 'The reason is plain: our travellers are in general young men of fortune, and are led by their tutors; and both of them, from the youth of one and the narrow education of the other, are as incapable of observation as if they were conducted through France and Italy blindfold'.[48] Some such tutors, however, were better educated than this jibe would suggest, and some of the most accomplished eighteenth-century travelogues (by Patrick Brydone and John Moore, for instance) are by men in this category.

Chloe Chard's recent claim that 'the concept of the Tour ... determines the way in which travel in Europe is envisaged and undertaken from the beginning of the seventeenth century up until 1830 or so', and her elevation of the preoccupations of a privileged élite to a central position in cultural discourse, present a partial view.[49] The non- (frequently, indeed, anti-) aristocratic flavour of much eighteenth-century travel writing can hardly be stressed too much. In this respect, the eighteenth century is not unusual: Steve Clark has observed recently that travel writing 'has taken a mixed and middlebrow form throughout its history ... Anyone can have a go, and usually does'[50]. It is therefore surprising how many otherwise excellent studies of travel writing still tend to overemphasize the Grand Tour component. James Buzard's account of nineteenth-century travel and tourism assumes a pre-1800 landscape of travel writing defined solely by the Grand Tour and its 'overt class and gender prerogatives'; and Dennis Porter is likewise concerned solely with this aspect of eighteenth-century travel.[51]

Increasingly, the middle classes not only dominated the realms of published travel literature, but claimed most insistently to embody Englishness or Britishness, in contrast to the unpatriotic cosmopolitanism of the aristocracy. This site of conflict will be explored in Chapter 1, where the geographical and ideological outlines of the genre will be mapped, and where the intersection of class with gender in national constructions will be described. Here also the discourse of English eccentricity or 'originality' will require analysis, especially as it relates to the increasing tendency from the 1760s onward to inject novelty into hackneyed itineraries by constructing a distinctive narrative

---

[46] Lord Chesterfield, *Letters to his Son and Others*, ed. R. K. Root (1929; repr. 1986), 153.

[47] Bruce Redford, *Venice and the Grand Tour* (1996), 81.

[48] *MR*, 34 (1766), 420.

[49] Chard, *Pleasure and Guilt on the Grand Tour*, 11.

[50] Clark, *Travel Writing and Empire*, 1.

[51] James T. Buzard, *The Beaten Track: European Tourism, Literature, and the Ways to 'Culture', 1800–1918* (Oxford, 1993), 18; Porter, *Haunted Journeys*.

subject. At this point, the vexed question of national nomenclature raises its ugly head: specifically, the extent to which 'English' and 'British' are synonymous. Discussing this same problem, Linda Colley has described the English-Welsh-Scottish composition of Britishness as 'like the Christian doctrine of the Trinity, both three and one, and altogether something of a mystery'.[52] The importance of such 'local distinctions' varied tremendously depending on the context of their use: during the Wilkes controversy, for example, the importance of 'English' liberty as opposed to allegedly pernicious 'Scottish' influence was loudly proclaimed. However, the vehemence of this separatist rhetoric of the 1760s underlines the extent to which, outside the immediate context of political controversy, the terms 'English' and 'British' were becoming interchangeable. Even Tobias Smollett, one of Wilkes's loudest critics and a Scot to boot, describes himself in the *Travels through France and Italy* (1766) as 'a man of a true English character', which he defines as 'soon tired of impertinence, and much subject to fits of disgust'.[53] In general within the discourses of eighteenth-century travel, 'English' and 'British' are deployed synonymously: or, indeed, 'English' (as Smollett's case illustrates) may be applied to a Welsh or Scots person, and notions of English eccentricity or liberty silently appropriated. This semantic vagueness (or, as Paul Langford has recently described it, 'terminological chaos') is hardly surprising in the context of travel writing which is concerned with the European 'other' rather than the regional. As Peter Sahlins has observed, national identity, 'like ethnic or communal identity, is contingent or relational: it is defined by the social or territorial boundaries drawn to distinguish the collective self and its implicit negation, the other.'[54] Langford observes that 'Much of the success of Britishness derived from the way in which it offered a layer of identity compatible with potentially conflicting loyalties. Numerous Scots took advantage of a formula which left them national self-respect while participating in the commercial and professional possibilities of an empire whose metropolis was London, not Edinburgh. So too, did many Irish.'[55] In certain cases, clearly, the specificities of British region *are* significant within a travelogue: thus, whilst I have attempted to impose some kind of consistency in the following study by using the term 'British' wherever possible, I have also endeavoured to remain properly alert to the more complex and significant uses of other terms.

---

[52] Colley, *Britons*, 13.

[53] Tobias Smollett, *Travels through France and Italy* (1766; ed. Frank Felsenstein, Oxford, 1979), 60.

[54] Paul Langford, *Englishness Identified: Manners and Character 1650–1850* (Oxford, 2000), 13; Peter Sahlins, *Boundaries: the Making of France and Spain in the Pyrenees* (Berkeley and Los Angeles, 1989), 271; cited in Colley, *Britons*, 5–6.

[55] Langford, *Englishness Identified*, 13. See also Eric Evans, 'Englishness and Britishness: National Identities *c.*1790–1870', in Alexander Grant and Keith J. Stringer eds, *Uniting the Kingdom? the Making of British History* (1995), 223–43.

As well as exploiting the growing interest in British individuality, which is related to the powerful cultural myth of political liberty, both xenophobic and sentimental travel narratives mobilize the powerful discourse of masculinity in order to bolster their claims to moral and political virtue. Aristocratic travellers are ubiquitously denigrated as 'effeminate', whilst the middling sort stress their own 'manly' Britishness. Chapter 2 will examine a selection of texts from the prolific and argumentative 1760s which present various energetic assertions of national and authorial masculinity. Not surprisingly, formulations of manliness become more complex with the rise of sentimental travel writing – the subject of Chapter 3 – when straightforward aggression and bluster are challenged by the idiom of sensibility. The sentimental traveller's masculinity is asserted not through physical confidence so much as sympathetic eroticism: this, however, risks degenerating into a parody of aristocratic sexual conquest at one extreme, or enfeebled emasculation at another.

Naturally, the increasing prominence of gender as well as class in definitions of national virtue presents particular problems for the small but significant number of women travel writers who begin to publish travel narratives after 1770. From this time, middle-class formulations of national virtue increasingly locate the source and sustainer of morality and patriotism within the domestic sphere, and in the person of the generally stationary wife and mother. Women travel writers are necessarily alert to these pressures, though not always cowed by them, as Chapter 4 will illustrate. The final chapter shows how the intricate literary and ideological fabric of eighteenth-century travel writing is further complicated by cultural shifts and political upheavals during the French Revolution. As early as the 1780s, the increasingly problematic resonances of sensibility (for men as well as women) had meant that narrative whimsy and singularity were becoming suspect: even before the Revolution, eccentricity began to shade into deviance, and the relationship between individual subjecthood and national identity was becoming more problematic. The Revolution injected a specific urgency into these cultural and stylistic developments, which inevitably took on a stronger political colouring after 1789.

The early stages of the French Revolution witness an optimistic re-visioning of national character and affinities: the French appropriation of that great British principle, liberty, prompts a celebration of international sympathies. However, later stages of the Revolution prompt revulsion, and a reinforcement of national stereotypes, particularly that of the free, 'manly' and domestic middle-class British. Travel narratives by men and women during the Revolutionary decade are written from a variety of social and political perspectives, and bring into sharp focus the extent to which accounts of 'abroad' replay domestic controversies. They also intensify the problematic relationship between the individual subject and the nation, which is further complicated by the conflicting claims of solitude and domesticity in the early Romantic era. The intersection of these competing pressures in some transitional texts from the later 1790s is briefly delineated in the Epilogue, which diagnoses and seeks in part at least to explain the eclipse of travelogue after 1800 by more consciously 'literary' forms as the most congenial contexts within which notions of personal and national identity can be explored. Recent reassessments of Romanticism have emphasized continuity with preceding decades as much as revolutionary change, and the trajectory of this study is in sympathy with such rereadings, whilst having as its primary aim the recuperation of a hitherto neglected yet centrally important aspect of eighteenth-century literature and culture.[56]

---

[56] Thomas Woodman ed., *Early Romantics: Perspectives in British Poetry from Pope to Wordsworth* (1998), 2. On continuity between 'eighteenth-century' and 'Romantic', see also Michael Meehan, *Liberty and Poetics in Eighteenth-Century England* (1986) and Marilyn Butler, *Romantics, Rebels and Reactionaries: English Literature and its Background 1760–1830* (1981; repr. Oxford, 1992).

Chapter 1

The world, the texts and the critics

The aim of this chapter is to recreate the geographical, political and cultural contexts within which British accounts of Europe were produced, read and reviewed between 1750 and 1800.

In terms of geographical scope, European travelogue is relatively limited, given that this was an age of increasing global exploration which spawned an extensive literature of its own. However, as the chapter's opening section will argue, the limited geographical scope of the texts with which this study is concerned is inversely related to the genre's wide congregation of authors, and its expansive potential for textual ingenuity. Indeed, while much of the period's literature of voyage and exploration is self-consciously couched in the language of Enlightenment empiricism, that of European travel is markedly more open to the expressive and individualistic possibilities of first-person narrative. These possibilities are further enlarged during the second half of the century, as the classical discourse which had dominated the literature of European travel gives way to less exclusive registers, both reflecting and encouraging the activities of increasing numbers of middle-class travellers in Europe.

Geography is always, of course, bound up with politics, and the political outlines of European travel 1750–1800 will be briefly outlined, showing how events such as the Seven Years War and the French Revolution influenced both the scope and the style of travel writing, prompting travellers to investigate new areas of Europe and to address, for example, the political and affective influence of Rousseau's theories or of Dutch humanitarianism.

Shifting political sympathies during this period are closely related to developing concepts of British national identity. The emergence of the discourse of individuality and eccentricity will be traced in some detail, since it is not only central to an understanding of British travel writing in general, but also, and especially, it is a strongly enabling framework within which otherwise invisible or anonymous writers are empowered to forge an authorial identity. The public literary arena, especially as supervised by the *Monthly* and *Critical* Reviews, is influential in accommodating and even encouraging the cheerful proliferation of distinctively characterized travel writers during the second half of the eighteenth century.

This proliferation is largely a middle-class phenomenon, just as the emergent discourse of national character tends to be appropriated by the middling sort, often in explicit challenge to the perceived effete anonymity of aristocratic cosmopolitanism. The discourse of patriotic middle-class masculinity is just one of a range of discursive registers available to travel writers, which the chapter's closing section will briefly delineate. Travel writing could accommodate a wide range of discourses – for example, those of mercantile common sense, natural history, cultural consumption, valetudinarianism – which, taken together or separately, offered an excitingly wide range of narrative and stylistic options to aspiring writers.

Expanding worlds, expressive possibilities

The global context of British travel during the eighteenth century is vast. Between 1750 and 1800 alone, the known world expanded at a prodigious rate.[1] Cook's comprehensively documented discoveries opened up a new continent and entirely new peoples for Western investigation, provoking religious and philosophical disorientation.[2] Trading interests in India started to put in place the machinery which would eventually underpin the Raj and indeed the British Empire as a whole. Wars were fought in the Americas and the Caribbean, and British investment in the slave trade and its associated profits continued to increase. Related interests meant that the western shores of Africa became increasingly familiar to the British public (although the interior of the dark continent remained largely unknown, as the disbelief which greeted James Bruce's *Travels to Discover the Source of the Nile* in 1790 illustrates). And countries hitherto lurking on the mysterious fringes of civilized Europe became increasingly familiar through the journeyings and publications of merchants into Russia and Turkey, archaeologists into the Mediterranean and Near East, and diplomats, scientists and historians into the remoter areas of Scandinavia, Iberia, and Eastern Europe.

The published literature of such travels – quite apart from more incidental coverage in newspapers, journals and imaginative fiction – was extensive. Even if it was not widely read in its original format (generally heavy and expensive quartos, often sponsored by institutions such as the Admiralty, in Cook's case, or the Society of Dilettanti), its value was acknowledged. Reviewing Hawkesworth's *Account* of Cook's voyages in 1773, the *Critical Review* observes that the work's publication 'under the auspices of government' demands 'more minute examination than is usually exercized by the generality

---

[1] See Glyndwr Williams, *The Expansion of Europe in the Eighteenth Century: Overseas Rivalry, Discovery and Exploration* (1966); P. J. Marshall and Glyndwr Williams, *The Great Map of Mankind: British Perceptions of the World in the Age of Enlightenment* (1982).

[2] J. C. Beaglehole, *The Exploration of the Pacific* (1934; repr. Stanford, 1968); Alan Moorehead, *The Fatal Impact: an Account of the Invasion of the South Pacific, 1767–1840* (1966); Lynne Withey, *Voyages of Discovery: Captain Cook and the Exploration of the Pacific* (1987); Neil Rennie, *Far Fetched Facts: the Literature of Travel and the Idea of the South Seas* (Oxford, 1995); and *The South Pacific in the Eighteenth Century: Narratives and Myths* (*Eighteenth-Century Life* special issue, NS 18 [1994]).

of readers', since the editor has paid 'greater attention to the purpose for which the work might be useful, than to the gratification of general curiosity'.[3] The fact that Hawkesworth was paid a controversial £6,000 may also lie behind this reviewer's stringency.[4] Similarly, the *Critical* in 1769 welcomes an informative account of the Spanish West Indies, declaring that 'We look upon every well authenticated original geographical description, like that before us ... as forming part of a great Mosaic composition, which ... must at last exhibit to us a complete picture, or somewhat very near it, of the terraqueous globe, and consequently interesting to all mankind, but to the learned in particular'.[5] The materials of this 'great Mosaic' were popularized for the non-learned reading public not only through the Reviews, but also by the twenty-five or so multi-volume collections of voyages and travels which appeared during the eighteenth century. In 1777, the *Monthly Review* pronounces one such collection, the *Modern Traveller*, 'well calculated for the million, but particularly for young persons: as no kind of reading is more pleasing, and at the same time more instructive. They may, therefore, with great propriety be given as presents to the younger reader of either sex.'[6] Smollett's *Compendium of Authentic and Entertaining Voyages* (7 vols, 1756) was one of the earliest and most influential compilations, inaugurating 'a succession of concise, orderly, convenient, and inexpensive collections, designed to make these important historical materials available to the mass of readers', which 'gradually reduced the disorderly mass of travel-literature to the form of static, systematized accounts of particular countries'.[7] In these works, it is not uncommon for the original first-person narration to be replaced by an objective third-person (such is certainly Smollett's editorial method), and for all subjective observations and personal colouring to be either removed, or modified into generalizing statements.

This procedure may be related to the Enlightenment impulse, influentially formulated by Foucault, to forge a 'general science of order', bringing together the grammars and discourses of different scientific fields, and constructing a monolithic European centre of knowledge.[8] However, this discursive realm

---

[3]   *CR*, 36 1773, 240, reviewing John Hawkesworth, *An Account of the Voyages Undertaken ... for Making Discoveries in the Southern Hemisphere ... by Commodore Byron, Captain Wallis, Captain Carteret, and Captain Cook* (3 vols, 1773).

[4]   See Philip Edwards, *The Story of the Voyage: Sea-Narratives in Eighteenth-Century England* (Cambridge, 1994), 85.

[5]   *CR*, 28 (1769), 153–4.

[6]   *MR*, 56 (1777), 392.

[7]   Louis Martz, *The Later Career of Tobias Smollett* (New Haven, 1942), 16–17; 9.

[8]   Michel Foucault, *The Order of Things: an Archaeology of the Human Sciences*, (first published as *Les Mots et les Choses* [Paris, 1966], 1970; repr. New York, 1973) 136–7. See also Marshall and Williams, *The Great Map of Mankind*, 50. It should be borne in mind, however, that Foucault's homogenizing argument is somewhat

exists in parallel with a precisely opposite tendency in British travel writing that describes more familiar, European territories. In this branch of the genre narrative ingenuity, even authorial oddity, become crucial components of the text's interest (the full, political implications of this trend will be addressed later in this chapter), and the prevailing tendency is therefore *against* uniformity. Smollett's own *Travels through France and Italy* (1766) offers a well-known example of ill-tempered self-dramatization, a procedure completely at odds with his editorial mode as compiler of collections. Well before 1766, in fact, we find evidence that Smollett had a keen sense of these two distinct modes of travel writing: in 1753–4 (while simultaneously working on the *Compendium*) he edited the first-person narrative of Alexander Drummond's *Travels* within Europe and the Levant, which cultivates a whimsical narrative persona who is sentimentally attached to his pet chameleon (of which he executes a charming sketch, included amongst the otherwise erudite and archaeological plates), and distinguished by an erotic interest in female beauty (whether in the flesh or in the form of antique sculpture). A contemporary reviewer remarks on the surprisingly 'sprightly turns, which one would not expect from a man so much in years as the author represents himself'.[9]

If Smollett's career provides evidence of the genre's twin poles, we find them existing within the same volume in Boswell's *Account of Corsica*, which opens with a compilation of extant writings on Corsica before proceeding to Boswell's own *Journal* of his visit, and the biographical *Memoirs of Pascal Paoli*. Johnson, always alert to the preferences of the common reader, favoured the latter sections: 'Your history [the *Account*] was copied from books; your journal rose out of your own experience and observation. You express images which operated strongly upon yourself, and you have impressed them with great force upon your readers'.[10] In 1771 Charles Burney omitted 'miscellaneous observations' from his *The Present State of Music in France and Italy*, but fleshed out the sequel, *The Present State of Music in Germany, the Netherlands, and United Provinces* (1773) with descriptive passages and

---

undermined (in the case, for example, of Pacific voyage narratives) by the publication of conflicting accounts of the same voyage (most spectacularly in the case of the *Bounty* voyage).

[9]   *MR*, 11 (1754), 211. Smollett was commissioned to edit the *Travels through Different Cities of Germany, Italy, Greece, and Several Parts of Asia, as far as the Banks of the Euphrates; in a Series of Letters* (1754) by Drummond's brother George (Provost of Edinburgh), and paid 100 guineas for the work, which suggests that substantial changes were made. See my entry on Alexander Drummond in *New Dictionary of National Biography* (forthcoming, Oxford, 2004), and G. M. Kahrl, *Tobias Smollett: Traveler–Novelist* (Chicago, 1945), 87.

[10]   James Boswell, *Life of Johnson* (1791), ed. G. B. Hill and L. F. Powell (6 vols, Oxford, 1934–64), ii. 70.

anecdotes of life on the road in European society, including Boswellian conversations with Rousseau and Diderot. This, he says, 'procured me many more readers than mere students and lovers of music'.[11] The *Monthly Review* commends the additional material and observes that 'the present narrative is more connected and *flowing*, as well as more frequently diversified, by the insertion of many observations of a miscellaneous nature'.[12]

The preference of the general reading public for personalized, playfully literary accounts of European travels (which were also smaller and cheaper than the encyclopaedic variety of voyage and exploration literature) is particularly evident once middle-class tourism begins to take off during the 1760s.[13] On a practical level, travel on the Continent became increasingly comfortable in the second half of the century, with improving roads, inns, and means of transport.[14] Ordinary travellers, as well as aristocratic owners of private vehicles, could now travel with reasonable ease and safety, at least in the better-known parts of Europe (Eastern Europe, Iberia and Russia remained dangerous and arduous itineraries, travelled mainly by the well-connected, in possession of letters of introduction to courts along the way). Comparative military calm after 1763 made Continental travel still more appealing. The 1763 Treaty of Paris, although seen as controversial and submissive in some quarters, was broadly welcomed. It not only brought an end to immediate hostilities, but also bestowed immense territorial gains (in the Americas) and international prestige on Britain. So, while the peace made Continental travel physically more feasible, victory rendered it patriotically enjoyable. Travellers of the 'middling sort' explored France and the Low Countries in increasing numbers, and those who could afford it ventured further afield into the German and Italian states. Guidebooks soon appeared to exploit this new gap in the market, both reflecting and influencing the development of certain favoured routes around Europe. If during the first half of the century recreational travel was dominated by the classical Grand Tour, during the second (although Grand Tourists continued their activities) it was appropriated by a far more diverse body of travellers. The middling sort tended to travel with wives, families and colleagues, and thus presented a different ensemble from the hierarchical and

---

[11]   Percy A. Scholes ed., *Dr Burney's Musical Tours in Europe* (2 vols, 1959), i. xxx.

[12]   *MR*, 48 (1773), 458.

[13]   Most of the travel narratives featured in this study were published in octavo or duodecimo, and would have cost between one and ten shillings. The growth of circulating libraries and book clubs, as well as the extensive publication of excerpts in reviews and newspapers, further complicates and extends the availability of travel literature for the reading public.

[14]   See Charles L. Batten, *Pleasurable Instruction: Form and Convention in Eighteenth-Century Travel Writing* (Berkeley and Los Angeles, 1978), 2; Jeremy Black, *The British and the Grand Tour*, (1985), 38–87.

masculine make-up of the aristocrat's travelling household, which would have included his tutor and an array of servants.

This mid-century change in the social make-up of European tourists is naturally reflected in the literary discourses which dominate published travelogues. Until around 1750, the discursive fields of travel literature were overwhelmingly masculine and, generally (at least in European contexts), classical. Richard Lassels, in the 'Preface' to *The Voyage of Italy* (1670), to which many later travellers refer, declares that 'I write to young men, and for them'; and, rhetorically anticipating a reader's objection 'that I fill my booke with too much *Latin*', he points out 'that I am writing of the *Latin* country; and that I am carving for *Schollers*, who can digest solid bitts, having good stomacks'.[15] Classic learning and classic ground are the central concerns. In similar vein was Addison's *Remarks on Several Parts of Italy* (1705), which rapidly became the most popular and influential eighteenth-century travel book, running to at least thirteen editions before 1800. (Revealingly, however, ten of these are before 1770, and the three further editions between 1770 and 1800 all appear within collections of canonized travel writings.) The 'Preface' to *Remarks* outlines the classical procedure, as Addison explains that

> before I entered on my voyage I took care to refresh my memory among the *Classic* Authors, and to make such collections out of them as I might afterwards have occasion for. I must confess it was not one of the least entertainments that I met with in travelling, to examine these several Descriptions, as it were, upon the spot, and to compare the natural face of the country with the Landskips that the Poets have given us of it.[16]

As one might expect from the future *Spectator* writer, Addison also pays some attention to 'manners', but in a curiously schematic and unobservant fashion. He commends Italian sobriety and the airy humour of the French, but describes no individuals or personal encounters. Characterizing the Genoese, Addison observes that 'while the Barrenness of their country continues', the 'Manners of the inhabitants do not change': he therefore cites from the *Aeneid* to illustrate these, charmingly translated as follows: 'Yet, like a true *Ligurian*, born to

---

[15] Richard Lassels, *The Voyage of Italy ... with Instructions concerning Travel* (1670), 'A Preface to the Reader, concerning Travelling' (fonts reversed, pages unnumbered).

[16] Addison, *Remarks on Several Parts of Italy, &c. In the Years 1701, 1702, 1703* (1705); in A. C. Guthkelch ed., *Miscellaneous Works* (2 vols, 1914) ii. 18 (fonts reversed). C.f. *Spectator*, 364 (28 April 1712), in which Steele discusses the uses and abuses of the Grand Tour, and highlights as one of the few worthwhile purposes of travel 'the Improving our Taste of the best Authors of Antiquity by seeing the Places where they lived, and of which they wrote; to compare the natural Face of the Country with the Descriptions they have given us, and observe how well the Picture agrees with the Original' (*The Spectator*, ed. Donald F. Bond [5 vols, Oxford, 1965], iii. 369).

cheat' (*Remarks*, 22–3). Horace Walpole in 1740 complained that 'Mr Addison travelled through the poets, and not through Italy; for all his ideas are borrowed from the descriptions, and not from the reality'.[17] Classical citation functions as a shorthand for visual description, as in this passage: 'I shall conclude this chapter with the descriptions which the *Latin* Poets have given us of the *Apennines*. We may observe in them all the remarkable qualities of this prodigious length of mountains' (*Remarks*, 191). And even when, unsurprisingly, a landscape has somewhat altered since classical times, Addison will insert a nostalgic reference regardless:

> As for the thick woods, which not only *Virgil* but *Homer* mentions, in the beautiful description that *Plutarch* and *Longinus* have taken notice of, they are most of them grubbed up since the promontory has been cultivated and inhabited, though there are still many spots of it which show the natural inclination of the soil leans that way. (*Remarks*, 135)

Nature and Homer were, he found, the same.

This classical nostalgia is a powerful presence in eighteenth-century literature, not only that of travel: Gibbon's account of the conception of *Decline and Fall* is perhaps the best known example. Malcolm Andrews notes the essentially moral thrust of the classic response to ancient sites, particularly ruins, which raise ideas of past human glory, only to usher in reflections on mutability. In contrast, travellers during the second half of the century (of whom Gibbon is certainly not typical) 'would be less inclined to *interpret* than to indulge random melancholic associations or admire the rugged contours of broken masonry and the mixed tints of lichen and moss'.[18] The picturesque response requires a less erudite frame of reference than that of classical nostalgia (Addison rarely translates his Latin quotations). The discourse of aesthetics was popularized by Addison's 'Pleasures of Imagination' essays in the *Spectator* – ironically, given the later divergence of the classical and aesthetic discourses. Although it was actually grounded in exclusivities of class, gender, and wealth, aesthetic discourse was appropriated by a broader social spectrum of travellers, for whom it provided a far more accessible discursive framework than that provided by the classics. Burke's refinement of

---

[17] Letter to West, 2 October 1740. *Horace Walpole's Correspondence*, ed. W. S. Lewis (48 vols, New Haven and Oxford, 1937–83), xiii. 231. Similarly, the *Monthly Review* in 1775 criticizes Richard Twiss (author of *Travels through Portugal and Spain*) as 'too apt', like Addison, 'to shew his reading and happy recollection, rather than his own observations; in aid of which, QUOTATION is too often dragged in' (*MR*, 53 [1775], 195).

[18] Malcolm Andrews, *The Search for the Picturesque: Landscape Aesthetics and Tourism in Britain, 1760–1800* (1989; repr. Aldershot, 1990), viii; see also 39–66.

Addison's categories also made available to the reading public a vocabulary of affective response dependent more upon Milton and mountains than upon Homer and Longinus, in the *Philosophical Enquiry into the Origin of our Ideas of the Sublime and Beautiful* (1757). And travellers were increasingly able to find aesthetic touchstones in the visual picturesque of Claude and Rosa (as popular prints circulate in increasing numbers), as well as the Gothic poetry of Gray, Akenside and the Wartons. Virgil and Homer retreat.

The fall from grace of the classical discourse of travel is irreverently reflected in Sterne's mockery in *Tristram Shandy* of 'the great Addison who did it with his satchel of school-books hanging at his a—'.[19] In 1775–6, Richard Chandler's massive record of archaeological research (sponsored by the Society of Dilettanti), *Travels in Asia Minor*, receives extensive coverage in the reviews, but the *Critical* acknowledges (not without a certain whiff of superiority) that there will be limits to its appeal:

> Such readers as have any taste for contemplating the remains of Grecian magnificence, will peruse this work with a degree of enthusiastic pleasure known only to those who are conversant with the venerable subjects of classic learning ...[20]

As this remark suggests, the expansion of the reading public beyond the classically educated classes was an important factor in the changing directions of travel writing. Growing public interest in more Whiggish aspects of commercial and political culture also undermined the pre-eminence of the classical perspective. As early as 1731 the *Gentleman's Magazine* announced that the 'rational Design of Travelling' is 'to become acquainted with the Languages, Customs, Manners, Laws and Interests of foreign Nations; the Trade, Manufactures, and Produce of Countries; the Situation and Strength of Towns and Cities'.[21] A similar recipe is prescribed as late as 1760 in Johnson's *Idler*, which observes that 'He only is a useful traveller who brings home something by which his country may be benefited. He that would travel for the entertainment of others, should remember that the great object of remark is human life. Every nation has something peculiar in its manufactures, its works

---

[19] Editions of Addison's *Remarks* appeared in 1705, 1718, The Hague 1718, 1726, 1733, 1745, 1748 (in Somers's tracts, vol. i), Glasgow 1755, 1761, 1767, 1778 (in *The World Displayed*, vol. xix), 1785 (in *A New and Complete Collection of Voyages and Travels*), 1797 (in William Mavor, *An Historical Account*, vol. xii). For Sterne's satiric portrait, see *The Life and Opinions of Tristram Shandy, Gentleman* (1760–67), ed. Ian Campbell Ross (Oxford, 1983), 388.
[20] *CR*, 42 (1776), 193–4.
[21] *GM*, 1 (1731), 321.

of genius, its medicines, its agriculture, its customs, and its policy'.[22] By the 1770s, however, accounts of 'human life' have increasingly begun to privilege the more sociable areas of 'manners and customs'. Although these had been included in earlier travellers' accounts, they become a central rather than ancillary feature of travel writing during the later eighteenth century. Much attention is paid to sexual morals, the status of women (with nuns and courtesans featuring heavily in many discussions of foreign mores), and social institutions like schools, hospitals, and charities. These changing preoccupations relate of course to the growing cultural influence of sensibility, which dictates increasingly that the virtues and vices of societies and nations can be plotted along a social and sexual, rather than high political, axis.[23]

All of these developments mean that travel writing increasingly accommodates the casual, humble and amateur tourist, as well as the educated and professional classes, and authors by trade – like Sterne and Smollett – who appreciate the lucrative potential of the genre. Travelogues proliferate during the late 1760s and the 1770s, initially to the delight of the Reviews, but eventually prompting a certain weariness with repetitive accounts of the beaten track of Europe. In 1776, the *Critical Review* is moved to make the following complaint:

> Every one that goes abroad, now a-days, whether for health, or pleasure, for idleness or business, seems to think themselves called upon by the public, to render it a minute account of their occupations, avocations, observations, and lucubrations, during their pilgrimage. Nay some, I have been informed, have so well prepared themselves for this work, before hand, that they have written half their book ere they set out, in order to save themselves the trouble of lugging the one they had copied from, about with them, from stage to stage. One person, I was assured, deferred his journey, for a twelvemonth, till he had finished his travels.[24]

Serendipitously, just as reviewers and readers alike are beginning to weary of the predictable itineraries, observations, and sentiments of middle-class travel writing, the map of Britain's European sympathies is dramatically reorientated. In 1778, France joined the American rebels, and war was declared. Between then and the 1783 Treaty of Versailles, as with the earlier period of the Seven Years War, 1756–63, opportunities for European travel were drastically reduced on a purely practical level, and it became once again ideologically problematic to lavish attention on the national enemy. The book

---

[22] *Idler*, 97, 23 February 1760, in Samuel Johnson, *'The Idler' and 'The Adventurer'*, ed. W. J. Bate, John M. Bullitt and L. F. Powell (New Haven, 1963), 300.
[23] See G. J. Barker-Benfield, *The Culture of Sensibility: Sex and Society in Eighteenth-Century Britain* (Chicago, 1992).
[24] *CR*, 42 (1776), 196.

trade responded with some ingenuity to these developments. Old works were reissued with altered titles possibly designed to swindle collectors of European travel writing.[25] Less duplicitously, a number of travelogues which had been written before hostilities broke out were published after 1778, and gained a poignant irony from their tardiness. John Moore's *A View of Society and Manners in France, Switzerland, and Germany* (2 vols, 1779), for example, contains an intelligent discussion of the likelihood of war with France, and includes an appeal to his correspondent (a Member of Parliament): 'for heaven's sake do you and your friends in parliament fall on some measure to prevent [the French] from engaging the affections of our industrious brethren of America' (ii. 435–6). An interesting counterpoint to Moore's account is William Jones's *Observations in a Journey to Paris*, published in 1777 (2 vols); Jones envisages the French rather than the Americans as 'brethren' of the English, and pleads for the avoidance of war. His text is peppered with sympathetic portraits of French individuals, and urges that 'especially at this time, when, having many and dangerous, and *unnatural* enemies at a distance, (which are even worse than the *natural*) it would be good for us to find as many friends as we can near at home' (ii. 106).

As it turned out, English travellers did indeed cultivate European friends during the ensuing years, but not in France. The period 1778–83 sees a large number of publications on parts of Europe beyond the now stale itineraries of France and Italy. Travel literature of the 1780s and 1790s is not only concerned to map new territories for investigation into natural history, manners and customs: there is also a marked tendency to establish new commercial, cultural and political affinities between Britain and newly interesting countries. Particularly in the wake of the French alliance with America, which profoundly disorientates international affinities, travel writers give voice to the British public's interest in redefining national sympathies and national character.

The expanded horizons of Continental travel reinvigorate travel literature during this transitional period between the sentimental era and that dominated by the French Revolution. Also during the 1770s, the British Isles become a practical and fashionable alternative to Continental travel: Gilpin's

---

[25] For example, Samuel Paterson's *Another Traveller!* (1768–9) is reissued in 1782 as *An Entertaining Journey to the Netherlands* (3 vols); Philip Thicknesse's *Useful Hints to those who make the Tour of France* (1768) reappears in 1782 as *Useful Hints to those who travel into France or Flanders, by the way of Dover, Margate, and Ostend.* Nathaniel Wraxall's *A Tour through the Western, Southern, and Interior Provinces in France* was published in 1784, and professes to describe those parts of France not 'usually trod by the English in their passage from Calais to Italy' (205); this was only possible since Wraxall is describing a journey made well before the war, and indeed the *Tour* is silently lifted from an earlier historical work of Wraxall's, *Memoirs of the Kings of France of the Race of Valois* (1776). No doubt the difficulty of access to France for several years previously made his account especially marketable in 1784.

Observations and Pennant's *Tours* appear during these years, establishing once and for all the picturesque and natural historical credentials of the British landscape.[26] Ireland, hitherto largely ignored, is described in various historical and topographical works in the early 1780s.[27] The more distant parts of the Continent offered a rich source of novelty: accounts of Spain, Sicily, Scandinavia and Russia appear in more substantial numbers during the 1780s, and are welcomed by the reviewers.[28] John Talbot Dillon's *Letters from an English Traveller in Spain, in 1778, on the Origin and Progress of Poetry in that Kingdom* (1781) presents Spain and Spanish literature as newly classic ground, and a rich source of comparative information for those interested in the native ballad traditions which Thomas Percy had recently researched and popularized (indeed, Percy corresponded briefly with Dillon on his Iberian discoveries).[29] More prosaically, Joseph Townshend's *Journey through Spain in the Years 1786 and 1787, with particular Attention to the Agriculture, Manufactures, Commerce, Population, Taxes and Revenue of that Country* (1791), whose Whiggish economic interests are weightily signified in this title, concludes with a grand vision of a Spain liberated from Roman Catholicism, despotism and trade restrictions, and enjoying a full and mutually beneficial 'commercial intercourse' with England (352–6).[30] Hardly realistic, Townshend's hopes nevertheless reflect contemporary British desires for new and empowering European alliances.

---

[26]   See Andrews, *Search for the Picturesque*, 241–7.

[27]   For example, Arthur Young's *A Tour in Ireland* (1780); an anonymous *History of the Political Connection between England and Ireland, from the Reign of Henry II to the Present Time* (1780); and an anonymous *Tour through Ireland* (also 1780).

[28]   On Spanish travels, see Ana Clara Guerrero, 'British Travellers in Eighteenth-Century Spain', *Studies in Voltaire and the Eighteenth Century*, 305 (1992), 1632–5. Henry Swinburne published *Travels through Spain, in the Years 1775 and 1776* in 1779, and *Travels in the two Sicilies in the Years 1777, 1778, 1779, and 1780* (2 vols, 1783–5). Accounts of northern Europe which appeared at this time include William Coxe, *Travels into Poland, Russia, Sweden, and Denmark. Interspersed with Historical Relations and Political Inquiries. Illustrated with Charts and Engravings* (2 vols, 1784), and Matthew Consett, *A Tour through Sweden, Swedish-Lapland, Finland and Denmark. In a Series of Letters, illustrated with Engravings* (1789). In 1775 appeared Jane Vigor's account of a residence in Russia, *Letters from a Lady* (1775), followed by John Richard, *A Tour from London to Petersburgh* (1781) and *Anecdotes of the Russian Empire. In a Series of Letters* (1784), by a 'Mr Richardson', who attended 'lord C——'.

[29]   See my entry on Dillon in *New Dictionary of National Biography*.

[30]   C.f. *Analytical Review* (*AR*), 5 (1789), 298, where Spain, 'this noble nation', is envisaged as 'about to rise, like a phoenix from her own ashes' into a new golden age of agricultural and commercial prosperity; and *MR*, NS 1 (1790), 13, where Spain is praised for having started to participate in 'that general diffusion of knowlege [*sic*] which so peculiarly distinguishes the present age', as the recent 'appearance of several volumes of travels' confirms.

Because of the higher costs and more difficult nature of journeys to remoter European regions, such tours were often undertaken less by the casual tourist than by more specialized professionals from the ranks of the middling sort, like natural historians, merchants or diplomats; even on occasion by aristocrats seeking to reinforce the exclusivity of the Grand Tour by relocating it to more exotic arenas.[31] Yet the middle-class tourist penetrates some surprisingly far-flung and inhospitable areas. Switzerland, which had remained neutral during the war and which by now offered the added attractions of Rousseauistic associations, becomes a particularly popular destination, remaining so well into the next century (when the spiritual as well as physical exertions demanded by mountaineering enhance its attractions for muscular British Christianity and the Humeian atheism of Leslie Stephen alike).[32]

The unique scenery and equitable government of Switzerland had long been noticed by British travellers en route to Italy, some of whom (including Boswell, John Moore, and William Coxe) had also visited Rousseau and Voltaire in exile there. (Not everyone was enthusiastic about such encounters with these 'comets in the moral world', who were seen as 'dangerous even for their abilities'.)[33] It is only in the later 1770s, however, that Switzerland comes into its own as the main subject of travel narratives. In 1779, William Coxe published his learned yet anecdotal *Sketches of the Natural, Civil, and Political State of Swisserland*, which saw a second edition in 1780 (and which the young Wordsworth carried with him as the guide for his Alpine itinerary in 1790).[34] Also in 1779, John Moore published *A View of Society and Manners in France, Switzerland, and Germany*, which although only partially concerned with Switzerland was influential in dignifying Swiss travel. Between 1779 and the end of the century, many works on Switzerland appeared, ranging from anecdotal observations, to guidebooks, to weighty folio collections of annotated plates, often translated from the French. Coxe himself in 1789 published a

---

[31] This may be seen to culminate in the Eastern movement of the aristocratic Grand Tour, which during the late eighteenth and early nineteenth century becomes intricately involved with Romantic Hellenism. See David Constantine, *Early Greek Travellers and the Hellenic Ideal* (Cambridge, 1984); also Robin Jarvis, *Romantic Writing and Pedestrian Travel* (1997), 17, on the 'downclassing' of the European Grand Tour which provoked the landed classes to decamp 'in search of more exclusive destinations'.

[32] See Francis O'Gorman, '"The Mightiest Evangel of the Alpine Club": Masculinity and Agnosticism in the Alpine Writing of John Tyndall', in Andrew Bradstock, Sean Gill, Anne Hogan and Sue Morgan eds., *Masculinity and Spirituality in Victorian Culture* (2000), 134–48.

[33] *A Letter to a Young Nobleman Setting out on his Travels* (1776), 23n. On the historically amicable relationship between Britain and Switzerland, see Mavis Coulson, *Southwards to Geneva: 200 Years of English Travellers* (Gloucester, 1988), 1–49; see also John Wraight, *The Swiss and the British* (Salisbury, 1987).

[34] See Duncan Wu, *Wordsworth's Reading 1770–1799* (Cambridge, 1993), 40. Wordsworth used the French translation of Coxe.

huge, three-volume quarto *Travels into Switzerland*, in which his own observations are supplemented from numerous other erudite sources in French, German and Latin. In 1792 the *Analytical Review* remarks with an air of understated exhaustion that 'Of tours in Switzerland we have lately had no small number'.[35]

Coxe's *Sketches* generated much critical interest in 1779, with reviewers commending his descriptions of 'the awful sublimity of this wonderful landscape' (*Sketches*, 15), as well as his accounts of Swiss politics and pastoral virtue. He is in general a staid and unforthcoming narrator, but he occasionally derives a 'sort of melancholy pleasure' in losing himself among nature's 'most awful and tremendous forms' (143). His most important contribution to the representation of Switzerland in British travel writing is his dynamic account of its political history. Switzerland's Protestant resistance to tyranny had for at least a century provoked the admiration of the British;[36] but it becomes peculiarly attractive to travellers during the late 1770s and the 1780s. 'Every step we now advance is treading, as it were, upon sacred ground', Coxe declares, 'as monuments continually occur of those memorable battles, by which the Swiss rescued themselves from oppression, and secured the enjoyment of their invaluable freedom' (129). The *Sketches* effectively 'classicize' Swiss politics and landscape, constructing Switzerland as a parallel inheritor, with Britain, of ancient Roman virtues which are overlaid on a native tradition of insular integrity guaranteed by Britain's literal insularity, and Switzerland's mountainous encirclement.[37] Arriving in Switzerland, Coxe feels 'great pleasure in breathing the air of liberty' (5), and exclaims 'I could almost think, for a moment, that I am in England' (6).

Another feature of the classicizing of Switzerland is the canonizing of Rousseau. For all the vilification heaped upon his personal eccentricities by the 1770s, Rousseau's celebration of Swiss landscape as a setting for human passion and noble sentiment is cited with increasing fervour. Coxe refers his reader to *La Nouvelle Héloïse* as if it were a travel guide: 'The beauties and varieties of this country you will find amply and faithfully delineated in that elegant letter of the *Nouvelle Heloise*, where St Preux relates his excursion into the upper Vallais' (220). Indeed, Coxe himself borrows the novel from a circulating library in Lausanne, and take it with him 'all the way I passed, examining the position of the country, and comparing it with the descriptions

---

[35] *AR*, 13 (1792), 479.

[36] See, for example, George Keate's enthusiastic *A Short Account of the Ancient History, Present Government, and Laws of the Republic of Geneva* (1761).

[37] The Swiss tendency to local attachment and homesickness, or 'Heimweh', was a well established cultural belief long before Coxe: see Alan D. McKillop, 'Local Attachment and Cosmopolitanism: The Eighteenth-Century Pattern', in Frederick W. Hilles and Harold Bloom eds, *Sensibility to Romanticism: Essays presented to Frederick A. Pottle* (Oxford, 1965), 191–218.

by that celebrated author'; he finds the scenery 'strongly marked' with the 'passions of love and despair' of St Preux and Julia (263–4). John Moore likewise traces the movements of the lovers, and finds 'the identical place where St. Preux sat with his telescope to view the habitation of his beloved Julia', declaring that 'Every circumstance of that pathetic story came fresh into my mind. I felt myself on a kind of classic ground' (*A View of Society and Manners in France, Switzerland, and Germany*, i. 255–6). Percy Bysshe Shelley in 1815 is by no means the last in this line of Rousseau enthusiasts, avidly reading *La Nouvelle Heloise* on the spot and remarking with some ambivalence that 'At least the inhabitants of this village are impressed with an idea, that the persons of that romance had actual existence'.[38]

Such reactions dignify not only the settings of Rousseau's works, but the affective responses they provoke in the traveller, which are described with increasing frequency from the 1780s onwards. In 1793 we find even the staid botanist, James Edward Smith ('Linnaean Smith' to his admirers) visiting the scenes of Rousseau's life. Echoing Moore, he pronounces that 'This indeed is classic ground. We could scarcely tear ourselves from it' (but he manages nevertheless to prise a piece of moss from Rousseau's tomb for a souvenir).[39] One might expect the example of *La Nouvelle Héloïse* to have encouraged stylistic vivacity and individuality; in fact, repetitive conformity seems to have ensued. By 1798, Helen Maria Williams observes of the countryside around Vevey that 'It would be hopeless to attempt a new sketch of these enchanting regions after the glowing description of Rousseau, which has already been so often detailed by the hundred sentimental pilgrims, who with Heloise in hand, run over the rocks and mountains to catch the lover's inspiration'.[40] Nevertheless, Shelley as late as 1815 is still running enthusiastically over rocks and mountains, pronouncing his journey to Vevey 'on every account delightful, but most especially, because I then first knew the divine beauty of Rousseau's imagination, as it exhibits itself in Julie' (107), and reporting, rather insanely, that 'We gathered roses on the terrace, in the feeling that they might be the

---

[38] Mary Shelley, *History of a Six Weeks' Tour through a Part of France, Switzerland, Germany, and Holland: with Letters descriptive of a Sail round the Lake of Geneva, and of the Glaciers of Chamouni* (1817), supplementary 'Letter III', 127–8, 131.

[39] James Edward Smith, *A Sketch of a Tour on the Continent* (3 vols, 1793), i. 103. C.f. Helen Maria Williams in 1798, 'The country around Vevay, where Rousseau has placed the scene of his charming romance, is become classic ground' (*A Tour in Switzerland*, ii. 179).

[40] Helen Maria Williams, *A Tour in Switzerland* (2 vols, 1798), ii. 179. James Buzard has observed how tourists following in Byron's footsteps during the early nineteenth century could experience a 'gratuitous sense of liberation in individual consciousness', whilst in fact being ushered along a production line of 'the same holiday routine'. See James T. Buzard, *The Beaten Track: European Tourism, Literature, and the Ways to 'Culture', 1800–1918* (Oxford, 1993), 130.

posterity of some planted by Julia's hand' (133). Mary Shelley's account of the same itinerary is, by contrast, notable for its lack of reference to Rousseau, and it seems likely that her husband's slightly outdated effusions are implied in her prefatory apologies for the 'enthusiasm of youth' which characterizes the ensuing account of 'scenes which are now so familiar to our countrymen, that few facts relating to them can be expected to have escaped the many more experienced and exact observers, who have sent their journals to the press' (iii).

If this insistence on Switzerland's 'classic' status is becoming tedious by the 1790s, readers could choose to discover instead (rather more surprisingly) the newly appreciated attractions of the Low Countries, which had likewise hitherto been little more than a staging post on the way to more appealing destinations. Ann Radcliffe observes in 1794 that the town of Nimeguen is 'classic ground to those, who venerate the efforts, by which the provinces were rescued from the dominion of the Spaniards'.[41] Admittedly, this may have been something of a fringe interest: but the Low Countries, for various reasons (not least their accessibility, but also perhaps their declining maritime power, which made them less of a threat), became a popular destination, and the theme of many travel accounts in the 1780s and 1790s. In 1790 their aesthetic potential, slightly improbably, is realized in Samuel Ireland's *Picturesque Tour through Holland, Brabant, and Part of France*. 'We should as soon have thought of making a picturesque tour through Lower Thames-street!', exclaims the *Monthly Review*;[42] but Ireland's Whig aesthetic is reasonably effective, in passages like this celebration of Rotterdam:

> Lofty trees, masts of ships, and elegant buildings, form all together a beautiful assemblage of objects, rarely to be met with in a commercial city. Here you may find a happy association of the means and the end of commerce: the house, or rather palace, of the merchant, ornamented by the ships that daily contribute to his opulence … (i. 23)

Other travellers focus more on the Dutch sense of civic responsibility. An anonymous *Trip to Holland* in 1786 (probably by Andrew Becket) somewhat laboriously insists on the sensibility of the Dutch, and the unfairness of their national reputation for dullness, whilst other texts from the 1780s, such as *An Hasty Sketch of a Tour through Part of the Austrian Netherlands, and Great Part of Holland* (1787: by 'an English Gentleman'), and *A Tour, Sentimental and Descriptive, through the United Provinces, Austrian Netherlands, and France* (2 vols, 1788), explore the enlightened systems of crime and punishment and of poor relief deployed by the Dutch: this latter *Tour* is even

---

[41] Radcliffe, *A Journey made in the Summer of 1794, through Holland and the Western Frontier of Germany, with a Return down the Rhine* (1795), 83.
[42] *MR*, NS 5 (1791), 94.

subtitled 'with some Observations on the Howardian System'.[43] The author of *An Hasty Sketch* admires the effective and humane poorhouses and prisons in Dutch towns, and his enthusiasm for Dutch 'humanity' is further strengthened by their outstanding 'conjugal felicity' and domesticity – both, at this time, virtues keenly associated with the British middle classes. Similarly, Samuel Jackson Pratt in 1795 stresses the numerous affinities between the Dutch and the British, observing that 'An Englishman in particular will here find himself at home. The face of the country, the general manners of the people, their modes of living, and their very language assimilates to Great Britain' (*Gleanings through Wales, Holland and Westphalia* 3 vols, 1795, ii. 323). Pratt repeatedly celebrates Dutch charity and industry, tapping into the established Whig discourse within which the Dutch had often functioned as an exemplary model of commercial republicanism.[44] Citing Thomson's praise (in the 'Autumn' section of *The Seasons*) of the blessings of 'Industry', commerce and the mechanic arts, he asserts that 'whoever visits Holland, will have reason to confess that every line has its force, its beauty, and its truth' (ii. 291–2).[45] Commercial prowess and moral virtue bind the two nations together, as Pratt's generous extension of the British poet's praise ('our delicious Thomson') illustrates.

The Anglo-Dutch affinity is contrasted, throughout Pratt's account, with the irrevocable alienation of Britain from the depravity of Revolutionary France. If Pratt's perspective on France is fairly representative of all but the most radical of English travel writers by 1795, the early years of the Revolution, by contrast, had fuelled an enormous public demand for travelogues which incorporated eye-witness reportage. A refocusing of theme was inevitable in the circumstances, as Thomas Ford Hill remarked in 1792, observing that travellers who 'formerly visited France, either to investigate living manners, or explore the remains of former times; nay, even that less meditating race, who went thither in search of mere amusement; have all had their attention turned at present in that country, to the study of politics; a study which they find almost

---

[43] John Howard had first published *The State of the Prisons in England and Wales, with Preliminary Observations, and an Account of some Foreign Prisons and Hospitals* in 1777 (Warrington). Four editions, successively enlarged by the indefatigable Howard's continued peregrinations, had appeared by 1792, as had also his *Account of the Principal Lazarettos in Europe* (Warrington, 1789). See John Lough, 'John Howard's Account of French Prisons and Hospitals 1775–1786', *Studies in Voltaire and the Eighteenth Century*, 284 (1991), 385–99.

[44] See Simon Schama, *Patriots and Liberators: Revolution in the Netherlands 1780–1813* (1977), 24–63.

[45] See James Thomson, Book III, 'Autumn', ll. 43–133, in *The Seasons* (1746), ed. James Sambrook (Oxford, 1981), 146–8.

necessary, to secure their personal safety'.[46] More timid travellers during the Revolutionary years could still visit the rest of Europe with relative safety, and continued to do so; though Ann Radcliffe for one is troubled by the streams of battered refugees flooding across into Germany, and retreats thankfully home, and Joseph Budworth urges the superior attractions of domestic tourism, on the grounds that 'a once-boasted, though now unfortunate, part of the Continent is become a scene of horror and devastation'.[47] By the autumn of 1790, the *Monthly Review* observes that 'excursions' within Britain 'are universally the fashion', and that this new 'passion ... pervades all ranks', as evinced by 'the multitude of *Guides, Tours, Journeys, Excursions,* &c. which are continually published'.[48] More exclusively, aristocratic Grand Tourists migrated south to Spain and Portugal and east to Greece and Turkey. The 1790s were transitional and troubling years for travel writing as for so many areas of cultural and literary experience. The Revolution exerted strange pressures on British cultural and political assumptions. It problematized the nature of individual and national liberty, and opened up the disquieting possibility that personal conviction may not necessarily coincide with national allegiances. The world of travel writing would never be quite the same again, and its discursive strategies were pushed to extremes of conservatism and radical disruption at this time, as the closing sections of this study will demonstrate.

The shifting outlines of the European tourist itinerary which we have here been tracing testify to the network of influences which shape the geographic and thematic development of eighteenth-century travel. Political contingency, cultural shifts, and literary fashions all have a part to play. In the published representation of British travel in Europe, another crucial element in the genre's evolution – one which brings together the quest for literary novelty with the projection of a public voice – is the emerging network of terms such as 'originality' and 'eccentricity', which unites political and literary concerns in the increasingly pervasive discourse of English or British 'character'. The origins of this discourse are worth tracing here, not least because they show how literary discussion actually helped to construct a cultural myth.[49] Whether

---

[46]   Thomas Ford Hill, *Observations on the Politics of France, and their Progress since the last Summer: made in a Journey from Spa to Paris during the Autumn of 1791* (1792), 1.

[47]   Joseph Budworth, *A Fortnight's Ramble to the Lakes in Westmoreland, Lancashire, and Cumberland* (1792), xiii–xiv (cited in Jarvis, *Romantic Writing and Pedestrian Travel*, 9).

[48]   *MR*, NS 3 (1790), 309–13.

[49]   Gerald Newman claims that the dominant 'English trait' during the eighteenth century was 'sincerity', which included innocence, honesty, originality, frankness and moral independence (*The Rise of English Nationalism: a Cultural History, 1740–1830* [1987; repr. 1997], 128–39); while the agglomeration of these sincere virtues was indeed influential, I would argue that the concept of 'originality' is of prevailing

the British character really became more 'eccentric' at this time, or whether its textual representation simply becomes more ingenious, is a moot point.

National character

The interest in English singularity or originality – 'eccentricity' was a later coinage, not fully in use till the 1790s – emerged from a conjunction of literary criticism and political events during the later seventeenth century. Stuart Tave's important study, *The Amiable Humorist* (1960) traces the replacement of the seventeenth-century concept of 'humour' as 'an aberration demanding satiric attack', by the eighteenth-century pride in that peculiarly British freedom which permitted and indeed fostered personal oddity.[50] British liberty and integrity was then retrospectively attributed to the whole of the nation's history, intersecting with the Norman Yoke theory. The emergence of these ideas – prompted first by the political upheavals of the 1640s and then, more potently, by the Glorious Revolution of 1688 – was initially registered in the poetics of comic drama, and Dryden's *Essay of Dramatick Poesie* (1668) is an important early formulation of the argument whereby the tolerant political atmosphere of the British Isles, in contrast to the repressive uniformity (in politics and the arts) of France, encourages the growth and free expression of individuality – albeit within a neo-classical and élitist framework.[51] Temple's influential essay 'Of Poetry' in 1690 developed Dryden's argument, but added that 'the unequalness of our climate' as well as English political liberty were responsible for the growth of English 'humours'.[52] Increasingly, also, British liberty came to be regarded as unique and indigenous, rather than as a reiteration of Greek or Roman models.

The eccentricity of the British was not inevitably seen as a good thing: Defoe in 1701 associates it with pride and tetchiness when he refers to 'That vain ill-natur'd thing, an *Englishman*'.[53] And somewhat later, Kant made a similar diagnosis, complaining that the English character consists in 'contempt

---

importance, at least in the context of literary representations of Englishness (and, by extension, Britishness).

[50]   Stuart M. Tave, *The Amiable Humorist: a Study in the Comic Theory and Criticism of the Eighteenth and Early Nineteenth Centuries* (Chicago, 1960), 91–105 and passim.

[51]   Howard D. Weinbrot, *Britannia's Issue: the Rise of British Literature from Dryden to Ossian* (Cambridge, 1993) presents a particularly compelling reading of the *Essay* in this context.

[52]   'Of Poetry', in Samuel Holt Monk ed., *Five Miscellaneous Essays by Sir William Temple* (Ann Arbor, 1963), 199.

[53]   *The True-Born Englishman: a Satyr*, in *The Shortest Way with the Dissenters and other Pamphlets by Daniel Defoe* (Oxford, 1927), 21–71; 37 (fonts reversed in second quotation).

for all foreigners, primarily because the English think that they alone can boast a respectable constitution that combines domestic civil liberty with might in external affairs'.[54] But at home, in general, the national predilection for individuality was presented positively. Temple was echoed in Congreve's 'Concerning Humour in Comedy' (1695) and, rather later, in Corbyn Morris's *Essay towards Fixing the True Standards of Wit, Humour, Raillery, Satire, and Ridicule* (1744). Similar ideas are exploited by the likes of Swift and Farquhar, influentially by Addison and Steele, and, fleshed out with speculations on native genius, by Edward Young in *Conjectures on Original Composition* (1759). As Tave puts it, this list 'could be extended indefinitely' to include most writers, whether 'of eminence, lack of eminence, or anonymity', during the eighteenth century.[55]

Tave describes eighteenth-century British 'humour' or 'character' as 'empirical, liberal and expansive, scientific, democratic and commercial'; it emphasized 'variety and the individual rather than conformity and the class'. Initially, this emerging discourse was politically inflected, since it was the Whig tradition of the Glorious Revolution which had made Britons 'proudly self-conscious of their liberties and wealth' (96). Corbyn Morris in 1744 describes the English eccentric or 'humourist' as 'a Lover of Reason and Liberty', and the 'Guardian of Freedom, and Scourge of such as do wrong', who 'flourishes only in a Land of *Freedom*, and when *that* ceases he dies too, the last and noblest *Weed* of the Soil of *Liberty*'.[56] By the middle of the eighteenth century, the discourse of national originality had expanded far beyond the theatrical and literary context (although it remains a powerful factor within these arenas, as the canonization of Shakespeare and the growth of strong national self-confidence in the literary world illustrates). It soon also began to transcend its Whiggish origins: by 1759 (the date of Young's *Conjectures*), even the Tory Johnson makes rhetorical use of this pervasive cultural myth, as his Dick Minim declares that 'we live in a country where liberty suffers every character to spread itself to the utmost bulk, and which therefore produces more originals than all the rest of the world together'.[57] As Michael Meehan has observed:

> The broad movement that can be discerned through the century is one of a nationalization of ideas that had their origins in party propaganda, but which lost the tang of factional dispute in

---

[54] Emmanuel Kant, *Anthropology from a Pragmatic Point of View* (1798), trans. Mary J. Gregor (The Hague, 1974), 169: cited in Paul Langford, *Englishness Identified: Manners and Character 1650–1850* (Oxford, 2000), 291.

[55] Tave, 263, n. 12.

[56] Morris, *Essay towards Fixing the True Standards of Wit* (1744), 20–21.

[57] *Idler*, 60 (9 June 1759); in Samuel Johnson, *'The Idler' and 'The Adventurer'*, 188.

employment against collective foes, against radicals at home and
enemies abroad, in the name of all that was truly English.[58]

Just as the factional element weakened, any precise or exact sense of political
'liberty' tended to become subsumed beneath a more general sense that
'liberty' consisted in, to use Meehan's phrase, 'the security that comes with the
rule of law', rather than in the right to actual democratic participation which
later ages (as well as seventeenth-century radical sects) would consider
essential to 'liberty'. 'Liberty' in its eighteenth-century sense gives to the
populace at large a virtual rather than an actual role in government: however, as
we shall see, the uses made of this indirect access to political influence were
often resourceful and influential.

A highly revealing summary of contemporary notions of the English
character in political context is provided by Hume in his essay 'Of National
Characters' (1748), where the author's own Scottishness doubtless influences
the tone of analytic detachment. The following passage warrants citing at some
length since it nicely illustrates the processes of comparison by which English
individuality is defined:

> We may often remark a wonderful Mixture of Manners and
> Character in the same Nation, speaking the same Language, and
> subject to the same Government: And in this Particular, the
> *English* are the most remarkable of any People, that ever were in
> the World. Nor is this to be ascrib'd to the Mutability and
> Uncertainty of their Climate, or to any other *physical* Causes;
> since all these Causes take Place in their neighbouring Kingdom of
> *Scotland*, without having the same Effect. Where the Government
> of a Nation is altogether republican, it is apt to beget a peculiar Set
> of Manners. Where it is altogether monarchical, it is more apt to
> have the same Effect; the Imitation of Superiors spreading the
> national Manners faster among the People. If a State consists
> altogether of Merchants, such as *Holland*, their uniform Way of
> Life will form their Character. If it consists chiefly of Nobles and
> landed Gentry, like *Germany*, *France*, and *Spain*, the same Effect
> follows. The Genius of a particular Sect or Religion is also apt to
> mould the Manners of a People. But the *English* Government is a
> Mixture of Monarchy, Aristocracy, and Democracy. The People
> are compos'd of Gentry and Merchants. All Sects of Religion are
> to be found amongst them. And the great Liberty and
> Independency, which they enjoy, allows every one to display the
> Manners, which are peculiar to him. Hence the *English*, of any
> People in the Universe, have the least of a national Character;
> unless this very Singularity be made their national Character.[59]

---

[58] Michael Meehan, *Liberty and Poetics in Eighteenth-Century England* (1986), 20.
[59] David Hume, *Essays, Moral and Political* (1748), 278–9.

This diagnosis of the '*moral* causes' of the English national character – which, paradoxically, resides in personal 'singularity' and an *absence* of shared 'national character' – sums up preceding and contemporary formulations, and is in turn echoed by countless writers in succeeding decades. Martin Sherlock, for example, affirms in 1780 that the 'first lesson' which an Englishman learns from his father, 'and the first lesson which he transmits to his son, is that independence is the inheritance of an Englishman. He is proud of being *himself*; of thinking, feeling, and acting *for* himself.'[60] Even Sterne, who professes to deconstruct national character in the interests of universal sympathy, celebrates 'that distinct variety and originality of character, which distinguishes [the English], not only from each other, but from all the world besides'.[61] As late as 1788, Joseph Priestley states that 'The English, they say, have least of an uniform national character, on account of their liberty and independence, which enables every man to follow his own humour.'[62] Whilst in the twentieth century, British 'eccentricity' tends to attach itself to the figure of the batty-but-loveable aristocrat, eighteenth-century formulations present a more democratic picture. Steele, for instance, emphasizes that this 'National Mark is visible amongst us in every Rank and Degree of Men, from the Persons of the first Quality and Politest Sense, down to the rudest and most ignorant of the People. ... Our very Street Beggars are not without their peculiar *Oddities*.'[63] As observed in my Introduction, moreover, the peculiar characteristics of English individuality were frequently appropriated by the Welsh, Scots and Irish, and assimilated into the term 'British'.

Not surprisingly, this view of the English or British character comes to be related to the teeming and varied pantheon of British writers, whose activities were seen as strong evidence of intellectual freedom and national self-confidence. In his 'Preface' to the *Harleian Miscellanies*, with reference to a long native tradition rather than a merely modern trend, Johnson observes that:

> among the Natives of *England*, is to be found a greater Variety of Humour, than in any other Country; and, doubtless, where every Man has a full Liberty to propagate his Conceptions, Variety of Humour must produce Variety of Writers; and, where the Number

---

[60] Martin Sherlock, *Lettres d'un Voyageur anglois* (2 vols, 1780), ii. 160; cited in Langford, *Englishness Identified*, 296.

[61] Laurence Sterne, *A Sentimental Journey through France and Italy by Mr. Yorick* (1768), ed. Gardner D. Stout, Jr (Berkeley and Los Angeles, 1967), 232.

[62] Joseph Priestley, *Lectures on History and General Policy* (Birmingham, 1788), 523; cited in Langford, *Englishness Identified*, 291.

[63] *Guardian*, 144, (26 August 1713), ed. John Calhoun Stephens (Lexington, KY, 1982), 474–5.

of Authors is so great, there cannot but be some worthy of Distinction.[64]

Perhaps deliberately, Johnson here is also delineating the realities of authorship in his own time, when writers, critics and readers were all too aware that the multitudes of publications were not all 'worthy of Distinction'. The *Monthly* and *Critical Reviews* claimed to offer guidance here, 'combating the opinions of the multitude, and exposing the applause, misplaced by caprice, on writers of no merit',[65] hoping thereby, in Smollett's words, to subdue the current 'Chaos of Publication'.[66] These ferocious pronouncements, together with the cut-throat realities of Grub Street, might have been expected to create a rather daunting audience for the would-be travel writer (as well as writers working in other genres), and it would be easy to assume that the reviewing arena functioned as an off-putting censor, especially for the non-professional writers with whom this study is mainly concerned. Such indeed is the argument of Morris Golden's essay on 'Travel Writing in the *Monthly Review* and *Critical Review*, 1756–1775', which argued in 1977 that 'As generalists and gentlemen, reviewers wanted to share the mental states of gentlemen, scholars, philosophers if possible, men disinterestedly motivated for the good of their countrymen', and that rational Enlightened discourse was therefore the only approach tolerated within travel writing: 'Even if idiosyncrasy made for temporary excitement, ... it is at least ludicrous and at worst offensive'.[67] More recently, Terry Eagleton has characterized the eighteenth-century reviewing enterprise as 'a reformative apparatus, scourging deviation and repressing the transgressive ... in the name of a certain historical emancipation'.[68] But this emphasis on the rational consensus of the 'classical public sphere' (Eagleton's phrase) seriously misrepresents what actually goes on within the pages of the Reviews, for all Smollett's authoritarian bluster. Both the *Critical* and the *Monthly* give voice to a great deal of material which by any standards must have seemed marginal to the rational Enlightenment project (if such a thing ever really existed), and frequently enter into quirky debate with authors which can extend over several months. The *Monthly* in particular, presided over by the Whig Dissenter Ralph Griffiths, welcomes writings which are not only eccentric but occasionally quite mad (Griffiths's 35,000-word review of Thomas Amory's fictive travels,

---

[64] 'Introduction' to *The Harleian Miscellany* (1744); in Allen T. Hazen, *Samuel Johnson's Prefaces and Dedications* (New Haven, 1937), 54–9; 55.

[65] *CR*, 12 (1761), 452.

[66] 'Proposals for Publishing Monthly, the Progress or Annals of Literature and the Liberal Arts' (30 December 1755), printed in Lewis Mansfield Knapp, *Tobias Smollett: Doctor of Men and Manners* (Princeton, 1949), 171–2.

[67] *Papers on Language and Literature*, 13 (1977), 213–23; 219.

[68] Terry Eagleton, *The Function of Criticism: from 'The Spectator' to Post-Structuralism* (1984, repr. 1991), 12–13.

The Life of John Buncle, in 1755, is a case in point). Indeed, almost in reaction against certain tendencies towards uniformity (as Joseph Loewenstein has observed, 'as the idea of a Standard obtrudes, the articulation of Difference becomes possible'[69]), idiosyncrasy is increasingly cherished during the 1760s and 1770s, not least because it testifies to the truth of the myth outlined above, of the British as a nation of distinctive individuals. Revealingly, the *Monthly Review* in 1771 describes its job as the presentation of 'just *characters* of the numerous works which daily issue from the press'.[70] In the case of travel writing, the merit of the text is increasingly bound up with the distinctiveness of its narrator, in the interests of the reader's enjoyment as well as national pride. The *Monthly*'s assessment of Philip Thicknesse's *A Year's Journey through France, and Part of Spain* in 1777, for example, shows how narrative energy is more important than informative content: 'the point and poignancy of his *manner*, generally give an agreeable zest to his remarks, and ... throw an air of novelty over many things with which we were before pretty well acquainted'.[71]

So, by presenting a distinctive, even downright odd, narrative persona, travel writers would simultaneously add marketable novelty to their texts, and testify to the liberty which British society offered for the infinite variety of its subjects. Furthermore, and by a convenient sleight of hand, personal distinctiveness proclaimed the writer to be a man or woman *not* shaped primarily by national character or prejudice. Their views could therefore be trusted as unbiased accounts of 'abroad': in the event, of course, they frequently reinforced British superiority, so that, as Jeremy Black puts it, most tourists returned to Britain as 'better-informed xenophobes', and many of them could agree with Johnson's remark that 'What I gained by being in France was, learning to be better satisfied with my own country'.[72] Edward Clarke in 1763 declares that his account of Spain will provide the reader with a 'fresh proof of the happiness, which he enjoys in being *born a Briton*; of living in a country, where he possesses freedom of sentiment and of action, liberty of conscience, and security of property'.[73] Importantly, then, the very fact that such judgements could be made in an informed way was implicit proof of the Briton's independence of thought – which, in the event, tended to express itself in patriotic clichés. The *Monthly* praises John Moore in 1779 as a model of this national quality, observing that 'Few writers, indeed, will be found more

---

[69]   Joseph Loewenstein, 'The Script in the Marketplace', in Stephen Greenblatt ed., *Representing the English Renaissance* (Berkeley, 1988), 265–78. Loewenstein is here alluding to Elizabeth Eisenstein, *The Printing Press as an Agent of Change* (2 vols, Cambridge, 1979), i. 79–85.

[70]   *MR*, 45 (1771), 169; my emphasis.

[71]   *MR*, 57 (1770), 207.

[72]   Black, *The British and the Grand Tour*, 186; Boswell, *Life of Johnson*, iii. 352.

[73]   Edward Clarke, *Letters concerning the Spanish Nation* (1763), 'Preface', vi.

untainted by prejudices of any kind than this agreeable Traveller; and, on this account, his testimony is the more valuable in favour of the customs and institutions of his native country'.[74] As succeeding chapters will demonstrate, however, broad satisfaction with being British did not preclude admiration for certain Continental practices and attitudes: for instance, as Ian Gilmour has observed, 'to take pride in British prosperity and liberty and to contrast them with absolute monarchy, Popery and wooden shoes was one thing; to claim that the system as it was in the 1760s and 1770s was the perfect and glorious embodiment of the principles of 1688 was quite another'.[75] Comparisons between Britain and Europe are frequently made which enable writers subtly to criticize British complacency. In a sense, they earn the right to do so by first establishing themselves as an interesting – and interested – British subject.

While the belief that the British (especially the English) are internationally distinguished by being individually beyond the scope of national characterization becomes pervasive, and is articulated by writers from very diverse political and social backgrounds, it often goes hand in hand with a cheerful readiness to apply stereotyped national characters to the rest of the world. Smollett's *The Present State of All Nations* (8 vols, 1768–9) is a sustained and comprehensive exercise in national labelling, briefer versions of which are dotted casually throughout the pages of travel writing. According to such formulations – as mocked by Joseph Baretti in 1770 – 'the Italians are naturally jealous, the French naturally volatile, the Germans naturally heavy', and so on. Curiously, it is not unusual to find within the same text complaints about the unfairness of national stereotyping, and casual indulgence in this very practice. A frequent strategy is to protest the unfairness, for example, of the French reputation for flippancy, urging instead that they are a sentimental nation. But the assumption of a French national character is never questioned.

The tendency to indulge in national stereotyping was to some extent perceived as class-related. Hume makes an interesting distinction (frequently reiterated in travel writing) between 'vulgar' prejudice and the kind of discernment practised by 'men of sense':

> The Vulgar are apt to carry all *national Characters* to Extremes; and having once establish'd it as a Principle, that any People are knavish, or cowardly, or ignorant, they will admit of no Exception, but comprehend every Individual under the same Character. Men of Sense condemn these undistinguish'd Judgments; tho' at the same Time, they allow, that each Nation has a peculiar Set of

---

[74] *MR*, 60 (1779), 464.

[75] Ian Gilmour, *Riots, Risings and Revolution: Governance and Violence in 18th Century England* (1992), 329.

Manners, and that some particular Qualities are more frequently to
be met with among one People than among their Neighbours.[76]

Similarly, the *Critical Review* in 1772 refers to 'that blind prejudice, and that
rooted antipathy, which distinguish the vulgar of contending nations'.[77] The
notion of 'vulgar prejudice' is frequently reiterated in travel narratives, which
have to tread a delicate path between popular xenophobia on the one hand, and
aristocratic cosmopolitanism on the other (Hume's phrase 'Men of Sense' is
apposite here, delineating a rational compromise between extreme attitudes).
Kathleen Wilson has highlighted the 'virulent strain of anti-aristocratic
sentiment' which had entered political discourse by the mid-1750s, and which
dwelt particularly on the aristocracy's unpatriotic susceptibility to French
influence.[78] The potent anti-luxury discourse that circulated throughout the
second half of the eighteenth century frequently intersected with anti-
aristocratic discussions of travel. In a diatribe against the Grand Tour in 1768,
the *Gentleman's Magazine* warns against the national disintegration which
aristocratic enthusiasm for foreign manners threatens to bring about:

> when men bring home the vanity and luxury of France, and blend
> the follies of other nations with their own, their minds are wholly
> devoted to pleasure and interest; they are fired with ambition, the
> public good is neglected, the cement of unity is disjointed, and
> torn to pieces; there seems to be no other harmony amongst us, but
> that of a giddy unthinking mob, bent upon mischief, obedient to no
> laws, incapable of knowing their own interest, devoted to
> destruction, and led to be slaves by each pretending patriot, whilst
> universal confusion threatens to scourge the kingdom for its folly
> and vice. May heaven avert it ...[79]

Aristocratic travel – in contrast to the middle classes' more frugal
expeditions – was frequently castigated as extravagant and unpatriotic. The
aristocracy were perceived as lavishing vast sums of British money on foreign
products and services: furthermore, it was widely felt that their sexual
promiscuity abroad threatened the vigour of the ruling classes through the
importation of venereal disease. At least as early as Lassels's *Voyage of Italy* in
1670, this particular anxiety had been expressed: '*Others desire* to go into *Italy*,

---

[76] Hume, 'Of National Characters', in *Essays, Moral and Political*, 267.

[77] *CR*, 33 (1772), 425.

[78] Kathleen Wilson, 'Empire of Virtue: the Imperial Project and Hanoverian Culture
c.1720–1785', in Lawrence Stone ed., *An Imperial State at War: Britain from 1689 to
1815*' (1994), 128–64; 145. See also Newman's suggestive account of 'eighteenth-
century cosmopolitanism and of its reverse ethic, national patriotism' (*The Rise of
English Nationalism*, 47).

[79] *Gentleman's Magazine* (*GM*), 38 (1768), 217.

onely because they hear there are fine *Curtisanes* in *Venice*. ... And thus by a false ayming at breeding abroad, they returne with those diseases which hinder them from breeding at home.'[80] The nobility's highly visible passion for collecting was another source of controversy, becoming a central plank of the hysterical discourse of luxury which spread like a contagion, carried by a great variety of media: books, pamphlets, periodicals and newspapers.[81] Intricately bound up with this economic and nationalistic discourse was the question of gender: specifically, the claims of the middle classes more truly to embody the virtues of the nation were increasingly bolstered by the assertion of a solid masculinity, in contrast to the effeminate degeneracy of the aristocracy, and the French (a common polemical conjunction). As Margaret Hunt puts it:

> Middling moralists obsessively identified traits that were alleged to be aristocratic (luxury, interest in things French, lack of application, moral laxity) with softness and effeminacy. Conversely they identified any and all values alleged to be non-aristocratic (plain speaking, usefulness, perseverance in the face of adversity, rationality, systematic pursuit of virtue) with masculinity.[82]

The literature of European travel presents a particularly interesting arena for this ideological battle, as the territory of the aristocratic Grand Tour was progressively invaded by travellers of other classes, for whom the publication of a sensible and manly narrative could function as an assertion of superior civic virtue and patriotism. The 'native manliness of our disposition' becomes a common formulation, especially in times of political crisis.[83] British singularity becomes almost indistinct from British masculinity.

An unusual example of the discursive conflict between aristocratic effeminacy and patriotic masculinity is William Beckford's *Dreams, Waking Thoughts, and Incidents* (1783). The main body of Beckford's text is fancifully sensuous, by turns classical and romantic, and disdainful alike of political issues and the ordinary citizen – the 'distant buzz of the town'.[84] He also offers

---

[80] 'A Preface to the Reader, concerning Travelling' (fonts reversed, pages unnumbered).

[81] See John Sekora, *Luxury: the Concept in Western Thought, Eden to Smollett* (Baltimore, 1977).

[82] Margaret Hunt, *The Middling Sort: Commerce, Gender, and the Family in England, 1680–1780* (Berkeley and Los Angeles, 1996), 71.

[83] The quotation is from John Andrews's fiercely nationalistic *Comparative View of the French and English Nations* (1785), 244: the *View* reflects the impact of recent hostilities.

[84] William Beckford, *Dreams, Waking Thoughts and Incidents: in a Series of Letters, from Various Parts of Europe* (1783); in Guy Chapman ed., *The Travel-Diaries of William Beckford of Fonthill* (2 vols, Cambridge, 1928), i. 83.

an insulting account of the Low Countries (characterizing them as dirty, smoky and stupid), which would no doubt have offended those readers just getting used to the notion of Anglo-Dutch affinities.[85] Beckford's travels are self-consciously, almost defiantly, aristocratic; and the homoerotic longings (for the minor, William Courtenay) which the text betrays would have done nothing to counter contemporary concern about aristocratic deviance. Nevertheless, intriguingly, Beckford appends a jingoistic coda to *Dreams* in which he apologizes for his apparent 'political indifference, as if I had affected the character of a citizen of the world ... No: I boast myself an Englishman' (i. 234), and proceeds to offer a highly clichéd survey of Europe's national characters, concluding that English good sense and valour will inevitably triumph over French dissipation in 'this unhappy conquest' (i. 237). Under pressure from his family, keen to quieten the rumours of homosexual scandal, Beckford withdrew *Dreams* from publication on 15 April 1783.[86] The Beckford clan may well also have realized that his parodic deployment of manly patriotism would likewise have generated public hostility. Finally, his explicit repudiation of the Grand Tour's function as a rite of passage into adulthood would have irritated his own class and confirmed the prevalent middle-class view of aristocratic travel as futile and emasculating. In an unpublished letter to his mentor, the painter Alexander Cozens, Beckford declares that 'I am now approaching the age when the World in general expect me to lay aside my dreams, abandon my soft illusion and start into public life. How greatly are they deceived, how fiercely am I resolved to be a Child for ever'.[87] And *Dreams, Waking Thoughts, and Incidents* as a whole is characterized by a similar tone of adolescent rebelliousness – 'Everybody stared, last night at the Opera when I told them I was going to bury myself in fallen leaves, and hear no music but their rustlings' (i. 170).

The example of *Dreams, Waking Thoughts, and Incidents* illustrates how particular discourses were seen to be available to travel writers, and how

---

[85]   Elizabeth Mavor also suggests that the anti-Dutch flavour of *Dreams* may have been seen as potentially damaging to the political ambitions which Beckford's family entertained for him, given that the British government was then negotiating a treaty with the Dutch. See Elizabeth Mavor ed., *The Grand Tour of William Beckford* (Harmondsworth, 1986), 141, and Thomas M. Curley, 'William Beckford and the Romantic Tradition of Travel Literature', *Studies in Voltaire and the Eighteenth Century*, 305 (1992), 1819–23.

[86]   See Redford, *Venice and the Grand Tour*, 132, and Robert J. Gemmett ed., *Dreams, Waking Thoughts, and Incidents* (Cranbury, NJ, 1971), 24–8.

[87]   Brian Fothergill, *Beckford of Fonthill* (1979), 96. Redford for one has argued that Beckford's valorizing of imagination over education in *Dreams* is revolutionary, and his exaltation of childhood may likewise be seen as ahead of its time (*Venice and the Grand Tour*, 132). In 1822, the 'Preface' to Samuel Rogers's influential poem *Italy* celebrates the literally rejuvenating powers of travel: 'All is new and strange. We surrender ourselves, and feel once again as children' (cited in Buzard, *The Beaten Track*, 101).

gender and class were key factors in one's choice of discursive framework. Quite apart from manly patriotism, authors had access to a range of discourses which signified public utility as well as individual sensibility. Beth Fowkes Tobin has shown how writers like Arthur Young, in his several *Tours* around the British Isles, developed a rhetoric of good husbandry and agricultural expertise, in conscious contrast to the irresponsible aristocratic rural pursuits of huntin', shootin', fishin', and landscapin'. They thus contributed to a 'redefinition of masculinity that valorized the capacity to quantify, commodify, and organize': or, to use the terms coined by Davidoff and Hall, they enacted their useful manhood with 'pen and ruler', in opposition to the destructive aristocratic reliance on 'sword, gun, and sexual conquest'.[88] To these last three might be added 'purse', for the exorbitant cost of upper-class recreations was a frequent theme, at a time when economic as well as moral anxieties about the spread of luxury were increasingly alarmist, and the middle classes were feeling the pinch of exorbitant indirect taxation: between 1757 and 1783, the National Debt grew from less than 80 million to over 240 million, largely due to the costs of the Seven Years War and the American War. Taxes on commodities, levied with increasing severity in order to service the Debt, tended to hit the middle and lower classes hardest. The coincidence of rising taxation with many high-profile cases of aristocratic decadence (Lord Baltimore's trial for rape in 1768, Lord Lyttelton the younger's notorious and widely reported Grand Tour debaucheries in the 1770s, and the publication of Lord Chesterfield's *Letters* in 1774) consolidated the growing conviction amongst the middling sort that this was an era in which national well-being, moral and economic, was seriously threatened by the extravagance and decadence of an unpatriotic aristocracy.[89] Aristocratic recreations abroad, especially those associated with urban tourism (collecting, gambling, extravagant socializing), were also highly susceptible to being construed as effeminate, since they lacked even the performative masculine vigour of English country sports.[90] In contrast, the range of manly and useful travelling

---

[88] Beth Fowkes Tobin, 'Arthur Young, Agriculture, and the Construction of the New Economic Man', in Beth Fowkes Tobin ed., *History, Gender, and Eighteenth-Century Literature* (1994), 179–97: 181; 190. See also Leonore Davidoff and Catherine Hall, *Family Fortunes: Men and Women of the English Middle Class, 1780–1850* (Chicago, 1987), 205.

[89] See Paul Langford, *A Polite and Commercial People: England 1727–1783* (Oxford, 1989), 640–1. Smollett's *The Expedition of Humphry Clinker* (1777) is a lively contribution to the contemporary distrust of materialism and luxury.

[90] See David D. Gilmore, *Manhood in the Making: Cultural Concepts of Masculinity* (1990). Gilmore argues that whilst manhood is distinct from biological maleness and has to be actively demonstrated through trials and rituals specific to any given society, femininity is more usually construed as a biological given which merely requires some cultural refinement.

activities available to other travellers would rarely entail more than the mere cost of the expedition. During the second half of the eighteenth century, several specialist angles on European travel developed into discursive realms in their own right, any number of which might intersect within the narrative self-construction of a particular travel writer. These may be briefly delineated.

The discourses of travel writing

Perhaps most respectable among the available discourses of eighteenth-century travel writing were those of mercantile and economic good sense. These would manifest themselves as an assiduous detailing of 'Trade, Manufactures, and Produce of Countries', and of their trading potential.[91] Defoe's *Tour thro' the Whole Island of Great Britain* (3 vols, 1723–5) is one of the earliest examples of this mercantile discourse (albeit confined to the British Isles). Josiah Tucker's *Instructions for Travellers* (1758) urges Britons abroad to collect data on agricultural conditions, taxation systems, labour costs, demography, and so on. Margaret Hunt has observed that Adam Smith's *Wealth of Nations* (1776) was heavily indebted to numerous travelogues for its comparative and global economic awareness: Smith 'had in his personal library almost every major piece of published travel writing by a French or English write of the seventeenth or eighteenth centuries'.[92] The frameworks of natural history and mineralogy (popularized by the German John James Ferber) were likewise valued for the economic potential they would reveal, as well as for their contribution to the more disinterested pursuit of encyclopaedic knowledge for its own sake: the *Monthly Review* welcomes a translation of Ferber's *Letters concerning Mineralogy* in 1776 for its opening up of a useful 'field of knowledge that has been hitherto untrod by the learned'.[93] Military observations, especially those which conduced to an increased understanding of Continental powers, were abidingly popular and relevant, and were increasingly fleshed out with more general comparative observations on politics and government, especially once this discursive arena had been opened up to more amateur speculation by the popularizing (in the Reviews and elsewhere) of controversialists like Rousseau and Voltaire, and historians like Hume, Gibbon and Robertson. Reflections on comparative liberty and tyranny are ubiquitous in travel writing, and although many of them simply relate to the traveller's vague sense of Britiish freedom, they do tend to become more analytical as the century progresses, and as developments such as the enlightened despotisms of

---

[91] *GM*, 1 (1731), 321.
[92] Margaret Hunt, 'Racism, Imperialism, and the Traveler's Gaze in Eighteenth-Century England', *Journal of British Studies*, 32 (1993), 333–57.
[93] *MR*, 55 (1776), 548.

Austria and Prussia, the French Revolution, and the British government's repressive measures during the 1790s problematize traditional easy contrasts between home and abroad.

A separate yet related discursive realm within which the responsibilities of the state are scrutinized might be described as the discourse of humanitarianism, which becomes particularly prominent during the later 1760s and the 1770s. This reflects an increased concern with poverty, crime, and women's sexual vulnerability, and with the need to quantify and categorize such problems. Not surprisingly, this discourse is frequently adopted by self-consciously sentimental travel writers, as humanitarianism becomes an increasingly acceptable aspect of middle-class, 'softened' masculinity. Humanitarianism then meshes with the practical, calculating discourse of utilitarianism during the later 1770s and 1780s: the 'Howardian' *Tour, Sentimental and Descriptive* (2 vols, 1788) of the Low Countries makes utilitarian philanthropy its defining feature, and many other narratives have more occasional recourse to it.

The broad expansion of interest in 'manners and customs', to use a traditional phrase, gives rise to its own discursive realm, which incorporates early approaches to anthropology and comparative sociology. The dominant theme of this discourse is sexual morality, and its prevailing tendency is to associate Britain's international supremacy with the allegedly superior position of British women, who demonstrate more virtue and generate more respect than women in any other country. Foreign nations display a range of deviations from this ideal, embodied in the ubiquitous figures of the courtesan, the sodomite and the *cicesbeo*, which pop up in almost every account of continental incontinence, as does the figure of the nun immolated against her will and thereby prevented from fulfilling her natural functions as wife and mother.

These rather emotive discourses are often leavened by the middle-class tourist's enthusiastic pursuit of cultural experiences, where the aristocratic tendency to purchase and collect is implicitly contrasted with the patriotic traveller's more spectatorial stance. This was, of course, disingenuous, for although on a less sumptuous scale, middle-class travellers as well as their aristocratic counterparts frequently indulged in consumerist acquisitiveness abroad. However, galleries and museums function as increasingly popular arenas wherein the tourist can enact taste and judgement at virtually no expense. As with the domestic culture of consumption, this is an activity within which women's public display of good taste – reflecting their private virtue – is particularly sanctioned, such that in 1776 Anne Miller publishes three volumes of *Letters from Italy*, whose 'remarks' upon the paintings and sculptures 'that pleased me most' are especially commended by the Reviews.[94] The developing

---

[94] Anne Miller, *Letters from Italy, describing the Manners, Customs, Antiquities, Paintings, &c. of that Country, in the Years MDCCLXX and MDCCLXXI, to a Friend*

discourse of aesthetics also opens up new descriptive possibilities for responses to landscape, whether sublime or picturesque. While it may well be true, according to Elizabeth Bohls's analysis, that the ideological foundations of aesthetic discourse construct its subject as a land-owning male, the published world of eighteenth-century tourism reveals the appropriation of the aesthetic spectator's position by a wide range of writers. Some have recourse to aesthetic discourse in order (regardless of rank or gender) to assert their status as British consumers of foreign spectacle; others use it to envisage a more radical transcendence of self and nation. Finally, significant offshoots of the discourse of general cultural tourism include the growing field of comparative literary research (of which Montagu's discussion of Turkish poetry, Dillon's literary history of Spain, and the investigations of Baretti and Southey into Spanish and Portuguese literature are examples); and the unique cultural territory covered in Charles Burney's 'musical tours' of Europe.[95]

Narrowing the focus still further, from the objects of the traveller's observations to the subjective experience of travel, we find here too distinct discursive formulations of national character. Ludicrous as it may seem, Smollett's hypochondria is relevant here, since spleen and its related disorders were by this time established as peculiarly British afflictions, and as signs not merely of superior sensibility, but also of superior intelligence: furthermore, it was becoming increasingly fashionable amongst the middling sort to suffer from hypochondria, formerly an upper-class malady.[96] Few valetudinarian travellers are as quite as obsessive as Smollett (whose fantastically detailed record of the temperatures in the South of France might seem almost a parody of the quantifying discourse of British, anti-aristocratic, manliness). Yet valetudinarian travel becomes increasingly fashionable, and allows the super-sensitive British to display simultaneously the physical evidence of their sensibility and, paradoxically, their intrepid spirit. A nice embodiment of this paradoxical conjunction is Mariana Starke's *Travels in Italy* (1800), which includes exhaustive descriptions of the cultural attractions which the traveller is obliged to seek out, together with 'instructions for the Use of Invalids' such as the following useful injunction: 'Invalids should not attempt to ascend Vesuvius' (ii. 138).

In some ways encompassing all of these discursive fields is, of course, the phenomenon of sensibility, which exerted several influences over travel

---

residing in France, by an English Woman (3 vols, London, 1776), i. 101. See *MR*, 55 (1776), 104–5.

[95] Charles Burney, *The Present State of Music in France and Italy; or, the Journal of a Tour through those Countries* (2 vols, 1771); *The Present State of Music in Germany, the Netherlands, and United Provinces* (2 vols, 1773).

[96] See John Mullan, *Sentiment and Sociability: the Language of Feeling in the Eighteenth Century* (1988; repr. Oxford, 1990), 203–6.

writing. At the simple level of literary production, the enthusiastic reception of
A Sentimental Journey in 1768 initiated a wave of sentimental trips, tours and
journeys, whose authors found a congenial and easily imitable stylistic model
in Sterne (these will be described in more detail in Chapter 4). Sentimental
encounters with affecting tableaux of human experience, rather than
enumeration of traditional tourist sites, dominated such works. More broadly,
sensibility's far-reaching influence on gender legitimized the kind of softened –
even feminized – middle-class masculinity which would demonstrate a
sensitive awareness of cultural relativity and universal humanity. In turn, the
foreign arena offered not only opportunities for the indulgence of sentimental
feeling, but also a map onto which the national co-ordinates of sensibility could
be plotted, intersecting with the domestically potent factors of class and gender.
Sensibility was, as Barker-Benfield and others have shown, a European
phenomenon: but its emergence in Britain was intricately bound up with
developing notions of national character and virtue. An important dimension
here is the emphasis in definitions of British manhood on chaste
heterosexuality, as opposed to foreign and aristocratic effeminacy or sexual
excess.[97] In this context, the undercurrents of sexual desire (rarely
consummated) in sentimental travel writing serve to strengthen the cultural
conviction of healthy English masculinity.

   Barker-Benfield has observed that while men were legitimately softened by
domesticity, manners, and humanitarianism (all of which, one might add, they
were then able to display and exercise on foreign travels), sensibility's
ideological effect on women was disabling rather than enabling, as the sexually
desiring aspect of female sensibility became increasingly problematic. As a
result, women were increasingly confined to the domestic sphere (where, it has
recently been argued, their alleged influence was in fact drastically curtailed as
sentimental masculinity asserted a right to interfere even in the hitherto largely
'private', feminine affairs of the family).[98] The virtue of a whole class and
nation came rhetorically to depend upon the moral stability of the feminine,
domestic sphere.[99] These developments might have been expected to preclude

---

[97]   See Hunt, *The Middling Sort*, 114–15.
[98]   See Shawn Lisa Maurer, *Proposing Men: Dialectics of Gender and Class in the
Eighteenth-Century English Periodical* (Stanford, 1998).
[99]   Such at least was the argument of countless conduct manuals and polemical
pamphlets. The extent to which ideological prescription actually reflected or affected
social practice remains open to question. See Robert B. Shoemaker, *Gender in English
Society, 1650–1850: the Emergence of Separate Spheres?* (1998), 318. See also Dena
Goodman, 'Public Sphere and Private Life: toward a Synthesis of Current
Historiographical Approaches to the Old Regime', *History and Theory*, 31 (1992), 3–
20, who observes that during the eighteenth century, '"public and private", "male and
female", were mere terms, ideal poles whose meanings were constantly and fruitfully
contested' (20).

women's active participation in travel writing, and yet between 1770 and 1800 almost twenty travelogues by women were published, generally to critical acclaim. Although tiny as a proportion of published travelogues during the century, this is still a significant figure.

There are several reasons for the emergence of the woman travel writer. Firstly, given that around 1770 readers and reviewers begin to complain of boredom with the European itinerary, the observations of female travellers were welcomed as a source of novelty. These were years during which women's presence as published writers in the literary arena was gaining wide acceptance in a variety of genres. Travel writing as a genre embraced, as we have seen, a range of discourses, some of which, although originally formulated as particularly appropriate for middle-class men, were readily adaptable for respectable female use. The broad shift from classical to sentimental, and the increased interest in 'manners and customs', art and landscape, and stories of human interest, all accommodated women writers. Secondly, on an ideological level, presenting oneself as an agreeable travelling companion for one's husband not only sanctioned publication, but also testified to the admirable condition of women in Britain. The only women travel writers not to dwell on their status as obedient wives are either aristocrats (Mary Wortley Montagu and Elizabeth Craven) or radicals (Helen Maria Williams and Mary Wollstonecraft). However, the continued exclusion of women from many discursive areas germane to travel writing, and their peculiar status as non-subjects within the domestic political context, means that women's travel writing is frequently pulled 'in different textual directions, and their writing exposes the unsteady foundations on which it is based'.[100] This is Sara Mills's diagnosis of women's travel writing within a colonial context, but its relevance to accounts of Europe is clear. One of the 'unsteady foundations' which is exposed by women's travel writing (whether by over-insistence or frank contradiction) is the cultural construction of gender and national character. In fact, such acts of exposure are not unique to travel writing by women, but can be found regardless of gender in texts by writers from a range of social and cultural backgrounds, at moments when not only the discourse of gender but also that of class or party politics may clash with that of national character (arguably, as we have seen, the genre's dominant discourse at this time).[101]

---

[100] Sara Mills, *Discourses of Difference: an Analysis of Women's Travel Writing and Colonialism* (1991), 3.

[101] See Joan Wallach Scott, 'Gender: a Useful Category of Historical Analysis', in Joan Wallach Scott ed., *Feminism and History* (Oxford, 1996), 152–80. Scott notes that power relations between nations and between classes have historically 'been made comprehensible (and thus legitimate) in terms of relations between male and female' (173).

If gender, class and nation are the dominant thematic concerns of this study, the formal issue of genre needs always to be borne in mind. As Markman Ellis has observed, 'the choice of genre effects [sic] not only how something is said, but also what is said, and to whom'.[102] Travel writing accommodates a variety of discourses and stylistic emphases. It is also a form which adapts and pirates ideas from genres both 'highbrow' (philosophy, history) and downmarket (fiction, journalism, gossip): these acts of incorporation frequently involve significant mistranslation or subversion of other cultural formulations. Thus, travel writing on Europe provided an influential and accessible arena for the articulation of ideological struggle, or, at times, consensus, and it is a world which has been invisible for too long.

---

[102] Markman Ellis, *The Politics of Sensibility: Race, Gender and Commerce in the Sentimental Novel* (Cambridge, 1996), 23.

Chapter 2

Class, character and controversy in the 1760s and 1770s

This chapter will illustrate in some detail the increasing displacement of aristocratic Grand Tourists by generally middle-class writers, whether amateur or professional, sentimental or splenetic, Whig or Tory. The invasion of the field by emphatically non-aristocratic writers, and the part played by the Reviews in this development, is the subject of the chapter's first section, which also addresses the question of how national and authorial character become more class-inflected and increasingly come to deploy the gendered virtues of common sense and patriotism. Prominent literary feuds between Tobias Smollett and Philip Thicknesse, and between Samuel Sharp and Joseph Baretti, bring these issues into sharp focus, and will be described in later sections.

The 1760s and 1770s were energetic and argumentative years for British travel writing. Especially after around 1765 (once the effects of the 1763 Peace of Paris had filtered through into the published products of Continental tourism), the genre proliferated cheerfully, encouraged and monitored by the *Monthly* and *Critical* Reviews, who during these years were themselves seeking to consolidate the authority of literary journals in general, whilst competing with each other for pre-eminence. The entry into the field of travel writing by established writers like Smollett and Sterne added further credibility to the genre, the popularity of which was simultaneously emboldening non-professional writers to publish accounts of their trips to Europe – whether for fame, or fortune or both. As one might expect, this authorial heterogeneity prompted discussion – within both texts and reviews – of the relative merits and demerits of professional or amateur literary status. Such debates frequently degenerated into slanging matches which opportunistically mobilized notions of personal integrity, public status, class, and national character.

The disputatious vigour of many travelogues and their reviews during these years is striking, and testifies to the genre's high and controversial profile within the expanding literary arena. Travel writing becomes a site of struggle for competing claims to moral virtue – claims which are frequently expressed in the gender-inflected language of class and nation. It becomes clear during these years that travel writers' perspectives on Europe are inevitably seen to impinge on social and political controversies at home, whether these involve broad class-based hostilities or more specific party politics (for example, the Wilkes controversy, and the ubiquitous debates over 'liberty' which this provoked). In this respect, the 1760s and 1770s set up an influential paradigm for travel writing and its reception in later decades, according to which constructions of the European 'other' function powerfully to define – or destabilize – consensual formulations of British national identity in relation to class, gender, and reputation or 'character'.

Class and authorial character

Although some aristocratic travelogues were well received during the 1760s and 1770s, any pre-eminence which the classical Grand Tour may have enjoyed in the world of published travels began seriously to be undermined. The rising status of professional authors, and the genre's accommodation of keen amateurs, contributed to a declining interest in the upper-class experience of Europe. The *Monthly Review* became particularly impatient with the pretensions of 'the mob of gentlemen who write with ease',[1] as is amusingly illustrated by its reception of *A Tour to the East* (1767), an account of a voyage through the Mediterranean to Turkey and home through Eastern Europe by Lord Baltimore. This is a slight and loosely-structured work, padded out with 'Select Pieces of the Wit, Wisdom, and Poetry of the East'. The descriptions are half-hearted to the point of boredom, substituting classical quotation for observation in a languid, sub-Addisonian manner. A storm off the South Italian coast, for instance, merely provokes Baltimore to note that 'we passed by the cavern of old *Eolus*, but not without being buffeted by his myrmidons' (7). His 'Preface' verges on self-parody, and the formulaic profession of aristocratic diffidence about the propriety of publishing comes across as an élitist disdain for the book trade: 'I wrote the following journals for my own private amusement, without any thoughts of their publication. I have not had the least assistance therein, consequently they must be full of incorrectness. However, as they may be of use, I have permitted them to be published' (iv). Baltimore's hauteur envisages a highly specific audience, and is hardly likely to endear him to the common readership: 'The relation in these sheets is short and contracted, but to those of a liberal education, I hope, full enough; what I saw in my travels recalled strongly to my remembrance the classical erudition I was so happy as to receive at *Eton College*' (ii–iii). The *Monthly Review* is distinctly unimpressed, pointedly admitting Baltimore's *Tour* only as far as its 'Monthly Catalogue', dismissing it in a brief critical paragraph, and employing a *Shamela*-esque short-hand:

> Lord B. [*sic*] no doubt, intended to oblige the public by printing the remarks he made in his tour to the east; and the public is

---

[1]   *MR*, 67 (1782), 100, reviewing the anonymous *Travelling Anecdotes through various Parts of Europe* (2 vols, 1782) which are described as 'affected and fantastic' (93).

certainly obliged to him for his kind intention, – but for nothing
more: the observations he has made being of very little
importance, and his book a mere trifle, compared with the
accounts before published by writers who were neither ashamed
nor afraid of being considered as *authors*. 'I am no author, (says
he) have a variety of affairs to attend on, as well as a very
indifferent state of health:' – then why the — did his Lordship run
his head against the press?[2]

The *Critical Review* is rather more deferential towards Baltimore's text,
referring throughout its notice to the 'noble author' or to 'his lordship', and
commending as a 'benevolent principle' his decision to publish. This
expression of gratitude acknowledges the general reluctance of the aristocracy
to venture into print, and it is intriguing how the *Critical Review* valiantly
discerns in Baltimore's hauteur an appreciation of the literary market's
burgeoning respectability: 'Persons of rank and quality cannot give a better
proof of their regard for literature, than by becoming authors themselves',
declares the reviewer.[3] At other times, in fact, the *Critical* could adopt a much
more hostile approach to dilettanti authors, and robustly celebrate the efforts of
professional writers and middle-class amateurs. Similarly, the *Monthly*'s
review of Baltimore does not mean that the journal was inherently anti-
aristocratic: in 1773, for example, it gives a very favourable review of the
posthumously published *Letters from Italy, in the Years 1754 and 1755*, by
John, Earl of Cork and Orrery. However, Orrery is praised for his personal
characteristics, not his rank; and the fact of his having previously figured in the
world of learned publication also earns respect. The reviewer observes that the
letters 'derive more than a common claim to attention, from the name of the
ingenious and noble Writer, already well known for his Translation of Pliny's
Epistles', and praising the author's family, 'which has been more ennobled by a
kind of hereditary love of science and literature, than by the adventitious
honours of titles and strings, – the *best* wishes by which some men are
distinguished'.[4] So, although Johnson's observation to George III that the
Critical Review was 'for supporting the constitution, both in church and state',
whereas – as he remarked to Boswell – the *Monthly* was for 'pulling down all
establishments', is broadly true, each journal was capable of entertaining a

---

[2]   *MR*, 37 (1767), 312. Lord Oxford observed that Baltimore's *Tour* 'no more deserved
to be published than his bills on the road for post-horses' (*Dictionary of National
Biography* 3rd edn, 22 vols, Oxford, 1967–8), iii. 720). Baltimore consolidated his
cavalier public image when he was tried (although finally acquitted) for the highly
Lovelace-esque abduction and rape of an unfortunately named young milliner, Sarah
Woodcock, in 1768. See the extensive coverage of the case in *GM*, 38 (1768), 42; 92;
140; 142; 180–88.

[3]   *CR*, 24 (1767), 172.

[4]   *MR*, 49 (1773), 81.

variety of political viewpoints in their critical judgements, not only because of the range of journalists they employed (all of whom remained anonymous, however), but also because of the ever-changing social and political contexts within which texts were reviewed.[5]

The *Critical* as well as the *Monthly* displays an increasing tendency to praise the integrity of professional writers and middle-class travellers, in explicit or implicit contrast to the moral and aesthetic value of Grand Tour accounts. In fact, as we have seen, these did not appear very numerously, and the aristocratic 'raree-shew books' berated in the *Critical*'s review in 1766 of Smollett's *Travels* seem to have existed more in the public imagination than in publishing fact. Hence, perhaps, the tone of surprised ridicule in the *Monthly*'s review of Baltimore's *Tour*, the clichéd classicism of which clearly struck its reviewer as astonishingly trivial and irrelevant. Nevertheless, according to the *Critical Review* in 1766, Smollett's *Travels* heralded a new era for the genre, and Smollett himself was hailed as a destroyer of 'error and false taste however dignified by length of time or authority of names; in short' – continues the reviewer – 'we here see a work executed upon an ethic plan'.[6]

If the Grand Tour came to be viewed with moral and aesthetic suspicion, it was increasingly condemned in political terms as irrelevant or indeed unpatriotic. Bruce Redford sees 1700–60 as the 'heyday' of the Grand Tour, with 1760–90 as a period of gradual decline.[7] This may be linked to the revival of universities and the rise of public schools as more effective educating procedures, as well as the promulgation of a specifically British cultural

---

[5]   James Boswell, *Life of Johnson* (1791), ed. G. B. Hill and L. F. Powell (6 vols, Oxford, 1934–64), ii. 40; iii. 32. The anonymity of the literary reviews during the eighteenth century meant that each journal presented to the reading public a uniform and in some ways inscrutable editorial collective. The reviewing 'we' was not always presented as a formidable monolith, however: most famously perhaps, the reception of Sterne (both *Tristram Shandy* and *A Sentimental Journey*) by the *Monthly Review* was conducted in terms which made it clear that the same reviewer had dealt with each volume, thus fostering a sense of relationship between text, review, and reader. See Alan B. Howes ed., *Sterne: the Critical Heritage* (1974), 5–11; 46–204. More generally, fluctuations of tone and register occur within the 'house-style' of each of the reviews. The *Monthly*'s editor, Ralph Griffiths, annotated his personal copies of the journal (now in the Bodleian Library, Oxford) so as to indicate by initials the contributing reviewer of each article. This information, together with a great deal of related research, enabled Benjamin Nangle in the 1950s to construct an index of all reviews in the *Monthly*, including their authorship. Although this constitutes an invaluable research tool in certain contexts, it should be borne in mind that the eighteenth-century reading public did not have the benefit of such information. See Benjamin Nangle, *The Monthly Review, First Series, 1749–1789: Indexes of Contributors and Articles* (Oxford, n.d.); and *The Monthly Review, Second Series, 1790–1815: Indexes of Contributors and Articles* (Oxford, 1955).

[6]   *CR*, 21 (1766), 322.

[7]   Bruce Redford, *Venice and the Grand Tour* (1996), 15.

identity to replace the cosmopolitan ideal. In 1763, the clergyman and 'Fellow of St John's College, Cambridge' Edward Clarke, who accompanied the Earl of Bristol as Ambassador to Madrid, and was himself well-informed about the classical world, actually expresses distaste for 'elegant' pursuits such as 'reading *Virgil* upon the banks of the *Mincio*' in favour of more productive investigations into 'the present state of SPAIN', which 'might prove of some utility to the public in general' (*Letters concerning the Spanish Nation*, i). These preoccupations are explicitly presented as more patriotic than those of aristocratic cosmopolitanism, since they offer empirically useful information (on religion and government in particular), and will more broadly provide the reader with 'a fresh proof of the happiness, which he enjoys in being *born a Briton*; of living in a country, where he possesses freedom of sentiment and of action, liberty of conscience, and security of property' (vi). The utility of this political focus is nicely contrasted with the futile and declining interests of the Grand Tourist:

> Writers of authentic accounts of countries, though beneath the attention of elegant genius, and not rising to the higher claims of taste and *virtù*, may notwithstanding be more serviceable to the public, than the purchaser of a decayed *Titian*, the recoverer of a rusty *coin*, the copier of a defaced *inscription*, or the designer of an old *ruin*. (ii)

Other writers (and their reviewers) emphasize less the informative value than the patriotic economy of middle-class travel. A comparatively late travelogue (the title is misleading), Thomas Cogan's *John Buncle, Junior, Gentleman* (2 vols, 1776–8), makes humorous play with these tensions, contrasting the fashionable mode of sentimental travel (which will be explored in more detail in the next chapter) with expensive dilettantism:

> I really prefer gathering up good useful sentiments as I traverse the country, to collecting of pictures, picking up of cockle-shells, catching of butterflies, creeping after insects, culling of simples, measuring of steeples, or any other travelling occupation in which, an ambitious trifler may also seek renown.[8]

---

[8] *John Buncle, Junior, Gentleman* (2 vols, 1776–8), i. 85–6. Cogan's narrative purports to contain the first-person travel narrative of the son of 'John Buncle', who had been the eponymous hero of Thomas Amory's strange novel-cum-travelogue, *The Life of John Buncle* (2 vols, 1756–66), which Ralph Griffiths had reviewed with great enthusiasm (*MR* 15 [1756], 497–512; 35 [1766], 33–43, 100–123). Amory's text, describing the 'transactions' of John Buncle the elder during his indefatigable expeditions in search of Unitarian maidens in the northern landscapes of England, had clearly become a byword for eccentric travel by 1776, and Cogan exploits this in his cheerily spurious title.

Cogan enumerates the advantages of his approach:

> In the first place, it is the *cheapest*. The largest collection of
> thoughts which a man can decently lay in, need not cost him more
> than his travelling expences. So that he must run many miles
> indeed, before he runs out any thing of a fortune.—Which, by the
> way, is not always the case with the other gentry, who are often in
> the utmost danger of hanging half their estate upon the *proboscis*
> of a *Beetle*, the *antennae* of a *Butterfly*, or the *convolution* of a
> *Shell*; and of giving more for a *painted* Landscape, than the
> proprietor gave for the original territory. (i. 86)

As well as being vilified for their extravagant shopping, Grand Tourists
were criticized simply for the vast sums they spent on subsistence abroad.
During the years immediately following the Seven Years War, streams of
'Milords' as well as crowds of humbler tourists poured across the Channel, and
social tensions inevitably arose, bringing into sharper focus the decadence of
the aristocracy at home as well as on vacation. *The Gentleman's Guide in his
Tour through France* was published in 1766, 'By an Officer in the Royal Navy,
who lately made that Tour on a Principle which he sincerely recommends to all
his Countrymen, *viz.* not to spend more Money in the Country of our natural
Enemy, than is requisite to support with Decency the Character of an
Englishman'. The *Critical Review* praises this enterprise, and adds that 'the
prodigality and lavishness of the English abroad is a national reproach to every
foreigner of sense and reflection', while the *Monthly Review* also notes that the
'character of an Englishman abroad, is that of a rich, foolish extravagant
fellow', and that this characterization therefore lays all Britons open to French
exploitation.[9] Philip Thicknesse complains about the 'multitude of low-bred
rich people' whose extravagance encourages the French to exploit *all* English
travellers: for their 'vanity and folly I must pay at every town I pass, or reside
in'.[10]

Repeatedly in such discussions, Grand Tourists are represented as an ill-
behaved and unthinking gaggle, lacking any discernible 'character' beyond the
folly of their class. Frequently, this stupidity is figured in farcically bestial

---

[9]   *CR*, 21 (1766), 464; *MR*, 35 (1766), 31. The thrust of the *Gentleman's Guide* speaks
explicitly to post-1763 concerns, but its encouragement of low-budget travel for the non-
aristocratic classes had been anticipated in 1753 by *The Traveller's Companion and
Guide through France, Flanders, Brabant, and Holland*, praised by the *Monthly Review*
as a 'work much wanted, and never before published, being calculated for the benefit
and information of all strangers going into those countries, either on business or
pleasure, and to prevent their being imposed on; for by following this book, they will
travel at near one half of the expence' (*MR*, 8 [1753], 511).
[10] Philip Thicknesse, *Observations on the Customs and Manners of the French Nation*
(1766), 89.

terms. For instance, the reviewer in the *London Magazine* of Smollett's *Travels* in 1766 hopes that the work 'may be of infinite service to our country, by giving some check to the follies of our Apes, male and female, of French fashions and politeness, with whom we are over run'.[11] The narrator of Samuel Paterson's sentimental travelogue, *Another Traveller!* (2 vols, 1768–9) describes the arrival of a typical herd of English Grand Tourists in Brussels:

> What company was that that arrived just now at the *hotel d'Angleterre*?—A crew of noisy Englishmen—they have left *London* upon a ten days party—to see a play, to laugh heartily at the friars, to steal a nun apiece (if possible) or failing therein, each to have his battered Brussels wh— and a skin full of Burgundy.— Englishmen are always at home—hark! they begin to roar already.[12]

If this passage (representative of many accounts) presents the roaring Milords as indistinguishable from one another in their rapacious virility, other writers by contrast rhetorically infantilize Grand Tourists. The *Monthly Review* in 1766 describes them as 'men of Fortune' who 'transport themselves from country to country, and ramble from town to town, without speculation, or improvement; as children turn over books for the sake of the cutts'.[13] Smollett complains in his *Travels* (also in 1766) about 'a number of raw boys, whom Britain seemed to have poured forth on purpose to bring her national character into contempt'.[14] Paterson and Smollett – like many other travel writers during these years – define themselves in moral opposition to the deviant aristocracy by stressing their own virtuous and adult masculinity. In Smollett's *Travels*, as in other travel narratives from the 1760s and 1770s, manly integrity goes hand-in-hand with the projection of an eccentric narrator, in implicit contrast to contemporary perceptions of Grand Tourists as herds of characterless cosmopolites or boors. The opening paragraphs swiftly establish Smollett's

---

[11] *London Magazine*, 35 (1766), 243.

[12] Samuel Paterson, *Another Traveller! or Cursory Remarks and Tritical Observations made upon a Journey through Part of the Netherlands in the latter End of the Year 1766* (2 vols, 1768–9), i. 236. In the nineteenth century, pejorative animal imagery of this kind is re-appropriated by self-consciously 'cultured' travellers to describe the ill-bred, plebeian 'tourist' hordes, *Blackwood's Magazine*, for example, complaining of the 'droves of these creatures' (cited in Paul Fussell, *Abroad: British Literary Travelling Between the Wars* [Oxford, 1980], 40).

[13] *MR*, 34 (1766), 127, reviewing a translation from the Swedish of Hasselquist's *Voyages and Travels in the Levant*, and distinguishing between these 'men of Fortune' and those 'men of Science' who 'enrich themselves and others by their collections and their remarks'.

[14] Tobias Smollett, *Travels through France and Italy* (1766), ed. Frank Felsenstein (Oxford, 1979), 251.

credentials as an upright citizen and the moral centre of his closely-knit family: not only is he fleeing the threat of 'civil dissension' posed by the Wilkes controversy (an issue to which we shall return later in this chapter), but he is taking with him his 'little family' and his 'trusted servant, who had lived with me a dozen of years, and now refused to leave me'. Furthermore, the trip is presented as an attempt at emotional recovery from an unspecified 'domestic calamity' – actually the death of Smollett's only daughter – and as undertaken largely to please his wife, who 'earnestly begged I would convey her from a country where every object served to nourish her grief' (2). Modern readers may find the sentimental domesticity of these opening paragraphs hard to square with the cantankerous tone of the *Travels* as a whole. John Mullan has explained this curious conjunction (in a range of influential literary and medical discourses during the eighteenth century), showing how the resonances of 'spleen' are complex, and how the term can denote heightened sensibility rather than its obverse.[15] Splenetic short-temper, therefore, should not be seen as diametrically opposed to sensibility, but as another of its manifestations. Furthermore, spleen and sensibility, whether together or separately, were frequently described as 'the English malady' – available by extension to all Britons – and viewed as conditions peculiar to the British, related to the changeable and generally damp climate, and especially common among the over-educated classes. This is an important nexus of ideas, which can in fact be further nuanced in the terms of the present study by highlighting the way in which Smollett's persona in the *Travels* enables him not only to assert his hypersensitive hypochondria, but also, semi-paradoxically, to present himself as splenetic in a peculiarly British and energetic fashion.

Like Lord Orrery's posthumous account, Smollett's *Travels* were greeted as the product of a writer whose 'abilities' are 'universally known'.[16] The *London Magazine* announced to its readers that 'Here no affected, pert journalist presents his crude observations; every thing is the product of learning and experience, and the thorough knowledge of mankind which the Dr is well known to have acquired'.[17] Reflecting on authorial integrity, the *Monthly* observes in 1763 that

> When men of learning and character publish accounts of their travels, the public never fail to distinguish their productions from the common details of Voyagers, and Tour-makers in general, who seldom inform us of any thing more important than the quality of the wine in one place, the nature of the roads in another, the price of provisions in a third, the ornaments of a church, the paintings in

[15] John Mullan, *Sentiment and Sociability: the Language of Feeling in the Eighteenth Century* (1988; repr. Oxford, 1990), 202–40.
[16] *MR*, 34 (1766), 420.
[17] *London Magazine*, 35 (1766), 243.

Prince what d'ye all-him's collection, the exhibitions of a theatre, and the diversions of a Carnival.[18]

Writers whose travel narrative was their first or only venture into print therefore had to exercise some caution. Some of the problems faced by obscure authors are winsomely described by Cogan's *John Buncle, Junior* (himself successfully hailed by the *Critical Review* as 'one of those facetious and eccentric gentlemen who afford entertainment even by their oddities'),[19] as he highlights the resourcefulness of the book-trade in marketing books by unknown writers:

> When we publish the works of an author, whose *name is up*, as we phrase it, then indeed we dress them out in the plainest garb imaginable, prudently reserving our ornaments for those who stand more in need of them ...
>   Again, if an author has not yet arrived to so great a degree of eminence, why we charitably hope the best, as in *your* case; and by a spirit of prophesy,—which I confess sometimes fails us—we announce him to the world as the *Ingenious*, the *Learned*, the *Celebrated*, carefully displaying all his titles and offices, down to the chaplainship of a regiment; if they appear either posts of honour or of intelligence.
>   These bays we generally reserve for Historiographers, Biographers, writers of voyages and travels, and the rest of the troops that are *in our own pay*, Mr. Buncle. (i. 8–9)

Albeit less overtly, an unknown young Scot named James Boswell had earlier realized the potential of the travelogue as a genre by which a writer's reputation might be made almost overnight. Boswell's account of Corsica was widely and enthusiastically reviewed on its appearance in 1768, and he swiftly consolidated his new-found celebrity in frequent ostentatious appearances as 'Corsican Boswell'. *Corsica* saw three editions and four translations before 1800, and until 1785 when *The Journal of a Tour to the Hebrides* was published, it was as the author of *Corsica* that Boswell was known to the reading public. The *Monthly*, for example, in a 1775 review of Johnson's *Journey to the Western Islands of Scotland*, identifies Boswell in a footnote as 'Author of a Tour of Corsica'. The strategies of self-presentation by which 'Corsican Boswell' hurled himself into the literary limelight into 1768 – as well as his use of the travelogue to put forward a particular political case – crystallize several of the issues under discussion here.

The full text of Boswell's tripartite *An Account of Corsica, the Journal of a Tour to that Island; and Memoirs of Pascal Paoli* is rarely read or studied

---

[18] *MR*, 28 (1763), 215.
[19] *CR*, 45 (1777), 239.

today. Yet the opening section, the *Account of Corsica*, which provides a natural and political history of the island, was well received in 1768: it was commended by the *Monthly Review* as a 'useful' compilation of 'ample materials' not otherwise widely available (most of them were French works), and it put Corsica firmly on the map of Europe for British readers. Nevertheless, the *Account* is entirely omitted from the Yale edition, on the grounds of its unoriginality, and lack of autobiographical reference.[20] Boswell's separation of personal experience and researched information serves him badly in the twentieth century, but in his own day was effective, because the *Account* established him as a conscientious author and thus disposed his audience favourably towards the more outspoken, individualistic sections of the volume. Despite the delusions of grandeur in the 'Preface', where he describes the 'ardour of publick curiosity' (*Account of Corsica* [1768], ix) which has encouraged him to publish, Boswell enjoyed no public reputation prior to the publication of *Corsica*, but instead constructed *within* his text the same kind of standing which Smollett already enjoyed as compiler and man of letters before the publication of his *Travels*.

Describing in his 'Preface' the collection of source material for the *Account*, Boswell proclaims not only his erudition and industry, but also his social connections: Mr Burnaby, the chaplain to the British factory at Leghorn, lends Boswell a diary of his own earlier tour to Corsica, and the English consul at Leghorn, as well as various Italian gentlemen including Count Rivarola, and Pascal Paoli himself, share their knowledge with the young Scot: 'These gentlemen have all contributed their aid in erecting my little monument to liberty' (xiv). Similarly, the volume's 'seasonable quotation from the Classicks' serves a double purpose, 'adding dignity to Corsica, by shewing its consideration among the ancients' (xviii), but also, of course, displaying Boswell's educational accomplishments. And by displaying his knowledge of the travelogue's Addisonian heritage, Boswell earns the right to deviate from the purely classical mode into the more outspoken and political concerns of the *Journal* and *Memoirs*.

It is a critical commonplace that in writing the *Memoirs of Pascal Paoli* Boswell performs his biographical apprenticeship for the *Life of Johnson*.[21] Just

---

[20] In the first (Glasgow) edition of 1768, 1–258 comprise the *Account of Corsica*, including an 'Appendix of Corsican State Papers'. The three chapters of the *Account* describe the climate, topography, agriculture and history of Corsica, and its present government, religion and national character. *The Journal of a Tour to that Island* and the *Memoirs of Pascal Paoli* occupy 259–382 (roughly a third of the volume). The Yale edition, *Boswell on the Grand Tour: Italy, Corsica and France 1765–1766*, ed. Frank Brady and Frederick A. Pottle (New Haven, 1955), prints the *Journal* and the *Memoirs*, with many additional letters and documents of biographical interest, but not the *Account*.

[21] See Thomas M. Curley, 'Boswell's Liberty-Loving *Account of Corsica* and the Art of Travel Literature', in Greg Clingham ed., *New Light on Boswell: Critical and*

as important an impulse behind both of Boswell's 'lives', however, is the construction of a public identity for the biographer. Boswell brilliantly conflates hero-worship and self-importance when he reiterates Pascal Paoli's pronouncement that 'A man come from Corsica will be like a man come from the Antipodes' (320). The 'Preface' makes still more explicit the book's role in creating a celebrity out of its author: 'I have an ardent ambition for literary fame', Boswell announces, and observes further that 'A man who has been able to furnish a book which has been approved by the world, has established himself as a respectable character in distant society, without any danger of having that character lessened by the observation of his weaknesses' (xx). Boswell is studious to characterize himself as different from the typical Grand Tourist; Ralph Griffiths notes approvingly that 'he, unlike our young men of quality, who only visit the scenes of foreign luxury and dissipation, pitched upon Corsica'.[22] Boswell himself phrases it rather more elegantly in the opening of the *Journal*:

> Having resolved to pass some years abroad, for my instruction and entertainment, I conceived a design of visiting the island of Corsica. I wished for something more than just the common course of what is called the tour of Europe; and Corsica occurred to me as a place which nobody else had seen, and where I should find what was to be seen nowhere else, a people actually fighting for liberty, and forming themselves from a poor inconsiderable oppressed nation, into a flourishing and independent state. (261)

Boswell enlists British sympathies for the Corsican resistance to French rule by emphasizing the affinities between the British and the Corsicans, both patriotic inhabitants of island states perpetually threatened by French invasion. Audaciously, Boswell envisages 'the blunt kindness and admiration with which the hearty, generous, common people of England would treat the brave Corsicans' once military support against France has been proffered (321). And the rather old-fashioned classical validation, through Addison, of Corsica's national significance was well calculated to recruit readers at the opposite end of the social scale from the 'common people of England' to the noble political cause of Corsican liberty. Similarly, Boswell's long abstract discussion of 'liberty' in the 'Introduction' to the *Account* (which the *Monthly Review* excerpts in full) exploits the fashionable and gratifyingly 'Enlightened' interest in Rousseau's philosophy. (It also capitalizes rather opportunistically on Rousseau's controversial personal status, since his feud with Hume was being assiduously documented in the national press and the reviews.) Finally, in the

---

Historical Essays on the Occasion of the Bicentenary of 'The Life of Johnson' (Cambridge, 1991), 89–103.
[22] *MR*, 39 (1768), 45–6.

light of 1760s politics, during which British 'liberty' had become a hostage to virulent class-based factionalism in the Wilkes furore, Boswell's relocation of the principles of liberty to Corsica is masterly.[23] Whereas Wilkes (for example, in a speech to the Court of Common Pleas in April 1768, following the *North Briton*, 45 uproar), pronounced his interest in the 'liberty of all peers and gentlemen and what touches me more sensibly, that of all the middling and inferior set of people who stand most in need of protection' and declared the current controversy to be 'of such importance as to determine at once whether English liberty shall be a reality or a shadow', Boswell effectively strips the term of its controversial associations with class conflict and emphasizes instead the primitive and insular origins of 'liberty' in the context of foreign invasion rather than domestic faction.[24] Indeed, domestic solidarity rather than disputation is what emerges as the central political virtue of Paoli's Corsica, and Boswell's text (which tactfully fails to mention his personal friendship with Wilkes) in this light may be seen covertly to advocate domestic conciliation.[25] In the 'Introduction', as indeed throughout the volume, Boswell dramatizes himself as a youthful enthusiast for liberty, to pre-empt criticism of his presumptuous lobbying of the British ministry on Corsica's behalf:

> I am persuaded that my readers will grant me every indulgence, when they consider how favourable is the subject. ... they will readily make allowance for the enthusiasm of one who has been among the brave islanders, when their patriotic virtue is at its height, and who has felt as it were a communication of their spirit. (8–9)

So, although the terms 'liberty' and 'patriotism' are bandied about freely in Boswell's *Corsica*, the text works vigorously to return the terms to an international, and domestically neutral context. Ralph Griffiths for one seems to have apprehended this idealistic refocusing of issues central to the Wilkes controversy, as he observes with quiet amusement that 'We have here what, in the eye of many a misinformed English Reader, may look like a prodigy; a *North* Briton fervently devoted to LIBERTY, and that with a degree of zeal almost romantic'.[26]

---

[23] See, for example, the report in *GM* 38 (1768), 140 of events on the night of Monday 28 March, when, following Wilkes' election, the populace 'grew outrageous' and broke the windows of Lord Bute's house and all those around: 'Wilkes and Liberty was the cry, and all who refus'd to eccho it back, were knocked down.'

[24] Cited in Ian Gilmour, *Riots, Risings and Revolution: Governance and Violence in 18th Century England* (1992), 307.

[25] The fact that Boswell's travelling companion around Italy was the son of Lord Bute is no doubt also relevant in this context.

[26] *MR*, 39 (1768), 43. The *North Briton* was, of course, the title of the radical anti-ministerial organ authored by Wilkes and Charles Churchill, number 45 of which had

That Griffiths was surprised at the absence of a factional agenda in a Scots-authored European travelogue owes something to the crucial role which the Wilkes controversy had been presented as playing in Smollett's *Travels* two years earlier.[27] The literary opportunist Philip Thicknesse (caricatured as 'Dr Viper' in Samuel Foote's play *The Capucin* of 1775) attacked the *Travels* with intense vitriol in the same year, 1766, prompted not only by Smollett's political bias but by a network of related concerns which pull together the issues of class and public character under examination here.[28] It is to this somewhat bizarre literary antagonism that we now, therefore, turn.

Smelfungus and Dr Viper : the Smollett–Thicknesse affair

The following section will explore the controversial relationship between the travel writings of Tobias Smollett and Philip Thicknesse. Having first addressed the explicitly political aspect of the antagonism, the discussion will broaden out in order to show how authorial good character (defined to some extent with reference to class) and the ability to engage in rational debate become signs of British male subjecthood which Thicknesse attempts valiantly to reconfigure. His critical reception – which was voluminous – suggests that he was only partially successful here, and indeed to some extent Thicknesse functions as a deranged stooge who serves to throw into relief the patriotic reasonableness increasingly claimed for the British national character. Nevertheless, the space devoted to his eccentric ravings by both Reviews is also an arena within which the more extreme implications of personal and literary liberty are debated.

Despite its twentieth-century reputation simply for xenophobic vitriol, Smollett's *Travels through France and Italy* was greeted by contemporary critics as the work of a 'man of sense, divested of partiality, reasoning with freedom and candour upon every occurrence, and without the smallest temptation to be biassed', and 'the work of a man of genius and learning'.[29] The *Critical Review* praises Smollett particularly for presenting things Parisian 'in a very different light from that of any other representation we have read, and with a freedom that could be dictated by independency alone, and that honest indignation which must arise in a sensible breast at the partiality with which

---

lambasted the king's craven subservience to his Scottish ministers Bute and Mansfield, prompting the arrest of Wilkes and his supporters for seditious libel. See Gilmour, *Riots, Risings and Revolution*, 301–41.

[27] Smollett's own pro-Bute journal, *The Briton* (1762–3), had inspired Wilkes to the ironic naming of his oppositional *North Briton*.

[28] See Philip Gosse, *Dr Viper: the Querulous Life of Philip Thicknesse* (1952), 167 and passim. Foote's play was originally entitled *A Trip to Calais*.

[29] *CR*, 21 (1766), 406; *MR*, 34 (1766), 429.

every thing relating to France and Frenchmen is commonly exhibited'.[30] A few months later Thicknesse responded with a work entitled *Observations on the Customs and Manners of the French Nation, in a Series of Letters, in which that Nation is vindicated from the Misrepresentations of some Late Writers*. Although his main target is in fact Smollett rather than Smollett's misrepresentations, and although the pro-French position suggested by his title is ambiguous – he is full of enthusiasm for the French nobility and monarchy, but dismisses the peasantry with exaggerated contempt – there is nevertheless a political dimension to Thicknesse's indignation. The nature of British liberty, in relation or comparison to French tyranny, is a persistent theme of the *Observations*, and the Wilkes controversy is alluded to several times (although, in fact, we discover that Wilkes himself offended Thicknesse by failing to respond to a note sent to him at Paris).[31] Thicknesse's opposition to Smollett's anti-Wilkes and pro-Bute position is vigorous, and combines (in a typically Thicknessian formulation) political principle with personal opportunism: Thicknesse had recently tried to blackmail Bute by threatening to publish some letters by the minister's late mother-in-law, Lady Mary Wortley Montagu.[32] Bute had, however, foiled this attempt, thus further fuelling Thicknesse's pre-existing Scottophobia, which would in any case have embraced Smollett.

Smollett opens his *Travels* with the hyperbolic suggestion that although 'domestic calamity' was one reason for his choosing to visit France, it was actually the Wilkes furore which had finally forced him to leave Britain. He thus establishes himself as a persecuted yet loyal national subject, and quietly erases the context of Anglo-Scottish antagonism which had fuelled the Wilkes controversy: 'You know with what eagerness I fled from my country as a scene of illiberal dispute, and incredible infatuation, where a few worthless incendiaries had, by dint of perfidious calumnies and atrocious abuse, kindled up a flame which threatened all the horrors of civil dissension' (2). It seems that part at least of Smollett's motivation for a hostile representation of France (and Italy, though to a lesser extent) was the desire to highlight, by contrast, British prosperity and liberty. This particular vein of patriotism would be especially apposite at such a time, since it would serve to deflect criticism of threats to British liberty, and would therefore help deconstruct the Wilkite analogy between French and British aristocratic tyranny. Jeremy Black has suggested that after 1763, political considerations at home 'altered the focusing

---

[30] *CR*, 21 (1766), 323.

[31] *Observations*, 153.

[32] This instance of literary blackmail is documented (with obvious bias) by Thicknesse in a pamphlet entitled *A Narrative of what passed between General Sir Harry Erskine and Philip Thicknesse, Esq; in consequence of a Letter written by the Latter to the Earl of B—, Relative to the Publication of some Original Letters and Poetry of Lady Mary Wortley Montague's, then in Mr. Thicknesse's Possession* (1766). Erskine was a major-general in the army at this time and widely considered Bute's favourite.

of xenophobia' from the Continent to Scotland, personified in Bute and Mansfield.[33] Smollett, a Scot and a hack of Bute's, reinforces Francophobia in his *Travels* in order to deflect hatred from Scotland. It should, however, be noted that Wilkes and his supporters were themselves vehemently anti-French, contemptuous of France's nobility and peasantry alike. *North Briton* 45 objected violently to the 1763 Treaty of Paris. Anti-French rhetoric could be mobilized to very different ends, to support widely divergent notions of patriotism.

Smollett seizes every opportunity to harp on the evils of French government. At times his pretexts seem absurd, though his point may be serious. For example, the most British complaint that in Burgundy 'we sometimes found it very difficult to procure half a pint of milk for our tea' leads him into the following train of thought:

> The peasants in France are so wretchedly poor, and so much oppressed by their landlords, that they cannot afford to inclose their grounds, or give a proper respite to their lands; or to stock their farms with a sufficient number of black cattle to produce the necessary manure, without which agriculture can never be carried to any degree of perfection. Indeed, whatever efforts a few individuals may make for the benefit of their own estates, husbandry in France will never be generally improved, until the farmer is free and independent. (67)

In the South of France, there are absolutely 'no black cattle; and milk was so scarce, that sometimes we were obliged to drink our tea without it' (76). The effects of tyranny are again brought home to us. However, Smollett's travelogue overall expresses a broadly optimistic hope of political reform. In one of several curiously prescient passages of political discussion, Smollett envisages the disappearance of the ancien régime:

> There are, undoubtedly, many marks of relaxation in the reins of the French government, and, in all probability, the subjects of France will be the first to take advantage of it. There is at present a violent fermentation of different principles among them, which under the reign of a very weak prince, or during a long minority, may produce a great change in the constitution. In proportion to the progress of reason and philosophy, which have made great advances in this kingdom, superstition loses ground; antient prejudices give way; a spirit of freedom takes the ascendant. (299)

---

[33] Jeremy Black, 'Tourism and Cultural Challenge: The Changing Scene of the Eighteenth Century', in John McVeagh ed., *All Before Them, 1660–1780* (1989), 185–202; 194.

It is striking how Smollett here envisages a peaceable, commonsensical revolution – much like that of 1688, it would seem. The rising tide of enlightened reason is further strengthened, in Smollett's vision, by the activities of the 'commons', who, 'enriched by commerce and manufacture, grow impatient of those odious distinctions, which exclude them from the honours and privileges due to their importance in the commonwealth' (313). Bourgeois rationality, then, which is oddly similar to British good sense, is likely to triumph over tyranny, whose power is thus rhetorically underplayed, just as the possibility of political violence is conspicuously absent. The relevance of this to British domestic politics, at a time when 'all the horrors of civil dissension' in the streets of London seemed a real possibility, is clear.

It was perhaps not so clear to Thicknesse, whose *Observations* seem to exploit the travelogue's potential for controversy and self-publication, without bothering to provide the requisite signs of reasonable, sociable Britishness. Thicknesse always hovered on the fringes of rationality and legality: he was a lifelong opium addict who believed that old age could be staved off by 'inhaling the breath of young women, whenever they lay in my way', and his literary activities included plagiarism, libel and blackmail.[34] The *Observations* are not only bizarrely amusing, but they also testify to the extent to which travelogue could accommodate individualism of an extreme kind at this time. Where Smollett, as spokesman for the middling sort of Briton, regrets that Grand Tourists bring Britain's 'national character into contempt' (251), Thicknesse attacks them for purely self-interested reasons, complaining that their extravagance encourages the French to hike up their prices and thereby cause great inconvenience to Philip Thicknesse: 'for [their] vanity and folly I must pay at every town I pass, or reside in' (*Observations*, 9). This penny-pinching querulousness characterizes all of *Observations* and Thicknesse's later *Useful Hints for those who make the Tour of France, in a Series of Letters* (1768), both of which are peppered with passages of personal invective or self-vindication relating to the numerous quarrels in which he involved himself, and generally quite irrelevant to the travelogue as such.

The hysterical individualism of *Observations* and *Useful Hints* is bound up with a class identity which is inconsistent to the point of irrationality. On the one hand, Thicknesse satirizes the idle excesses of the French court as well as the decadent antics of the aristocratic Grand Tourists. On the other, he describes the daily routine of the French monarchy at Versailles with fawning detail, congratulating himself on his proximity to their futile activities, and he also presents his contempt for Smollett as a class issue by casting aspersions on the social spheres in which Smollett allegedly moved: 'An English lady of fashion who resides here, to whom I lent Smollet's [*sic*] Travels, says, he certainly lodged at ale-houses, and conversed with the lowest class of

---

[34] Gosse, *Dr Viper*, 290 (citing Thicknesse's *Memoirs*), and passim.

mechanics that frequent such houses' (*Observations*, 91). Throughout his works, Thicknesse adopts a self-conscious tone of upper-class disdain, and engages in name-dropping, connection-hunting, and complaining about peasants. Indeed, for the French poor he has nothing but contempt, observing at one point that 'The common beggars, indeed, are more numerous than with us; but common beggars have very little title to compassion, are of no use to society, and, as General Hurst used to say to them, when they said they were starving: "Die! Die! the sooner you are dead the better"' (*Observations*, 53–4).

If his hatred of the poor seems wilfully groundless, Thicknesse's hostility towards the reviewing establishment – whom he accuses of 'Partiality ... *atrocious* ignorance, incapacity, and *******' (*Useful Hints*, unnumbered prefatory page) – is, by contrast, assiduously backed up with rafts of accusatory evidence. The *Critical* comes in for particular vitriol, as Thicknesse constructs an elaborate conspiracy theory around Smollett's earlier involvement with the journal. The first letter of *Useful Hints* is a seventeen-page diatribe against Smollett, dotted with pairs and triplets of exclamation marks against even the most petty of observations: complaining about Smollett's stove arrangements at Nice, for example, Thicknesse shrieks 'the Doctor burnt, in the space of *four weeks*, FIFTEEN THOUSAND weight of wood!!! exclusive of pine-tops to light this bonfire!—The poor cook! I wonder! Is HE alive!!' (13). This attack is preceded by one on the *Critical Review*, which is berated for employing personal satire. Thicknesse's own cheerful use of this approach is justified, in his view, on the grounds that he is a private citizen who happens to publish, while Smollett is a 'writer *by trade*', and therefore has a greater public responsibility:

> When the *arch critic* himself puts forth any thing; when *Toby the martinet in literature*, honours the world with an account of *his travels*, the public are gulled and imposed upon, if they do not meet with TRUTH; purity of style, delicacy of sentiment, and sterling judgment throughout the whole performance; from a writer by profession every propriety is expected, every absurdity is glaring. (2)

Not that Thicknesse has any respect for the 'trade' of writing; he sneers at the *Critical* reviewers as men 'who are *to be had*, like common prostitutes, for hire' (2). Given that no other writer of the time made such opportunistic and amoral use of the book trade than Thicknesse, this is more than slightly hypocritical. But he nevertheless adopts a pseudo-aristocratic position of personal diffidence and disdain for the tawdry world of the book trade, complaining that 'The chieftain of the Reviewers, perceiving that I was indifferent as to an attack made upon what I am sensible I do not possess, (any abilities as an author) laid aside *reviewing* the WRITINGS, to abuse and vilify the WRITER ...' (2). This aggrieved paranoia inspires Thicknesse to the childish but

mildly amusing ploy of plagiarizing several of the concluding remarks of
Smollett's travel letters as conclusions for his own. *'There's for you! A la
Smolletta!'* he crows triumphantly at one point, having explained that

> as I am sensible how much depends upon the manner in which (to
> speak in the style of an auctioneer) a letter is *knocked off*, by a
> graceful and well-turned conclusion, I am determined, in spite of
> the sin of plagiarism, to conclude this, and my subsequent letters
> above the reach of *Scotch criticism*: for who among them will dare
> to censure me, when I say,—'These I own are frivolous incidents,
> scarce worth committing to paper; but they may serve to introduce
> observations of more consequence; and in the mean time I know
> nothing will be indifferent to you that concerns Your humble
> servant'[35]

He also plagiarizes the *Monthly Review*'s critique of Smollett in the Pantheon,
word for word: citing Smollett's comparison of the rotunda to 'a huge cockpit,
with a hole at the top', the reviewer and Thicknesse both inquire why he did
not liken it to 'an inverted porridge-pot, with a hole in the bottom'.[36] The
Monthly Review had not in fact been especially hostile towards Smollett's
Travels, though it was less adulatory than the *Critical*. Notwithstanding his
blanket condemnation of the literary prostitution represented by both Reviews,
Thicknesse is happy to enlist the *Critical*'s rival onto his side, taking full
advantage of the publicity afforded by the reviewing arena.

The response of the *Critical* to Thicknesse's frenzied accusations is a
masterpiece of amused irony. Having first emphasized the journal's impartiality
by observing that 'Dr Smollett ... has not, for several years past, had the least
concern with the Critical Review', the reviewer proceeds to explain
Thicknesse's eccentric paranoia by diagnosing him as insane. The onset of his
madness is quite precisely located, as the reviewer informs readers that 'Letter
V is written from the top of a mountain so high, that the writer loses sight of
common sense'.[37] Thicknesse's affliction is referred to with elaborate
compassion throughout this review, and is recalled in that of *Useful Hints* two
years later, when the reviewer reiterates the journal's

> most sensible concern at his having not yet recovered that sight of
> common sense which he lost upon the top of a high French
> mountain. However, as he seems to enjoy some lucid intervals, we
> will talk with him in a manner that shall not touch upon the springs
> of his disorder; and therefore, for fear of reviving it, we shall omit
> all his abuse of Dr. Smollett, which fills up the first letter of the

---

[35] *Useful Hints*, 24–5, plagiarizing the conclusion to Letter I of Smollett's *Travels*.

[36] *Useful Hints*, 11, plagiarizing *MR*, 34 (1766), 428.

[37] *CR*, 22 (1766), 432–4.

publication before us, because we scorn to encounter Mr. T. with
the odds of the public opinion and judgment on our side.[38]

Common sense, 'public opinion and judgment', and indeed Smollett himself,
are all established as moral and critical stabilities which Thicknesse is
powerless to shake, although his attempts to do so may provide amusement for
the reading public. The ideological and personal instability of *Observations* and
Useful Hints, and the complete failure (or refusal) of their narrator to present
himself as a consistent British subject, remove the texts from the scope of
rational, consensual criticism. Mock charity is presented as the only viable
critical approach.

In complete contrast, Smollett's travelogue overflows with articulations of
patriotic subjecthood, and deploys several analytical perspectives of a self-
consciously British, empirical and rational nature. The letters which make up
the *Travels* skilfully weave together a range of discursive threads which would
have been highly appealing to the middle-class reader's hunger not only for
information and opinion, but also for a set of congenial attitudes and
pronouncements. Smollett's seamless recycling of passages from earlier
guidebooks, as well as his own copious descriptions, establishes the *Travels* as
empirically valuable: and then the deployment of a range of respectably manly
and patriotic discourses further consolidates his claim to virtue and 'genius'.
He confesses that he once 'had thoughts of writing a complete natural history'
of Nice and its environs, and although he has had 'neither health, strength, nor
opportunity, to make proper collections' (177), his benevolent intentions of
contributing to the expansion of knowledge are nevertheless poignantly
registered. More successful are his assiduous recordings of temperatures in
Nice (charted in an Appendix), his exhaustive accounts of available foodstuffs
in the south of France, and his speculations on the suitability of particular
climates and diets for valetudinarian travellers. The quest for health (through
diet, climate, or sea-bathing) in a hostile and alien environment further
highlights, in a rather extreme form, his peculiarly British physical intrepidity.
Similarly, the frequent references to French aristocratic decadence (for
example, in Letter IV's attack on the 'vain, proud, poor, and slothful' noblesse
of Boulogne, who are 'helpless in themselves, and useless to the community',
27), invoke the emotive anti-luxury, anti-aristocracy discourse which circulated
ubiquitously during the middle years of the century.[39] While for modern readers
Smollett's deployment of such rhetoric may smack of simple xenophobia – as
in his pronouncement that 'France is the general reservoir from which all the
absurdities of false taste, luxury, and extravagance have overflowed the

---

[38] *CR*, 25 (1768), 277–8.
[39] See John Sekora, *Luxury: the Concept in Western Thought, Eden to Smollett*
(Baltimore, 1977).

different kingdoms and states of Europe' (52) – in 1766 it resonated more of a domestic and manly patriotism, and Sterne's caricature of Smollett as the perpetually displeased Smelfungus should not be taken as a representative response. For readers of the *Critical Review*, as well as many who formulated their judgements independently, Smollett's *Travels* were congenial in presenting a 'naked view of objects and characters, and such a view as must endear England to Englishmen'.[40]

A few months later, the *Critical* echoes this tribute in praising the author of *Letters from Italy*, Samuel Sharp, as 'one of those few writers, whose labours ought to endear England to Englishmen'.[41] If the Smollett–Thicknesse dialogue reveals the extent to which rational, manly good sense was valued as central to British subjecthood, a similarly hostile textual exchange (again, powerfully intervened in by the reviews) between Samuel Sharp and Joseph Baretti reveals the extent to which those civic and personal qualities were increasingly construed as so peculiarly British as to be unavailable to an Italian. It is to the Sharp–Baretti controversy, and the 'nationalization' of virtue engineered by the reviews as much as the travelogues of these writers, that we now turn.

'Natural, manly, and forcible': Samuel Sharp versus Joseph Baretti

Whereas Thicknesse and Smollett were unequally matched in terms of their standing in the literary world, Sharp and Baretti were both writers of some reputation in other genres before they ventured into the territory of European travelogue. In 1753 Baretti had published *A Dissertation upon the Italian Poetry*, and he was a member of Johnson's literary circle. Sharp was a man of science rather than of letters, a distinguished surgeon and medical lecturer, and a member of the Royal Society. The *Monthly Review* observes in a footnote to its review of his travelogue that Sharp is the 'Author of *Operations in Surgery*, and *A Critical Enquiry into the Present State of Surgery*', implying that he can therefore be trusted to provide a reliable anatomy of the Italian manners which are the subject of his *Letters from Italy, Describing the Customs and Manners of that Country, in the Years 1765, and 1766* (1766).[42] Sharp's account (particularly the second edition of 1767) provoked a response from Baretti, *An Account of the Manners and Customs of Italy; with Observations on the Mistakes of some Travellers, with Regard to that Country* (2 vols, 1768).

Sharp's *Letters* do not display the literary sophistication or picaresque epistolary rhythms which distinguish Smollett's *Travels*, but in 1766 their self-proclaimed focus on 'customs and manners', rather than the more traditional

---

[40] *CR*, 21 (1766), 406.
[41] *CR*, 22 (1766), 285.
[42] *MR*, 35 (1766), 329.

topics of Italian travelogue (antiquities, galleries, and museums) earned them considerable critical respect. The *Monthly* provides extensive excerpts from the *Letters*, and numbers its author amongst those valuable books of travels 'written by men of acknowledged penetration and veracity'.[43] In fact, Sharp's allegedly penetrative voice is blunt and occasionally irascible, as he describes the economic, moral and sanitary well-being of the cities he visits, and – usually in inverse proportion to these – the pernicious influence of the Roman Catholic church. In *A Sentimental Journey*, Sharp is caricatured as 'Mundungus', who 'made the whole tour ... without one generous connection or pleasurable anecdote to tell of'.[44] Taking a more positive view of Sharp's fungoid affinities, the *Critical* associates the shaping principle of his *Letters* with Smollett's 'ethic plan', and commends the patriotic tendency of both travelogues, which are, we learn, 'written on the same principles, and tend to the same end, viz. that of dispelling the clouds of prepossession and prejudice, which in defiance of common sense, and even corporeal feeling, have so long induced' – anti-Continental diatribes, perhaps? No, these irrational prejudices have in fact for too long induced 'the good people of this island to squander their time and money in Italy'.[45]

Roused to patriotic indignation by Sharp's *Letters* and their critical acclaim, Baretti's *Account* uses Sharp's text as a springboard for a dense sequence of highly detailed refutations. A single remark of Sharp's can provoke pages of counter-argument. The *Account* is structured thematically (whereas Sharp's had followed a journey format), with chapters on nuns, priests, costume, recreation, climate, sexual customs, and so on. Baretti's treatment of each of these topics confutes the stereotyped versions provided by English travellers, whose reports he exposes as shameless fictions written to formulae dictated by a narrow-minded junta of British printers and booksellers. Baretti explains how the prejudice and xenophobia of Sharp and his ilk derive from their ignorant and superficial experiences abroad, and that in their writings, 'falshood is palmed for truth upon the credulous, and thus are men confirmed in a narrow way of thinking, and in those local prejudices, of which it ought to be the great end of travelling, and books of travels, to cure them' (i. 3). In his travel book proper written some years later (1770), Baretti again emphasizes the role of the book trade in encouraging English chauvinism, noting the 'contempt' of 'the populace of England' for 'all other countries, (into which contempt they are

---

[43] *MR*, 35 (1766), 431: the review occupies 329–40 and 430–39.

[44] Laurence Sterne, *A Sentimental Journey through France and Italy by Mr. Yorick* (1768), ed. Gardner D. Stout, Jr (Berkeley and Los Angeles, 1967), 119.

[45] *CR*, 22 (1766), 291.

betray'd by many of their daily scribblers, who are incessantly reviling all other countries)'.[46]

Sharp's view of Italy is certainly fairly contemptuous, presenting an unholy trinity of religion, class, and sex as the main areas of Italian corruption. Although to some extent his hostility is designed more to disabuse the English of their enthusiasm for Italian culture than simply to attack Italy for its own sake, he does in the process undermine several institutions and practices which Baretti sees as central to Italian national character and virtue. Foremost amongst these is the role of the Roman Catholic church in the nation's spiritual and economic life. Sharp complains how he 'cannot look on their golden altars, and their fat monks, without reflecting on their deserted *Campania*, and starving laity' (69). Sharp is more hard-nosed than most eighteenth-century travellers (excluding, perhaps, Philip Thicknesse) in his criticism of the church's responsibility for poverty, which he makes explicit in the following observation:

> there is an abundance of charitable foundations; however, the swarms of beggars are surprisingly great. The trade of begging, in all Catholic countries, will necessarily prosper, so long as that species of charity, which is bestowed on beggars, contrives to be inculcated by their preachers and confessors, as the most perfect of all moral duties. (29–30)

Baretti responds, it would seem explicitly, to this diatribe. In the *Account* he describes the numerous charitable foundations supported by the Catholic church, and comments that

> Nor is the admittance into our hospitals rendered difficult by caviling or narrow regulations, as is often the case in other countries, where charity is so diligently anatomised, that many good things are not done, for fear improper objects should partake of them. The Italians scorn such paultry discriminations, and every person who is, or will be, an object of their charity, is by them considered as poor enough to deserve a share of it. (ii. 102)

Baretti here interweaves national hostility with personal attack: the nicely chosen verb 'anatomised' points directly to Sharp as the purveyor of 'paultry discriminations', and English rationality is implicitly contrasted to the instinctive Italian tendency to generosity and compassion. Elsewhere in Baretti's account the 'calculating' (albeit in a slightly different sense) nature of Sharp's ethics is further derided, and indeed rhetorically extended to English travel writers as a breed. For instance, responding to grossly exaggerated

---

[46]   *A Journey from London to Genoa, through England, Portugal, Spain, and France* (4 vols, 1770), i. 65.

estimates of the numbers of Italian girls women forced into convents – Sharp calculates 36,000 in Tuscany alone, which is corrected down to just 600 – Baretti exclaims:

> See now, my good readers, what dependance you must have on the veracity of your travel-writers, though their accounts be constantly uniform, and constantly delivered in the most petulant strain of affirmation! They see nothing; examine nothing; but copy one another in a most shameless manner. (ii. 5)

Repeatedly, the literary misdemeanours of English travellers are taken as evidence or emblem of their personal moral failings. Baretti's critique of Sharp's description of 'the Italian ladies' is an extreme but not unrepresentative example of this strategy: 'he vomits slander all the time he thinks himself speaking oracles; for in the corrupted city of Venice itself, there are very many ladies possessed of the most exalted virtue. It is true that they are not commonly known to the English travellers' (i. 92). A similar conflation of Sharp's low social acquaintance with seedy inaccuracy (a trick which, as we have seen, Thicknesse neatly applies to Smollett, and which is becoming something of a trope in eighteenth-century travel writing) occurs when Baretti observes that Sharp's information on the mores of the Italian nobility is derived from his 'temporary footman in Naples', 'the chief oracle consulted by his good master about the customs and manners of Italy' (i. 92, 83).[47] The nationalistic feud is here complicated by the introduction of class hostilities, apparently calculated to undermine Sharp's claims for the moral superiority of the professional middle-class traveller.

Not surprisingly, the critical reception of Baretti's *Account* was somewhat strained. For the *Monthly*, its empirical value is undeniable, and the *Account* is acclaimed as of 'considerable merit', and 'containing a great variety of entertainment, and much information'.[48] This information is valuable precisely because it confutes the ill-natured and prejudiced accounts of previous writers. Yet the interest of Baretti's remarks also lies in their aggressive relationship to Sharp's text, and the *Monthly* tempers its appreciation of Baretti's observations with stern disapproval of his 'illiberal manner, and strong prejudices', and berates him for violating 'the rules of decency and good breeding, to such a degree as must expose him to the censure of every liberal-minded reader'.[49] The *Critical*'s review of the *Account* was xenophobic to the point of hysteria,

---

[47] For a comparable use of this disparaging strategy, compare Mary Ann Hanway's complaint that Johnson's account of Scotland has been 'raked' from 'the very lowest dregs of the people, with whom, I should be sorry, to suppose he kept company' (*A Journey to the Highlands of Scotland*, 1777, 156).

[48] *MR*, 38 (1768), 448; *MR*, 39 (1768), 63.

[49] *MR*, 39 (1768), 63; *MR*, 38 (1768), 448.

as we shall see presently: but meanwhile, Sharp was already plotting his own riposte, which he published in 1768, a curious piece of triumphalist satire which contrasts remarks in the *Account* with various observations in Baretti's Italian literary magazine, *Frusta Letteraria* (published at Venice between 1763 and 1765), in order to point out contradictions in Baretti's own assessments of Italian culture.[50] The full title of Sharp's text is *A View of the Customs, Manners, Drama, &c. of Italy, as they are described in The Frusta Letteraria; and in The Account of Italy in English, written by Mr Baretti: compared with The Letters from Italy, written by Mr Sharp*. It is an extended exercise in condemning Baretti out of his own mouth. Sharp cites and annotates choice excerpts from the *Frusta Letteraria*, which, in its often scurrilous content, had offended much of the Italian literary establishment. He juxtaposes these excerpts with passages from the *Account* in which Baretti had berated Sharp's dismissive treatment of Italian letters, passages in which Baretti is at his most high-minded and defensive about Italian cultural achievements.

The *Monthly Review* notes the publication of Sharp's text in the 'Monthly Catalogue' for October. It makes no explicit judgement, instead concluding with the remark: 'How far this method of answering Mr. Baretti is satisfactory, the Reader will be enabled to judge by what is said of the nature and design of the *Frusta Letteraria* in the following article'; which is a three-page review of a still more recent addition to this literary battle, *An Appendix to the Account of Italy, in Answer to Samuel Sharp Esq.*, 'By Giuseppe Baretti'.[51] The length of the review owes as much to an incidental and rather confusing quarrel between Baretti and the *Monthly* (over whether or not Voltaire could write English) as to the Sharp–Baretti controversy itself. Despite the *Monthly*'s disagreement with Baretti on this point, the main body of the review genially allows him, in lengthy quotations, to confute Sharp's arguments. Baretti observes a crucial flaw in Sharp's method of citing from the *Frusta Letteraria* in order to demonstrate its self-contradiction:

> ... let every word in it be mine, still Mr. Sharp ought to have had candour enough to inform his readers, that the *Literary Scourge* was not written in my own, but in an assumed character. It was written in the name and character of an old, ill-natured, and ferocious soldier ...
>
> This soldier is called *Aristarco Scannabue*; that is, *Aristarchus the Dunce-Killer*. By the Introduction, and still more by many passages in the work itself, it appears that this personage is drawn as hating almost every thing done in Italy, and approving almost of

---

[50] See Catharina Johanna Maria Lubbers-van der Brugge, *Johnson and Baretti: some Aspects of Eighteenth-Century Literary Life in England and Italy* (Groningen, 1951), 66–7.

[51] *MR*, 39 (1768), 320–23.

nothing but what is done abroad, especially in England and France.[52]

Sharp is made to look extremely foolish – dunce-like, indeed – and distinctly out of his depth in the literary and self-referential world which Baretti invokes.[53] The apparently straightforward association of writer and text which had fuelled Baretti's attack on Sharp's travel book is inadequate to Sharp's attempted riposte. Intending to hoist Baretti with his own petard, Sharp instead has the rug pulled out from under his feet. The juxtaposition of the notices in the *Monthly Review* consolidates Baretti's position and serves further to exclude Sharp from the ranks of the literarily sophisticated.

The *Critical Review*'s treatment of the Aristarco affair has Baretti as the villain of the piece, and diverts the controversy into an aggressively nationalistic channel. Reviewing Baretti's *Appendix*, the *Critical* pooh-poohs his duplicitous use of Aristarchus: 'Mr. Baretti in this defence aggravates his former transgressions against sense, reason, learning, and every liberal sentiment, and skulks behind the masked character of Aristarco Scannabue.'[54] Notwithstanding Baretti's disclaiming protestations, which it cites, the *Critical Review* opines that 'this pretended dunce-killer's mask … has served Mr. Baretti … to most excellent purpose, as it has given him an opportunity to unload his breast of that spite and malignity which lay rankling within him against the English nation'.[55] So, whereas the *Monthly* treats the clash of opinion and character as a light-hearted and literary entanglement, within which national differences are less significant than the ability to engage in literary allusion and Scriblerian indirection, for the *Critical* it becomes a nationalistic feud in which the reviewers are bound indignantly to defend British good sense against cowardly and duplicitous Italian attacks. Baretti's nationality complicates his literary status. Being and speaking Italian enables, one might expect, an account of Italy far superior in insight to any produced by English travellers. This, indeed, is the premise and claim of Baretti's *Account*, which emphasizes also the unreliability of 'strange judgments on men and things, taken from sudden and superficial impressions' (i. vii–ix), and the dangers of the English tendency to splenetic travel, which means that 'all objects will be misrepresented by moroseness and ill-nature, the ordinary concomitants of bad health' (i. 13). However, Baretti's corrective observations on Sharp's remarks are viewed by the *Critical* as 'a most audacious insult upon the constitution and church of England; because the avowed intention of the

---

[52] *MR*, 39 (1768), 321; Baretti, *Appendix*, 2–3.
[53] For Aristarco Scannabue, see Warburton's note of 1742 to *Dunciad*, IV, 210, where he glosses Pope's 'Aristarchus' (Bentley) as a 'famous Commentator, and Corrector of Homer, whose name has been frequently used to signify a complete Critic'.
[54] *CR*, 26 (1768), 230.
[55] *CR*, 26 (1768), 230–31.

author is to defend his own countrymen, and to recommend their manners, practices, and religion, at the expence of every thing which ought to be dear not only to a lover of liberty, but a rational being'.[56]

Rational libertarianism is in fact conspicuous by its absence from the *Critical*'s review of Baretti's *Account*, which is one of the most xenophobic passages in eighteenth-century periodical writing. The review presents Baretti as a bigot, a dunce, and, perhaps worst of all, an Italian. Streams of invective are supplemented with extracts from Baretti's text, passages which 'Mr. Sharp, in his late pamphlet, seems to have overlooked'.[57] These are cited to bolster the enthusiastic review of Sharp's *View* which immediately follows.[58] Throughout both reviews, Sharp's moral uprightness is associated not only with his nationality but with his superiority to the mercenary world of the book trade within which Baretti is disparagingly located (despite, ironically, Baretti's own professed contempt for that same world):

> Mr. Sharp's moral character, it is well known, stands unimpeached. The fortune he has so worthily acquired by his eminence in a liberal and useful profession, places him above all suspicion of writing for bread; and the account he has given us of the Italians entitles him to a considerable rank among men of letters and discernment. As we are utter strangers to the moral as well as personal character of his antagonist, we shall leave him and his friends to answer for both; but without violating the laws of impartiality, or trespassing upon the rules of candid criticism, we can safely assert, that in England he is a foreign adventurer, in Italy a despicable bigot; that his work appears with every character of being a job either for a party or a bookseller, perhaps for both ...[59]

Whereas Sharp has proved himself a gentleman and a scholar, Baretti is, 'to give him the most favourable appellation, a literary harlequin, but destitute of skill and abilities to perform his part'.[60]

In this emphasis on moral corruption, figured sexually in phrases such as 'foreign adventurer', as well as on duplicity, Baretti becomes metonymically representative of modern Italy – as does the figure of the *cicisbeo*, on whom Sharp's *View* dwells at some length. According to Sharp and many other British travel writers, virtually every married Italian noblewoman was perpetually attended by a young gigolo whose duties (sexual as well as social) symbolized the absolute decay of social morality in Italy. The subservience of

---

[56]   *CR*, 26 (1768), 23.
[57]   *CR*, 26 (1768), 21.
[58]   Review of Baretti's *Journey*, 17–24; of Sharp's *View*, 24–8.
[59]   *CR*, 26 (1768), 17.
[60]   *CR*, 26 (1768), 28.

the *cicisbeo* to his mistress makes him into a figure of ambivalent sexuality, and the alleged ubiquity of the practice in Italy functions in Sharp's account as a graphic embodiment of national degeneracy. The virtual institutionalizing of cicisbeism which Sharp describes in Venice causes the reviewer to 'forget all the lofty ideas we had conceived in our youth, of its being *built by the hands of gods instead of men*; for it is a place equally contemptible and detestable'.[61] This moment of disillusionment powerfully dismantles the aristocratic allure of Venice, firmly establishing British middle-class sexual morality as the benchmark of national virtue, and the source of Britain's implied national superiority.[62]

By contrast, the *Monthly* is actually critical of Sharp's chauvinism, observing that 'What we term domestic happiness, would be no happiness at all to an Italian; and nothing would be attended with more *dreadful consequences to their society*, than to oblige them to be happy in our way'.[63] When, in 1770, Baretti – curiously undiscouraged by all this controversy – publishes a substantial travelogue describing *A Journey from London to Genoa, through England, Portugal, Spain, and France* (4 vols), these questions of national differences, freedoms, and morality surface once more in both text and review. The cultural relativism displayed in the *Monthly*'s rebuke to Sharp's chauvinism is becoming a more potent strand within the discourse of European travel.

A carefully structured work rather than a reactive response like the *Account*, the *Journey* was, in general, well received by the *Critical* and the *Monthly*. The fact that the *Journey*'s arena was outside Italy relieved Baretti and his reviewers of the immediate nationalistic pressures which had shaped the earlier work. Indeed, by 1770 Baretti is keenly cultivating powerful English affiliations for himself. The *Journey* is somewhat fulsomely dedicated to the members of the Royal Academy, and its 'Preface' pays tribute to 'my most revered friend Samuel Johnson', who not only suggested that Baretti keep a textual record of his journey, but also 'exhorted me to write daily, and with all possible minuteness', and 'pointed out the topics which would most interest and most delight in a future publication'. Also, somewhat improbably (and in contradiction to remarks made later within the *Journey*), the 'Preface'

---

[61] *CR*, 22 (1766), 286.

[62] Redford, *Venice and the Grand Tour*, 6–7 describes the 'allure' of Venice as 'magnetic yet subversive', and cites *Dunciad*, IV, 307–10 as the touchstone of such ambivalence, since Pope sets Venice as erotic playpen in subtle opposition to Venice as formerly glorious republic:

> But chief her shrine where naked Venus keeps,
> And Cupids ride the Lyon of the Deeps;
> Where, eas'd of Fleets, the Adriatic main
> Wafts the smooth Eunuch and enamour'd swain.

[63] *MR*, 35 (1766), 337.

apostrophizes 'imperial England' as 'thou illustrious mother of polite men and virtuous women! Thou great mart of literature!' (i. 2–3). The brief opening sequence describing England is similarly enthusiastic, pronouncing, for example, 'the rural beauties of Devonshire ... not inferiour to the best parts of Piedmont and Lombardy' (i. 21). Baretti's biographer, comparing the Italian and English versions of the *Journey* (first published in Italy as *Lettere ai tre fratelli* in 1766), shows that in the latter a number of unfavourable opinions on the English which Baretti had shared with his Italian readership were either omitted or mitigated.[64] The controversy generated by the *Account* is assiduously avoided, not least because Baretti seems to have realized how powerfully a congenial travelogue could function as a passport to acceptance by polite lettered society (as Boswell's *Corsica* had so successfully shown).

The concerns of the *Journey* are wide-ranging, and generally sociable. Baretti records folk song, oral poetry, dance traditions and courtship rituals, thus bringing together the increasingly acceptable discourses of literary-historical investigation and philanthropic sensibility. The *Critical Review*, which, surprisingly, presents a long and favourable appraisal of the *Journey*, acknowledges its appealing discursive range: 'Here are objects for men of all tastes; for the antiquary, the philologist, the poet, and the politician'.[65] Furthermore, Baretti leavens erudition with more sentimental, anecdotal encounters with women (including nuns) and peasants (including some blind beggars). He frequently draws attention to the variegated texture of his travelogue, in passages like the following:

> consider that I cannot every moment have an earthquake ready at hand, nor pompous patriarchs at every step ... Such grand topics do not occur every day, and of something I must fill my letters, or break the plan of my journal. Thus I write about literature when I am just come out of a library, and scribble about my landlady when at an inn. A man who is giving a full account of his travels I hope you consider as an historian; and you know that historians, like death, must knock *aequo pede*, at the beggar's as at the king's door. (ii. 141–2)

This focus on a broad range of social and cultural topics is praised by the *Critical*, as are Baretti's romantic encounters with Iberian females, especially 'the fair Paolita': to 'lay before us the emotions of the human heart, is to give

---

[64] The *Journey* was written in Italy between 1760 and 1766, and published there in 1766 as *Lettere ai tre fratelli*, but the Italian version was revised after a second visit to Spain in 1768–9 for the publication of the English text in 1770. See Lubbers-van der Brugge, *Johnson and Baretti*, 7; 41; 63–5.

[65] *CR*, 30 (1770), 196. The review as a whole occupies *CR*, 30 (1770), 194–208 (September); 241–56 (October, leading article); 335–48 (November).

us a philosophical entertainment, on whatever occasion they are excited'.[66] The review opens with an abstract discussion of travel literature's power to dispel prejudice and inculcate a sense of 'all mankind as brethren, the workmanship of one Supreme benign Creator'.[67] So far so good: but in fact the reviewer then proceeds to berate Baretti for pushing these universalist notions too far, whereupon he is pronounced 'a poor moralist, and a worse politician'.[68] In the reviewer's opinion, all mankind may well be brethren, but they are not the same. In opposition to Baretti's belief in a universal human nature, the reviewer asserts the vital influences of 'education' and 'habit', and, in particular, national political temper: 'The Turk, in his political character, is actuated by fear; the Englishman by freedom; and each of them, as he is thus influenced, shows the formation of his nature, his intrinsic and distinguishing character.'[69] Baretti's downplaying of political considerations in favour of philosophical speculation prompts critical indignation. The offending passage is a meditation on the carefree existence of the Portuguese peasantry:

> Thus live the Portuguese, without thinking much of to-morrow; that plaguy *to-morrow*, which, along with *liberty*, is always uppermost in the head of an Englishman. ... Whether the proportion of happiness is greater in Portugal than in England, or the contrary, I have no means of calculating; but the Portuguese do not look as if they were disturbed by desire of change, or fear of want. (i. 304–5)

The reviewer is fired to indignation by this speculation: 'If the English are not happier than the Portuguese, they are the most stupid and perverse people under the sun. For is not Liberty, Knowledge, and rational religion, more favourable to happiness than despotism, ignorance, and superstition?'[70] In sum, then, the response of the *Critical* makes it clear that as a gentleman, literary antiquary, and faintly absurd sentimentalist, Baretti may almost be acceptable as a British or at least politically neutral subject; but the discursive realms of nationality, liberty, and 'rational religion' are firmly delineated as a British preserve. For John Hawkesworth, who reviewed Baretti's *Journey* in the *Monthly*, even the realms of whimsy and sentiment are deemed inaccessible to Baretti. Notwithstanding the *Monthly*'s hostile critique of Baretti's earlier work,

---

[66] *CR*, 30 (1770), 197.

[67] *CR*, 30 (1770, 196.

[68] *CR*, 30 (1770), 348.

[69] *CR*, 30 (1770), 252. The reviewer was doubtless also irritated by Baretti's universalizing vision of human nature in historical context, and his suggestion (with reference to earlier empires in world history) that England's present position of 'superiority over all the present nations' will inevitably lead into decline and fall (iii. 2–5).

[70] *CR*, 30 (1770), 205.

Hawkesworth regrets the degeneration of Baretti's style from the *Account*'s 'natural, manly, and forcible' manner into one which is characterized as 'affected, puerile, and feeble; almost every page abounds with the impertinences of a petty importance, and is rather the conceited prattle of a talkative coxcomb, than the plain narrative of a sensible traveller'.[71] The gendered terminology of Hawkesworth's judgements is striking, and perhaps perplexing: it makes more sense in the light of his further observation that whereas in the *Account* Baretti had imitated Johnson's style, in the *Journey* he has 'manifestly imitated the manner of Sterne', and that 'though as an imitator of Johnson he is respectable, he is disgusting and ridiculous as an imitator of Sterne'.[72] The sentimental position is implicitly associated with its British original, Sterne, and deemed inaccessible to the 'affected, puerile, and feeble' pen of Baretti.

The apparent polarization of Johnson and Sterne, manly and puerile, is deceptive: Baretti's puerility and feebleness is related to his inept imitation of Sterne, rather than imputed to Sterne's own procedure. Indeed, perhaps surprisingly for modern readers, sentimental travel writing was seen by contemporaries as projecting an intricate relationship between sincerity, imaginative sympathy, and manly Britishness. We find intimations of this nexus of ideas even in Smollett's *Travels*, where the French are perpetually described as 'volatile' and 'unthinking', in implicit contrast to the solidity and reflectiveness of the British, and where 'politeness', or 'the art of making one's self agreeable', is wrested away from its traditional practitioners, the French, and described as

> an art that necessarily implies a sense of decorum, and a delicacy of sentiment. These are qualities, of which (as far as I have been able to observe) a Frenchman has no idea; therefore he never can be deemed polite, except by those persons among whom they are as little understood. (*Travels*, 57)

Imaginative sympathy is likewise 'nationalized', as Smollett announces that

> of all the people I have ever known, I think the French are the least capable of feeling for the distresses of their fellow creatures. Their hearts are not susceptible of deep impressions; and, such is their levity, that the imagination has not time to brood long over any disagreeable idea, or sensation. (58–9)

---

[71] *MR*, 43 (1770), 219. Arthur Young, in 1792, relates contemptuously that 'the bagatelles of Baretti, amongst the Spanish muleteers, were read with avidity' (*Travels in France*, 3, fonts reversed).

[72] *MR*, 43 (1770), 222.

Curiously, here, we find a close parallel to the misgivings about French 'polish' which Yorick hesitantly expresses to the Count in the 'Character: Versailles' section of *A Sentimental Journey*:

> A polish'd nation, my dear Count, said I, makes every one its debtor; and besides urbanity itself, like the fair sex, has so many charms; it goes against the heart to say it can do ill; and yet, I believe, there is but a certain line of perfection, that man, take him altogether, is empower'd to arrive at—if he gets beyond, he rather exchanges qualities, than gets them. I must not presume to say, how far this has affected the French in the subject we are speaking of—but should it ever be the case of the English, in the progress of their refinements, to arrive at the same polish which distinguishes the French, if we did not lose the *politesse de coeur*, which inclines men more to human actions, than courteous ones—we should at least lose that distinct variety and originality of character, which distinguishes them, not only from each other, but from all the world besides. (230–32)

Both Smollett and Sterne rhetorically emasculate the French: Smollett bluntly highlights their levity and superficiality, while Yorick (innocently or provocatively?) links their 'urbanity' with the 'charms' of 'the fair sex' and with a blandly anonymous form of courtesy which stands in contrast to the 'distinct variety and originality of character' and the '*politesse de coeur*' of the English.

What emerges, then, from Smollett's *Travels*, Sterne's *A Sentimental Journey*, and a wide range of related texts and contexts, including those discussed in the preceding pages of this chapter, is an influential formulation of manly, middle-class, British sensibility which, although primarily developed within the discourse of travel, is rapidly assimilated into many other areas of literary and cultural experience. Travel writing and its reception becomes an important site for competing claims to represent the interests of the nation – claims which inevitably reflect the authors' own affiliations and biases. As we have seen, many travel writers disingenuously claim a happy freedom from bias and prejudice while quietly naturalizing these very positions. If the writings examined in the preceding pages make unconsciously creative use of bigotry, dishonesty and hypocrisy, those scrutinized in the next chapter are much more anxiously aware of the problematics of travel writing. As with sentimental fiction of the period, sentimental travels are peculiarly self-conscious, perpetually drawing attention to their own ideologically perplexing foundations while seeking to transcend or disown them. Sentimental travel writing interrogates, often with remarkable subtlety, the cultural and political complacency to which the discourses of national character and conventional morality are prone.

Chapter 3

Sentimental travels: 'so much the *ton*'

> there is a balance, said he, of good and bad every where; and
> nothing but the knowing it is so can emancipate one half of the
> world from the prepossessions which it holds against the other—
> that the advantage of travel, as it regarded the *sçavoir vivre*, was by
> seeing a great deal both of men and manners; it taught us mutual
> toleration; and mutual toleration, concluded he, making me a bow,
> taught us mutual love.[1]

This edifying lecture is delivered to Yorick by the French officer he meets at the opera, and is a response to the English cleric's disgust at the sight of an Abbé sticking his hand up the skirts of 'a couple of grissets'. The Sternean cocktail of sex, satire and sentiment is characteristic of *A Sentimental Journey*, a text whose profound engagement with the problematic aspects of travel, nationality, and sympathy is repeatedly complicated not only by specific political irony, but also by the seamier side of sensibility. Nor should we assume that the complexities of Sterne's text were lost on its first readers. This chapter will offer a reading of *A Sentimental Journey* which seeks to recapture its contemporary resonances. These can be explored further with reference to various imitations and critiques of Sterne's travelogue in the decade following its publication, which will be examined in later sections of the chapter. The sentimental travelogues under discussion here appeared in tandem with, and implicit (sometimes overt) contradiction to, the disputatious and xenophobic writings featured in the previous chapter, offering alternative modes of travel and of appropriate masculine behaviour. Eighteenth-century responses to *A Sentimental Journey* clarify some of the issues merely insinuated in Sterne's work, and show how the sentimental mode in travel writing offered new possibilities for the construction of individual and national identities. Barker-Benfield has observed how many popular novels written by men during the 1760s and 1770s were 'preoccupied with the meanings of sensibility for manhood', although, curiously, their intended readership was predominantly female.[2] Similarly, Markman Ellis has recently highlighted the active intervention of sentimental novels (by men and women) in social and political controversies.[3] Travel literature at this time is still directed at a largely

---

[1]   Laurence Sterne, *A Sentimental Journey through France and Italy by Mr. Yorick* (1768), ed. Gardner D. Stout, Jr (Berkeley and Los Angeles, 1967), 181.
[2]   G. J. Barker-Benfield, *The Culture of Sensibility: Sex and Society in Eighteenth-Century Britain* (Chicago, 1992), 142.
[3]   Markman Ellis, *The Politics of Sensibility: Race, Gender and Commerce in the Sentimental Novel* (Cambridge, 1996).

(although not exclusively) male audience: its exploration of manly behaviour in a broader political and international context therefore provides an important counterpoint to the more familiar and domestic realm of experience addressed in the fiction of the period. As Ellis observes, 'the choice of genre effects [*sic*] not only how something is said, but also what is said, and to whom' (23). More frankly addressed to a largely male audience, yet prescribed also as suitable reading for women and younger readers, travel writing positions itself at the heart of contemporary debates concerning national identity, the acceptable extent of sympathy, the validity of gender and class divisions, and the pitfalls as well as the pleasures of authorship. It enables amateurs as well as professional writers to address a reading public, and in so doing endorses broader intervention in public affairs, albeit on the level of textual rather than legislative activity.

Learning better manners: rereading *A Sentimental Journey*

Broadly speaking, there are two dominant critical approaches to *A Sentimental Journey*, which neither separately nor together tell the whole story. On one view, *A Sentimental Journey* is seen as a development of Volume vii of *Tristram Shandy* and read as a novelistic satire on travel which provides a sentimental and bourgeois corrective to xenophobic or aristocratic versions of travel.[4] As proponents of this approach have convincingly demonstrated, Sterne's 'sentimentalizing' of travel is provoked not only by the urge to counter Smollett's xenophobia but also by the critical reception of *Tristram Shandy*. The bawdy satire of Tristram's Grand Tour is replaced in *A Sentimental*

---

[4]   See Alan H. Vrooman, 'The Origin and Development of the *Sentimental Journey* as a Work of Travel Literature and of Sensibility' (PhD diss., Princeton University, 1940); Stout's 'Introduction' to *A Sentimental Journey*, 1–47; Robert W. Uphaus, 'Sentiment and Spleen: Travels with Sterne and Smollett', *Centennial Review*, 15 (1971), 406–21; Thomas M. Curley, 'Sterne's *Sentimental Journey* and the Tradition of Travel Literature', in John McVeagh ed., *All Before Them, 1660–1780* (1989), 203–16; and Frédéric Ogée, 'Channelling Emotions: Travel and Literary Creation in Smollett and Sterne', *Studies in Voltaire and the Eighteenth Century*, 292 (1991), 27–42, who suggests that while the opening chapters parody Smollett's xenophobia, the deferred 'Preface' correctively steers the text towards an alternative mode of travel writing. Most recently, Chloe Chard has explored the formal aspects of the text's satirical thrust, and observed that *A Sentimental Journey* 'ends with a triumphant displacement of hyperbole by the digressive details of social exchange: just as the traveller is embarking on the traversal of the Alps, he is sidetracked into a complex "Case of Delicacy" with a woman in an inn' (Chloe Chard, *Pleasure and Guilt on the Grand Tour: Travel Writing and Imaginative Geography 1600–1830* [Manchester, 1999], 8).

Journey by the kind of sentimental encounter which the *Critical* and *Monthly Reviews* had praised in *Tristram Shandy*.[5]

If this approach to the text runs the risk of uncritically celebrating Sterne's sympathetic reworking of travel, the other prevailing view of *A Sentimental Journey* is far more hostile, accusing Sterne of enshrining the ideological contradictions which underpin bourgeois sensibility. For Robert Markley, in an influential recent interpretation, *A Sentimental Journey*, like 'most eighteenth-century sentimental narratives, ... suppresses questions about how one acquires the wealth to be able to afford one charitable act after another'.[6] However, Markley's critique of bourgeois sensibility classifies *A Sentimental Journey* as a 'sentimental novel [inscribed] in a parody of the picaresque mode' (229). This description takes no account of the text's evident relationship to the literature of European travel, and Markley's reading interrogates Sterne's representation of social inequities as if he had written *A Sentimental Journey through England and Wales*. Evidently, there *is* an element of displacement in Sterne's text: the projection onto French society of the inequity which sentimentalism laments, yet exploits, can be read as an evasive strategy. But one might also fruitfully explore the foreignness of Yorick's experiences, which is central to Sterne's subtle probing of the relationship between individual and national consciousness. The following pages will tease out the directly political implications of the text, in both domestic and international contexts. As one might expect from Sterne, it will emerge that *A Sentimental Journey* manages simultaneously to destabilize and reinforce existing notions of patriotism, individuality, and middle-class masculinity.

Yorick's arrival in Paris is an important interlude. It presents a moment of stasis in which the traveller's solitude prompts reflective self-definition:

> I own my first sensations, as soon as I was left solitary and alone in my own chamber in the hotel, were far from being so flattering as I had prefigured them. I walked up gravely to the window in my dusty black coat, and looking through the glass saw all the world in yellow, blue, and green, running at the ring of pleasure.—The old with broken lances, and in helmets which had lost their vizards— the young in armour bright which shone like gold, beplumed with each gay feather of the east—all—all tilting at it like fascinated knights in tournaments of yore for fame and love.—

---

[5] See Stout's 'Introduction' to *A Sentimental Journey*, 10–11. *MR*, 32 (1765), 138 (in a review of Volumes vii and viii of *Tristram Shandy*), advises Sterne that his 'excellence' lies 'in the PATHETIC'.

[6] Robert Markley, 'Sentimentality as Performance: Shaftesbury, Sterne, and the Theatrics of Virtue', in Laura Brown and Felicity Nussbaum eds., *The New Eighteenth Century: Theory, Politics, English Literature* (1987), 210–30; 211. See also Judith Frank, '"A Man who Laughs is never Dangerous": Character and Class in Sterne's *A Sentimental Journey*', *English Literary History*, 56 (1989), 97–124, for a Marxist and Foucauldian reading.

> Alas, poor Yorick! cried I, what art thou doing here? On the very
> first onset of all this glittering clatter, thou art reduced to an atom—
> seek—seek some winding alley, with a tourniquet at the end of it,
> where chariot never rolled or flambeau shot its rays—there thou
> mayest solace thy soul in converse sweet with some kind *grisset* of
> a barber's wife, and get into such coteries! —
> —May I perish! if I do, said I, pulling out the letter which I had to
> present to Madame de R * * *.—I'll wait upon this lady, the very
> first thing I do. So I called La Fleur to go seek me a barber
> directly—and come back and brush my coat. (155–7)

The romantic, chivalric 'world' Yorick visualizes here is redolent of
aristocratic leisure (and sexual activity – 'running at the ring of pleasure'). It is
a vision of a trans-European exotic past, from which the middle-aged English
cleric, clad in a sober 'black coat', is emphatically excluded. This moment of
isolation, rare in *A Sentimental Journey*, raises the dizzying possibility that one
may be 'reduced to an atom'; the imagined 'converse sweet' of sentimental
intercourse with 'some kind *grisset*' provides therefore a vital sense of social
identity. Yorick rallies, and resolves to seek out the aristocratic Madame de
Rambouliet as an antidote to his existential crisis. In the event, however, he is
decoyed by a sentimental encounter with the beautiful *grisset* intuited in this
passage. Only after a further distraction in the form of the *opera comique* does
Yorick find himself in a coach with Madame de Rambouliet, an occasion
notable for nothing more edifying or sentimental than her desire for '*Rien que
pisser*' (182). Clearly, Yorick's natural path is the winding alley and the
converse sweet provided by the more decorous and sensitive petty bourgeoisie,
as he had apprehended in his epiphanic moment at the window.

This moment of realization is replayed at key moments in the text. In Paris,
Yorick is introduced by Mons. Le Compte de B**** to several 'people of rank'
(261), and dallies for three weeks amongst superannuated chevaliers and high-
born ladies of dubious moral fibre, but soon grows tired of such company: 'the
better the *Coterie*—the more children of Art—I languish'd for those of Nature:
and one night, after a most vile prostitution of myself to half a dozen different
people, I grew sick—went to bed—order'd La Fleur to get me horses in the
morning to set out for Italy' (266). The next episode is Yorick's encounter with
Maria de Moulines and her faithful dog, which fulfils his needs exactly and
moves him to exclaim 'I am positive I have a soul' (271). Finally of course, it
is the Fille de Chambre's end, not that of her mistress, to which Yorick
connects.

But although thus valued more highly than the tasteless enjoyments of the
Grand Tourist, Yorick's sentimental encounters with the French bourgeoisie
and peasantry are complicated by being figured also as economic transactions.
Ralph Griffiths's enthusiastic account of *A Sentimental Journey* in the *Monthly*

confirms that this aspect of Sterne's text was noted at the time. Griffiths discusses the work as a travel narrative, not as a novel:

> Of all the various productions of the press, none are so eagerly received by us Reviewers, and other people who stay at home and mind our business, as the writings of travellers;—over whom, by the way, we readers have prodigious advantage; for *they* undergo the fatigue, inconvenience, and expence, while *we*, in all the plenitude of leisure and an elbow-chair, enjoy the pleasure and the profit, at so small a charge as—the price of the book. Why here, now, we have many dozens of shrewd observations and choice sentiments, the *ground*work of which must have cost our friend Yorick many a bright glittering guinea: all which our other friend, Becket, who is the most reasonable of human booksellers,—is content to let us have at less than seven farthings a-piece![7]

Here, the commodification of the book breaks down further into the exact costing of particular 'observations' and 'sentiments'. Griffiths's calculations mirror Sterne's isolation and evaluation of particular encounters within *A Sentimental Journey*, where the middle-class commodification of sentiment replaces the aristocratic penchant for collecting *objets d'art*. Chapters within *A Sentimental Journey* often function as verbal tableaux, such that Griffiths in the *Monthly* is moved to exclaim 'What an affecting, touching, masterly picture is here! 'Tis *The monk-scene*,—Calais'.[8] Yorick describes the monk as an artifact, 'one of those heads, which Guido has often painted', frozen in 'the attitude of Intreaty' (71–2). 'Attitude', a neutral technical term within the discourse of aesthetics, is a loaded one in social intercourse. Its use by Yorick suggests the cleric's own pretentiousness (which of course masks his evasion of the economic realities which underly the gestures): it is as if he is momentarily corrupted by the dilettante objectification practised by the connoisseur. Similarly, as Chloe Chard has pointed out, the description of Maria weeping for her goat is a visual pun on the figure of the weeping Dacia admired by more classically-minded travellers in Rome, a pun which simultaneously substitutes sentiment for aesthetic contemplation, and elides the differences between the two idioms.[9] Later, Yorick's interest in 'the *nakedness* of … hearts' as distinct from their 'different disguises of customs, climates, and religion' is described as a 'thirst … as impatient as that which inflames the breast of the connoisseur' (217–9): again, the sentiment is tainted by the values invoked within the figure of speech.

From very early on in *A Sentimental Journey*, the association of improved manners with the aristocratic Grand Tour is dismantled. Having deployed

---

[7] *MR*, 38 (1768), 174.
[8] *MR*, 38 (1768), 177.
[9] Chard, *Pleasure and Guilt on the Grand Tour*, 153–6.

spurious arguments over deserving and undeserving poor, in order to avoid dispensing charity to the monk, and having attempted to rally his own spirits with a raffish sequence of exclamations ('My heart smote me the moment he shut the door—Psha! said I with an air of carelessness, three several times'), Yorick reflects penitently: 'I have behaved very ill; said I within myself; but I have only just set out upon my travels; and shall learn better manners as I get along' (75). The sentimental traveller's tutors are drawn from the ranks of monks, paupers, and women. However, the uses made by Yorick of assorted social outcasts in *A Sentimental Journey* are undoubtedly problematic.

Those moments of sentimental transaction which redefine nationally beneficial commerce have been indicted by recent critics as indices of sensibility's moral dereliction. Such a reading is nothing new: the *Critical Review* notes that Yorick seems to have travelled 'in a delirium', which

> had, moreover, the happy temporary effect of making the sufferings of others the objects of his mirth, and not only rendering him insensible to the feelings of humanity, but superior to every regard for taste, truth, observation, or reflection.[10]

Less critically, Ralph Griffiths in the *Monthly* acknowledges Yorick's trading in charitable feeling: singling out for particular praise the incident at Montreuil in which the beggars outside the inn press upon the departing Yorick, moving him to distribute his *sous* with sentimental liberality, Griffiths remarks that 'the heart of the humane reader will revel in all the luxury of benevolence', and he excerpts the entire chapter.[11] Sensibility is bound up with social and financial inequity, and therefore finds it difficult to escape from the commercial frame of reference it professes to despise. In this context as in so many others, however, *A Sentimental Journey* highlights its own paradoxes. In the scene with the beggars, for example, Yorick's observation that 'of all others, resumed I, the unfortunate of our own country, surely, have the first rights; and I have left thousands in distress upon our own shore' (73) is deployed as an evasive tactic, yet also highlights with some acuity an unsettling political fact. Thus, on one level at least, the predicament of the French peasantry presents a mirror image of their British counterparts: a sly inversion of, for example, Smollett's habit of drawing contrasts between British bucolic prosperity and Continental beggary. Furthermore, Yorick's mixed (generally sexual) motives and the dubious sincerity of his charitable actions provide *A Sentimental Journey* with an inbuilt critique of the sentimental impulse as an end in itself, such that the Marxist attack on the text seems really to be stating the obvious, and also failing to address its more politically suggestive aspects.

---

[10] *CR*, 25 (1768), 182.
[11] *MR*, 38 (1768), 183.

If the politics of charity are perplexingly handled in *A Sentimental Journey*, the myths of national character are likewise interrogated and problematized so as to unsettle the complacent reader. International relations are figured in transactions which, though unequal, are at least conducted between individuals rather than mere representations of the national stereotype. Figures such as the monk, the Shakespeare-loving Comte, and of course the tragical Maria were well calculated to become part of the gallery of Sterne's adored 'characters' in much the same way as Uncle Toby et al. had captured the sentimental hearts of *Tristram Shandy*'s readers. Yorick's very name is important here, standing as it does for a universal British virtue which the canonization of Shakespeare at this time was rapidly establishing, yet managing simultaneously to delineate a highly individualized figure. As we shall see, several of Sterne's 'imitators' similarly adopt whimsical pseudonyms which enable them to function not merely as eccentric individuals, but as representatively *British* eccentrics. Sentimental travellers distinguish themselves from their more xenophobic compatriots by cultivating individuated relationships with humble foreigners (as opposed to notables whose names may be dropped to social advantage), thus simultaneously upholding the integrity of the individual whilst also making it clear that the British (sentimental) traveller is uniquely positioned, by virtue of superior sensibility as well as political freedom, to appreciate such individuality.

During his travels in France, Yorick has to unlearn British rationality in favour of feeling, a faculty which he gradually appropriates from the French. Thus, although he has 'predetermined not to give [the poor Franciscan] a single sous' (70, he is educated out of this position by a combination of conscience and sexual desire for the 'fair lady' he wants to impress. Her rebuke of his analytical reflections on their being thrown together 'in such a cordial situation' (96) invokes a contrast between head and heart, figured in national terms:

> When the situation is, what we would wish, nothing is so ill-timed
> as to hint at the circumstances which make it so: you thank Fortune,
> continued she—you had reason—the heart knew it, and was
> satisfied; and who but an English philosopher would have sent
> notices of it to the brain to reverse the judgment? (96)

The rest of *A Sentimental Journey* charts the rehabilitation of instinct or feeling over reason in the English/British character, effectively reappropriating virtuous impulses from the French. The lines between national character are thus blurred in order for the British model to be redrawn. But, as so often with Sterne, the very notions of lines, boundaries, and definitions are problematic. This becomes clearer if we examine a sequence of episodes within the text which carry a submerged and yet potent weight of specific political critique, which reveal how frail are the foundations of British identity, as construed politically and as defined in opposition to the Continent.

Sterne is not generally thought of as a political animal. Studies of his work tend to draw out his erotic or philosophical scintillation, or his religious agenda. At first sight, *A Sentimental Journey* is far from a political text: and yet it is possible to tease out an important set of political allusions and ironies. These operate within the broad context of Whiggish sympathies, overlaid by specific interests generated by Sterne's relationship with John Wilkes. We know that Wilkes and Sterne were reasonably close friends. Sterne's biographer notes that 'Lydia Sterne, after her father's death in 1768, looked upon Wilkes as one of her father's closest friends'; and she wrote to remind him of his promise to collaborate with John Hall-Stevenson on a biography of Sterne (which never in fact appeared).[12] Hall-Stevenson, the 'Eugenius' of *Tristram Shandy*, was a prolific if uneven author, some of whose 'best accomplishments as a poet were the satires he wrote in support of Wilkes'.[13] Among Hall-Stevenson's productions is *A Pastoral Puke: a Second Sermon Preached before the People Called Whigs* (1764), which berates the Whigs for their internal dissension. The *Monthly Review* praises this work, remarking that 'When Tristram Shandy went to France, he certainly left his mantle with this his natural brother in jocularity'.[14] The affinity is political as well as stylistic. After Sterne's death, Bishop Warburton writes to Charles Yorke: 'Poor Sterne, whom the papers tell us is just dead, was the idol of the higher mob, who have left the care of the public to Wilkes and the lower.'[15] The political difference between the two men is perceived as one of degree, not kind. Sterne travelled on the Continent with Wilkes's ardent supporter and co-agitator, Horne Tooke; although at times he professed his boredom with 'Wilkes and Liberty', it seems likely, as Carol Kay has noted, that Sterne was involved in pro-Wilkes protest.[16] While in Paris in 1764, Sterne spent a good deal of time with the

---

[12] Arthur H. Cash, *Laurence Sterne: the Later Years* (1986), 233, 348–9. See also 181–2 on the friendship in Paris.

[13] Arthur H. Cash, *Laurence Sterne: the Early and Middle Years* (1975), 182. See also Lodwick Hartley, 'Yorick's Sentimental Journey Continued: a Reconsideration of the Authorship', *South Atlantic Quarterly*, 70 (1971), 180–90, which establishes Hall-Stevenson's innocence of the *Continuation* and his support for Wilkes. Hartley's article 'Sterne's Eugenius as Indiscreet Author: the Literary Career of John Hall-Stevenson', *Proceedings of the Modern Languages Association*, 86 (1971), 428–45, provides many suggestive insights into Hall-Stevenson's literary and political influence on Sterne. In 1761 *Fables for Grown Gentleman* launched Hall-Stevenson 'into the field of political satire on what was to be the Wilkite side before Churchill entered the same arena' (430), and in July 1762 he was corresponding with Wilkes about *The Briton* and *The North Briton*.

[14] *MR*, 30 (1764), 415.

[15] Cash, *Laurence Sterne: the Later Years*, 333.

[16] Carol Kay, *Political Constructions: Defoe, Richardson, and Sterne in Relation to Hobbes, Hume, and Burke* (Ithaca, 1988), 242.

exiled Wilkes, whom French intellectuals welcomed as a heroic spokesman for Enlightenment ideals. Cash confirms that the intimacy between Sterne and Wilkes – which of course adds an extra ironic twist to the Sterne–Smollett opposition – 'can hardly be doubted'.[17]

Cash sees Wilkes's relationship with Sterne purely in terms of his dubious moral influence, and is anxious to distance Sterne (in search of 'his own sort of sentimental love') from Wilkes's rakish promiscuity.[18] On 'Wilkes and Liberty', Cash is silent. *A Sentimental Journey* makes no mention of Wilkes, but it does include (in the same chapter as a recollected dialogue with 'Eugenius') a discourse on Liberty, with an upper-case 'L' and the rest of the word in small capitals – a significant departure from the more neutral (typographically and politically) tribute to British 'liberty and good sense' in the sermon on conscience in *Tristram Shandy*, which was written in 1759, before the word took on such immediate political resonances.[19]

'LIBERTY' in *A Sentimental Journey* is introduced in the chapter 'The Passport. The Hotel at Paris', which describes Yorick's encounter with the caged starling and his apprehension of the horrors of imprisonment. Fears of the Bastille are inadequately dissipated as Yorick rationally analyses the reality of imprisonment there: '—And as for the Bastile! the terror is in the word— ... with nine livres a day, and pen and ink and paper and patience, albeit a man can't get out, he may do very well within' (196). He attempts to reverse the processes of imaginative terror which Burke had outlined:

> —Beshrew the *sombre* pencil! said I vauntingly—for I envy not its powers, which paints the evils of life with so hard and deadly a colouring. The mind sits terrified at the objects she has magnified herself, and blackened: reduce them to their proper size and hue she overlooks them ... (197)

But the 'hey-day of this soliloquy' is interrupted by the voice of the starling – 'I can't get out' – which immediately awakens Yorick's 'affections': 'Mechanical as the notes were, yet so true in tune to nature were they chanted, that in one moment they overthrew all my systematic reasonings upon the Bastile' (197–8). This prompts a paean to 'LIBERTY',

> whose taste is grateful, and ever wilt be so, till NATURE herself shall change—no *tint* of words can spot thy snowy mantle, or chymic power turn thy sceptre into iron—with thee to smile upon him as he eats his crust, the swain is happier than his monarch, from whose court thou art exiled ... (199–200)

---

[17]   Cash, *Laurence Sterne: the Later Years*, 181.

[18]   Cash, *Laurence Sterne: the Later Years*, 182–3.

[19]   Laurence Sterne, *The Life and Opinions of Tristram Shandy Gentleman* (9 vols, 1760–67), ed. Ian Campbell Ross (Oxford, 1983), 112.

Stout notes that this passage echoes Sermon II, x, where Sterne, in his consideration of slavery, cites 'the history of the Romish church and her tyrants'. Stout suggests that 'it is characteristic of the cosmopolitan tolerance of Yorick's *Journey* that in echoing this passage Sterne omits the references to the tyranny of the "Romish church"'.[20] In fact, this apparent 'cosmopolitan tolerance' is impelled by a refocusing of attack. The sentence describing the happy swain munching his crust in sunny liberty is curiously ambiguous: just where is this scene taking place? Probably not in France, since the flow of the passage praising Liberty, in the manner of numerous contemporary travel writings, directs Yorick and the reader towards England. So, is it the English court from which Liberty is exiled? Given the political flavour of the day, this seems highly probable. We might even detect a glancing reference to that most famous of exiles, John Wilkes. Yorick is unable to free the starling; the cage door is 'twisted and double twisted so fast with wire, there was no getting it open without pulling the cage to pieces' (197). This seems to be an allusion, similar in method to the allegory of the coats in *A Tale of A Tub*, to the difficulty of political and constitutional reform.

In this passage, the joint forces of sensibility (focused on the starling) and subjectivity (Yorick's psychological construction of the real and illusory horrors of imprisonment) serve to distract attention from the political resonances; so successfully, indeed, that Stout sees the passage as evidence simply of *A Sentimental Journey*'s greater tolerance. More recently, Markman Ellis has read it as an anti-slavery statement, with the starling functioning as a 'metonymic emblem of African slavery': in this context, Ellis argues, it is significant that Yorick apostrophizes a 'white' goddess of Liberty.[21] Suggestive as Ellis's reading may be, the passage seems to be more centrally concerned with mounting an ironically indirect attack on domestic threats to British liberty, threats emanating from the court-centred faction which had exiled Wilkes. In this light, Yorick's observation, a little later, to Mons. Le Compte that 'our court at present is so full of patriots, who wish for *nothing* but the honours and wealth of their country' (227) is hilariously ironic, especially if the 'patriots' busily enriching 'their' country are taken to be the ruling junta of Scottish ministers; and in this context, Yorick's continuation, 'and our ladies are all so chaste, so spotless, so good, so devout' (227), mischievously alludes to the popular belief that the Princess of Wales and Lord Bute were shameless adulterers.

Devious as this network of allusions may seem (we recall Yorick's puzzled attempts to decipher the fragment of writing used to wrap his butter: 'the difficulty of understanding it increased but the desire', 251), the pro-Wilkes

---

[20] Stout, *A Sentimental Journey*, 199n. See *The Sermons of Mr Yorick* (2 vols, Oxford, 1927), i. 122.

[21] Ellis, *The Politics of Sensibility*, 73–4.

agenda of *A Sentimental Journey* was doubtless easier to detect for contemporary readers, finely attuned to the ironic resonances of terms such as 'patriot' as well as the fabular and winsome mode of much political writing in this context.[22] One at least of Sterne's imitators seems to have recognized the point of his satire: in 1771 was published *A Short Ramble through some Parts of France and Italy*, by 'Lancelot Temple, Esq.' (actually John Armstrong). Armstrong's imitation of Sterne is purely stylistic, and his politics are decidedly Tory. This becomes clear in a pathetic account of galley slaves at Marseilles, which then modulates into an anti-Wilkes diatribe:

> many of those poor Creatures have lost their Liberty, and are condemned to a life of nasty misery and ignominy for small Offences; such as the unexpiable Crime of having murdered a *royal* Hare or Partridge, or a most *noble* Pheasant.—What a precious Blessing is Liberty? But like Health, People are perhaps never properly sensible of its Value till they have lost it. However, a Debauchee who has no Family nor Connexions, may use his own Constitution as freely as he pleases; but no *Patriot* has any right by an indecent intolerable Abuse of his own Liberty to sport away mine.[23]

The passage as a whole owes obvious debts to Sterne (even down to the presence of helpless birds); but its politics – anti-French as well as anti-Wilkes – present a deliberate challenge to those of *A Sentimental Journey*.

The liberal political agenda of *A Sentimental Journey* is winsomely complicated by a sequence of encounters and reflections which address the issue of national character and its relation to liberty by paradoxical means. Yorick's enthusiastic intercourse with the French bourgeoisie is presented as a triumph over linguistic and cultural barriers. In the 'Preface in the Désobligeant', Yorick complains that

> 'tis so ordered, that from the want of languages, connections, and dependencies, and from the difference in education, customs and habits, we lie under so many impediments in communicating our sensations out of our own sphere, as often amount to a total impossibility.
> It will always follow from hence, that the balance of sentimental commerce is always against the expatriated adventurer ... (78)

---

[22] On the political applications (often now difficult to detect) of animal fable in this period, see Mark Loveridge, *A History of Augustan Fable* (Cambridge, 1998).
[23] *A Short Ramble*, 56–7. Armstrong, better known as a poet, had in fact been a friend and supporter of Wilkes until a quarrel in 1763. In 1770 he visited the dying Smollett at Leghorn (*Dictionary of National Biography* [3rd edn, 22 vols, Oxford, 1967–8], i. 566–8).

Yet it becomes clear that Yorick as sentimental adventurer successfully redresses this balance. He creates a universal language through which to determine and describe his route, as he feels his way across Europe:

> —What a large volume of adventures may be grasped within this little span of life by him who interests his heart in everything, and who, having eyes to see, what time and chance are perpetually holding out to him as he journeyeth on his way, misses nothing he can *fairly* lay his hands on— (114)

The language of gesture is available to the sensitive subject even at home: Yorick announces that 'when I walk the streets of London, I go translating all the way' (171). How much more of a challenge it is, however, to colonize the '*nakedness*' of hearts abroad, a nakedness discernible beneath 'the different disguises of customs, climates, and religion' (218):

> The thirst of this, continued I, as impatient as that which inflames the breast of the connoisseur, has led me from my own home into France—and from France will lead me through Italy—'tis a quiet journey of the heart in pursuit of NATURE, and those affections which rise out of her, which make us love each other—and the world, better than we do. (219)

Too often read as a sentimental vision of universal humanity, this passage actually functions more anthropologically, demonstrating at least as much interest in cultural differences as in underlying similarities. As a philosophical formulation of the purpose of travel, it needs to be read in conjunction with Yorick's own earlier assertion (provoked by the curious figure of speech employed by his barber) that

> I think I can see the precise and distinguishing marks of national characters more in these nonsensical *minutiae,* than in the most important matters of state; where great men of all nations talk and stalk so much alike, that I would not give ninepence to chuse amongst them. (160)

Coming into play again in this passage is the opposition of aristocratic cosmopolitanism and middle-class national distinctiveness. And yet, although, as we have seen, *A Sentimental Journey* derives much of its texture from the implicit recognition that French individuals (characters, even) earn their part in the story, Sterne also mobilizes the discourse of British 'singularity' or individuality in order to underline its independence upon political liberty. To this end, the myth of British distinctiveness and foreign national uniformity is brought into play.

As we have seen in previous chapters, English singularity is conceptualized as both a result and a sign of national freedom and virtue. That 'distinct variety and originality of character ... distinguishes them [the English], not only from each other, but from all the world besides' (232), as Yorick explains to Mons. Le Compte in response to the question 'And how do you find the French?' (230). To illustrate his point, Yorick fishes 'a few king William's shillings as smooth as glass' out of his pocket:

> See, Mons. Le Compte, said I, rising up, and laying them before him upon the table—by jingling and rubbing one against another for seventy years together in one body's pocket or another's, they are become so much alike, you can scarce distinguish one shilling from another.
> The English, like ancient medals, kept more apart, and passing but few peoples hands, preserve the first sharpnesses which the fine hand of nature has given them—they are not so pleasant to feel—but in return, the legend is so visible, that at the first look you see whose image and superscription they bear.—But the French, Mons. Le Compte, added I, wishing to soften what I had said, have so many excellencies, they can the better spare this—they are a loyal, a gallant, a generous, an ingenious, and good temper'd people as is under heaven ... (232–3)[24]

English singularity is metaphorically elevated to a supra-economic plane (medals, not coins), and granted the dignity of antique virtue and correctness. The French, by contrast, are worn smooth by ceaseless mutual contact. This no doubt refers to the greater physical demonstration of their social affections. They are more pleasant to feel. However, the evident sexual resonances of this observation are not – for once, perhaps – the dominant note of this moment in *A Sentimental Journey*, which is more concerned with political symbolism. For the French uniformity of character is related to deficient liberty: the coins with which Yorick represents the French are 'king William's shillings', and their smoothness is due to the erasure of the figurehead of English liberty.[25] This metaphor, somewhat confusingly, prevents a straightforward contrast, since it is the English coins which illustrate the French character. They thus signify also the potential application of the metaphor to the English themselves: individuality and liberty are interdependent, and the symbolic erosion of King William threatens to become literal in the turbulent political climate of the 1760s.

---

[24] There is a curious reversal here of Shaftesbury's assertion that 'All politeness is owing to liberty. We polish one another, and rub off our corners and rough sides by a sort of amicable collision', *Essay on the Freedom of Wit and Humour*; cited by Stephen Copley and David Fairer, '*An Essay on Man* and the Polite Reader', in David Fairer ed., *Pope: New Contexts* (Hemel Hempstead, 1990), 204–24; 212.

[25] This point is made by Carol Kay, *Political Constructions*, 262–3.

At this point, it is worth returning to the starling, who likewise symbolizes the potential corruption into French ways of the English political system, and the much vaunted liberty on which it depends. As a postscript to the episode at Versailles, Sterne provides a 'short history' (looking beyond the actual temporal scope of *A Sentimental Journey*) of 'this self-same bird' (204). Since his 'little song for liberty' is 'in an *unknown* language at Paris' (204), Yorick explains,

> In my return from Italy I brought him with me to the country in whose language he had learn'd his notes—and telling the story of him to Lord A—Lord A begg'd the bird of me—in a week Lord A gave him to Lord B—Lord B made a present of him to Lord C— and Lord C's gentleman sold him to Lord D's for shilling—Lord D gave him to Lord E—and so on—half round the alphabet—From that rank he pass'd into the lower house, and pass'd the hands of as many commoners—But as all these wanted to *get in*—and my bird wanted to get out—he has almost as little store set by him in London as in Paris. (204–5)

As the symbolic deployment (fables, almost) of the shillings and the starling suggest, the myth of English national character is powerfully deployed within the complicated domestic political scenario within which *A Sentimental Journey* positions itself, in order to highlight simultaneously the value and vulnerability of English liberty. And yet in its reworking of the motifs of travel – again, in line with the text's liberal political agenda – Sterne's dismantling of aristocratic cosmopolitanism in favour of middle-class sincerity (figured as heterosexual in inclination if not execution: doubly virtuous) ends up attributing 'character' and sincerity to the bourgeois French 'other'. This ideological paradox presents yet another level of teasing ambivalence to incorporate into our understanding not only of *A Sentimental Journey*'s complexity, but also of its astonishing and promiscuous popularity in 1768.

The Birmingham Register, or Entertaining Museum for 19 May 1764 announces 'We hear that Mr. W[ilkes] and Tristram Shandy, both now in Paris, are going to make the tour of Italy, etc. together'.[26] Given Wilkes's rakish debaucheries in Paris as elsewhere, and his and Sterne's evening amusements with Parisian actresses, it is perhaps as well for Yorick's virtue that this planned trip never took place. But its erotic potential may serve as a fitting point on which to close this discussion of *A Sentimental Journey*, and move on to examine the response of succeeding writers to the political and erotic possibilities offered by Sterne's text.

---

[26] *The Letters of Laurence Sterne*, ed. Lewis Perry Curtis (1935; repr. Oxford, 1965), 212.

Plain citizens and common pilgrims: other sentimental travelogues

The premature ending of *A Sentimental Journey*, and of its author's life, was just the beginning of a tide of imitations which lasted into the early nineteenth century. The majority of Sternean imitations were of the *Sentimental Journey* rather than of *Tristram Shandy*.[27] Yorick's journey prompted not only imitators but pilgrims. The anonymous author (probably William Jones) of *Observations in a Journey to Paris, by Way of Flanders, in the Month of August, 1776* (2 vols, 1777) visits the Franciscan chapel at Calais. Remembering Yorick's encounter with the friar there, and his later visit to the friar's grave, the narrator is momentarily puzzled:

> I thought it rather unfortunate for the credit of this lamentation, that the monks are buried under a stone pavement in the chapel—till I recollected that *Yorick*'s friar, at his own particular request, was buried in a church-yard at some distance from Calais. (i. 28)

This passage is representative: many of the imitators and admirers of *A Sentimental Journey* treat it as literal truth, as travelogue rather than fiction. The multiplication of similar examples would not be illuminating here: more germane to this study is an appraisal of Sterne's stylistic and political imitators.

The indefatigable bibliographer of Sterneana, J.C.T. Oates, observed in 1968 that 'to judge from the book-lists and magazines, all England and most of Europe during the last thirty years of the eighteenth century were infested with sentimental travellers'.[28] The ease with which sentimental journeys could be churned out is suggested by the *Monthly Review*'s weary remark in 1779:

> *Trips*, and *Tours*, and *Excursions*, and *Sentimental Journeys*, are become so much the *ton*, that every rambler, who can write (tolerably or intolerably), assumes the pen, and gives the Public a journal of the *occurrences* and *remarks* to which his peregrinations have given birth.[29]

Note here the informal and inconsequential qualities attributed to such travels: *A Sentimental Journey* had a strongly enabling influence on writers of little erudition or social status, who were also encouraged by the growing association of literary unsophistication with sincerity in travel narrative (and indeed other genres at this time). For these delicate reasons, the *Monthly Review* in particular (and especially in the early years of Sterne's influence) seems

---

[27] Alan B. Howes, *Yorick and the Critics: Sterne's Reputation in England, 1760–1868* (New Haven, 1958), 67.
[28] J. C. T. Oates, *Shandyism and Sentiment, 1760–1800* (Cambridge, 1968), 14.
[29] *MR*, 60 (1779), 191.

reluctant simply to condemn, even while it acknowledges the low literary standard of many 'imitations'. Literary unsophistication frequently goes hand in hand with a humble, indeed parochial itinerary – typical titles are *A Sentimental Journey to Bath, Bristol, and its Environs* (1778), or *Sentimental Excursions to Windsor, and other Places* (1781). As well as the whimsically derivative 'sentimental' journeys which flooded the market after 1768, more traditional and erudite texts appeared which also adopt sentimental styles and topics. The following sections of this chapter will discuss texts drawn from both these groups.

The most tedious 'imitations' of Sterne are those which make fewest efforts to create at least the illusion that the text is based on an actual journey. Often, the imitation is purely stylistic. The *Critical Review* notes of a 1788 *Continuation* that 'the only imitation of Sterne in this production, is in the breaks, and dashes, and scanty pages, in all which the imitator infinitely exceeds the original': the *Monthly* concurs, adding that 'Sterne had but one blank leaf in a volume; but this book (if you measure by *meaning*) is all blank, from the beginning to FINIS'.[30]

Several works claim to be a genuine *Continuation of Yorick's Sentimental Journey*: the first of these appeared as early as 1768 and was attributed (wrongly, as recent scholarship has shown) to Hall-Stevenson.[31] This text, and another published in 1788, consists largely of sexually titillating anecdotes, to which the rites of Catholicism add a curious frisson and source of double entendre. They make the obligatory claims to artlessness and simplicity, and describe a series of erotic encounters with Catholic women. Temptations and acts of devotion, devoid of Sterne's ambiguity, abound. The following passage, from the 1788 *Continuation*, characteristically describes a 'sentimental' visit to a church with a new female acquaintance:

> We were both on our knees before I perceived my hand was still locked in that of the fair pilgrim.—What wouldest thou have said, *Eugenius*, to have seen me prostrate with her? (54–5)

The decadence of such works has led to the blanket condemnation of Sterne's 'imitators'. But some of these works are in fact remarkably accomplished; furthermore, they provide revealing insights into the way *A Sentimental Journey* may have been read in its time, and develop the sentimental possibilities of travel in unexpected ways.

The most sophisticated, and the first to appear, was Samuel Paterson. In 1769, under the pseudonym 'Coriat Junior', he published a pamphlet aimed at the *Monthly* reviewers, entitled *An Appeal to the Candid and Spirited Authors*

---

[30] *CR*, 66 (1788), 584; *MR*, 79 (1788), 468.
[31] Hartley, 'Yorick's Sentimental Journey Continued'.

of the Critical Review, against Ignorance, Malevolence and Detraction.[32] The *Monthly* attributes the author's 'chagrin' to 'his having been number'd among the imitators of Sterne'.[33] The pamphlet asserts the originality of Coriat Junior's two-volume travel narrative, *Another Traveller!*, published in 1768 and 1769. The *Critical Review* itself considers Coriat's originality 'unanswerably proved by the subjoined affidavits of creditable booksellers and printers, and by them subscribed'.[34] These testify that *Another Traveller!* was in fact 'put to press in the month of August, 1767', several months before the publication of *A Sentimental Journey*, and that publication was only delayed by the author's 'multifarious business'.[35] Paterson was indeed an active bookseller and auctioneer, and his earliest biographers describe *Another Traveller!* as 'the result' of a book-buying 'tour through Holland and Flanders'.[36]

The *Critical Review*'s acceptance of Coriat Junior's originality no doubt relates to that journal's negative reviews of the Smollett-bashing *Sentimental Journey*. The *Monthly*, as one might expect, engages more playfully with the pamphlet, observing that 'the resentment of this Gentleman is like that of a wayward child', and wagging a finger at his 'lust of praise':

> We have bestowed great commendation on the Author, but we have not, it seems, allotted him enough. Though we gave him (too partially, as some of our Readers think) the preference to Sterne, in certain respects, yet, because in others, we entered an exception in favour of that admired ORIGINAL, Mr. Coriat has lost a little of his good humour.[37]

---

[32] Paterson takes his pseudonym from Thomas Coryate, 'The Odcombian Legge-stretcher' (from Odcombe in Devon), who walked from Venice to London in 1608. He published an account of his journey in *Coryats Crudities, Hastily Gobbled up in Five Moneths Travells* (1611): this is a patchwork of observation and plagiarism, perhaps most interesting today for the fifty-nine prefatory verse tributes contributed by the likes of Jonson, Donne, Thomas Campion, and Inigo Jones – all poking fun at Coryate's self-publicizing, which in 1608 is seen as Odcombian rather than English. See Michael Strachan, *The Life and Adventures of Thomas Coryate* (1962).

[33] *MR*, 40 (1769), 167.

[34] *CR*, 28 (1769), 387. The full title of Paterson's book is *Another Traveller! Or Cursory Remarks and Tritical Observations made upon a Journey through Part of the Netherlands in the latter End of the Year 1766*. It was published in two volumes, in 1768 and 1769, but the title page of Volume i bears the date 1767 (probably mendaciously). It saw a second edition in 1769, and was reissued in 1782 as *An Entertaining Journey to the Netherlands*.

[35] *CR*, 28 (1769), 387–8.

[36] See *Dictionary of National Biography* (3rd edn, 22 vols, Oxford, 1967–8), xv. 467–8 and John Nichols, *Literary Anecdotes of the Eighteenth Century* (9 vols, 1812–15), iii. 438–40.

[37] *MR*, 40 (1769), 166.

The reviewer is sceptical of Coriat's protestations, noting that the 'very ample specimens of [Sterne's] *peculiar manner of travelling*, in his later Volumes of Tristram Shandy, published long enough before either the *Sentimental Journey*, or Mr. Coriat's performance', could well have furnished him with a model for Shandean travels.[38]

The 'Preface' to *Another Traveller!* jestingly apologizes for daring to publish 'a couple of *Shandean* duodecimos', and explains that 'travelling is the mode, and ... it is no less the mode to print travels' (i. vii–viii). Paterson's close involvement in the book trade no doubt contributed to the textual self-consciousness of *Another Traveller!*, whose narrator frequently discusses the mechanics of writing, marketing, and criticism with a series of tetchy interlocutors. Sterne was not alone at this time in realizing the lucrative potential of combining the Shandean style with the modish genre of travel narrative. However, to describe *Another Traveller!* as 'Shandean', as do both the 'Preface' and the *Monthly*, suggests that it is redolent more of ludic fiction and satire than of 'genuine' travel narrative. This is misleading. Paterson's text is simultaneously one of the most engaging and apparently 'authentic' sentimental renderings of a journey published in the 1760s or 1770s. Sentimental reflection and the physical experience of travel are held in an assured balance. Descriptions of routes, towns, cathedrals and personal encounters are interwoven with ponderings on authorship, publishing, sentiment, prejudice, and other abstract topics. Coriat Junior journeys by land, sea, and canal from London to Antwerp and its environs. He invariably makes use of public transport, whether this be coach or barge, and thereby encounters a rich variety of fellow-travellers, British and foreign. Descriptions of the towns and cathedrals where he alights, and accounts of his personal encounters (with charitable monks and beautiful nuns in particular) are interwoven with dramatized dialogues and reflections:

> My intention is to diversify this short travel as much as possible—to make it narrative, descriptive and sometimes allegorical—always with a little meaning and seldom without a moral. ... the very moment I discover that I have nothing to say, I shall lay down my pen—I have no opinion of forcing, under the notion of assisting nature, and, from my soul! I abominate Dr. *Slop*'s forceps! (i. 174)

For all Paterson's indignant claims, the earlier publication of *A Sentimental Journey* does effectively undermine his claims to originality. At this early stage in the proliferation of sentimental travels, however, the issue of invention is less important than the inherent value of the new approach. Ralph Griffiths's enthusiastic and lengthy account of *Another Traveller!* in the *Monthly* opens thus:

---

[38]   *MR*, 40 (1769), 167.

Sentimental Travels seem now to be coming into vogue; and,
indeed, we shall rejoice to see a final period put to those dull details
of post-stages, and churches, and picture-catalogues, with which
books of travels heretofore chiefly abounded ...

The sprightly, the humorous, the sentimental Yorick, was the
first who had sense and taste enough to quit the beaten pack-horse
path; and the ingenious author of the present travels has the good
fortune to follow him at no despicable rate. There have been many
imitators of that celebrated original; but none who, in our opinion,
have caught so much of his manner and spirit as Mr. Coriat, Junior
...[39]

A passage from *Another Traveller!* suggests a distinction between literary and
personal originality. It consists of a dialogue between Coriat Junior and his
anxious, nagging bookseller, Johnson, over the slow progress of his
manuscript. Johnson is especially worried by an advertisement he reads out
from the *St James's Chronicle*:

'Speedily will be published—*A sentimental journey, by* Mr.
YORICK'
Good!—I am heartily glad of it!—for then we shall have
something worth reading!—How can this affect us, but with
delight?
'Are you not abashed?—And will not malicious folks say?'—
— — —
Let them say what they will—for after him, and a thousand
worse, ANOTHER TRAVELLER will still be read!—There is room
enough in this big world for him and me too—Shadows fill no
place—Mr. YORICK will be read for his wit—I must be heard for
my cause. (i. 443)

In contrast to the competitive backbiting which characterizes the literary world
of Smollett and Thicknesse, Sharp and Baretti, the sentimental arena is sociable
and inclusive; the sentimental traveller has a generic identity as well as an
individual defining characteristic – 'Mr. YORICK will be read for his wit—I
must be heard for my cause'.

As with Yorick, Coriat Junior's fictive persona is important in this curious
conflation of the individual and the representative. Paterson's playful allusion
to the seventeenth-century traveller Thomas Coryate is expanded by Coriat
Junior into a celebration of his namesake's 'modesty and humility', as well as
his satiric wit. We are informed that 'Tom possest one part of *Falstaffe*'s
character in a very eminent degree; and if he was not over witty himself, he was
the true cause *that wit was in other men*'.[40] The comparison with Falstaff

[39]   *MR*, 39 (1768), 434–5.
[40]   *MR*, 39 (1768), 435–6; *Another Traveller!*, i. 113.

reinforces the symbiotic relationship between British singularity and typicality which 'Coriat Junior' and 'Yorick' also signify; like Sterne's Yorick, Coriat is at once an individual and a fragment of shared British culture; paradoxically, a *representative* of national *singularity*, and Britain's moral spokesman. Many 'sentimental' travel writers likewise deploy pseudonyms. As we saw in the preceding chapter, Thomas Cogan presents himself as 'John Buncle, Junior' (capitalizing on the popularity of Thomas Amory's whimsical fictional character, and demonstrating how the original John Buncle had become a byword for English oddity), whilst a clergyman from Leeds (author of religious tracts as well as a travelogue) writes as 'Cornelius Cayley', a vowel-laden name obscurely suggestive, like Samuel Jackson Pratt's 'Courtney Melmoth', of sensitive benevolence. To these characters we shall in due course return.

Coriat Junior's distinctive 'cause' seems to be no less than a radical revision of British attitudes to abroad:

> *I beg leave then to proceed in my own way*—and tho' it is become so much the fashion among my countrymen of late to decry foreign customs and manners, and to cry up whatever is of *British* growth, whether right, or wrong; I shall nevertheless take the liberty so far to differ from them, as to commend whatever in my judgment has appeared commendable, without dread of the forfeiture of my allegiance; and even to do justice to a monk where I have found him worthy, and I hope without the imputation of being a papist.
>
> By such candid proceeding I flatter myself it is not impossible but that I may be able with reason to remove the illiberal prejudices of some of my readers, and to laugh away the childish notions of others. (i. 32–3)

This rational optimism sits uneasily with the pessimistic determinism associated with sensibility, which presents the sentimental individual as painfully subject to the abuse of the irredeemably non-sentimental herd (Henry Mackenzie's *The Man of Feeling* in 1771 represents the quintessence of such vulnerability). Boarding the ship for Ostend, Coriat Junior and his companion stand politely back, only to find that every other passenger presses forward, 'and my companion and I were fain to lay, the one upon a bulk, the other upon the cabin floor'. This upsetting experience prompts the following reflections:

> Such are the disadvantages which the modest man frequently labours under, to which the impudent is an utter stranger—the forward and bold constantly avail themselves of the backwardness of the humble and modest, turn their punctilios into jests, and, in short, reap every advantage at their expence, save one—arising from a certain sensibility, which as they can never feel, so it is impossible to make them comprehend. (i. 29)

Significantly, the 'forward and bold' here are Coriat Junior's countrymen: he is rarely thus abused by the Flemish. Similarly, Courtney Melmoth's more laboured *Travels for the Heart* (1777) berates a particularly noxious example of pig-headed English xenophobia in the person of a Lombard Street merchant who has been boasting about English commercial dominance:

> Fie, fie, and a thousand blushes upon such for the poorness of their heads, and the pitylessness of their feelings—but I am writing *for the heart*, and have therefore no leisure to address those who are without one.[41]

Such passages establish the sentimental traveller's difference from other British men or women. This difference contributes to the narrator's individuality; yet, consisting as it does in sensibility, it is shared with the assumed reader. It is also class-inflected, implicitly middling. The sentimental mode of travelling replaces, in *Another Traveller!*, the cumbersome baggage of the aristocratic Grand Tour:

> Give me only a reasonable portion of philanthropy—as much as I can conveniently carry about me, let me travel which way I will, and I am satisfied.
> I abominate incumbrances of every kind—and you see plainly, that if I had assumed any other character than that of a well-meaning cosmopolite, that I must have carried my library along with me.
> Men of science are positively nothing without their tools.
> (i. 321–2)

Eating, drinking, travelling, conversing, even attending church with the 'inhabitants' provides not only a cheaper way of travelling, but also a means by which the harsh corners are rubbed off the 'prejudices' cultivated by the grand and aloof journeyings of most of Coriat Junior's countrymen (i. 161–2). Again, however, there is a strong element of determinism, this time social. The wealthy and aloof will always travel in the same way. The pleasures of sentimental travel are zealously, though subtly, guarded:

> You are to understand that I am a plain citizen of the great world; not a gay fellow of the little one—a common pilgrim in the beaten track; not a courtly passenger in the bye path:—an humble tenant of the wide forest and the open field; not a lord of the lawn, the grove, and the terras; who carefully shuns the din and plash of the populace, and studiously avoids interfering with the lot of those beneath him; lest, by degrees, he should be insensibly wrought upon, to contemplate the nothingness of his own. (ii. 167–8)

---

[41] Courtney Melmoth, *Travels for the Heart. Written in France* (2 vols, 1777), i. 70.

Here, European universality is explicitly redefined. The cosmopolitan culture of the aristocratic Grand Tour is relegated to a 'little' world, and the 'well-meaning cosmopolite' is distinguished by philanthropy, not classical or courtly culture. In a similar sleight of hand, Coriat Junior reclaims the strength of feeling signified by 'prejudice', a term generally resonant of xenophobia, for sentimental purposes: describing the Flemish practice of exhibiting the corpses of hanged malefactors, Coriat Junior announces that he is 'particularly prejudiced against that inhuman practice' (i. 205). Likewise reclaiming the term, and alert to the class implications of such a reclamation, John Buncle, Junior announces that it is his 'ardent desire to cultivate right principles', and 'to clear my mind from vulgar prejudices; to approve and vindicate what I can discern excellent in a cobler [sic], and detest villainy in a king' (i. 70).[42]

The promotion of sensibility is nicely bound up with the assertion of individuality (as well as class), as Coriat Junior declares that 'to contemplate the condition of others, are the only means by which I shall arrive at the knowledge of myself' (i. 332–3). Moments such as these in *Another Traveller!* are unsubtle in comparison to Sterne: but, lacking Sterne's ambiguity and complexity – his 'wit' – Coriat Junior is bolder in his social criticism, the exposition of his 'cause'. Paterson exploits for sentimental ends the traditionally educative function of travel writing. 'If a man has a mind to indulge serious reflections, let him write a book on purpose' complains one of the voices in *Another Traveller!*, to which Coriat replies: 'Yes, as you say—and then he will be pretty sure that nobody will read them—I tell you mine are just in the right place—for here many may stumble upon them, who never dreamt of any such thing' (i. 152).

Perhaps Paterson's most evident preoccupation is Catholicism, towards which he adopts an ambivalent stance, oscillating between fascination and distaste. Volume ii (1769) was very possibly written, or at least altered, after reviews of Volume i had commended as 'affecting' his 'reflections upon nuns and nunneries'.[43] Within Volume ii, however, a fictive reader dares to condemn the sympathetic portraits of monks and priest, prompting Coriat to retort that 'I

---

[42]   Paterson's text may be seen as a classic instance of Whig sentimentalism: as recently defined by Julie Ellison, this 'rests on the early eighteenth-century claim that integrity in the public sphere is demonstrated by one's emotional and somatic sensitivity' ('Redoubled Feeling: Politics, Sentiment, and the Sublime in Williams and Wollstonecraft', *Eighteenth-Century Studies*, 20 [1990], 197–215; 212, n. 1).

[43]   *CR*, 26 (1768), 348. The *Monthly* had excerpted long examples of Coriat's nun passages. Cf. Baretti, who expresses puzzlement that although monks and friars 'afford the most curious subject for speculation in human nature, yet not one in a hundred of the English travellers, when in Italy, or in other Popish countries, ever shows the least desire of knowing the distinguishing marks of such an odd and surprising set of mortals', beyond observing (like Sharp) 'that they are superstitious and have fat guts' (*An Account of the Manners and Customs of Italy* [2 vols, 1768], ii. 76).

have not yet spoke a word about religion, blockhead! I have only been characterizing men' (ii. 35). Again, the sentimental approach strives to engage with individuals rather than ideologies.

Coriat Junior's presentation of Catholicism has specific political resonances as well as a sentimental agenda of broader tolerance. Ralph Griffiths in the *Monthly* excerpts in its entirety a chapter entitled 'An Apology for Wooden Shoes', those potent symbols (especially popular in satiric prints) of Continental despotism and misery. During the 1760s' wave of anti-Scottish feeling, clogs were sometimes attributed also to the Scottish peasantry. Paterson chooses to celebrate the practical value of wooden shoes, and notes that 'Humanity pleads strongly in their favour'; they are, moreover, far preferable to the barefooted oppression evident 'in the northern part of this loved island, where property is so partially divided that all are lords, or beggars; shoes are almost as scarce as parishes' (i. 364–5). This attack on the well-heeled Scots (evoking in particular Lords Bute and Mansfield) again suggests that the pro-Wilkes agenda of *A Sentimental Journey* was recognized by contemporaries. But, as with Sterne, Paterson's dissidence expands beyond high politics into a broader critique of domestic social policy.

The way in which *Another Traveller!* represents Catholic seclusion is noteworthy. Many visits to convents and monasteries are documented. Paterson will refer to confinement as 'that pernicious practice', and 'a road which nature shudders at', yet frequently enjoy the 'pleasure of conversing' with monks and, more especially, nuns (i. 353–4). This ambivalent assessment of Catholicism is explicable if one considers separately its charitable functions and its immobilization of women: nuns, certainly as Coriat sees it, play no part in the socially virtuous practices of hospitality and charity which are evident in the many monastic institutions visited. Of these virtues, as displayed at the Abbey of Affligem, he notes:

> By some unaccountable fatality, these primitive virtues stand their ground—and rail at the believer, wrapt in a particular-fashioned habit, as long as we like, we can never strip him of something that lies under it—That by which so many good people are daily benefitted, must needs be praise-worthy—and, indeed, to which, as to articles of faith, we must subscribe whether we will, or no. (i. 318)

(Given Coriat's conscious Shandyism, it is difficult not to see an innuendo in this passage – 'something that lies under it' – but its function is unclear.) A little later, it is suggested that we can all share in the 'heavenly offices' of charity. The term refers back to the (specifically) monastic duties Coriat has just described at the Abbey, but is expanded to signify a wider benevolence, such that by carrying out such offices, we are fulfilling our role as 'members of the great world, and links of general society' (i. 331). Few of Coriat's compatriots, including Sterne, provide such a pragmatic evaluation of Catholicism, one which brings together sympathetic universalism and active charity, and which unsentimentally acknowledges the 'primitive virtues' beneath the widely ridiculed trappings of religion. This strand of *Another Traveller!* relates to the discussion, increasingly pressing in later eighteenth-century Britain, of poor relief, and of the form and function of charitable institutions.[44] In these terms, Catholic institutions, especially their outward influence, are viewed positively as models for social behaviour.

Their inward organization with respect to women is, however, far less palatable to Coriat Junior. In part, this is because female seclusion precludes any social or charitable function. But, more broadly, it represents a deep social and psychological threat, and female retirement is emphatically rejected as a choice of life. Coriat suggests that seclusion may properly be embraced once a woman has lived out her useful purpose in society, and after 'the loss of husbands, who were their partners, or their plagues; of children, who might have been their comforts, or their curses' (i. 175–6). It is clear that the practices of Catholicism are being used to validate, by contrast, the dependence and social usefulness of the British domestic female. This is made more explicit in the particular case of an Englishwoman named Grace Fox, who was, apparently, seduced into her convent by the 'present pious bishop of *Bruges*. ... His lordship, no doubt was happy in thinking that he had gained a soul—but I dare say he never once reflected how many good subjects the king my master may have lost through his zeal, and Heaven perhaps as many saints' (i. 94–5).[45] Where female independence of British social constraints is concerned, Coriat's sentimental tolerance and adventurous social critique desert him.

While Paterson picks up on the issues of politics, charity, and women which *A Sentimental Journey* had obliquely raised, other 'imitators' respond to different aspects of Yorick's experiences. In 1773, Cornelius Cayley, a Leeds clergyman, published *A Tour thorough Holland, Flanders, and Part of France*, which had been previously published in serial form in 'the Leeds news-paper'.[46] Capitalizing on the sermonizing potential of the sentimental journey (and resolutely rejecting the erotic), Cayley's text is saturated with Christian moralizing, so that the European jaunt becomes a rich source of spiritual analogy; arriving in Amsterdam, for example, the narrator is moved to exclaim

[44] See A. W. Coats, 'The Relief of Poverty: Attitudes to Labour, and Economic Change in England, 1660–1782', *International Review of Social History*, 21 (1976), 98–115; David Owen, *English Philanthropy, 1660–1960* (Cambridge, MA, 1965); and Gertrude Himmelfarb, *The Idea of Poverty: England in the Early Industrial Age* (1984).

[45] Cf. i. 175 where Coriat Junior refers to the 'horrible impiety of dispeopling Heaven, by entombing fair damsels alive; under the notion of increasing the kingdom of Saints'.

[46] *A Tour thorough Holland*, 114.

'Ah! thinks I, If this city is so beautiful, what must the new Jerusalem be—the city of the living God!' (13). He preaches toleration (at one point intervening between a Frenchman and an Italian engaged in doctrinal dispute), and admires the humane Dutch for their 'care of the poor' (38), as well as their civic cleanliness – 'Ah, Leeds! when wilt thou imitate it?' (27). In France, he lays the blame for French poverty squarely at the door of the aristocracy, and makes explicit and pointed comparisons with the English state of affairs:

> It is well if the rage of inclosing commons, and ingrossing farms in
> ENGLAND, do not at length make our villages as poor and destitute
> as in *France*. A procedure, that is as impolitic as wicked; and far
> from being agreeable to that benevolence of heart, which will never
> oppress the industrious poor to enrich a few individuals. But whilst
> the spirit of luxury, gaming, and dissipation so much prevails
> amongst the great, we must not expect these evils will be remedied,
> tho' quite obvious to all. (101)

The social conscience of sentimental travelling finds unexpected voice in a comparatively late account, *A Descriptive Journey through the Interior Parts of Germany and France, including Paris: with Interesting and Amusing Anecdotes*, 'By a young English Peer, of the highest Rank, just returned from his Travels' (1786) – actually Francis Russell, 5th Duke of Bedford. The 'Advertisement' sets out the sentimental agenda of the *Journey* in terms reminiscent of *Another Traveller!*:

> In order to gratify a commendable curiosity, viz. the knowledge of
> human nature in (comparatively speaking) an unaccommodated
> state, our young Traveller frequently preferred a Diligence, or
> Stage-Coach, to the pompous equipage and parade of a Man of
> Fashion; and the plain, but wholesome food, and humble
> companions, generally found at an *Auberge*, or Public Inn, to the
> elegant accommodations, and luxurious viands, which are usually
> placed before a Man who is princely in his fortune, and but one
> degree below Royalty itself. (vi–vii)

The text which follows, however, signally fails to provide the promised menu, presenting instead a catalogue of courtly visits to libraries and galleries, cabinets of curiosities, palaces, princes, gardens and assemblies. The author moves in the lofty circles which his rank – 'but one degree below Royalty itself' – would lead one to expect, and in fact is rather disgusted by the realities of public transport:

> The day was fine, and the ride of course would prove agreeable: but
> the company was infernally offensive; as is too often the case in
> public carriages. A Capucin and a wh—e, two Jews, an Officer, and
> myself, formed the society ... (22–3)

The social sympathy outlined in the 'Advertisement' is little more than a sop to the common reader: it suggests nevertheless the extent to which sentimentalism has entered the discourse of travel.

Further evidence, possibly of sentiment's actual domination of travel writing, and certainly of its modish appeal, is provided by its espousal in 1777 by – of all people – Philip Thicknesse. In 1777, he published his final travel narrative, *A Year's Journey through France, and Part of Spain*. This is an elegant two-volume octavo costing a guinea (*Observations* was a badly printed single octavo, just over 100 pages long and priced at two shillings, *Useful Hints* a single octavo at four shillings). Thicknesse somehow managed to enlist 430 subscribers for *A Year's Journey*, including the Duchess of Cumberland, and secured an advance of £580.[47] It is an altogether more respectable enterprise. The tone is far mellower and more courteous. Even Smollett – now deceased – is treated with muted tolerance: 'poor man! he was ill' (i. 3). The *Monthly Review* remarks on the author's 'original turn for sarcastic drollery', but adds that 'we do not mean this in the most unpleasant sense of the term'; rather, the volumes display their author's 'agreeable zest'.[48] Even the *Critical Review*, while displeased by Thicknesse's 'private and personal' reflections, is generally approving.[49]

Volume i is prefaced with a curious address 'To the Reader', in which Thicknesse gives thanks for his own health and laments the recent deaths of various friends (i. xiii–xvii). The world of public contention and prejudice, personal or political, is explicitly repudiated, and his own death symbolically anticipated:

> for in what, and where do all these worldly trifles end?—in sorrow, sickness, and in DEATH—O eloquent, just, and mighty DEATH! … thou has drawn together all the far-fetched greatness, all the pride, cruelty, guilt, and ambition of man; and covered it over with these two narrow words—

> 'HIC JACET'

There follow several small line-drawn boxes, symbolic coffins, within which are inscribed the names of various of Thicknesse's friends and relations; the final box contains the inscription 'HIC JACET PHIL. THICKNESSE' (i. xvii). Much of the text is devoted to an account of the monasteries or 'hermitages' at Montserrat, described with a humane religious tolerance increasingly in vogue in the 1770s – briefly marred, however, by Thicknesse's casual theft of 'a pound of chocolate' from one of the hermits' cells (i. 193). The *Monthly*

---

[47] Philip Gosse, *Dr Viper: the Querulous Life of Philip Thicknesse* (1952), 175.

[48] *MR*, 57 (1777), 207.

[49] *CR*, 43 (1777), 449.

Review commends, and presents copious extracts from, these sections. There are also far fewer attacks on peasants and individuals (within or beyond the text) than in Thicknesse's earlier travelogues, and an autumnal note of regretful exile from England. The trip was allegedly undertaken to save money following the disastrous outcome of a lawsuit in which Thicknesse had long been embroiled. The 'Preface' elaborates these circumstances at some length, and Thicknesse melodramatically announces that he was 'driven out of my own country, with eight children in my train' (i. xv). This is a partial echo of Smollett's plaintive explanation of exile at the beginning of the *Travels* ('traduced by malice, persecuted by faction, abandoned by false patrons, and overwhelmed by the sense of a domestic calamity, which it was not in the power of fortune to repair');[50] and Thicknesse's 'eight children' make a spectacular appeal to the candour and sensibilities of a late 1770s readership. The text as a whole is equable and informative, not inspired by any particular grievances (although one or two are aired along the way), and free from the frantic daring which had characterized his earlier travel narratives. Thicknesse's own ageing partly explains the change in tone: but given his opportunistic awareness of the literary marketplace, the replacement of scurrilous muscle-flexing with this sentimental posture speaks volumes about the dominance of sensibility within travel writing by this date.

Sentiment under scrutiny

The extent of Sterne's influence, and the pervasiveness of sentimentalism generally, are further illustrated by the permeation of sensibility into serious texts produced by learned and well-connected writers: members of the Royal Society, and diplomats, for instance. As popular examples of each of these types, we turn now to Nathaniel Wraxall's *Cursory Remarks made in a Tour through Some of the Northern Parts of Europe* (1775) and Patrick Brydone's *A Tour through Sicily and Malta* (2 vols, 1773), written only a couple of years after Sterne and Paterson. Both these works describe relatively unknown parts of Europe. They reflect the expanding geographical horizons of travel at this time, even while (paradoxically) their ironic engagement with sentiment foreshadows the insularity which is to dominate in the 1780s, a decade in which (as Chapter 5 will describe) sentiment and eccentricity come increasingly under attack.

Despite the title of Wraxall's account, which clearly exploits the growing public thirst for affective and immediate travel narratives, *Cursory Remarks* is generally erudite. It is traditional and sober in organization, and packed with

---

[50] Tobias Smollett, *Travels through France and Italy* (1766), ed. Frank Felsenstein Oxford, 1979), 2.

information on comparatively unfamiliar parts of Europe (Denmark, Sweden, Russia). Wraxall moved in diplomatic and royal circles, travelling as an intermediary between George III and supporters of George's sister, the exiled Queen Caroline of Denmark. *Cursory Remarks* focuses especially on the private dramas behind political controversies and court scandals in the countries which he visits: in later life he was to achieve notoriety as a political memoirist.[51] His narrative reads like a source book for historical romances. The book is dedicated to Viscount Clare, for his 'patronage in this ... first attempt to appear before the tribunal of the Public' (iv). Wraxall's particular interest in affecting tales of aristocratic distress is symptomatic of his wider preoccupation with feminine beauty and virtue, distressed or otherwise. This sits somewhat oddly with discussion of matters military, political, and agricultural. The *Critical Review*, though choosing not to excerpt certain 'detail[s] of gallantry' in favour of historical information (and thus perhaps encouraging curious readers to purchase the full text themselves), generally commends 'this agreeable, and sentimental traveller'.[52] The *Gentleman's Magazine*, however, complains that 'could he be prevailed on to strike out all mention of every woman that he would have us believe reigned the sovereign of his affections for an hour, in a very rapid succession ... [the *Tour*] would appear to much greater advantage'.[53]

As these conflicting critical responses would suggest, Wraxall's text and indeed his narrative persona are strangely divided. On the one hand, he professes and displays a voracious hunger for new and useful information, on topics such as the partition of Poland and the architecture of St Petersburg: on the other, sudden passions can thoroughly distract his attention from matters historical and topographical, and produce a narrative hiatus. Even his pursuit of knowledge is described in strongly emotional and sentimental terms, as 'that insatiable avidity, that divine and indescribable delight which ... I attempt in vain by language and description to kindle in other bosoms, where nature has not given a similarity of feeling' (268–9). The emotional terminology here is perhaps intended to render the empirical approach more attractive to a post-Sterne readership; but it also suggests that the narrative self-consciousness

---

[51] His most controversial publication was the *Historical Memoirs of my own Time, from 1772 to 1784* (2 vols, 1815), which present anecdotes of the political world and the London social scene. They generated enormous public interest and critical outrage, being denounced by the *Quarterly Review* as 'pompous gossip and inflated trash' (*QR*, 13 [1815], 213) and by the *Edinburgh* as a 'union of nastiness and obscenity' (*ER*, 25 [1815], 190). Wraxall was careful to publish subsequent volumes only posthumously (as *Posthumous Memoirs*, 3 vols, 1836). See my entry on Wraxall in *New Dictionary of National Biography* (forthcoming, Oxford, 2004).

[52] *CR*, 39 (1775), 451–2. As late as 1789, he is still referred to as 'the sentimental Wraxal [*sic*]' in *CR*, 68 (1789), 44.

[53] *GM*, 46 (1776), 24.

fostered by the sentimental mode has extended into all areas of travelling experience, transforming a previously communal interest into a more individualistic passion. (The reference to the vanity of arousing similar interest in naturally unsympathetic bosoms is, moreover, a version of the determinism which operates in unashamedly 'sentimental' texts, like Samuel Paterson's.)

Enthusiasm for knowledge is frequently sacrificed to Wraxall' other passion, sexual sympathy. A revealing insight into the relationship between these two topics follows a lingering description of the Princess Royal of Prussia, imprisoned at Stettin:

> I have been so engaged in speaking and thinking of this unfortunate princess, that I have not yet mentioned a word of Stettin. Indeed, to say the truth, I know very little about it. There are a great many houses, and a great many streets, two very large churches, a river, a quay, and, as they tell me, a very extensive commerce. The inhabitants are about 16,000. This is the sum total of my knowledge respecting the place. (390)

Wraxall notches up encounters with beautiful young women – one of whom is only eleven, but her 'whole figure was a beauty in miniature' (11) – as other writers would enumerate their scientific or archaeological discoveries. His descriptions of charitable encounters never fail to stress that sexual attraction is his chief motivation.[54] In a passage excerpted by both the *Monthly* and the *Critical*, a cluster of 'very pretty forms' among a crowd of Swedish peasants who press round him have a powerful effect:

> I must own that I distributed my schellings more in proportion to their beauty, than their age, infirmities, or poverty. Such is the inchantment of this captivating endowment, that I attempted in vain to resist it's [*sic*] influence: my head condemned me, but my heart counteracted all its dictates, and warped my benevolence in compliance with its own feelings. (92–3)

Similarly, he dispenses coins to a French prisoner at Elsinore who enthuses about the '*aimable*' queen Matilda also confined there:

> I could not resist the force of his compliment to an English and an injured queen—I put my hand in my pocket, and gave him some half dozen stivers; nor was it, I must own, either general

---

[54] Contrast Yorick in *A Sentimental Journey*: 'I had then but three sous left: so I gave one, simply *pour l'amour de Dieu*, which was the footing on which it was begg'd—The poor woman had a dislocated hip; so it could not well be, upon any other motive' (133). Clearly, this is the exception that proves the rule for Yorick, the bizarre pun upon 'footing' and 'hip' contributing to the strangeness of the moment.

philanthropy, or private commiseration, which drew most of them
out—It was Matilda gave them, and I bid him thank her, not me. (9)

This self-conscious compulsion to analyse the motivation of voluptuous charity
is striking. In emphasizing the agency of Matilda – a queen – over the
commoner impulses of 'general philanthropy' or even 'private commiseration',
Wraxall is resisting the levelling tendencies of sentimental giving. Similarly, in
his frequent close encounters of the romantic kind, Wraxall's gallantry
functions to distance him from the more earnest and bourgeois associations of
sensibility. There is a deliberate aristocratic rakishness in his posturing. So,
even while the influence of sentimental travels obliquely provides Wraxall with
a vocabulary – and a ready market – his seigneurial response to female
vulnerability deliberately ignores the problems of inequity and exploitation
which tend to be addressed by less 'aristocratic' sentimental travels.

Both the *Critical Review* and the *Gentleman's Magazine* link Wraxall's
travel book with that of Patrick Brydone, whose *Tour through Sicily and Malta*
had appeared in 1773. In each journal, the perceived affinity is one of stylistic
informality; the *Critical* notes that both writers employ 'the epistolary form'
and write in a 'lively manner'.[55] Patrick Brydone, a lowland Scot and a Tory
who later served in the North ministry, had a classical education and a military
training. He was both a Freemason and an expert on electricity. During the late
1760s he travelled in the Swiss Alps conducting electrical experiments, and
also travelled as tutor to William Beckford of Suffolk (to whom the letters of
the *Tour* are addressed).[56] The publication of the *Tour*, with its wealth of
information on Sicily's agriculture and antiquities, volcanoes, religious
festivals and social habits, coincided with Brydone's election to the Royal
Society.[57]

The *Critical Review* notes the 'enthusiasm' with which Brydone describes
his scientific and vulcanological researches, and his 'lively and entertaining
manner'.[58] In the *Monthly*, Ralph Griffiths's praise of Brydone's narrative is
inseparable from his assessment of Brydone's character, and presents a glowing
portrait of Enlightenment man:

---

[55] *GM*, 46 (1776), 24; *CR*, 39 (1775), 443.

[56] Not to be confused with the later William Beckford of Fonthill (no relation), author
of *Vathek* (1786) as well as *Dreams, Waking Thoughts, and Incidents: in a Series of
Letters, from Various Parts of Europe* (1783).

[57] For biographical information, see Paul Fussell, 'Patrick Brydone: The Eighteenth-
Century Traveler as Representative Man', *Bulletin of the New York Public Library*, 66
(1962), 349–63. Fussell notes that the existing entry in the *Dictionary of National
Biography* is unreliable. See my entry on Brydone in *New Dictionary of National
Biography* (forthcoming, Oxford, 2004).

[58] *CR*, 35 (1773), 299, 301.

[Captain Brydone's] letters prove him at once the gentleman, the scholar, and the man of science: a rational observer, a philosophical enquirer, and a polite and pleasing companion. His style is natural and easy, his language free and flowing (though not always correct) and his manner cheerful and lively; yet properly varied to suit the several subjects, whether gay or serious, as they occur in the course of the Traveller's adventures.[59]

Paul Fussell cites Griffiths' character sketch to support his reading of Brydone as a 'consummately representative man' of the eighteenth century (363). But Fussell's concept of the eighteenth century is one-sided: Brydone is presented as a man of Augustan sensibilities, with a Johnsonian or even Swiftian sense of human absurdity, while the wave of sentimentalism in travel writing from the late 1760s onwards is not addressed. In fact, Brydone's text engages on a sophisticated level with contemporary trends towards sensibility, if only to impose a conservative equilibrium. He not only puts the vocabulary of sublime enthusiasm to good use in his account of Mount Etna, but also employs an intimate and affective style throughout: 'We see every thing which he saw, we feel all that he felt, we share in his fatigues, and we partake of his raptures'.[60] This encomium from Ralph Griffiths seems directly to echo (and reverse) Brydone's own diffidence about conveying his 'impression[s]' to the reader, 'Few things I believe in writing being more difficult than thus "s'emparer de l'imagination," to seize,—to make ourselves masters of the reader's imagination, to carry it along with us through every scene, and make it in a manner congenial with our own' (i. 100). Whereas Wraxall engages with sentimentalism only to fragment it and appropriate it to his rakish persona, Brydone bridges the gap between erudition and sentiment more comprehensively, here assimilating sympathy and clubbability.

In his accounts of religious and social practices, and occasionally in anecdotes of personal encounter, the language of sensibility is deployed for affective immediacy and to explore the power and limits of sympathy: yet, finally, a more commonsensical position asserts itself.[61] The personally alienating and politically adventurous aspects of sensibility are edged out of the narrative by a brisk tone of authority and sociability. This approach has a politically conservative basis. One of the most discordant passages in the *Tour*, near the end of Volume ii, is a long diatribe against Whiggishness; specifically, against current anti-Scots feeling and its licentious expression in the British press. Brydone rails against the 'despicable incendiaries', who are 'the most

---

[59]   *MR*, 49 (1773), 22–3.
[60]   *MR*, 49 (1773), 120.
[61]   Similarly, as Fussell has noted (357), Brydone's sublime and poetic accounts of Etna always finally advance a naturalistic cause for a sublime effect, an explanatory procedure later developed in the Gothic fiction of Ann Radcliffe.

abandoned and profligate wretches in the nation', and pays elaborate tribute to George III, 'the most virtuous and benevolent prince on earth' (ii. 267–8). The contrast with Sterne's sly pro-Wilkes sympathies could not be greater, and further attests to the political leanings of sensibility, of which Brydone is aware, and to which his narrative provides a check. So, his simultaneous use and critique of the sentimental mode within a generally scientific narrative (with classical interludes also – there is much quotation and allusion, more elegant and apposite than Addison's) ensures Brydone a very wide readership and a favourable reception, by whichever criteria are applied. This is no doubt why his *Tour* was so astonishingly popular (there were seven English editions in Brydone's own lifetime). Other factors must also have contributed to its popularity: its elegant readability; the variety of topics covered, ranging from Homer to volcanoes, to turtle-catching, to nuns; the lively, 'sublime' descriptions of volcanoes and electricity (which the *Monthly* and *Critical* both excerpt at length); and, quite simply, the highly marketable novelty of his itinerary: 'this little expedition has never been considered as any part of the grand tour and ... will probably present many objects worthy of your attention, that are not mentioned in any of our books of travels' (i. 3).[62]

Brydone's discussion of Catholic devotion displays a sophisticated application of sensibility, and a critique of its political implications. An amused account of the Christianization of Sicily's pagan remains – 'what was Venus or Proserpine, is now Mary Magdalene, or the Virgin' (i. 143) – modulates into a more intimate consideration of Catholic idolatry:

> I own I have sometimes envied [the Catholics] their feelings; and in my heart cursed the pride of reason and philosophy, with all its cool and tasteless triumphs, that lulls into a kind of stoical apathy the most exquisite sensations of the soul.—Who would not chuse to be deceived, when the deception raises in him these delicious passions, that are so worthy of the human heart; and for which, of all others, it seems to be the most fitted?—But if once you have steeled it over with the hard and impenetrable temper of philosophy; these fine-spun threads of weakness and affection, that were so pliable, and so easily tied, become hard and inflexible; and for ever lose that delicate tone of sensibility that put them into a kind of unison and vibration with every object around us: For it is certainly true, what has been said of one part of our species, and may almost with equal

---

[62] Kenneth Churchill has remarked on the 'constant recurrence in almost every "Italian" novel or story [in the later eighteenth century, and early nineteenth] of the name Rosalia (or Rosalie, Rosolia, Rosalina); apparently taken from the account of the feast of Santa Rosalia at Palermo in Brydone's *Tour' (Italy and English Literature 1764–1930* [1980], 19).

justice be applied to the whole,
                 'That to their weakness half their charms we owe'.[63]

This allusion to Sterne's 'great sensorium', which extends the Burkean response to female feebleness into a universal affection, is adventurous: Brydone skilfully employs the adoration of female images as a symbol by which Catholic practices are brought within the sentimental reader's understanding. Sacred icons are scarcely different from the female object of sentimental emotion, and both promote 'delicious passions' and socially cohesive vibrations. Baretti in fact had already outlined this affinity, observing that 'Our [Italian] modes of religion force our eyes on beautiful mothers tenderly embracing their children, and on saints and angels melting with devotion; and thus contribute to render us affectionate and gentle'.[64]

The levelling tolerance of the Brydone passage is, however, significantly modified by what follows:

> Now, pray, don't you think too, that this personal kind of worship is much better adapted to the capacities of the vulgar, than the more pure and sublime modes of it; which would only distract and confound their simple understandings, unaccustomed to speculation; and that certainly require something gross and material, some object of sense to fix their attention? (i. 149–50)

Brydone then cites a passage from Pope's *Essay on Man* as an example of a 'pure and sublime' mode of worship.[65] The 'sublime language of our poet' (i. 149), describing the dizzying immanence of the deity, is held up to demonstrate the kind of abstract speculation which would completely bewilder 'a country fellow':

> But, set up before him the figure of a fine woman, with a beautiful child in her arms; and tell him that she can procure him every thing he wants;—He knows perfectly what he is about; feels himself animated by the object, and prays to her with all his might. (i. 151)

The manly, educated, and British reader, who will respond to the resonances of 'our poet', will prefer the sublime yet rational representation of the deity. The cruder appeal of feminine beauty to the religious feelings is for the foreigner or

---

[63] *Tour*, i. 148–9. The misquotation is from Pope, 'Epistle to a Lady', line 42, '''Tis to their changes that their charms they owe'.

[64] Baretti, *An Account of the Manners and Customs of Italy* (2 vols, 1768), ii. 91.

[65] *Essay on Man*, I, 269–74; 279–81. Brydone does not make the attribution: clearly, as fellow Britons, we are supposed instantly to recognize the source.

rustic.[66] And the encouragement of such feelings in the interests of social stability is implicitly approved.[67]

Brydone is, then, capable of skilled appropriation of sensibility in order to illustrate a particular point: but the very occasional nature of his sentimental passages testifies to his scepticism. The obligatory nun passage in the *Tour* further demonstrates Brydone's impulse to demystify sentimentalism. Whilst Baretti had reworked the topos in order to emphasize the Roman Catholic virtue of the nun rather than the poignant emotions of the traveller (celebrating the 'converse' of nuns because of their 'innocence and goodness'),[68] Brydone – from the perspective of the British man of sense – deconstructs the elaborate mechanisms whereby the very impotence of the sentimental observer adds to his exquisite enjoyment. Brydone and his party converse through a grate 'for some hours' with some affable nuns, who display a 'soft melancholy in their countenances' but fail to 'acknowledge the unhappiness of their situation'. Their alienation from useful and pleasurable life 'cannot fail to move our pity; "And pity melts the mind to love"' (i. 56–7).[69] There is, moreover, 'another consideration' which increases 'these feelings' (of love, or pity, or both?):

> that is, our total incapacity ever to alter her situation. The pleasure
> of relieving an object in distress, is the only refuge we have against
> the pain which the seeing of that object occasions; but here, that is
> utterly denied us, and we feel with sorrow, that pity is all we can
> bestow.
>   From these, and similar considerations, a man generally finds
> himself in bad spirits after conversing with amiable nuns. (i. 57–8)

The generalized peevishness of this last remark asserts, self-defensively, the man of sense over the man of sensibility.

Brydone's critique of sentimental indulgence finds a parallel in his treatment of the 'paean to liberty' topos. 'Sacred liberty! thy blessings alone are blessings of the soul' he exclaims, formulaically; but then he brings himself up short in his execrations of the Spanish oppressors in Sicily:

---

[66] Jemima Kindersley was similarly to observe in 1777 that the 'glare and shew' of Roman Catholicism, 'which catches the eye, and leads the imagination of the vulgar', was admirably adapted to render African slaves in Brazil 'the most virtuous common people in the world' (*Letters from the Island of Teneriffe, Brazil, the Cape of Good Hope, and the East Indies*, 51), but (unlike Brydone) she thereby provoked an angry theological denunciation in the form of *Letters to Mrs Kindersley*, by the Rev. H. Hodgson, BA (1778). See Chapter 4 below, page 148.

[67] Elsewhere, however, Brydone is the model of 'rational' objectivity, blaming the superstitious excesses of Catholicism for deism among the upper classes, whose 'refined and cultivated understanding' recoils from papal dogma and vulgarity (ii. 133).

[68] Joseph Baretti, *A Journey from London to Genoa* (4 vols, 1770), i. 194.

[69] I have been unable to identify this quotation.

> Now that I am in the humour of it, I could curse them till sun-set, could it be of any service to these poor creatures, but I am afraid I should only put myself in a passion to no end. (ii. 22)

Both these passages invoke an extensive array of shared cultural assumptions, sentimental and patriotic, radical and conservative. At such moments, Brydone skilfully evokes conventional responses in his reader, only to provide a critique of the reaction he envisages, and highlight its self-indulgence. His text brings together with great subtlety the sentimental and the empirical: in dramatizing their interplay, he presents us with the traveller as a product of the conflicting discourses and perceptive frameworks available within the genre. He is, finally, a conservative writer, but his conservatism gains strength and flexibility through acknowledging more radical sympathies.

A passage written from Palermo, describing his nostalgia for British sociability, exhibits Brydone's assured deployment of sympathetic discourse to more insular and patriotic ends (the echoes of Hartley here no doubt owe as much to Brydone's scientific background as to his sentimental interests):

> although the society here is greatly superior to that of Naples, yet,—call it prejudice—or call it what you will, there is a—*je ne sçai quoi*,—a certain confidence in the character, the worth, and friendship of our own people, that I have seldom felt any where on the continent, except in Switzerland.—This sensation, which constitutes the charm of society, and can alone render it supportable for any time, is only inspired by something analogous, and sympathetic, in our feelings and sentiments; like two instruments that are in unison, and vibrate to each other's touch: for society is a concert, and if the instruments are not in tune, there never can be harmony ... where discords predominate, which is often the case betwixt an English and an Italian mind, the musick must be wretched indeed. (ii. 64–5)

We are reminded of what Sterne referred to as 'the *politesse de coeur*' (both writers reach for a French phrase to define this elusive quality); that quality which defines British individuality, British social cohesion, and, finally, British superiority. Even the eccentric Philip Thicknesse refers in his *Useful Hints* (1768) to the '*je ne sçai quoi* about every Englishman abroad', which convinces one of the superiority of English 'honour, honesty, and hospitality' (142).

Brydone (like Smollett) is a Scot, and is therefore especially concerned with the cultural integration of Britain. His text makes explicit the limits and the political resonances of international sympathy. These resonances are suggested but disguised in *A Sentimental Journey*. Brydone can articulate the full implications of sympathy abroad, because sentimental discourse is only ever for him a means to an end – whether that end be the production of a text catering to all tastes, or the construction of a sensible yet solid Britishness; or, indeed, both.

The limits of sympathy

I hope so far in this chapter not only to have given an idea of the range and variety of sentimental travel narratives, but also to have shown how several of the generally denigrated 'imitators' of Sterne display literary sophistication and develop the more adventurous undercurrents of *A Sentimental Journey*, whether from a dissident or a conservative perspective. In terms of sexual politics, sentimental travelogues respond in a variety of ways to the problematic nature of middle-class masculinity in the eighteenth century, which required the simultaneous experience and suppression of desire. Sterne makes playful use of this paradox while Paterson plays down the sexual aspect of sentimental travel. Wraxall, aristocratically, presents himself as rakishly unconstrained by middle-class anxieties concerning desire and responsibility, while Brydone lays bare the class stratifications implicit in contemporary formulations of British masculinity and sexual feeling.

Another significant preoccupation which emerges from these texts is the question of how far abroad sensibility could extend itself. Such questions were under continual discussion in this period, prompted by the realities of war and peace as well as by philosophical articulations in the works of, for example, Hume and Adam Smith. Chris Jones has explored later eighteenth-century debate over the permissible extent of sympathy, and there is no need to duplicate his survey here.[70] The geographical scope of sensibility is, however, of importance to this study. The writings of Hume and Smith – both Scots – have a conservative agenda and form a significant part of the network of discourses involved in fashioning the British nation and national character.

Hume notes in the *Treatise* that habit, proximity, and, above all, ties of blood, neighbourhood, and nationality, make the most powerful claims on our sympathy.[71] Smith also confines the realistic exercise of charity within one's neighbourhood, region, or nation. He does this by positing a separate kind of patriotic attachment, stating that

> the love of our own country seems not to be derived from the love
> of mankind ... We do not love our country merely as a part of the

---

[70] Chris Jones, *Radical Sensibility: Literature and Ideas in the 1790s* (1993).
[71] David Hume, *A Treatise of Human Nature* (1739–40), ed. P. H. Nidditch and L. A. Selby-Bigge (1888; repr. Oxford, 1990), 352.

great society of mankind: we love it for its own sake, and independently of any such consideration.[72]

This does not, apparently, limit our capacity for international sympathy:

Though our effectual good offices can very seldom be extended to any wider society than that of our own country; our good-will is circumscribed by no boundary, but may embrace the immensity of the universe. (235)

Smith then explains that our faith in a 'benevolent and all-wise God' allows us to suffer misfortune with patience, in the knowledge that our partial evil must be contributing to the universal good. Moreover, this same benevolent and all-wise God makes it unnecessary for us to extend our own beneficence beyond realistic bounds, since:

The administration of the great system of the universe, however, the care of the universal happiness of all rational and sensible beings, is the business of God and not of man. To man is allotted a much humbler department, but one much more suitable to the weakness of his powers, and to the narrowness of his comprehension; the care of his own happiness, of that of his family, his friends, his country ... (237)

As if challenging such formulations, Coriat Junior prays that on his travels he will be confronted with 'ACCIDENTAL EVIL', so that he can do 'ACCIDENTAL GOOD', and thus confirm his part in the providential scheme, which otherwise appears to 'our short sight the meer effects of BOUNTEOUS ACCIDENT'.[73] He thus implicitly rejects the limitations which conservative versions of sympathy would impose.

Clearly, one encounters problems once the arena of sympathy is abroad. On one level, the complacent tendencies of sensibility are flattered by the spectacle of French or Italian poverty and misery, since this convinces the traveller of the superiority of the British constitution. But this reassuring equation between bad government and widespread poverty can prove troubling. Yorick, trying to avoid dispensing charity towards the monk at Calais, remarks that 'the unfortunate of our own country, surely, have the first rights; and I have left thousands in distress upon our own shore' (*A Sentimental Journey*, 73). As we have seen, this statement is complicated by Yorick's dubious motivation, but its impact is powerful nevertheless. Just how far superior, then, is the British constitution, or the current British government? Such questions are rarely

---

[72] Adam Smith, *A Theory of Moral Sentiments* (1757), ed. D. D. Raphael and A. L. Macfie (Oxford, 1976), 229.
[73] Paterson, *Another Traveller!*, i. 332.

addressed directly, but the prominence of foreign poverty, and its political implications, prompt observations which disturb the complacency of the Briton abroad. The prevalence of beggars in France reminds Charles Burney of

> our great manufacturing towns, where the heads of houses acquire great fortunes in a short time, and the workmen who are paid 3 or 4 times the wages of a day labourer, are so worthless, that their children have no subsistence but what they acquire by beggary in the streets, or the road.[74]

This observation, significantly, is excised from the published version of Burney's travels, which was calculated to appeal to heads of houses rather than day labourers. In this respect, the humble Cornelius Cayley is more adventurous.

Abroad, one has no immediate political agency. This presents problems for the civic aspect of middle-class masculinity, which measures itself in terms of action and performance. As compensation for political impotence, perhaps, the freedom which travel provides for the exercise of sensibility in foreign countries permits a peculiar intensification of sympathy. Sympathy for the distressed can be indulged without having to interrogate one's own role in the political system which creates social distress. Yet sympathy also fosters understanding. Just as beggars, distressed women, and small injured animals become domestic triggers for sentimental response, nuns, gibbets, and clogs, symbols of Catholic oppression, become convenient foreign stimuli for feelings of pity (where earlier in the century they would have been more likely to provoke disgust). The sentimental fetishization of such objects – such as the snuffbox Yorick receives from the monk, and which he preserves like 'the instrumental parts of my religion, to help my mind on to something better' (101) – is not unlike the function of Catholic idols, relics and rituals, as described by British travellers.

Catholicism is discussed with increasing understanding and tolerance by travellers of a sentimental cast. In a sense, this affective analysis of Catholic ritual defuses its terror: it does not reduce criticism of the way in which religion is used as a tool of absolutism, but it promotes sympathetic understanding rather than contempt for its uneducated devotees, whose feelings, though

---

[74] Percy A. Scholes ed., *Dr Burney's Musical Tours in Europe* (2 vols, 1959), i. 46. Cf. the similar use of this sting-in-the-tail approach by Arthur Young in his 1792 *Travels through France*: 'All the country, girls and women, are without shoes or stockings; and the ploughmen at their work have neither sabots nor feet to their stockings. This is a poverty, that strikes at the root of national prosperity; a large consumption among the poor being of more consequence than among the rich: the wealth of a nation lies in its circulation and consumption; and the case of poor people abstaining from the use of manufactures of leather and wool ought to be considered as an evil of the first magnitude. It reminded me of the misery of Ireland' (18).

misguided, at least evince humanity. Increasingly, the devout peasant is preferred to the cynical saloniste, and the necessity of the comforts provided by the structure of the Catholic church is acknowledged. We have seen this in Brydone; but even a hard-nosed writer like Richard Twiss, more interested in economics than sentiment in his *Travels through Portugal and Spain* (1775), is moved to stress that 'I have not endeavoured to ridicule the persons believing, but the objects of their belief'.[75] Sympathy for the oppressed poor is perhaps a guilty response to the privileged enjoyments of travel, and Charles Burney's response (published, this time) is again suggestive:

> The fine arts are children of affluence and luxury; in despotic governments they render power less unsupportable, and diversion from thought is perhaps as necessary as from action. Whoever therefore seeks music in Germany, should do it at the several courts, not in the free imperial cities, which are generally inhabited by poor industrious people, whose genius is chilled and repressed by penury; who can bestow nothing on vain pomp or luxury; but think themselves happy, in the possession of necessaries. (*Dr Burney's Musical Tours*, ii. 42)

We are reminded of Francis Russell, the 'young English peer' whose aristocratic travelogue is prefaced with a guilty gesture towards charitable tolerance.

The traveller's capacity for sympathy abroad, then, offers a challenge to the local and patriotic constraints which conservative sensibility would impose. The sceptical modification of sentimentalism by writers like Brydone and Wraxall shows how its relationship with domestic issues of class and political affiliation was keenly appreciated. Sentimental travel narrative expands not only the boundaries of international tolerance, but also the arena of British political debate; and the sentimental traveller (or indeed the critic of sentimental travel) crafts a narrative identity appropriate to his particular version of British nationality.

Travels for the heart

1777 saw the publication of a Shandean narrative by 'Courtney Melmoth' (the pseudonym of Samuel Jackson Pratt, a writer notorious for leaping onto the bandwagons of lucrative literary fashions). *Travels for the Heart. Written in France* (2 vols) not only explores the relationship between sentiment and patriotism in a curious way; it also offers a fresh perspective on the role of

---

[75]   Richard Twiss, *Travels through Portugal and Spain, in 1772 and 1773* (1775), ii.

gender in travel and travel writing, at a time when travel narratives by women were just beginning to appear.

Melmoth's narrator is accompanied on his *Travels* by a semi-fictional Amelia, who embodies all that is opposed to 'the impressions of patriotism, and propriety' (i. 186). Her excitement at the prospect of the trip actually impels him to cross the channel, as they pore over a map together:

> When she pointed to the environs of Paris, as if to the text of her voluptuous commentary upon the charms of that city, especially as her wrist was not without a bracelet, and that bracelet not without a flattering figure, by no means in the attitude of refusal, the animal spirits coursed along the veins with such celerity, that I felt them throb at the very ends of my fingers; and, at the conclusion, every thing within me played a tune so brisk and vivacious, that, had every wave been a rock, I do verily think, so wrought upon as I was, I could not have thrown the cold water of refusal, upon the beautiful warm blood which glowed on the face of those animated hopes of the heart. (i. 204–5)

This is not an isolated moment in Melmoth's text, and may owe something to Yorick's encounter with the lady at the door of the *remise*, whose 'silk gloves' are suggestively 'open only at the thumb and two fore-fingers' (90), prompting him to experience a 'pleasurable ductility about her, which spread a calmness over all my spirits—Good God! how a man might lead such a creature as this round the world with him!' (92).

Earlier in *Travels for the Heart*, the sensibility of the female heart is set up in contrast to the 'notions of a London-bred citizen', which are jingoistically xenophobic – 'England, England, Old England for ever!' (i. xxxiv–xl; 63). The female body becomes a map of sensibility which displays the attractions of and the willingness to travel:

> And, herein consists the indiscribeable [*sic*] superiority of the female organization. Every artery about them, is hung more airily; the avenues which nature hath opened to the heart, though perhaps more involved in mazes, are yet so like a wilderness of sweets, that we have many more inducements to clear the way, and examine them: add to all this that certain voluptuous particles swim along the beautiful labyrinths that are formed by the veins, and always fit them for a spirited proposal at a moment's notice. (i. 60–61)

The 'proposal' in this case is a tour to Paris, but the equation of travel with sex is clear (how fortunate that Amelia enjoys the protective guidance of our narrator rather than any less scrupulous adventurer). For all the activity which this female spiritedness suggests, though, it is significant that female sensibility does not initiate: it stimulates and responds, thus overcoming male 'patriotism, and propriety'. The representatives of xenophobia within Melmoth's text are all male, and there is a lengthy account, praised and excerpted in the *Critical Review*, of some debauched Grand Tourists, whose crude Francophobia is rebuked not by the narrator but by Amelia – and by a Franciscan monk (ii. 118).[76] Melmoth's narrator exploits the sentimental and feminized mode of travel writing without compromising or having to redefine his own manly Britishness.

Melmoth uses Amelia as a mouthpiece for sentimental sympathy, and within the text her role is therefore an active and outspoken one. When we examine travel narratives actually written by women, however, a more complicated picture emerges. Diffidence and apology often figure in women travel writers' textual self-representation, not least because the very act of travel disrupted the increasingly domestic and circumscribed realm of acceptable feminine activity. Of course, the question of gender here is complicated by the issue of class: the following chapter will explore the relationship between these determinants, and the way in which they shape the small but increasing number of travel narratives published by women after 1770.

---

[76] See *CR*, 44 (1777), 350–52.

Chapter 4

The rise of the woman travel writer

A woman sees the world, as it were, from a little elevation in her
own garden, where she makes an exact survey of home scenes, but
takes not in that wider range of distant prospects which he who
stands on a loftier eminence commands. (Hannah More, *Strictures
on Female Education*, 1799, ii. 25–6)[1]

If the 1760s and 1770s are notable for the battle lines drawn up between
xenophobic and sentimental travellers, and for the growing complexity of travel
writing's ideological engagements, the years between 1770 and 1800 see the
publication of around twenty travelogues by women, including several voyage
narratives.[2] This chapter will explore the peculiar contexts of this development,
with reference to those travelogues published by women before the French
Revolution in 1789. The final chapter of the book will explore the impact of
events in France on British travel writing (by both men and women): the
Revolution crystallizes many of the preoccupations outlined so far in this study,
but also, as one would expect, forces some of the genre's formal and
ideological premises to breaking point. The role of the present chapter is to
chart some key notions concerning femininity, class, and national identity
which emerged forcefully within travel writing and other cultural forms (in
particular, conduct literature) in the pre-Revolutionary era, and which crucially
informed British responses to developments in France.

Before 1770 only two travel narratives by women were published, Elizabeth
Justice's *A Voyage to Russia* in 1739 and Lady Mary Wortley Montagu's
Embassy Letters, published posthumously in 1763, over forty years after their
initial composition. But in 1777 the *Critical Review* notes, with characteristic

---

[1]   Full title: *Strictures on the Modern System of Female Education. With a View of the
Principles and Conduct Prevalent among Women of Rank and Fortune* (2 vols, 1799).
[2]   Voyage narratives are in general beyond the scope of the present study, but should
here be mentioned. In 1777 Jemima Kindersley published *Letters from the Island of
Teneriffe, Brazil, the Cape of Good Hope, and the East Indies*. Anna Maria
Falconbridge's *Two Voyages to Sierra Leone* (1794) is now available in an annotated
edition, with Mary Ann Parker's *Voyage round the World* (1795), as *Maiden Voyages
and Infant Colonies: Two Women's Travel Narratives of the 1790s*, ed. Deirdre
Coleman (1999). See Mary Louise Pratt, *Imperial Eyes: Travel Writing and
Transculturation* (1992), 102–6 on Falconbridge. Some texts described as 'travel
writing' by later cataloguers have a rather tenuous relationship to the genre, for example
Mary Tonkin's account of trips to France on espionage, *Facts. The Female Spy: or Mrs
Tonkin's Account of her Journey through France, at the Order of Charles James Fox*
(1783); and an intriguing pamphlet entitled *A Letter, addressed to a Female Friend. By
Mrs Sage, the first English Female Aerial Traveller* (1785).

understatement, that the 'Letters of female travellers are now become not unusual productions'.[3] Women, then, were becoming beneficiaries of the enlarging possibilities for travel and tourism described in earlier chapters, and of the changing scope of travel narrative, away from erudite classical traditions in favour of more sociological, affective, and miscellaneous preoccupations. Women travel writers often provide less hostile accounts of Europe (and, indeed, of Wales and Scotland) than some of their male counterparts. A review in the *Analytical Review* of *A Tour to Milford Haven, in the Year 1791*, by 'Mrs Morgan', observes that if the author's observations be read 'without any high expectation of novelty of information, or depth of speculation', they will offer amusement by virtue of 'the general air of chearful good humour, which runs through these letters; particularly with the delight which the writer every where expresses at the natural beauties and wonders of Wales, and the good humoured satisfaction with which she contemplates the manners of it's [*sic*] inhabitants'.[4]

This characteristic disposition to be pleased relates to women travellers' emergence as writers at a time when the sentimental mode has largely displaced the xenophobic: but in fact few women mobilize sensibility to any great degree, doubtless because of its associations (as outlined in the previous chapter) with particular formulations of manliness – including sexual impulses – as well as its tendency towards social critique. Women travel writers during the 1770s seem to mediate between the extremes of spleen and sentiment, asserting a middle ground of reliable, commonsensical British womanhood. They may thereby provide an implicit critique of the aristocratic excesses of the Grand Tour: indeed, not unlike some of their middle-class or professional male counterparts (Smollett, for example), their emphasis on conjugal or family-based travel stands in virtuous opposition to the selfish individualism of the Grand Tourist. Mariana Starke's *Travels in Italy* indicates its middle-class target market, and its implied opposition to noble extravagance, in its sub-title: 'With Instructions for the Use of Invalids and Families, who may not chuse to incur the Expence attendant upon Travelling with a Courier'.[5] Anne Miller visits the famous Grotto del Cane near Naples, where numerous Grand Tourists would keenly witness a dog being lowered into a sea cave in order to be asphyxiated by the interestingly noxious gases: in an uncharacteristic outbreak of charity, Miller requests that the dog *not* be 'put into the grotto for me, as I was not in the least degree curious to see the effect of the experiment'.[6]

[3]   *CR*, 43 (1777), 439.
[4]   *AR*, 21 (1795), 491.
[5]   *Travels in Italy, between the Years 1792 and 1798; containing a View of the Late Revolutions in that Country ... likewise pointing out the Matchless Works of Art* (2 vols, 1800).
[6]   *Letters from Italy, describing the Manners, Customs, Antiquities, Paintings, &c. of that Country, in the Years MDCCLXX and MDCCLXXI, to a Friend residing in France,*

Lady Mary Wortley Montagu penned various private complaints about Grand Tourists, worthy of Smollett in their splenetic tone, describing the breed as 'the worst company in the world' and 'the greatest blockheads in nature, ... their whole business abroad (as far as I can perceive) being to buy new cloaths, in which they shine in some obscure coffee-house, where they are sure of meeting only one another; and after the important conquest of some waiting gentlewoman of an opera Queen ... return to England excellent judges of men and manners'.[7] However, these observations were not published in Montagu's lifetime, and certainly not included in the gracious volumes of the *Embassy Letters* published in 1763. In general, women's travel writings were generally welcomed by the reviewers not for any critical insights they might provide into masculine and aristocratic modes of travel, but rather for the novel perspectives they offered on well-worn itineraries, often by virtue of their perceived interest in topics such as 'manners and customs', and in some cases because of the woman traveller's access to areas of experience (in Montagu's case, the harem) closed to their male counterparts.

Most women's travelogues were favourably reviewed, despite the fact that in 1771 the *Critical Review* had complained that 'So many authors of late years, have published their travels into France and Italy, that works of this kind are come to be regarded as a stale commodity among the booksellers'.[8] In its notice of Anne Miller's *Letters from Italy* in 1776, the *Critical* outlines the qualifications now required to render such an account interesting:

> Justness of remark, and fidelity of detail, are not the only qualifications requisite in those who would convey a representation of foreign countries. They ought also to be endowed with a certain vivacity of disposition, which may derive additional entertainment as well as instruction from the incidents that occur in their journey; though care should be taken that this quality do not deviate into an ostentatious display of frivolous pleasantry or superior acuteness, which never fail to prove uninteresting, and perhaps even disgusting, to the reader.[9]

What is striking here is the way in which the traditional masculine qualities of rationality and accuracy are cautiously complemented by more feminine characteristics: 'a certain vivacity of disposition' is to be welcomed, but kept firmly in check, lest it degenerate either into an excess of female pertness ('an

---

by an English Woman (3 vols, 1776), ii. 337–8. Although published anonymously, the *Letters'* authorship was no secret, and was publicized in the *Monthly Review*'s account of the work (*MR*, 55 [1776], 104).

[7] *The Complete Letters of Lady Mary Wortley Montagu*, ed. Robert Halsband (3 vols, Oxford, 1965–7), iii. 166; ii. 177.

[8] *CR*, 32 (1771), 143.

[9] *CR*, 41 (1776), 355.

ostentatious display of frivolous pleasantry'), or a threatening incursion ('superior acuteness') into male territory.[10] Shrewdly, Miller chooses to distinguish her narrative chiefly by its focus on painting and sculpture, a field of cultural interest originally popularized by Jonathan Richardson Junior and Senior in their *Account of some of the Statues, Bas-reliefs, Drawings and Pictures in Italy* in 1722.[11] Miller brings the appreciation of art within the reach of middle-class and female travellers. She offers a selection of works of art 'that pleased me most', rather than a 'regular catalogue of the pictures and curiosities' (i. 101). The works described at length (rather than merely listed or complained about) are invariably of a morally improving nature, and the 'indecent collection' in the gallery at Turin is carefully eschewed, Miller instead approving the decision of the 'good old king' to have three separate paintings of Venus, all by Guido, 'cut in two, and from the breast downward burnt ... the rest of their persons, we may suppose, were as full of merit as might be expected, being the production of so great a master; but that is left to the imagination' (i. 124).

Naturally, the emergence of women travel writers during the later eighteenth century is also related to a general increase in female literacy, literary activity, and publication within a variety of genres, too well known to require rehearsing here.[12] Although, in these emergent stages of women's literary publication, many women poets and novelists deploy strategies of denial and apology for their decision to publish, there is a peculiar defensiveness in women's travel writing from this period, concerning the acts both of travelling and of publishing. The authorial self-consciousness of most women travel writers reflects pressures generated by the social contexts of the genre, and indeed by the clash between the premises of travel writing and the assumptions concerning women's role and place which most other contemporary cultural forms tended to foster. As if to naturalize the position of woman travel writer,

---

[10] Compare the *Monthly Review*'s cautious praise for Jemima Kindersley's *Letters from the Island of Teneriffe*, in which the absence of 'philosophical penetration' – clearly a masculine characteristic – is compensated for by the feminine virtues of 'ease and simplicity, and ... every mark of fidelity' (*MR*, 57 [1777], 243).

[11] Bruce Redford highlights the way in which the Richardsons' *Account* taught an 'elementary vocabulary of analysis' and cultivated an 'awareness of genre, period, and school' (*Venice and the Grand Tour* [1996], 37). It was an influential text in creating a taste for connoisseurship beyond the realm of the antique.

[12] See Margaret Ezell, *Writing Women's Literary History* (1993); Janet Todd, *The Sign of Angellica: Women, Writing and Fiction, 1660–1800* (1989), and Todd ed., *A Dictionary of British and American Women Writers 1660–1800* (1987); Jane Spencer, *The Rise of the Woman Novelist: from Aphra Behn to Jane Austen* (Oxford, 1986); Cheryl Turner, *Living by the Pen: Women Writers in the Eighteenth Century* (1992); Roger Lonsdale ed., *Eighteenth-Century Women Poets: an Oxford Anthology* (Oxford, 1989); J. R. de J. Jackson, *Romantic Poetry by Women: a Bibliography, 1770–1835* (Oxford, 1993); Isobel Armstrong and Virginia Blain eds, *Women's Poetry in the Enlightenment: the Making of a Canon, 1730–1820* (1999).

female participants in the genre generally eschew the stylistic oddity and political frankness which was beginning to constitute male travel writers' main claims to novelty. Perhaps for this reason, such works have been neglected by modern literary scholars, with the exception of the handful of women who travelled to distant lands and whose writings have received some attention from a post-colonial perspective, and of Lady Mary Wortley Montagu, whose celebrated *Embassy Letters* (published posthumously in 1763) are, not surprisingly, profoundly uncharacteristic of most women's travel writing from the later half of the century.[13]

Although – as we have seen – European travel writing as a genre enabled the articulation (covert or otherwise) of dissident or controversial opinion, it was able to do this precisely because its empirical basis and acclaimed instructive capacity gave it a privileged position within the literary hierarchy. As the travel writer and clergyman John Owen put it in 1796, 'No taste is more prevailing than that for books of travels; none, perhaps, not professedly moral is less productive of mischief'.[14] This may, paradoxically, be another reason for its comparative neglect within the recent feminist revision of the eighteenth-century canon, which has perhaps been more interested in more contentious genres, like fiction, or more private (and therefore, this argument, runs, more subversive) ones, like autobiography. Felicity Nussbaum, for example, has celebrated those texts (largely diaries) in which eighteenth-century women 'construct a private space that questions the gendered positions available for women (and men) and as a place to contest the closure of "self" and text'.[15] The assumption here seems to be that we can learn nothing about such issues from more 'public' genres, such as travel writing. But, on the contrary, travel writing's position at the heart of the respectable canon makes women's engagement with its assumptions and conventions of particular interest, not least because of the fault lines between the ideological foundations of travel and national identity on the one hand, and of women's function and significance on the other.

Intriguingly, the emergence of women's travel writing during the eighteenth century coincides with a veritable torrent of literature, in the form of sermons, tracts, conduct books, and didactic novels, which locate the source of moral and national virtue in the domestic sphere, and appoint as its guardian the wife and mother. This body of writing is largely addressed to the increasingly self-

---

[13] See Pratt, *Imperial Eyes*, 102–6, and Coleman ed., *Maiden Voyages and Infant Colonies*. Recent bibliography on Montagu is extensive. See note 63 below.

[14] John Owen, *Travels into Different Parts of Europe, in the Years 1791 and 1792* (2 vols, 1796), i. vi.

[15] Felicity Nussbaum, 'Eighteenth-Century Women's Autobiographical Common-places', in Shari Benstock ed., *The Private Self: Theory and Practice of Women's Auto-biographical Writings* (1988), 147–71; 156. See also Nussbaum, *The Autobiographical Subject: Gender and Identity in Eighteenth-Century England* (Baltimore, 1989).

conscious middle classes, and it is travel writing by middle-class women writers, rather than aristocrats, which most assiduously seeks to assimilate itself to the morality of the domestic sphere. The first main section of this chapter will examine the problematic relationship between women's travel writing and these more proscriptive genres, to show both the pressures and the freedoms which travel writing could provide to women seeking a published voice. The central section of the chapter will then look at Mary Wortley Montagu's account of Europe and Turkey in the light of a later, critical response to the *Embassy Letters* published by the redoubtable yet scandalous Lady Craven in 1789. This comparison illuminates not only the increasingly imperial sensibility of later decades of the century, but also their trend – even in upper-class contexts – towards that distinctive propriety (notably absent from Montagu's consciously 'Enlightened' account) whose emphasis on traditionally gendered virtue was to underpin British opposition to the French Revolution, as well as the moral project of colonialism. Finally, we will turn to several accomplished middle-class women travel writers, including Hester Piozzi in 1789, whose works reveal (in Piozzi's case, through concealment and parody) the extent to which the status and capabilities of women are becoming central planks in British national identity during the 1770s and 1780s. Paradoxically, in drawing attention to their eschewal of political controversy, these women travel writers powerfully endorse the increasingly potent and gendered myth of Britain's superior moral virtue, thereby performing an important political function.

'So inspiring a theme': the place of British women

In comparison with the number of published travel accounts by men, the proportion of publications to journeys undertaken by women during the eighteenth century is tiny. We know that countless women did actually travel abroad: eloping with lovers, pursuing a healthy climate, seeking a new home and employment, exploiting the much lower cost of living abroad, or simply accompanying their travelling husbands (Mrs Smollett and Mrs Thicknesse – neither of whose journeys can have been easy – spring to mind).[16] Few of them, however, made literary capital out of their experiences, though many of them must have kept journals and written letters home (Lady Phillipina Knight notes in a letter from Paris in 1776 that she and her daughter 'each journalise in a

---

[16]   A handful of women travelled through Britain and American spreading opposition to slavery from the 1750s onward. See Clare Midgley, *Women Against Slavery: the British Campaigns, 1780–1870* (1992), 14–15.

little book').[17] Several travel journals and letters written by eighteenth-century women were subsequently published in the nineteenth and early twentieth centuries, often by interested descendants, and such works display varying degrees of literary self-consciousness.[18] *The Household Book of Lady Grisell Baillie* includes an account of a Continental tour in 1731–2; *The Memoirs of Ann, Lady Fanshawe* describes Portugal and Spain, where Lady Ann's husband was Charles II's ambassador until his sudden death in Spain in 1666; Lady Henrietta Pomfret's correspondence describes her travels and residence in France and Italy (where she entertains Lady Mary Wortley Montagu) between 1738 and 1741; *A Series of Letters between Mrs Elizabeth Carter and Miss Catherine Talbot* includes an account of Elizabeth Carter's travels in France, the Low Countries and the Rhineland in 1763 and 1782; while *Lady Knight's Letters from France and Italy* describes the travels and residence abroad of Lady Phillipina Knight and her daughter, Ellis Cornelia, who later wrote serious historical and topographical accounts of Rome, France, and Spain.[19] The Knights, like the Countess of Pomfret, lived abroad partly for financial reasons; it was far cheaper for distressed gentlefolk to maintain a suitable standard of living in, say, Rome, than in London. Lady Knight finds an apartment in Rome for thirty-six pounds a year, and servants are correspondingly cheap (*Lady Knight's Letters*, 53). She declares that 'Rome is certainly the best place in the world for the widow's cruse of oil to hold out', and points out that if they had remained in England, 'my dear girl and I must there be shut up in absolute retirement with a single woman servant, or board in some uncomfortable manner' (102; 105). Genoa is cheaper still, their 'habitation there costing eleven pounds a year (137). Two Scottish women wrote notable manuscript accounts of their travels which have subsequently been published: Margaret Calderwood, 'a well-born Scots lady', wrote up her journals of a trip to Holland and the Low Countries in 1756 into four volumes of narrative, which she sent home at intervals from Brussels; and Janet Schaw produced a polished manuscript record of a voyage from Scotland to the West Indies and America in the mid 1770s.[20]

---

[17] *Lady Knight's Letters from France and Italy, 1776–1795*, ed. Lady Eliott-Drake (1905), 7.

[18] For a full listing, see Jane Robinson, *Wayward Women: a Guide to Women Travellers* (Oxford, 1990).

[19] *The Household Book of Lady Grisell Baillie, 1692–1733*, ed. Robert Scott Moncrieff (Edinburgh, 1911); *The Memoirs of Ann, Lady Fanshawe, 1600–72*, ed. H.C. Fanshawe (1907); *Correspondence between Frances, Countess of Hartford (afterwards Duchess of Somerset) and Henrietta Louisa, Countess of Pomfret, between the years 1738 and 1741* (3 vols, 1805); *A Series of Letters between Mrs Elizabeth Carter and Miss Catherine Talbot, from the Year 1741 to 1770* (4 vols, 1809).

[20] *Letters and Journals of Mrs Calderwood of Polton from England Holland and the Low Countries in 1756*, ed. Alexander Fergusson (Edinburgh, 1884); Janet Schaw, *Journal of a Lady of Quality; being the Narrative of a Journey from Scotland to the*

Although such texts are peripheral to this study, they do illuminate the circumstances within which women travelled, wrote of their journeys, and decided whether or not to publish. Lady Knight writes from Toulouse in December 1776 that:

> It's no small entertainment to Cornelia and me to write a journal, which we are doing after the manner of the Bath Guide; we have got very forward in it and have the vanity to think you and Captain Drake would have great diversion from it, but it would not answer to send it to you by bits. (25)

This 'journal' is distinct from the letters to Mrs Drake published as the edition of *Lady Knight's Letters* in the early twentieth century, and seems not to have survived; it may not, in any case, have been a long-lived project. Nevertheless, the reference to a 'journal' suggests that these women were engaging in a consciously literary activity and modelling their work on a published text, but with an audience of two persons in mind. There is no way of knowing how common this practice was. Similarly, Margaret Calderwood occupied herself during the winter of 1756 at Brussels in revising her letters into continuous volumes for the entertainment of friends at home. Calderwood is briskly self-conscious about the processes of literary composition, and the following reflections on the subject are revealing:

> All my volumes end abruptly, and so must this, as Lady Nelly goes to-morrow, and is to carry it ... I have not time to look over nor correct the last pages, which you will do before anybody else see [them]. I have only one thing in my works which any great author has had before me, that, like Shakspear, I write without a blot, that is, without correction or second thought ... (270)

This is an extraordinary passage, disparaging its own feminine garrulity and yet (albeit ironically) asserting considerable literary status. Calderwood's text is a polished one, more sophisticated than many published eighteenth-century travel writings in its fluent interleaving of descriptive minuteness, social anecdote, and cultural analysis. Similarly, Janet Schaw's *Journal of a Lady of Quality* was obviously intended for a significant manuscript readership. There are three extant manuscript copies of her text, clear evidence that substantial private circulation was envisaged.[21] The manuscripts employ blanks for the names of

---

West Indies, North Carolina, and Portugal, in the years 1774 to 1776, ed. Evangeline Walker Andrews and Charles McLean Andrews (1921; enlarged edn New Haven 1939), from British Museum MS Egerton 2423. See Elizabeth Bohls, 'The Aesthetics of Colonialism: Janet Schaw in the West Indies, 1774–1775', *Eighteenth Century Studies*, 27 (1994), 363–90.

[21] See *Journal of a Lady of Quality*, 1–3; 18–19.

almost every person mentioned within the text, including Schaw herself. This suggests that she envisaged a readership far beyond the circle of her family, and may even have been considering publication. Her twentieth-century editors claim that she was 'blessedly unaware, as she jotted down her opinions and descriptions ... that she was writing for posterity a document of rare interest and importance' (6), but this innocence seems highly unlikely.

Whatever her putative readership, Schaw consciously writes within a tradition of travel literature. She informs her reader that 'I think I have read all the descriptions that have been published of America, yet meet every moment with something I never read or heard of' (151); and in Portugal she positions herself within the world of published travel narratives:

> I do not recollect ever to have read a description of ... Lisbon by any hand, who has done it justice. Mr Twiss says a great deal, but his travels seem only a journal of his own bad humours, prejudices and mistakes, for I believe he would not willingly tell a falsehood, but I am at a loss to think where he found the dirty scenes he describes. I have been at no pains to avoid them, yet have met with no such thing. (250)

Although Schaw here shows herself fully at ease within the discourse of travel writing, deploying the terms ('falsehood', 'prejudice', 'humour') central to topical debates during the 1760s and 1770s, she elected not to publish. It is impossible to know how many other women were likewise invisibly engaged in travel writing. Their diffidence of publication was doubtless related to the residually masculine associations of the genre, in contrast to the (albeit slightly patronizing) acceptance of women writers within the more 'feminine' genres of poetry and fiction. Beyond the sphere of *belles lettres*, however, lurked a whole body of thought and writing which was establishing with increasing fervour that the proper position of women (and British women in particular) was at home. Of course, theory is not always matched by practice, and in this area in particular one should be cautious of assuming that proscription and prescription were always carried through into life. Conversely, one should be wary of suggesting that the eighteenth century was qualitatively different from other eras in its insistence on women's domestic location. Karen Lawrence has claimed transhistorically that 'the plot of the male journey depends on keeping woman in her place. Not only is her place at home, but she is effect is home itself, for the female body is traditionally associated with earth, shelter, enclosure'.[22] Nevertheless, as a discursive framework with a specific ideological freight, within which women writers of the eighteenth century had

---

[22] Karen R. Lawrence, *Penelope Voyages: Women and Travel in the British Literary Tradition* (1994), 1.

to operate, this network of ideas became particularly insistent, and warrants closer scrutiny.

The stress on the family as the fundamental unit of civic life (at least as old as Aristotle) was given a new lease of life in the early eighteenth century by the ideological separation within middle-class morality of male and female spheres of action, this separation being powerfully inscribed in the periodical and conduct literature which shaped the middle classes' emerging self-consciousness.[23] As recent studies of periodical literature and its extensive influence throughout the eighteenth century has shown, the civic virtues of private, familial, middle-class existence presented a powerful rebuke to the public vices of the aristocracy, whose luxurious decadence was increasingly figured as unpatriotic and frivolously Francophile.[24] It is ironic, then, that a powerful new formulation of women's circumscribed arena of activity came not from within the British Isles, but from France. The influence of Rousseau on the ideological confinement of women was considerable: the force of Wollstonecraft's diatribes against Rousseau's prescriptions for women's education as late as 1792 (in the *Vindication of the Rights of Woman*) indicates how widespread and sustained this influence was.[25] *La Nouvelle Héloïse* was rhapsodically received in England in 1760–1 (Edward Duffy finds thirty-three review accounts of the novel); and the literary establishment was thus predisposed to enthuse over *Emile* on its English publication in 1762–3.[26] Although the philosophical and political tenets advanced in *Emile* provoked

---

[23]   Davidoff and Hall's influential argument for the emergence of separate spheres after 1780 has been as influentially contested by Amanda Vickery, who argues that 'separate spheres' existed at least 100 years earlier. See Leonore Davidoff and Catherine Hall, *Family Fortunes: Men and Women of the English Middle Class, 1780–1850* (Chicago, 1987); Amanda Vickery, 'Golden Age to Separate Spheres? A Review of the Categories and Chronology of English Women's History', *Historical Journal*, 36 (1993), 383–414.

[24]   See Kathryn Shevelow, *Women and Print Culture: the Construction of Femininity in the Early Periodical* (1989) and Shawn Lisa Maurer, *Proposing Men: Dialectics of Gender and Class in the Eighteenth-Century English Periodical* (Stanford, 1998). Maurer argues that the so-called 'separation of spheres' was deceptive and ultimately sinister, since middle-class masculinity increasingly incorporated those sentimental nurturing qualities formerly attributed to women: men thus extended their moral domination within the private sphere, whilst simultaneously consolidating their sole right to a public existence.

[25]   See Joan B. Landes, *Women and the Public Sphere in the Age of the French Revolution* (Ithaca, 1988). Linda Colley refers to Rousseau's 'immensely influential' sexual politics in eighteenth-century Britain (*Britons: Forging the Nation, 1707–1837* [1992], 239–41). On the French intellectual background to Rousseau's theories on female education, see Jean H. Bloch, 'Women and the Reform of the Nation', in *Woman and Society in Eighteenth-Century France*, ed. Eva Jacobs et al. (1979), 3–18.

[26]   See Edward Duffy, *Rousseau in England: the Context for Shelley's Critique of the Enlightenment* (Berkeley, 1979), 1–53. The following discussion is indebted to Duffy's study. Ralph Griffiths was the first London bookseller to stock and advertize *La Nouvelle Héloïse*.

hostile criticism (Edmund Burke in the *Annual Register* branded the work 'impracticable and chimerical' and positively 'dangerous'), Rousseau's views on nursing and education, and in particular on marriage and on female education, were reviewed with enthusiasm.[27] Book V of *Emile* was widely acclaimed, as Duffy explains:

> This, the final book of *Emile*, is now generally regarded as a reactionary and antifeminist fantasy that is anything but essential to the program for mankind outlined by *Emile*. The eighteenth-century English, however, thought so highly of the fifth book that they gave its heroine a place in the title of the English translation. To the English reading public, Rousseau's book was not *Emile* but *Emilius and Sophia*. (17)

The *Critical Review* waxes lyrical about the marital union of Emilius and Sophia and, more seriously, recommends the text to be 'read by every lover, husband, and parent. Indeed we should prefer this to all the preceding volumes, for practical purposes, and those who read with a view rather of increasing their happiness than improving their intellects'.[28]

The construction of ideal womanhood in Book V of *Emilius and Sophia* remained central to English concepts of female education and virtue throughout the century. Female virtue becomes synonymous with domesticity and stasis, and vital to the cultivation of public (masculine) virtue and patriotism, 'as if it were not the lesser country, or, in other terms, our family, that formed the attachment between us and the larger country, or the government we live under; as if it were not the good son, the good father, the good husband, that constituted the good citizen'.[29] In Book V, Emilius is cast as the roving Telemachus, while Sophia, implicitly modelled on Eucharis, waits patiently at home. Moreover, the second half of Book V complements the treatise on women's education laid out in the first half with a highly conventional account of travel and its importance in a young man's education. Whereas for men, travel takes on a grand philosophical and character-building importance, we are urged that 'a prudent mother of a family, instead of being a woman of the

---

[27] Burke's remarks were published in *Annual Register*, 5 (1762), 225; cited by Duffy, 20. For positive response with lengthy excerpts from *Emile*, see especially *CR*, 14 (1762), 250–70; 336–46; 426–40, and *CR*, 15 (1763), 21–34.

[28] *CR*, 15 (1763), 30.

[29] *Emilius and Sophia: or, An Essay on Education*, trans. Thomas Nugent (2 vols, 1763), ii. 186. The modern Everyman edition puts it rather more succinctly: 'Can patriotism thrive except in the soil of that miniature fatherland, the home?' (1911; repr. 1989), 326. Thomas Nugent also wrote the extremely influential guidebook, *The Grand Tour* (4 vols, 1749).

world, lives as recluse a life as a nun'.[30] In *La Nouvelle Héloïse*, written
fractionally earlier than *Emile*, early sections of radical sexual emotion
modulate into a model of domestic bliss similar to that outlined in *Emile*; Julie
waits at home for St Preux to return from his travels.

In numerous conduct books for women from the late 1760s onwards, the
domestic circle is inevitably presented as woman's natural environment.[31] This
spatial location is paralleled in definitions of suitable areas of knowledge and
education for women. William Kenrick's anonymous *The Whole Duty of
Woman* (published in 1753 and many times reprinted) intones with pseudo-
Scriptural authority that

> Thy kingdom is thine own house, and thy government the care
> of thy family.
> Let the laws of thy condition be thy study, and learn only to
> govern thy self and thy dependants.[32]

James Fordyce is characteristic in inveighing against 'Learned Ladies' and
enjoining 'the plain duties and humble virtues of life', and this polarization of
learning and domestic duty is reiterated by countless writers in the ensuing
decades.[33] Thomas Gisborne's hugely popular *Enquiry into the Duties of the
Female Sex* reiterates in 1791 women's crucial role in the 'sphere of domestic
life' (2) and pronounces law, politics, learning, navigation, trade, and warfare

---

[30] *Emilius*, ii. 230. On the 'cautious conservatism of Rousseau's views on feminine
education', see P.D. Jimack, 'The Paradox of Sophie and Julie: Contemporary Response
to Rousseau's Ideal Wife and Ideal Mother', in Jacobs et al. eds., *Woman and Society in
Eighteenth-Century France*, 152–65.
[31] Among the most important of these are: James Fordyce, *Sermons to Young Women*
(2 vols, 1766), which saw six editions within a year; James Fordyce, *The Character and
Conduct of the Female Sex, and the Advantages to be derived by Young Men from the
Society of Virtuous Women* (1776); Hannah More, *Essays on Various Subjects,
Principally designed for Young Ladies* (1777); John Moir, *Female Tuition: or an
Address to Mothers, on the Education of Daughters* (1784; repr. 1786); John Bennett,
Strictures on Female Education; chiefly as it relates to the Culture of the Heart (1787);
anon., *Instructions for the Conduct of Females, from Infancy to old Age* (1789); anon.,
*Woman. Sketches of the History, Genius, Disposition, Accomplishments, Employments,
Customs, and Importance of the Fair Sex, in all Parts of the World* (1790); John Burton,
Lectures on Female Education and Manners (2 vols, 1793); Thomas Gisborne, *An
Enquiry into the Duties of the Female Sex* (1797; five editions by 1801); Hannah More,
*Strictures on the Modern System of Female Education. With a View of the Principles
and Conduct Prevalent among Women of Rank and Fortune* (2 vols, 1799).
[32] William Kenrick, *The Whole Duty of Woman*, 18. Kenrick – a frequent reviewer for
the *Monthly* – later translated *La Nouvelle Héloïse*.
[33] Fordyce, *Sermons to Young Women*, i. 202. See Evelyn Gordon Bodek, 'Salonières
and Bluestockings: Educated Obsolescence and Germinating Feminism', *Feminist
Studies*, 3 (1976), 185–99 and Sylvia Harcstark Myers, *The Bluestocking Circle:
Women, Friendship, and the Life of the Mind in Eighteenth-Century England* (Oxford,
1990).

all beyond the scope not only of women's experience but also of their intelligence (21). In *An Essay on the Character, the Manners, and the Understanding of Women, in Different Ages* translated from the French in 1781 by Jemima Kindersley (herself a female voyager of no small adventurousness who accompanied her husband on a voyage to India via South Africa), we are informed that 'if patriotism is little made for women, the general love of humankind, which extends itself over all nations and all ages, and which is a sort of abstract sentiment, seems still less to coincide with their nature'; and the limits of female feeling and intellect are brought together in the assertion that 'The minds of women do not take in so extensive a field ... extensive ideas appear to them out of nature. One man is more to them than a nation.'[34] During the 1780s in particular, the domestic location of female virtue becomes especially associated with British social stability, in contrast to the perceived subversion of gender roles in ancien régime France, where – as James Fordyce claimed in 1776 – 'the women are supreme: they govern all from the court down to the cottage' (*Character and Conduct of the Female Sex*, 27).

At the very end of the century, Hannah More provides an account of women's abilities which summarizes many preceding formulations:

> Both in composition and action [women] excel in details; but they do not so much generalize their ideas as men, nor do their minds seize a great subject with so large a grasp. They are acute observers, and accurate judges of life and manners, as far as their own sphere of observation extends; but they describe a smaller circle. A woman sees the world, as it were, from a little elevation in her own garden, whence she makes an exact survey of home scenes, but takes not in that wider range of distant prospects, which he who stands on a loftier eminence commands.[35]

From this remark, and from the conduct literature (and its reviews, which further extended its influence) of which it is so representative, a female ideal emerges to which the woman traveller and travel writer is antithetical. There is, in fact, almost no direct discussion of women as travel writers. This is no doubt because, as we have seen, the numbers of women travel writers were very small: they were not seen as either a body of like-minded individuals, or as any kind of coherent threat to domestic ideals. If there is no systematic critical thought on women *travel writers* at this time, there is, however, a great deal of controversy surrounding the developing vogue for travel, within Britain and

---

[34] *An Essay on the Character, the Manners, and the Understanding of Women, in Different Ages* (1781), from the French of Antoine Léonard Thomas (Paris, 1772). Kindersley had in 1777 published *Letters from the Island of Teneriffe, Brazil, the Cape of Good Hope, and the East Indies*.

[35] More, *Strictures on Female Education*, ii. 25–6.

abroad, by women (generally the well-heeled variety). Such 'travel' may be grouped into two categories: the practice of 'visiting', as described and lambasted by conduct books; and the increasingly fashionable activity of Continental tourism, sometimes on the pretext of travelling for one's health. This is a preoccupation not just of conduct literature, but also of magazines, newspapers and novels. Satirical attacks on the practice are similar (in method and ideological stance, though not in frequency) to the ongoing ridicule of the Grand Tour in the eighteenth century.

Various conduct books inveigh against women's passion for 'visiting', which is presented as a serious threat to domestic stability. John Moir advizes mothers that 'You can never make [daughters] good house-wives without attaching them early to the house';[36] and Thomas Gisborne's *Enquiry* contains a lengthy diatribe on the evils of women's absences from home – on local social visits and on longer journeys to London and abroad – and envisages national calamity:

> the numerous and protracted excursions from the family mansion,
> which fashion, the desire of displaying wealth, and the restlessness
> of a vacant mind, excite at present, are productive of consequences
> very unfavourable to individuals and to the public. (288)

These include the 'interruption of domestic habits and occupations' and 'the acquisition of an unsettled, a tatling, and a meddling spirit' (289). Most serious of all, however, is the threatened dissolution of all ties of local and domestic responsibility, as the absent woman abandons 'the place where she will possess peculiar means of doing good among the humbler classes of society' (290). Keeping women in their place is clearly related to keeping the humbler classes in theirs. Gisborne's ideological agenda is perhaps more extreme than that of earlier conduct literature, and no doubt reflects anti-Revolutionary paranoia. Hannah More's *Strictures* (1799) are similarly impelled by anti-Jacobin zeal. She attacks the general 'dissipation' of modern 'fashionable life' evident at assemblies and watering places: 'This inability of staying at home, as it is one of the most infallible, so it is one of the most dangerous symptoms of the reigning mania' (ii. 142). One wonders what Hannah More would have made of one of the oddest female voyagers of the later eighteenth century, Mrs Sage, 'the first English Female Aerial Traveller', who went up in a balloon with George Biggin Esq. (with whom she shares a bottle of cherry brandy *and* one of 'Florence wine'), relishes 'floating in the boundless regions of the air', and experiences 'a most pure and perfect tranquillity of soul, during the whole time we had withdrawn ourselves from every earthly connection, where not a noise

---

[36]   Moir, *Female Tuition*, 41.

was heard to break in upon our peace'.[37] Press reports of her agitation and fainting at the moment of ascent are hotly denied – 'I never in my life was more mistress of my reason than at this moment' (13) – and the balloon finally comes to rest in a field near Harrow, whence they are rescued by the boys and headmaster, with many 'acclamations of applause' (30) from these youthful embodiments of British tradition and propriety.

Despite their specific relevance to the 1790s, the vehement anti-travel arguments of writers like Gisborne and More also belong to the anti-luxury discourse which was firmly in place by the mid-eighteenth century. We have seen how the luxury question intersected with the discourse of travel in the debate over the values and demerits of expensive foreign travel for young Englishmen. From quite early in the eighteenth century, the question of women, travel and luxury begins to surface in such discussions. Initially, the emphasis is very much on women of quality, and their pernicious fondness for French fashions and moral levity, whether or not they actually travel to France. Fordyce, in *Sermons* (1766), warns against these corrupting passions, which are distracting his 'fair countrywomen' from their roles as wives and mothers, and thus eroding their love for their 'native country' (i. 38–9). In Smollett's *Humphry Clinker* (1771), we encounter the cautionary tale of Mrs Baynard, whose enormous appetite for luxury items forced her husband to 'carry her abroad to France or Italy, where he might gratify her vanity for half the expence it cost him in England'.[38] Unfortunately, Mr Baynard's strategy backfires horribly, as his wife's extravagance is fuelled to ruinous heights by their travels. Curiously, the fashionable vices she acquires in France are not so much those of female vanity and excess, but rather those pastimes (architectural improvement and landscaping) more usually associated with men. This underlines her monstrous wilfulness – and, perhaps, the very unnaturalness of travel for women:

> It now appeared, that her travels had produced no effect upon her, but that of making her more expensive and fantastic than ever:— She affected to lead the fashion, not only in point of female dress, but on every article of taste and connoisseurship. She made a drawing of the new façade to the house in the country; she pulled up the trees, and pulled down the walls of the garden, so as to let in the easterly wind, which Mr Baynard's ancestors had been at great pains to exclude. (292)

---

[37] *A Letter, addressed to a Female Friend. By Mrs Sage, the first English Female Aerial Traveller* (1785), 14; 16.
[38] Tobias Smollett, *The Expedition of Humphry Clinker* (1771), ed. Lewis M. Knapp (Oxford, 1966), 289.

If Smollett's sketch of this unnatural female seems far-fetched, it is instructive to turn to Elizabeth Percy (Duchess of Northumberland)'s anonymously published *Short Tour* (1775), which describes her trip around the Low Countries with breathtaking self-obsession. The Duchess 'was once reprimanded by the Queen for travelling with a greater retinue than the Queen herself'.[39] Her (mercifully short) book is essentially a name-dropping catalogue of social engagements at various Courts, with descriptions of towns and landscapes kept brief and dismissive: Cologne is 'a dirty, stinking city' (7). The following is a typical entry:

> Tuesday, April the 23d. I bought two charming ivories; sent to the Elector a couple of cucumbers which Price had brought from England. Dined at Court, twenty seven people at table. ... Went after and played at Berlan with the Elector, &c. as usual. (15)

Her other main focus is her gout, the agony of which is repeatedly stressed, and the details minutely described. At one point we are informed that 'the ancle was thirteen inches and a half, the instep eleven inches, and at the root of the toes it was ten inches and a half' (35–6); at another, of how she procures a new pair of crutches, 'with which I was so much charmed, and used so often, that I brought on a fresh fit of pain into my left foot' (34). Occasionally, the Duchess's twin obsessions gratifyingly coalesce, as in the following entry:

> Wednesday, May the 8th. Had the gout violently all night; was not able to rise till noon; continued in pain all day. The Princess of Orange sent, and the Prince of Weilbourg came in person to enquire after me. (32)

Happily, her enjoyment of socializing and of gambling increasingly prevail over her ailments, as she explains how

> I made a shift, by the help of my two sticks, to hobble from the coach, out of which the footman lifted me, to the Berlan, where I played (though in great pain all the time) with the Princess of Hesse Philipstahl, Sir Joseph Yorke, Colonel Saumaise, and Madame de Bretslaar, and won seventeen pence. (69)

And although she strains the nerves of her feet 'most cruelly' by walking over cobbles to buy Renaissance Old Masters in Antwerp, the pictures get bought. The *Short Tour* was ignored by the Reviews, who doubtless felt disinclined to offer it any further publicity. Lady Percy is the embodiment of the conduct books' greatest fears for the consequences of female travel.

---

[39] Todd, *Dictionary of British and American Women Writers*, 234.

Such fears are enumerated in John Andrews' *Remarks on the French and English Ladies* (1782), which devotes several anxious pages to the recent explosion of women travellers in France. Not only do the French fashions breed luxurious emulation (a point made also by the author of *Strictures on Female Education* in 1788), and thus exacerbate the immorality of travelling expensively in a 'rival nation'; but the 'frequent tours to France, of late years become so frequent' are far more dangerous now that women are 'of the party', since 'their superior [English] beauty renders them objects of almost idolatry among the French: every snare is laid to decoy them, that ingenuity, prompted by passion, can suggest' (260–63). These anxieties verge on paranoia, but the moral dubiety they cast over women travellers is not surprising in an age whose imaginative literature represented travel as the preserve of the rakish and picaresque hero, and something which women only undertook out of compulsion (as in the Gothic novel), or out of rather suspect motives, like the adventuresses of Daniel Defoe and Delarivière Manley, or the picaresque heroine of *The Entertaining Travels and Adventures of Mademoiselle de Richelieu ... Who made the Tour of Europe dressed in Men's Cloaths, attended by her Maid Lucy as her Valet de Chambre.*[40] That this moral dubiety reflected or extended into real life is suggested by Margaret Calderwood's complaint in Brussels in 1756 that

> All the British in this town (that is, the women) are mostly what I call adventuresses. There is a Mrs. Child, a divorced wife, married to one Child a man of fortune in England. ... There is a Mrs. Pope whose husband is an officer at Gibraltar, and she in the mean time travelled for her amusement, and has found a gallant here, one Sir Lambert Blackwell, a man of fortune, who, as his family is increased, is furnishing a large house; then Miss Townsend, who run away with an officer who has a wife, was here for some time, but is now, I beleive [*sic*], living at Antwerp.
>
> I have no great ambition to be acquainted with Madam Beaton's princes, nor with my own countryfolks; the first I cannot speak to; the last I will not speak to.[41]

The predominantly upper-class focus of these attacks on wayward women is significant, given that at this time it was very much the middle-class domestic sphere which was becoming the locus of national virtue, providing a bulwark against the twin evils of upper-class luxury and lower-class degradation.[42] In

---

[40] Generally attributed to Henry Erskine: its claim to be a translation from the French is false (3 vols, 1740). Cf. also the sprightly and dubious adventures of *The Female Soldier; or, the Surprising Life and Adventures of Hannah Snell* (1750).

[41] *Letters and Journals of Mrs Calderwood*, 288–9.

[42] See Kate Ferguson Ellis, *The Contested Castle: Gothic Novels and the Subversion of Domestic Ideology* (Chicago, IL, 1989), 10–11.

general, in the women's travel writing of this period, apology and anxiety concerning travel and publication is projected far more by writers who can be termed middle-class. Aristocratic women travelled with greater *sang-froid*, and while they might, like Lady Mary Wortley Montagu, see *publishing* as somehow vulgar, they would certainly make no apologies for their travelling activities.

The moral dubiety imputed to women travellers by conduct literature and its infiltration into other forms (including fiction) discernibly inform the women's travel texts of the period. It provides a framework within which women writers fashion an apologetic, not merely for publishing, but for the act of travelling itself. Mary Ann Hanway, who only travelled as far as the Western Islands of Scotland, paraphrases Goldsmith's *The Traveller* as she reflects that however far we travel, 'the mind still remains untravelled, and clings fondly to that dear, and domestic circle whom we have left over our own fire-sides'.[43] As she travels, therefore, she resolves to 'make my journey in some measure compensate the fatigue of undertaking it', and her letters home are the result, by means of which she can 'accommodate my friends with information' (vii): her text thus apologizes for and justifies travel by stressing the domestic preoccupation, if not practical location, of female virtue. Other women stress that their journeys were undertaken with their husbands, and therefore represent an extension of domestic obedience. Jane Vigor, Anne Miller and Ann Radcliffe all adopt this position, a poignant variation upon which is wrought by Mary Ann Parker, whose *Voyage round the World* (1795), undertaken with her sea-captain husband, was overshadowed by his sudden death at sea: her account is therefore credited to him but 'Performed and Written by his Widow, for the Advantage of a Numerous Family'. By contrast, Maria Guthrie's *Tour* to the Crimea was edited and published by her husband in 1802, after she herself had died in her fruitless search for better health around the Black Sea. She left her husband (a doctor and antiquary) in service at St Petersburg when she made her journey. At his request, she sent him long letters describing the antiquities and the modern topography of the region, with just the occasional hint of her own loneliness and illness – 'That the return of my health may soon lessen the distance between me and my family, is the prayer with which I finish this letter, and most of my others, although not so openly expressed.'[44] The letters are extraordinarily erudite, and made more so by her husband's additions: as he

---

[43] Mary Ann Hanway, *A Journey to the Highlands of Scotland* (n.d., probably 1777), vi. Cf. Oliver Goldsmith, *The Traveller* (1759):
Where'er I roam, whatever realms to see,
My heart untravelled fondly turns to thee;
Still to my brother turns with ceaseless pain,
And drags at each remove a lengthening chain. (ll. 7–10)
[44] *A Tour, Performed in the Years 1795–6, through the Taurida, or Crimea ... Described in a Series of Letters to her Husband, the Editor* (1802), 94.

explains in the 'Introduction', 'The fair Traveller … desired that he would add to her modern description of each city, &c. its antient history in the times of the Greeks, Romans, Goths, Genoese, Venetians, Tartars, &c.' (v). These additions are woven seamlessly into the text, and Mr Guthrie also provides some 150 pages of appendices, describing ancient religions, inscriptions, and medals. His wife's last journey displays his vast learning as much as her own; indeed, the two become indistinguishable. Guthrie's is an extreme case, but it does highlight the extent to which women travel writers' marital status (or lack thereof, in some cases) shaped not only their experience of abroad, but also the way in which they presented themselves in print.

A frequent strategy, whatever the writer's marital status, is to disclaim any intention to publish. Anne Miller is typical in claiming that her letters were written to a 'near and much esteemed relation', who later persuaded her to publish (*Letters from Italy*, i. v). As a rhetorical gesture, this was of course widely available to, and mobilized by, male writers, but to a large extent became irrelevant and even risked appearing hypocritical once the professionalization of letters (and indeed of travel writing) was under way: we recall the scorn of the *Monthly Review* for Lord Baltimore's effete protestations that he 'wrote the following journals for my own private amusement' (iv): 'then why the — did his Lordship run his head against the press?'[45] Disclaimers of premeditation and of profit motive sounded more natural from female pens, however. Mary Ann Hanway nicely embroiders the trope of reluctant publication in terms suggestive of unintellectual reproduction, relating in her 'Preface' how she 'saw my letters swelling gradually into a volume, with a new-born rapture which always attends the juvenile mind on such occasions' (xii, fonts reversed). Amongst eighteenth-century women travel writers, only Hester Piozzi failed to include any form of gender-based disclaimer or justification for daring to publish a travel account: and, as we shall see, she was judged more harshly on that account.

The first woman's travel narrative to appear in the eighteenth century, Elizabeth Justice's short and unsophisticated *Voyage to Russia* (1739), offers a detailed explanation for 'appearing in this publick Manner' (i). Having alluded to the marital and financial crises which impelled her to take a position as governess to an English family in St Petersburg, she also claims that she was urged to publish her account in order to defend her 'Honour' against slanderous accusations that 'I never have been in *Russia*; but make it a pretence only to cover a fantastical Inclination I had to ramble elsewhere' (v).[46] Justice's plea

---

[45] *MR*, 37 (1767), 312.

[46] In Justice's (anonymous) autobiographical novel, *Amelia, or, The Distress'd Wife: a History founded on Real Circumstances. By a Private Gentlewoman* (1751), we learn that her husband's unpleasant sister is the source of these compromising rumours. On the curious relationship between Justice's *Amelia* and Fielding's, see Elizabeth Kraft,

finds an unlikely echo in 1789, when the spectacularly ill-behaved Lady Craven declares that she is publishing her *Journey through the Crimea to Constantinople* in order to satisfy friends' curiosity, and to show the world 'where the real Lady Craven has been', her husband's mistress having for some years passed herself off as such on *her* travels around less exotic parts of Europe (France, Switzerland, and England).[47] The implied conjunction between 'rambling' and sexual incontinence is clear. A variation on this theme of enforced publication is offered by the case of Jane Vigor, whose *Letters from a Lady* describing her sojourn as the wife (successively) to three Englishmen in St Petersburg during the 1730s were published anonymously in 1775. Vigor herself is diffident to the point of affectation – 'a woman's observations are so ridiculous, that no one else ought to see them' (117) – and her obituary in the *Gentleman's Magazine* for 1783 suggests that 'she was in a manner obliged to publish, to prevent a spurious and incorrect copy from being obtruded on the world'.[48]

Avoidance of political controversy or strong opinion (especially of a negative or xenophobic nature) is another defensive posture adopted by many women travel writers. Reviewing Mary Ann Hanway's *Journey to the Highlands of Scotland* in 1777, both the *Monthly* and the *Critical* observe that there is nothing new in her account, but the *Monthly* concedes that it gives 'a lively and pleasing view of the country, which may serve as a counter part to the picture which Dr. Johnson has drawn with his *sombre* pencil'.[49] Hanway presents Johnson as a betrayer of his Scots hosts, and as one of the 'snarlers' or '*literary* travellers' who 'travel not with intent to give the world a fair account of manners and customs, but merely to exaggerate the bad and sink the good' (66–7). However, it is only fair to point out that her pro-Scots angle also relates to the demands of patronage, as the volume is dedicated to the Earl of Seaforth, with the professed aim of presenting 'a just representation of a country, that hath been honored by giving birth to your Lordship's illustrious ancestors' (ii–iii).

Both the *Monthly* and the *Critical* commend Hanway for her 'agreeable stile' and for being a 'lively correspondent'.[50] Critical accommodations of women's travel writing on similar stylistic grounds are common: Vigor's *Letters from a Lady* (1775) are praised for their 'easy and agreeable manner' and the 'spirit and liveliness of her style';[51] whilst Jemima Kindersley is commended for relating 'a variety of amusing particulars with much ease and

'The Two Amelias: Henry Fielding and Elizabeth Justice', *English Literary History*, 62 (1995), 313–28.
[47] Dedication: pages unnumbered, sig A3^v.
[48] *GM*, 53 (1783), 892.
[49] *CR*, 43 (1777), 238: *MR*, 57 (1777), 242.
[50] *MR*, 57 (1777), 242; *CR*, 43 (1777), 238.
[51] *CR*, 40 (1775), 166; *GM*, 53 (1783), 892.

simplicity', albeit offering 'few material facts not to be met with in the narrative of former voyagers, and little of that philosophical penetration so desirable in travellers'.[52] The slightly patronizing aspect of such praise is nicely mocked by Maria Guthrie, who voices impatience in a letter to her husband:

> pray remember, that I intend to put a great deal of method into my Tour, just to punish you men for your sneer at *the charming disorder that must reign in the narrative of a female traveller*; piquing yourselves, no doubt, on the charming order and arrangement that ever reigns around the lords of the creation, who at the same time cannot, without our help, even arrange their own studies, wherein books, charts, and manuscripts dispute the floor and dust ... (15–16)

This 'charming disorder' brings to mind Smollett's Lydia Melford, who parodically demonstrates women's unsuitability for the role of travel writer:

> this is a charming romantic place. The air is so pure ... the mountains covered with flocks of sheep, and tender bleating wanton lambkins playing, frisking and skipping from side to side ... the water so clear, so pure, so charmingly maukish. (*Humphry Clinker*, 26–7)

Hannah More, discussing reasons for women writers to suppress their urges, points out that an aspiring literary woman's 'highest exertions will probably be received with the qualified approbation, *that it is really extraordinary for a woman.*'[53] Women travel writers did tend to bolster low critical opinions by conforming, with varying degrees of sincerity, to modest and apologetic stereotypes. This is particularly true with respect to the topics they choose to cover and to avoid. They commonly proclaim their lack of qualification and confidence to discourse on 'male' subjects such as economics, politics, and military affairs. Mary Ann Hanway, for example, offers some brief reflections on the Jacobite rising in her Scottish *Journey*, which are then rapidly curtailed: 'But a truce with politics, they ill become a woman's pen; and I know not a more ridiculous character than a petticoat pedant, or politician'. The excuse she pleads for her comments is that they were prompted by irresistible feelings, aroused 'on the spot'; feminine sensibility justifies her timid excursion into patriotic discourse (61). Anne Miller makes playful use of her expected ignorance of certain subjects; she introduces a transcription of her husband's account of Genoa's economy and history, containing several refutations of Addison's remarks, as follows:

---

[52] *MR*, 57 (1777), 243.
[53] *Strictures*, ii. 12.

> M— is gone out, he has left his *portefeuille* behind, and I have
> seized the opportunity of copying some of its contents. You may
> be sure I shall give you a most faithful copy, nor presume to add or
> diminish. (*Letters from Italy*, i. 330).

Miller was no doubt wise to adopt such a pose. In 1777, Jemima
Kindersley's *Letters from the Island of Teneriffe* had aroused the ire of the
Revd H. Hodgson, who was moved to publish *Letters to Mrs Kindersley*, in
which he poured scorn on her speculations concerning the usefulness of Roman
Catholic devotion in maintaining the tranquillity of the negro slaves in Brazil.
In fact, Kindersley's sentiments, although clumsily expressed, are similar to the
musings of Patrick Brydone on the consolations of religion and superstition
amongst the peasants of southern Italy (although Kindersley is more outspoken
about the ideological role of religion), which seem not to have disturbed the
Rev. Hodgson. His unease seems related to her insidious female charms:

> You, Madam, have gained thoroughly the happy art of trifling with
> ease, elegance, and sweetness; but this renders you the more
> dangerous, and is a sufficient reason why your Letters ought to be
> read with great caution. (*Letters to Mrs Kindersley*, 6)

Such warnings notwithstanding, accounts like Kindersley's, as well as
travelogues by women describing more familiar European territories, were
frequently mined for illustrative examples in eighteenth-century discussions of
women and their role. Travel literature's increasing focus on 'manners', sexual
morality, and women's predicament in foreign societies rendered such texts
particularly valuable for the writers of conduct books, comparative histories
and anthropologies. Second-hand accounts of Roman Catholic nunneries and
the Muslim harem and seraglio are ubiquitous in such works, and are almost
always accompanied by a celebration of British women's 'liberty', such as
Hannah More's description of 'this land of civil and religious liberty, where
there is as little despotism exercised over the minds, as over the persons of
women'.[54]

In general, the comparisons opened up between British and foreign society
serve to bolster British boasts of superior female freedom as well as morality.
James Fordyce, in his *Sermons* of 1766, recommends 'Voyages and Travels' as
suitable reading for young women, and enthuses: 'How enlarging to our
prospects of mankind! How conducive to cure the contracted prepossessions of
national pride, and withal to inspire gratitude for the peculiar blessings
bestowed upon our country' (i. 275).[55] And the conviction that the position of

---

[54] *Essays*, 21.
[55] A small compendium, *The Flowers of Modern Travel* (2 vols, 1788) was 'Intended
chiefly for Young People of Both Sexes'.

British women within society was the best in the world was ubiquitous in travel writing, conduct literature, and general histories and anthropologies of foreign countries. As early as 1670, the compiler of *A Collection of English Proverbs* notes that 'England is the paradise of women. ... Hence it has been said that if a bridge were made over the narrow seas, all the women in Europe would come over hither'.[56] This belief is reiterated a century later by the author of *The Laws respecting Women, as they regard their Natural Rights, or their Connections and Conduct* (1778):

> England has been stiled the Paradise of women; nor can it be supposed that in a country where the natural rights of mankind are enjoyed in as full an extent as is consistent with the existence and well-being of a great and extensive empire, that [*sic*] the interests of the softer sex should be overlooked. ('Preface', vi)

The text which follows, however, is (with unconscious irony) a comprehensive account of Englishwomen's legal non-existence and social subordination.

Nationalistic formulations like these find less obviously ideological parallels in 'the growing conviction of leading Enlightenment thinkers that respect for women, and especially for the intellectual capacity of women, was an infallible mark of an advanced civilisation. ... Conversely, the subjection of women became the mark of a barbarous or even savage society in the estimation of some Enlightenment thinkers'.[57] By the 1770s, this belief has become a commonplace in discussions of women's character and status. In 1783, the *Monthly Review* judges John Andrews's literary talents (in his *Remarks on the French and English Ladies*) inadequate to his subject matter, since the 'female character is so inspiring a theme'.[58] Fordyce in 1776 asserts that civilized nations have always esteemed women, while savage societies have 'seldom behaved to women with much respect or tenderness', and his essay includes a historical and geographical survey of women's position in different societies, intended to clinch his argument.[59] This strategy can be found in many conduct and travel books, and is deployed to emphasize British women's glorious freedom and elevated status. Jemima Kindersley in 1777 describes the women of Brazil, who are

> brought up in indolence, and their minds uncultivated, their natural quickness shews itself in cunning. As their male relations do not

---

[56] John Ray, *A Collection of English Proverbs* (1670), 54, cited in Elaine Hobby, *Virtue of Necessity: English Women's Writing, 1649–88* (1988), 1–2.
[57] Arthur M. Wilson, '"Treated Like Imbecile Children" (Diderot): the Enlightenment and the Status of Women', in Paul Fritz and Richard Morton eds., *Woman in the 18th Century* (Toronto, 1976), 89–104; 96.
[58] *MR*, 70 (1783), 381.
[59] Fordyce, *The Character and Conduct of the Female Sex*, 6.

place any confidence in their virtue, they in return use their utmost
art to elude the vigilance with which they are observed; and, to
speak the most favourably, a spirit of intrigue reigns amongst
them. (*Letters from the Island of Teneriffe*, 41)

Hannah More in 1799 acknowledges 'the just encomiums of modern travellers,
who unanimously concur in ascribing a decided superiority to the ladies of this
country over those of every other'; but notes sternly that the appalling 'state of
manners' in 'those countries with which the comparison has been made' hardly
gives cause for complacency.[60]

Reading through the conduct literature of the second half of the eighteenth
century, one is struck by the increasing reference to travellers' accounts of
women's treatment abroad. This in turn reflects the growing tendency in travel
narratives to dwell on such matters, which, some argued, had been too long
excluded from the rubric of travel literature. William Alexander, the compiler
of *The History of Women*, laments in 1779 that 'unhappily, of all other parts of
the female history, that of their manners and customs is involved in the greatest
obscurity' (i. 338); he notes that the ancient historians largely neglected such
topics, and continues:

> Nor is the subject much better elucidated by the moderns, who, in
> their voyages and travels, for the most part, only inform us of the
> dress, complexion, and behaviour of the women in the countries
> they have visited; which, indeed, is commonly all that is in their
> power; for their ignorance of the language of the people they are
> describing, precludes them from every species of information, but
> what they receive by their eyes. The jealousy of the men, in many
> places, hinders them from all access to their women; and the short
> stay made by a traveller affords not the necessary time for
> information. (i. 339)

As if in response to Alexander's complaint, John Andrews in 1783 published
Remarks on the French and English Ladies, an unremarkable text probably
cobbled together out of researches undertaken for his earlier *Account of the
Character and Manners of the French; with occasional Observations on the
English* (1770). Andrews's altered focus in 1783 was no doubt adopted in
response to market demand, although the 'Preface' claims that the letters which
make up the *Remarks* were written to a private correspondent (gender
unknown) who had particularly requested observations on women.

Of course, Lady Mary Wortley Montagu is the eighteenth-century woman of
whom it was most often and enthusiastically pronounced that her gender
qualified her to describe scenes 'not to be paralleled in the narrative of any
male Traveller': namely, the Turkish bath, the harem, and the lifestyles of

---

[60] More, *Strictures on Female Education*, xi.

aristocratic Turkish women.[61] The *Embassy Letters* display a proud self-consciousness of Montagu's distinction within the genre: the letter describing the bath concludes with 'Adieu, Madam, I am sure I have now entertained you, with an account of such a sight as you never saw in your life, and what no book of travels could inform you of, as 'tis no less than death for a man to be found in one of these places'.[62] The work's subtitle stresses how its observations are '*drawn from Sources that have been inaccessible to other Travellers*'. As early as 1724, Mary Astell had drafted a preface to the *Embassy Letters* in which she confessed herself

> malicious enough to desire, that the world should see, to how much better purpose the LADIES travel than their LORDS; and that, whilst it is surfeited with *Male-Travels*, all in the same tone, and stuft with the same trifles; a lady has the skill to strike out a new path, and to embellish a worn-out subject, with variety of fresh and elegant entertainment. (i. viii)

Not surprisingly, Montagu's travelogue has received more critical attention in recent years than all other eighteenth-century women travel writers put together.[63] To add to this body of work seems at best audacious, at worst redundant. However, the broader contexts and the reception of the *Embassy Letters* have not been fully explored. The following section will focus on their post-publication contexts and critical fortunes, with particular reference to Lady Craven's attack on Montagu's veracity in 1789, in order to illuminate the rapidly changing intellectual and moral climate of eighteenth-century travel writing, and of the domestic culture with which travel writing was intertwined.

---

[61] *MR*, 28 (1763), 392.

[62] *Letters of the Right Honourable Lady M—y W—y M—e: written, during her Travels in Europe, Asia, and Africa, to Persons of Distinction, Men of Letters, &c. in different Parts of Europe. Which contain, among other curious Relations, Accounts of the Policy and Manners of the Turks; drawn from Sources that have been inaccessible to other Travellers* (3 vols, 1763), i. 164–5. Hereafter cited as *Embassy Letters*.

[63] See in particular Elizabeth Bohls, *Women Travel Writers and the Language of Aesthetics 1716–1818* (Cambridge, 1995); Jill Campbell, 'Lady Mary Wortley Montagu and the Historical Machinery of Female Identity', in Beth Fowkes Tobin ed., *History, Gender and Eighteenth-Century Literature* (Athens, Ga., 1994), 64–85; Isobel Grundy, '"The barbarous character we give them": White Women Travellers Report on Other Races', *Studies in Eighteenth-Century Culture*, 22 (1992), 73–86; Joseph W. Lew, 'Lady Mary's Portable Seraglio', *Eighteenth-Century Studies*, 24 (1991), 432–50; Cynthia Lowenthal, 'The Veil of Romance: Lady Mary's Embassy Letters', *Eighteenth-Century Life*, 14 (1990), 66–82; Lowenthal, *Lady Mary Wortley Montagu and the Eighteenth-Century Familiar Letter* (1994); Bruce Redford, *The Converse of the Pen: Acts of Intimacy in the Eighteenth-Century Familiar Letter* (Chicago, 1986), 19–48.

'A disgusting sight': re-alienating the 'Other' in Craven's *Journey*

Montagu's attractive visions of Turkey have come to embody a particular version of British Enlightenment culture and aesthetics. Bernard Lewis sees in Montagu's account the 'new myth, still in its embryonic form, of the non-European as the embodiment of mystery and romance'.[64] In many ways, however, Montagu's *Embassy Letters* are uncharacteristic of 'the eighteenth century' of which they are so often claimed to be paradigmatic. In 1789, Lady Elizabeth Craven, the other great British eighteenth-century woman traveller to Turkey, takes issue with many of Montagu's opinions in her own travelogue, *A Journey through the Crimea to Constantinople*, and pronounces indeed that Montagu 'never wrote a line of them'.[65] In her later *Memoirs*, and in the enlarged edition of the *Journey* published as *Letters from the Right Honorable Lady Craven* in 1814, Craven expands on this view, pronouncing that the *Embassy Letters* 'were most of them male compositions, pretending to female grace in the style, the facts mostly inventions'.[66] There had in fact been a spurious 'fourth' volume of Montagu's *Embassy Letters* published in 1767, perhaps written by John Cleland; but by the 1780s its spuriousness, and the authenticity of the 1763 volumes, were not in doubt.

Montagu's highly favourable impressions of abroad, especially of Turkey, and especially of Turkish women, are Craven's chief targets. Craven found an unexpected ally in the person of Lady Bute, Montagu's daughter, who, having failed to suppress the publication of the *Embassy Letters* in 1763, was delighted to find support (over twenty-five years afterwards) for her disowning of her mother's vulgar publishing activities. Ladies Craven and Bute later corresponded about the authorship of the *Embassy Letters*, Lady Bute agreeing heartily that 'most of the Letters were composed by men', and suggesting that Horace Walpole 'and two other wits' had written them.[67] No one else seems to have taken these assertions seriously; yet, questions of personal grievance and arrogance aside, this curious episode suggests how uncongenial Montagu's account has become to at least some later eighteenth-century readers. Craven's critical observations on Turkey, which to a large extent are a reactionary engagement with Montagu's, were taken seriously by the Reviews (including the *Analytical*), although they slyly mocked her style and arrogance. Moreover,

---

[64] Bernard Lewis, *Islam and the West* (Oxford, 1993), 83.

[65] *A Journey through the Crimea to Constantinople. In a Series of Letters from the Right Honorable Elizabeth Lady Craven, to his Serene Highness the Margrave of Brandebourg, Anspach, and Bareith. Written in the Year MDCCLXXXVI* (1789), 105.

[66] *Letters from the Right Honorable Lady Craven, to His Serene Highness the Margrave of Anspach, during her Travels through France, Germany, and Russia in 1785 and 1786* (1814), 289.

[67] *Memoirs of the Margravine of Anspach, written by Herself* (2 vols, 1826), ii. 116.

the *Monthly Review* commends her 'liberal reflections, which do honour to the writer, both as a lover of her own country, and as a citizen of the world'.[68]

The generally positive reception of Craven's text in 1789 owes something to her itinerary, since little else in the way of original travel writing on Turkey had been published since Montagu's text in 1763: James Porter's *Observations on the Religion, Law, Government, and Manners, of the Turks* (1768) was a compilation of previous travellers' accounts, and the focus of Richard Chandler's *Travels in Asia Minor* (1775) was archaeological. And Turkish affairs were much in the public eye in the late 1780s: although her journey was made during 1785–6, Craven's account was published during the Russian and Austrian war against Turkey (1787–92), during which British policy towards the Ottoman Empire was anxiously supportive.[69] More intriguing still for the reading public would have been the hope of insights into Craven's already notorious private life (made extremely public through the attentions of the *Town and Country Magazine* and other such gazettes).[70] The generally dour *Analytical Review* observes with some drollery that 'The letters of this sprightly female will naturally excite curiosity'.[71]

The mere existence of their narratives testifies to the privileged status of Montagu and Craven. Their rank made possible not only their access to European and Turkish high society – 'The Turks are very proud, and will not converse with a stranger they are not assured is considerable in his own country', claims Montagu (*Embassy Letters*, ii. 131–2) – but their very expeditions. Montagu travelled through Austria and Hungary to Constantinople, with 'thirty covered waggons for our baggage, and five coaches ... for my women' (*Embassy Letters*, ii. 110), and points out that:

> The journey we have made from Belgrade hither, cannot possibly be passed by any out of a public character. The desert woods of Servia, are the common refuge of thieves, who rob, fifty in a company, so that we had need of all our guards to secure us; and the villages are so poor, that only force could extort from them necessary provisions. (*Embassy Letters*, ii. 2)

---

[68] *MR*, 80, (1789), 209.

[69] See Stanford Shaw, *History of the Ottoman Empire and Modern Turkey* (2 vols, Cambridge, 1976), i. 258–60.

[70] See A. M. Broadley and Lewis Melville, *The Beautiful Lady Craven: the Original Memoirs of Elizabeth Baroness Craven afterwards Margravine of Anspach and Bayreuth and Princess Berkeley of the Holy Roman Empire (1750–1828). Edited with Notes and Historical Introduction containing much unpublished matter* (2 vols, 1914). See also my entry on Anspach, Elizabeth, Margravine of, in *New Dictionary of National Biography* (Oxford, forthcoming, 2004).

[71] *AR*, 3 (1789), 176.

Elsewhere, she describes her distress at the 'insolencies' of their escorts 'in the poor villages through which we passed' (i. 152). Craven travelled with a smaller entourage but rather less sensitivity. Her *Journey* is peppered with name-dropping, and pervaded by a strong sense of her own importance, as in this passage:

> At Soumi I conversed with a brother of Prince Kourakin's and a Mr Lanskoy, both officers quartered there; and to whom I was indebted for a lodging: they obliged a Jew to give me up a new little house he was upon the point of inhabiting. (*Journey*, 154)

The *Critical Review* concludes its account of Craven's *Journey* with the waspish pronouncement that the 'rest of the journey affords little subject of remark, except that whatever accommodations rank and beauty could demand, and despotic power could procure, lady Craven enjoyed'.[72] The circumstances under which Montagu's and Craven's texts were published testify to the critical significance not only of their rank, but also of their gender, and illuminate changing concepts of private and public identity between the early 1760s and the late 1780s.

The *Embassy Letters* emerged into the literary world like the elegant ghost of their recently deceased author, appearing in 1763 in three small octavo volumes. For all her contempt of authors who descended to the vulgar activity of publication (in a letter of 23 July 1753 she observes that it is 'not the busyness of a Man of Quality to turn Author'),[73] Montagu was clearly anxious that the *Embassy Letters* eventually be published. She kept the manuscript with her wherever she travelled, and on her final journey home entrusted them to an English clergyman at Rotterdam, with instructions to publish them after her death. It was her travel letters, rather than her poems or essays (some of which had been circulated in manuscript or even published anonymously during her lifetime), which Montagu was concerned to have preserved for posterity. The propriety of publishing is not an issue within Montagu's text, for all its prominence in her thought and activity elsewhere. Craven, however, engages vigorously with the issue. She seems to have had few qualms about the propriety of publishing; indeed, she somewhat showily published in a quarto volume illustrated with six engravings. Of the women travel writers who published in the eighteenth century, only Craven and Radcliffe (whose literary reputation was already well established) published in anything grander than octavo; and only Craven's book had plates. The *Gentleman's Magazine* is unimpressed, however, noting that 'What Lady C. here offers to the publick in

---

[72] *CR*, 67 (1789), 286.
[73] Halsband ed., *Complete Letters*, iii. 37.

a costly quarto might certainly have been very well compressed to the size of Lady Montague's Letters'.[74]

The letters which make up Craven's *Journey* are written to the Margrave of Anspach, with whom Craven had developed a 'more than sisterly affection' on her travels in Europe following her scandalous separation from Lord Craven in 1781.[75] Unfortunately, his wife the Margravine was still alive, albeit in a sickly fashion, and it appears that Craven decided on a grand tour of exotic locations in order to remove the embarrassment to the Margrave created by her continued residence at Anspach, and to kill time until both the Margravine and Lord Craven had expired: he in fact held out until 1791, at which point she promptly married the Margrave. They then returned to England, but her long absence and widely publicized adultery had enabled Lord Craven to turn their children against her: all six refused to acknowledge her. Moreover, she was no longer received at Court, which must have been a serious blow to a woman of her pretensions. In 1814, Craven – now the Margravine of Anspach – reissued the *Journey* with minor alterations and additions. The new title blazons the name and rank of her correspondent: *Letters from the Right Honorable Lady Craven, to His Serene Highness the Margrave of Anspach, during her Travels through France, Germany, and Russia in 1785 and 1786.* The virtuous nature of their relationship is indignantly defended in several additional letters, and in the new 'Preface', where we are informed that she 'constantly refused estates and titles' offered by foreign potentates lest she be called suddenly home by her husband and children:

> my husband had all his [*sic*; for 'my'] fine property in his own power, and therefore I could not consent to take any duties on me, when I felt, that my first duty, that of a mother, must make me forsake those duties my gratitude and pride might have made me take elsewhere—my duty as a mother lay in England. (*Letters*, v)

The 1814 edition also inserts references to her marital problems with Lord Craven and her deepening friendship with the Margrave; he is presented as a saintly refuge from the callous Lord Craven, who had prevented their children from writing to her, and whose appalling behaviour is clearly intended to exonerate her from any accusations of unwifely conduct. Craven casts herself in the role of restless exile, happy neither at home nor abroad, whose journeying is less a violation than a proof of propriety. The changes made to the 1814 edition engage with the increasingly severe moral climate of the late eighteenth century and early nineteenth, and negotiate the problematic space

---

[74] *GM*, 59 (1789), 237.
[75] *MR*, 53 (1789), 201.

between public propriety and 'private' affairs which the earlier *Journey* had, perhaps naïvely, opened up for public inspection.

Craven capitalizes (in both editions) not only on her personal notoriety but also on the increasingly affective scope of travel writing in the later eighteenth century. While Montagu's reasons for travel and her personal affairs are largely absent from the *Embassy Letters*, Craven's private dramas provide, quite publicly, a moral justification for her travels, as well as an almost novelistic source of semi-scandalous interest. Craven's text and apologetic signal her awareness of the moral sensitivity of such issues, but her aristocratic self-importance permits her to rise above bourgeois anxiety. When it comes, however, to describing Turkish women, Craven's moral sensibility is closer, as we shall see, to the middle-class propriety of the 1780s and 1790s than to any aristocratic largesse. Moreover, the emphasis she increasingly places on her submissive married relationship (Montagu, by contrast, barely mentions her husband, although she does briefly refer to her experiences of childbirth in Turkey) can be related to an emergent imperial sensibility, within which visible domestic affection in the Christian institution of marriage testifies to the moral superiority of the colonizer. As we shall see, other eighteenth-century women who journeyed in the less exotic regions of Europe bolster a similar sense of national virtue, and likewise locate it in conjugal obedience and happiness: in this respect, it is possible to see the ideological origins of gender and empire being formulated initially on a less expansive international scale.

Robert Halsband has observed that, whilst in the courts of western Europe Montagu mingled with princes and diplomats, at the Ottoman Court her sex deprived her of this privilege.[76] Craven is similarly excluded, but with chagrin: at one point she resorts to spying on the Sultan through a telescope. This exclusion partly explains the absence of political and diplomatic material in both women's accounts and their focus instead on the status of Turkish women, of whom they present strikingly different accounts. Both writers commend the respect and apparent liberty granted to Turkish women, but Montagu's account of their grace and beauty is vigorously contradicted by Craven. Montagu describes the women of the harem with admiration:

> They have naturally the most beautiful complexions in the world, and generally large black eyes ... They generally shape their eye-brows, and both Greeks and Turks have the custom of putting round their eyes a black tincture, that, at distance, or by candle-light, adds very much to the blackness of them. I fancy many of our ladies would be overjoyed to know this secret; but 'tis too visible by day. (*Embassy Letters*, ii. 31–2)

---

[76] Robert Halsband, *The Life of Lady Mary Wortley Montagu* (Oxford, 1956), 71.

Craven is less favourably impressed:

> I have no doubt but that nature intended some of these women to
> be very handsome, but white and red ill applied, their eye-brows
> hid under one or two black lines—teeth black by smoaking, and an
> universal stoop in the shoulders, made them appear rather
> disgusting than handsome ... The frequent use of hot-baths
> destroys the solids, and these women at nineteen look older than I
> am at this moment. (*Journey*, 225–6)

'Nature' here is implicitly associated with British standards of beauty, and
Craven frequently equates it with Western, and usually British, behaviour. The
Critical Review notes the prevalence of the adjective 'ugly' in her account.[77]
More recently, Montagu has also been accused of forcing Turkish women into
a Western frame of reference, most notoriously in this famous description of
the Turkish bath:

> They walked and moved with the same majestic grace, which
> Milton describes our General Mother with. There were many
> amongst them, as exactly proportioned as ever any goddess was
> drawn, by the pencil of a Guido or Titian,—And most of their
> skins shiningly white, only adorned by their beautiful hair, divided
> into many tresses, hanging on their shoulders, braided either with
> pearl or ribbon, perfectly representing the figures of the graces. (i.
> 161–2)

Such objectifying manoeuvres, Isobel Grundy and Cynthia Lowenthal have
argued, allow Montagu simultaneously to appreciate the exotic otherness of
Turkish women and to evade the more problematic issues of freedom and
happiness within the harsher realities of Turkish women's experience.[78]
Elizabeth Bohls, however, has recently presented a more radical version of
Montagu's aestheticizing strategies, arguing that she presents herself, daringly,
as an aesthetic subject (a privilege usually reserved for males) in order to
neutralize Orientalist stereotypes of women, and to re-present them as aesthetic
rather than erotic objects: statues and paintings rather than the lascivious
harpies of seventeenth- and eighteenth-century male-authored travels, by the
likes of Paul Rycaut and Aaron Hill.[79]

Craven's strategy, by contrast, is simultaneously to de-aestheticize the
Oriental female, and to render her morally dubious once more. Where Montagu
celebrates the steamy beauty of the Turkish bath, Craven is appalled by the

---

[77] *CR*, 67 (1789), 282.
[78] Grundy, "'The barbarous character we give them'"; Lowenthal, 'The Veil of
Romance'.
[79] Bohls, *Women Travel Writers and the Language of Aesthetics*, 23–45.

hordes of naked fat women, 'a disgusting sight' (*Journey*, 264). Craven's account of a 'Turkish' bath in fact occurs in Athens. This displacement testifies not only to Craven's tendency to lump together Greeks, Turks, Tartars and Cossacks as Eastern and primitive, regardless of politics or national identity – and indeed to use the term 'Turk' as a term of abuse for any objectionable Eastern individual – but also to the distance which Craven strenuously constructs between herself and the Eastern 'other', especially in Turkey and her dominions, where the pernicious influence of Islam is stressed. The *Critical Review* observes that Craven is interested not only in 'the stupidity and indolence of the Turks', but also in 'the effects of their despotism on the conquered Greeks'.[80] Craven's horror at the Turkish bath is similar to her 'disgusted' reaction to a Cossack belly dancer, who 'never lifted her feet off the ground but once in four minutes, and then only one foot at a time, and every part of her person danced except her feet' (*Journey*, 173). A description in Montagu's earlier account of a similar entertainment had, by contrast, employed the term 'proper' in an aesthetic sense devoid of moral implication, and envisaged a neutralizing coalescence of art and eroticism which would cast the insensitive Western prude as the villain of the piece:

> This dance was very different from what I had seen before. Nothing could be more artful, or more proper to raise *certain ideas*. The tunes so soft! the motions so languishing!— Accompanied with pauses and dying eyes! Half-falling back, and then recovering themselves in so artful a manner, that I am very positive, the coldest and most rigid prude upon earth, could not have looked upon them without thinking of *something not to be spoke of*. (*Embassy Letters*, ii. 89–90)

In the more 'proper' climate of the 1780s, Montagu's aesthetic Oriental women are re-becoming lascivious. Craven's implicit rebuke to her readers' curiosity echoes Jane Vigor's disapproval in 1775 of a query which reaches her from a male acquaintance at home as to 'whether I have been at a Russian bagnio', and which 'merits no reply, but the contempt that ought to be shown to men of his turn of mind, who fancy they have been witty when they have said an improper thing'.[81]

Both Montagu and Craven elaborate on the freedoms offered by the anonymous garb of Turkish women, but Craven dwells repeatedly on its possibilities for intrigue and licentiousness, even imagining sexual assignations being conducted during services at Santa Sophia, by figures 'wrapped up like a mummy' (*Journey*, 218). Montagu herself exploits the liberty which Turkish dress affords, wandering the streets of Constantinople 'every day, wrapped up

---

[80] *CR*, 67 (1789), 285.
[81] *Letters from a Lady*, 133.

in my Ferige and Asmak' (*Embassy Letters*, iii. 26). Craven would not countenance such assimilation:

> As to women, as many, if not more than men, are to be seen in the streets—but they look like walking mummies—A large loose robe of dark green cloth covers them from the neck to the ground, over that a large piece of muslin, which wraps the shoulders and the arms, another which goes over the head and eyes ... If I was to walk about the streets here I would certainly wear the same dress, for the Turkish women call others names, when they meet them with their faces uncovered—When I go out I have the Ambassador's sedan-chair, which is like mine in London, only gilt and varnished like a French coach, and six Turks carry it; as they fancy it impossible that two or four men can carry one; two Janissaries walk before with high fur caps on—The Ambassadors here have all Janissaries as guards allowed them by the Porte—Thank Heaven I have but a little way to go in this pomp, and fearing every moment the Turks should fling me down they are so awkward ... (*Journey*, 205–6)

Montagu's experience of Turkey stands in opposition to the restrictive idea of gendered space which was becoming a fact of life in eighteenth-century Britain, and London especially.[82] The trappings of Turkish femininity offer unlimited access to public spaces (and Craven also notes that 'as many, if not more' women than men occupy the streets). Craven's text rewrites the concept of separate spheres so that space and activity are divided along racial lines. Her 'if I was to walk about the streets here' is purely rhetorical. The Britishwoman is resolutely opposed to the anonymity of Turkish feminine costume (perhaps here the developing discourse of British individuality and strong 'character' is an influence). Consequently, her evident difference opens up perceptible hostility between the women of different races, which can only be contained, quite literally, within a sedan chair borne by Turkish males. And yet this too poses a threat, Craven 'fearing every moment the Turks should fling me down they are so awkward'. For her journey out of Turkey, Craven is given as an escort another threatening male, a 'Tchouadar, that is to say, a kind of upper servant, or rather creature of the Visir' (*Journey*, 285). This 'yellow looking Turk' (286) is a constant source of irritation to Craven, competing with her for the servants' attention and for the lion's share of the party's provisions. At one point she finds that he has used her kettle to make himself coffee:

> If any travellers were to meet us, they would certainly take him for some Grand Seigneur, and that I am of his suite, by the care taken of him, and the perfect indifference all, but my two companions

---

> and my servants, show for my ease and convenience ... I thought it
> right to point to two most excellent little English pistols I wear at
> my girdle, and assure him they would be well employed against
> any offence I met with. And when the interpreter had done I could
> not help calling him a stupid disagreeable Turk, in English; which
> he took for a compliment, and bowed his head a little ... (291)

Turkish degeneracy and luxury here emerge as sexual savagery, barely
containable through the brandishing of 'English pistols' worn in a highly
defensive position, 'at my girdle' (and through the futile yet cathartic effect of
English insults).

In 1763, the *Monthly Review* had praised the *Embassy Letters* in gendered
terms: 'There is no affectation of female delicatesse, there are no prettynesses,
no Ladyisms in these natural, easy familiar Epistles'.[83] Paradoxically, Montagu
is celebrated as a writer because she is not typical of her gender, even though it
is her gender which makes possible her most novel observations (her
descriptions of the harem). In 1789, by contrast, the *Critical Review* notes
archly that Craven 'saw objects in the true female view'.[84] If this is true, then
Craven is doing so partly in response to the increasing ideological separation of
male and female fields and abilities. Similarly, her highly restrictive notions of
sexual propriety are very much of her time. If we recall Craven's aspersions on
the authorship of Montagu's text, moreover, it becomes clear that narrowing
concepts of female activity colour Craven's reading of Montagu's text to the
extent that the *Embassy Letters*' tolerant view of Turkish manners evinces their
spuriousness.

Montagu's broader cultural tolerance is if anything still more offensive to
Craven than her views on women. Jill Campbell has described how Montagu
imagines Turkish culture as 'outside history, as a place where past and present,
the literary and the natural, coexist', and relates this to the anthropological
phenomenon observed by Johannes Fabian (in *Time and the Other*),

> by which Western travelers deny the contemporaneity of different
> cultures, coexisting in the same historical moment, and instead
> imagine the alien cultures they encounter as inhabiting the distant
> past of their own culture's history or prehistory.[85]

A letter to Pope, written at Adrianople, shows Montagu adopting precisely this
position:

---

[83] *MR*, 28 (1763), 385.
[84] *CR*, 67 (1789), 282.
[85] Campbell, 'Lady Mary Wortley Montagu and the Historical Machinery of Female
Identity', 74–5.

> I read over your Homer here, with an infinite pleasure, and find
> several little passages explained, that I did not before entirely
> comprehend the beauty of: Many of the customs, and much of the
> dress then in fashion, being yet retained. I don't wonder to find
> more remains here, of an age so distant, than is to be found in any
> other country, the Turks not taking that pains to introduce their
> own manners, as has been generally practised by other nations,
> that imagine themselves more polite. (*Embassy Letters*, ii. 44)

This is to Pope, and about poetry, and is therefore consciously idealistic. The letter invokes a cultural continuity which dissolves national boundaries and represents difference as innocence from the ravages of civilization: 'I never see half a dozen of old Bashaws (as I do very often) with their reverend beards, sitting basking in the sun, but I recollect good King Priam and his counsellors (*Embassy Letters*, ii. 45).

The *Embassy Letters* as a whole strives to articulate an innocence of history and politics – which are barely mentioned – and also of cultural judgement. Crucial to this project is the fragmentation of narrative identity which occurs within the *Embassy Letters*. Montagu's text differs markedly from Craven's in being addressed (rather unusually, in eighteenth-century travel literature) to a wide range of correspondents (fifteen in all, twelve of whom are women), ranging from her depressed sister, Lady Mar, to the Abbé Conti, to Alexander Pope, and including assorted female friends. All of Craven's letters, by contrast, are addressed to the Margrave (which may partly account for their celebration of her virtues and of the esteem in which she is held throughout Europe, Russia and Turkey). This formal difference makes for a greater stylistic variety within the *Embassy Letters* than in Craven's *Journey*. Montagu uses different literary and conversational registers for different correspondents, and deploys a range of descriptive topics. She addresses one letter to the Princess of Wales, writing as ambassadress for Christendom as well as Britain:

> I have now, Madam, finished a journey that has not been
> undertaken by any Christian, since the time of the Greek
> Emperors; and I shall not regret all the fatigues I have suffered in
> it, if it gives me an opportunity of amusing your R. H. by an
> account of places utterly unknown amongst us ... (*Embassy
> Letters*, i. 151)

To Lady Mar, Montagu writes anecdotal, humorous accounts of social and sexual customs, and visits to exotic notables like the Grand Vizier's 'lady' and the Sultana Hafiten. With assorted Ladies, she is chatty and occasionally risqué. All her detailed (and celebrated) accounts of Turkish women, in harem or public bath or private audience, are addressed to women. With the Abbé Conti and with Pope, not surprisingly, Montagu is at her most scholarly and philosophical. To the Abbé she writes of 'manners and religion' (*Embassy Letters*, ii. 1), government and welfare, antiquities and architecture, commerce, military parades, and Islam. To Pope she addresses witty and sometimes flirtatious letters on poetry and pastoral, resolutely denying him the almost erotic satisfaction which her letters to women friends offer in their accounts of her Turkish costume and luxurious lifestyle. One detects a distinctively plaintive note to Pope's declaration that 'I long for nothing so much as your Oriental Self ... I expect to see your Soul as much thinner dressd as your Body'.[86] Through this dazzling variety of subjects and styles, Montagu refracts her narrative identity into a prismatic multiplicity. The *Letters'* observing self becomes, quite literally, an embodiment of Enlightenment pluralism. Their multi-faceted narrator was no doubt an important factor in the enthusiastic reception of the *Embassy Letters*. Smollett in the *Critical Review* itemizes the narrator's separate attractions, declaring that the letters will display, 'as long as the English language endures, the sprightliness of her wit, the solidity of her judgement, the extent of her knowledge, the elegance of her taste, and the excellence of her real character'.[87] The freedom of the *Embassy Letters* from opinion, judgement, or 'vulgar prejudice' seems to have made them peculiarly attractive to the critical and reading public of the 1760s, to whom Montagu must have seemed a true citizen of the world. The *Embassy Letters* were published in 1763, the year of the cessation of the Seven Years' War in Europe: the war had in some ways undermined the viability of Enlightened ideals and seen them compromised by political contingency and nationalistic feeling. Montagu's visions of a distant and not immediately threatening foreign world perhaps reassured the reading public that Enlightened tolerance was still, albeit remotely, alive and possible. Alternatively, the confidence-boosting territorial gains made at the Peace of Paris may have fostered a relaxed and culturally tolerant mood among the reading and critical public. Furthermore, remarks like 'Upon the whole, I look upon the Turkish women, as the only free people in the Empire' (*Embassy Letters*, ii. 35) must have offered a pleasurable alternative to the bitter resonances of 'liberty' in its domestic context in 1763. The *Embassy Letters* were published and reviewed in May of 1763; *North Briton* 45 had appeared in April, and 'Wilkes and Liberty' was becoming a rallying cry.

For all the enlightened pluralism of the *Embassy Letters*, however, one might argue that there are letters in which Montagu's narrative persona is more emphatically British and where, correspondingly, things Turkish are presented in a more ambivalent light. The first is in a letter (her only) to the Princess of Wales, in which (as mentioned earlier) she writes as spokeswoman for Christendom. She describes her arrival in Turkish territory:

---

[86]   *Correspondence of Alexander Pope*, ed. George Sherburn (5 vols, Oxford, 1956), i. 494.
[87]   *CR*, 15 (1763), 435.

> The country from hence to Adrianople, is the finest in the world. Vines grow wild on all the hills, and the perpetual spring they enjoy, makes every thing gay and flourishing. But this climate, happy as it seems, can never be preferred to England, with all its frosts and snows, while we are blessed with an easy government, under a King, who makes his own happiness consist in the liberty of his people, and chooses rather to be looked upon, as their father, than their master. (*Embassy Letters*, i. 155)

This is a striking passage in Montagu's text – all the more so in that it sounds, almost parodically, like a great deal of other eighteenth-century travel writers, who draw such comparisons so frequently as to make them at best a trope, at worst a cliché, of the genre. The identity of Montagu's correspondent here largely explains the jingoistic tone. This letter is, however, hardly xenophobic: but the same could not be said of one to Pope, describing Austro-Turkish atrocities in the battle for Belgrade, which contains a virulent diatribe against the Turks:

> You see here that I give you a very handsome return for your obliging letter. You entertain me with a most agreeable account of your amiable connexions with men of letters and taste, and of the delicious moments you pass in their society under the rural shade; and I exhibit to you in return, the barbarous spectacle of Turks and Germans cutting one another's throats. But what can you expect from such a country as this, from which the muses have fled, from which letters seem eternally banished, and in which you see, in private scenes, nothing pursued as happiness but the refinements of an indolent voluptuousness, and where those who act upon the public theatre live in uncertainty, suspicion, and terror.[88]

This letter implicitly rejects the classical idealizing of Turkey which dominates most of the *Embassy Letters*, and declares indeed that 'I long much to tread upon English ground, that I may see you and Mr. Congreve, who render that ground classick ground'.[89] These Smelfungoid passages disrupt the tolerant pluralism of the other letters. Or, I should say, *would* disrupt: for although a recent editor of Montagu includes this letter, it did not in fact appear in the 1763 edition of *Embassy Letters*. It was first published in the spurious 'fourth volume', containing five fake letters and some genuine material (an essay, a letter, some verse), which appeared in 1767.[90] Robert Halsband has

---

[88] *An Additional Volume to the Letters of the Right Honourable Lady M—y W— M—e: written, during her Travels in Europe, Asia and Africa, to Persons of Distinction, Men of Letters, &c. in different Parts of Europe* (1767), 27–8.
[89] *An Additional Volume*, 32.
[90] The letter is inexplicably included in the Everyman selection of Montagu's *Letters*, ed. Clare Brant (1992).

documented the inauthenticity of most of the 1767 volume.[91] Discredited by the time Craven was writing, this literary imposture had nevertheless deceived 'even ... the critics' in 1767, as the *Monthly Review* in 1784 ruefully admits.[92] The 1767 volume is a fascinating hoax, and reveals the extent to which Montagu's pluralistic tolerance is already nostalgic, indeed outdated, by the later 1760s; or at least is co-existing somewhat uneasily with a more xenophobic, politically defensive sensibility. Revealingly, Lady Bute 'was convinced that the volume published in 1767 must be "genuine"'.[93]

In the bona fide volumes of the *Embassy Letters*, by contrast, Turkish indolence is invested with a complex philosophical value, embodying both classical (specifically, Elysian) tranquillity, and the possibility of a modern epicureanism:

> I am almost of opinion they [the Turks] have a right notion of life. They consume it in musick, gardens, wine and delicate eating, while we are tormenting our brains with some scheme of politicks, or studying some science to which we can never attain ... Considering what short liv'd weak animals men are, is there any study so beneficial as the study of present pleasure? I dare not pursue this theme ... (*Embassy Letters*, iii. 52–3)

Elsewhere, Montagu surrenders to 'the wicked suggestions of poetry', and observes 'the warmth of the climate ... naturally inspiring a laziness and aversion to labour' (*Embassy Letters*, ii. 40–2). For Craven in the 1780s, however, indolence is anything but 'naturally' inspired: her 'nature' favours industry and (where such industry is not indigenous) colonization. And her version of pastoral, as in this description of the valley of Baydar in Turkey, is decidedly imperial:

> a most enchanting and magnificent spot, intended by nature for some industrious and happy nation to enjoy in peace—A few Tartar villages lessen the wildness of the scene, but, in such a place, the meadow part should be covered with herds, and the mountainous with sheep ... (*Journey*, 190–91)

Her response to Turkish languor is one of prosaic disapproval: 'The quiet stupid Turk will sit a whole day by the side of the Canal, looking at flying kites or children's boats ... How the business of the nation goes on at all I cannot guess' (*Journey*, 207). Her visions of commercial imperialism are couched in the language of emancipation and vision:

---

[91]   Halsband ed., *Complete Letters*, i. xviii; i. 371.

[92]   *MR*, 70 (1784), 575.

[93]   Halsband ed., *Complete Letters*, i. xviii.

Can any rational being, dear Sir, see nature, without the least assistance from art, in all her grace and beauty, stretching out her liberal hand to industry, and not wish to do her justice? Yes, I confess, I wish to see a colony of honest English families here; establishing manufactures, such as England produces, and returning the produce of this country to ours—establishing a fair and free trade from hence, and teaching industry and honesty to the insidious but oppressed Greeks, in their islands—waking the indolent Turk from his gilded slumbers, and carrying fair Liberty in her swelling sails ... This is no visionary or poetical figure—it is the honest wish of one who considers all mankind as one family ... (*Journey*, 188–9)

The *Monthly Review* commends this passage for its 'liberal reflections, which do honour to the writer, both as a lover of her own country, and as a citizen of the world'.[94] This judgement testifies to the ideological gulf not only between Montagu and Craven, but between the values of mid-century and those of later eighteenth-century culture, moving towards a new world of imperial expansion within which the East is no longer merely an exotic playpen, but a land ripe for the type of colonial appropriation already well under way in India. The forceful narrative personality projected by Craven's text in 1789 signals the emergence of the moral centre which the British woman is to provide not only as a bulwark against the forces of European revolution but also, in the longer term, for the colonial project.

'One man is more to them than a nation': matrimony and nationality

Whilst Elizabeth Craven's aristocratic *hauteur* and her colourful private life provoke sly humour on the part of the reviews, the ideological stance of her *Journey* is nevertheless congenial to the late 1780s, and to the broadly middle-class common readership of travel literature. The relationship between gender, class and national virtue is central not only to Craven's account, but also to the work of three other woman travel writers from the 1770s and 1780s, to whom this closing section is devoted. Anne Miller, Jane Vigor and Hester Thrale Piozzi deal in very different ways with the particular social pressures exerted upon their travelogues by the demanding set of moral and cultural contexts outlined in earlier sections of this chapter.

In 1775 Dodsley published a small octavo volume entitled *Letters from a Lady, who resided some Years in Russia, to her Friend in England. With historical notes*, which saw a second edition in 1777. The letters are dated 1729–39 but were probably doctored for publication: their idiom and sensibility

---

[94]   *MR*, 80 (1789), 209.

are of the 1770s rather than of the earlier period. They are rated by the *Monthly Review* as 'somewhat in the lively manner of Lady Montagu, tho' they are certainly not equal to the letters of that celebrated lady', and the *Critical* commends Vigor's 'easy and agreeable manner'.[95] The *Monthly* expresses surprise at the work's anonymity, since, as the writer 'appears to have been the lady of the English minister there ... her name can be no secret, from dates and circumstances'.[96] Indeed, she was the wife first of Thomas Ward, British Consul-General for Russia from 1728, and, after his death, of Claudius Rondeau, British Resident at the Court of Moscow. Rondeau, 'a man naturally delicate, and bred among the politest circles', died in October 1739, and his widow then travelled home under the protection of a Quaker merchant William Vigor, whom she married in 1740.[97] Her first bereavement and her marriage to Rondeau are described in the *Letters*, as is the birth at St Petersburg of her first child.[98]

Both the *Gentleman's Magazine* and the *Monthly Review* mention Vigor's historical pictures of the Russian court as their distinguishing feature.[99] John Nichols writes in 1812 that her 'account of the Court of Russia is extremely curious, and the secret history of it is quite new'.[100] It is certainly a completely different view of Russia from that offered in 1739 by the humble governess, Elizabeth Justice, whose relationship to the Court is emphatically marginal, as the following passage suggests:

> All the News I can send you, is, that the *English* Resident gave a very elegant Entertainment on the King's Birth-day, which concluded with a Ball. I was not at it, for my Dress is still Brown Camlet, and I think that best for Retirement: I make up the Disappointment of Feasts, by attending a very polite Entertainment, that is, in Reading the *Spectator*. (1746 rev. ed., 60)

By contrast, Vigor (who at one point boasts that 'I am a spectator, and moralize on human weakness', 17–18) experienced Court life in an extremely 'public situation', which gave her 'the best opportunities of seeing and knowing the

---

[95]   *MR*, 53 (1775), 211; *CR*, 40 (1775), 166.

[96]   *MR*, 53 (1775), 211.

[97]   The description of Rondeau is from the 'Eleven Additional Letters' which were printed off in 1785 (after Jane Vigor's death) 'to be bound up with the others', 61. These letters offer some slightly more private information than those previously published, including the revelation that while still Mrs Ward, she had shared a Moscow house with Rondeau (and, mercifully, a 'female friend') during one of Ward's absences on business.

[98]   See my entry on Jane Vigor in *New Dictionary of National Biography* (forthcoming, Oxford, 2004).

[99]   *MR*, 53 (1775), 211; *GM*, 45 (1775), 531.

[100]   John Nichols, *Literary Anecdotes of the Eighteenth Century* (9 vols, 1812–15), iii. 209.

persons she describes'.[101] As a diplomat's wife she entertained ambassadors, and worked tapestries with the Russian royal family. The tales related in the *Letters* – of enforced marriages, sudden deaths, insults, tortures and executions – build up a picture of a barbaric feudal culture within which the boorishness of Russian patriarchs contrasts oddly with the saintly stoicism and aristocratic elegance of their womenfolk (and, implicitly, with the more enlightened condition of British society). The 'Historical Notes' added – by whom is unclear – as footnotes to the *Letters* illuminate the Court's personal histories rather than Russia's political history (which by 1775 had been competently documented by male travel writers).[102] Nor is there much reference to topics such as climate, topography, or national character, Vigor remarking to her correspondent that 'you actually make me do things that fright me; for asking an account of a country, or the characters of people, of me, is as out of the way as to consult a minister of state about the making of your gown' (123).

Vigor's female correspondent is, rather unusually in travel writing, presented as a powerful shaping force within the *Letters*. She is unmarried, and courted by a Mr B— whom she teases and controls, rather like Anna Howe in Richardson's *Clarissa*. She is repeatedly invoked as a figure of self-control and masculine firmness, and as a foil to the tremulous and volatile emotional state of Jane Vigor herself, particularly in the letters recounting Mr Ward's illness and death, of which this passage is typical:

> your sentiments are so much above the weakness of human nature, that you can hardly allow affections the weakness, that will attend on those whose minds are formed for soft passions; for yours, though very humane, I look on as of the masculine kind, and when you are afflicted, you would scorn the womanish relief of tears. (52)

The opening letter of the volume establishes this peculiarly gendered relationship between Vigor and her correspondent (none of whose letters are actually reproduced):

> You, who are mistress of so much philosophy, are excusable for fancying that, now the ceremony of our reception is over, I may be composed enough to give you some account of the place my rambling planet has thrown me into; but for me, who have strong passions, and the inseparable companion of them, weak reason, I cannot so soon forget my friends and country, but am (notwithstanding the mask I wore before my departure) feeling

---

[101] *GM*, 45 (1775), 531.
[102] John Bell, *Travels from St Petersburgh in Russia to Divers Parts of Asia* (2 vols, Glasgow, 1763); John Cook, *Voyages and Travels through the Russian Empire, Tartary and Persia* (2 vols, Edinburgh, 1770).

those passions with a double force that were restrained in the fatal hour of separation. (1)

Ingeniously, Vigor here (and throughout the *Letters*) presents herself as frail, homesick and patriotic, passively acquiescing in the 'rambling' destiny to which her wifely devotion subjects her. In one of the 'Eleven Additional Letters' published in 1785, she admits to weeping at the 'pleasing reverie' of homecoming, but hastily conceals her emotion from Mr Ward, 'for if I cannot assist him, I am at least determined not to distress him' (17). In effect, she becomes the sentimental object of travel writing, rather than the inquiring and adventurous subject. We are reminded of Maria in *A Sentimental Journey* who, deranged by the loss of her lover, had 'stray'd as far as Rome, and walk'd round St Peter's once—and return'd back ... found her way alone across the Apennines—had travell'd over all Lombardy without money—and through the flinty roads of Savoy without shoes', inspiring Yorick to declare protectively that 'in all thy weaknesses and wanderings I would seek after thee and bring thee back'.[103] Perhaps uniquely amongst eighteenth-century women travel writers, Vigor becomes the central embodiment of delicate sensibility within her own text. In this way she obviates the need to insert tales of sentimental distress which would cast her in the role of detached observer (a role very much bound up with the kind of masculine responses described in the preceding chapter), and sanctifies the role of the travelling wife. In its obituary notice, the *Gentleman's Magazine* confides protectively that Vigor 'possessed a degree of sensibility, and a tenderness of feeling, approaching almost to weakness'.[104] As if to counter the up-beat resonances of her published surname, and the narrative confidence with which the historical anecdotes are related, her own 'weak mind and strong apprehensions' (92) are repeatedly stressed within her account. Given that she managed three marriages within ten years, her emphasis on her quivering need for British masculine protection may be seen as strategically defensive.[105]

---

[103] Laurence Sterne, *A Sentimental Journey through France and Italy* (1768), ed. Gardner D. Stout, Jr (Berkeley and Los Angeles, 1967), 115.

[104] *GM*, 53 (1783), 892.

[105] See Claudia Johnson, *Equivocal Beings: Politics, Gender and Sentimentality in the 1790s: Wollstonecraft, Radcliffe, Burney, Austen* (Chicago, 1995). Johnson makes a revisionist case for 'sensibility' as less the 'feminization' of culture than the 'masculinization' of formerly feminine gender traits, such that 'the affective practices associated with it are valued *not* because they are understood as feminine, but only insofar as they have been recoded as masculine. ... finally, only men have legitimate access to the discourse of the heart'. Therefore, women's 'affectivity' is represented as 'inferior, unconscious, unruly, or even criminal', and their chief function is to provoke affective response in the male subject (14).

If the resources of sentimental travel writing are mobilized in order to provide a moral sanction for Vigor's travelling and indeed writing, the masculine attributes of her inquisitive correspondent are also exploited to cater to the more traditional, empirical requirements of the genre. Vigor will often use one of her friend's queries ('your desires are to me commands', 167–8) to determine the subject of her letter: 'You ask me, how I spend my time? I'll give you a journal of one day' (36). Similarly, a question about religion prompts a discussion of Orthodox rituals (19). Repeatedly, her friend's insatiable desire for information on things Russian overcomes Vigor's own homesick apathy and self-confessed 'weakness'. Of course, this weakness is one of the *Letters'* great ideological strengths, testifying not only to their author's highly feminine personal qualities, but also to their nationally representative value, as encapsulated in an encounter with some visiting Chinese dignitaries at St Petersburg, who tell Mr Rondeau that:

> they thought that the English had been wiser than to suffer their
> wives to come out and be at liberty, but they were glad they had
> seen me, as they had never seen an Englishwoman before, and they
> knew I had love and courage to come so far from my own country
> for any man upon earth. (84–5)

Deftly here, as indeed throughout the *Letters from a Lady*, Vigor makes a moral strength out of her own passivity. The text's literary sophistication, with its debt not only to memoir writing but also to sentimental fiction, gives it a curiously androgynous texture, as the brisk and intelligent provision of courtly anecdote is counterbalanced by the cultivation of homesick virtue and reluctant heroism. Completely lacking the robustness, erudition, and sense of cultural relativity which had underpinned the enormous critical and commercial success of Montagu's *Embassy Letters*, the *Letters from a Lady* were, nonetheless, extremely well received, and their positive critical reception bears witness to the more wintry moral climate which was beginning to creep across the British literary scene.

The same is true of Anne Miller's *Letters from Italy*. Published in 1776, they were accorded significant review space and generous praise. The Editor's 'Preface' praises the 'artless, ingenuous narration' of the *Letters*, and observes that 'farther embellishment of style, apposite quotations, abundant illustrations, &c. &c. might have been supplied by the same pen, ... had such decorations seemed expedient, or a display of the author's reading been an object of publication' (i. vi). In fact, as the *Critical Review* rather patronizingly observes, Miller 'writes as a person even not unacquainted with the names and productions of some of the most celebrated Roman authors', thus simultaneously displaying her own education and keeping it in its place.[106] She frequently deprecates her subject matter as mere 'amusement' (i. 25), and claims that she is 'neither qualified nor inclined to descant upon the merits of ... government, laws, &c' (i. 26). In stark contrast to Montagu, she habitually inserts her husband's opinions on topics like politics, fortifications and architecture, and describes his conversations with the likes of Voltaire and d'Alembert, of which she persuades him 'to relate to me every word' (i. 24).

This mixture of diffident modesty and quiet superiority is characteristic of the *Letters*. Their anecdotal, opinionated, and sometimes self-dramatizing approach is justified on the grounds that it provides 'a more natural picture of the manners, &c. of the people represented, than the unanimated narrative of a meer spectator might have conveyed' (i. ix). This obeisance to the empirical traditions of the genre is belied, however, by Miller's almost novelistic rendering of the perils of travel, and her self-ironizing construction of a fastidious and housewifely traveller. Her descriptions of Italian inns and cuisine are masterly exercises in the humorous grotesque: 'a very bad supper, composed of liver and brains, (to what animal they had belonged, I do not pretend to decide)' (i. 60); 'a hog's head, with the eye-lashes, eyes, and nose on; the very food the wretched animal had last eat of before he made his *exit* remained sticking about the teeth ... Need I say we went to bed supperless?' (ii. 89–90). Sometimes, these descriptions simultaneously poke fun at the hapless travellers' squeamishness, and at her desperate efforts to maintain British standards of decency:

> The blanket—I scarce dare look at it; but when we are about lying down to sleep (if that be possible) I shall, by the means of an enormous pair of tongs, endeavour to drag it into the corner of the room, as far as possible from the bed. (ii. 184)

Anticipating *Northanger Abbey* by some twenty years (before, indeed, Radcliffe's Italianate horrors), Miller occasionally casts herself, with sophisticated literary humour, in the fearfully imaginative role which Austen was to give to Catherine Morland. On the night-boat to Venice she wakes her husband to deal with her terrible discovery, 'tall man hanging up, much embarrassed in a quantity of clothes'. M— approaches with pistols:

> but judge of my surprise, when it appeared that the groans and lamentations proceeded from the ropes by which we were towed; and the hanging man was nothing but a parcel of weeds which had collected and stuck about them. (iii. 241–2)

---

[106] *CR*, 41 (1776), 361.

Similarly, in the catacombs near Rome, M— wanders ahead with the guide, while his wife's skirt catches on an iron bar:

> Just God, said I, perhaps M— is assassinated, and the servant joined with the guide in the perpetration of the murder, and I am miraculously held fast by the dead, and shall never leave these graves ... I soon extricated myself, and walking forward, luckily in the right path, found M— who was quietly copying an inscription. (iii. 54–5)

As one might expect from a woman thus capable of ironizing melodramatic excess, Miller is thoroughly unsentimental and politically conservative. Her 'spirit of tenderness and benevolence' and her allegedly 'impartial and liberal' attitude to foreigners, celebrated in the *Letters'* 'Preface', are in fact extended only to those of rank and elegance, in whose circles the Millers are proud to move, having been supplied with 'recommendatory letters' from the Cardinal de Choisseul, and thus with a 'general and particular knowledge of customs and manners amongst the first people of the country' (i. 192–3). Entering a male monastery in the Apennines, she observes with pride that 'no woman had ever been received into this convent beside myself, excepting Christine Queen of Sweden, the present Empress of Hungary, and the Queen of Naples' (ii. 88).

Anne Miller's contempt for the oppressed peasantry of Roman Catholic Europe, 'prancing and grinning at one in their dirt, misery, and *sabots*' (i. 14) is constant, as is her celebration of 'liberty' as the necessary nutrient of 'every patriotic and social virtue' (i. 14). The 'shocking' and 'unnatural' practice of cicisbeism is wearily accepted as one of 'the unavoidable consequences of all arbitrary and despotic governments' (i. 420). And her professed anthropological interest is constrained by an insular and snobbish propriety: she refuses to sit at the table d'hôte with its 'great deal of company', pronouncing (with unfortunate echoes of Gulliver) that 'we had rather eat a crust of bread in the stable with the horses, than sit down with all sorts of people that one do not know' [*sic*] (i. 50–51). She relates that she and her husband are the only people who fail to kneel at the elevation of the host on Easter Day at St Peter's, despite a curious stare from the Pope himself (iii. 21), and despite having earlier praised the way in which travel eradicates 'many prejudices and littlenesses of thinking' (i. 421–2).

Miller's remarks upon paintings and sculpture were perhaps the most critically valued aspect of the *Letters from Italy* in 1776, not only because they provided a template for acts of aesthetic appreciation hitherto seen largely as the preserve of the dilettanti or the extravagant Grand Tourist, but also because of their invigorating moral tone. As mentioned earlier, she endorses the acts of violation committed in the name of censorship upon several erotic paintings by Guido. She assiduously avoids reference to anything remotely titillating in painting or sculpture, eschewing the fascination with naked statuary which would characterize the connoisseur. In Florence she and her husband take a sequence of meticulous measurements of the Venus de' Medicis, yet manage to avoid making any reference to its aesthetic (let alone erotic) qualities: 'round her throat, at the thickest part, twelve inches and an half; her face, from her chin-bone (not including her double chin) to the root of her hair, five inches and an half' (ii. 112). No measurements are recorded for anything below the waist or above the knee, Miller no doubt being keen to avoid the moral dubiety attributed for example by John Moore to women with pretensions to connoisseurship:

> Ladies, who have remained some time at Rome and Florence, particularly those who affect a taste for virtù, acquire an intrepidity and a cool minuteness, in examining and criticising naked figures, which is unknown to those who have never passed the Alps.[107]

Notwithstanding Miller's evident affinities with the hard-nosed patriotism and professional briskness displayed in the previous decade by the likes of Smollett and Sharp, the *Monthly Review* declares that the *Letters from Italy* 'discover a solid understanding, liberal sentiments, and a cultivated taste'.[108] By the standards which had applied to male travel writers during the controversial but not infrequently open-minded 1760s, and the increasingly sentimental 1770s, Miller's position is in fact rather intolerant and reactionary. But it does mean that she runs absolutely no risk of appearing morally dubious or politically suspect. Just as Vigor camouflages her literary energies with the cultivation of a vulnerable femininity, the 'air of originality' which the *Monthly Review* discerns in the *Letters from Italy* is nicely counterbalanced by the politically conservative discourse of continental depravity and British common sense.

This balance is not so easily struck by Hester Piozzi, due to personal circumstance as much as political inclination. Her travelogue and its critical reception recapitulates but also complicates many of the issues which this chapter has pursued. *Observations and Reflections Made in the Course of a Journey through France, Italy, and Germany* (2 vols, 1789) has high literary pretensions. Piozzi rejects the epistolary form adopted by most women travel writers: 'I have not thrown my thoughts into the form of private letters; because a work of which truth is the best recommendation, should not above all others begin with a lie' (i. vi). Instead, *Observations and Reflections* is divided into chapters of irregular length, headed with the name of the town or city Piozzi is describing. It seems that she is here emulating Johnson's procedure in *A*

---

[107] John Moore, *A View of Society and Manners in Italy* (2 vols, 1781), ii. 424–5.
[108] *MR*, 55 (1776), 105.

Journey to the Western Islands of Scotland (1775): the *Monthly Review* refers to her as 'a lady celebrated for her studies in the Johnsonian school'.[109] Habitually, a chapter will open with the party's arrival in a new place, move into general reflections on situation, architecture, and the character of the people, and conclude with a more anecdotal account of galleries, libraries, villas and churches, and of social engagements and acquaintances. Descriptive passages are laced with literary allusion – to British and Italian poets, to travel writers including Addison, Moore and Corke, and to ancient and modern historians. Comparison with the manuscript account of the journey, and with the relevant volumes of her journal, *Thraliana*, reveals that in many places the 'immediacy' one would expect to see actively cultivated in a travel book is in fact excized in the transition into print, as part of Piozzi's eschewal of 'the form of private letters' – remarks such as 'I write from my Bed to which I am at length arrived' and 'These Reflexions are interrupted by my Arrival on the Banks of the Rhône' are ruthlessly cut.[110] The published text arguably suffers also from the removal of various evocative remarks on the dangers of travel, such as 'we are now going thro' Prague, Dresden &c. a long – (& as they say) a dangerous Journey – God send us safe to the end of it'; and (leaving Prague), 'God send us safe to Dresden they say the Road is horrible'.[111]

The literary formality and stature invoked by Piozzi's revisions are, however, at odds with the informal, consciously feminine style of the *Observations*, which provoked what now seems a disproportionate amount of critical hostility. Mary Wollstonecraft in the *Analytical Review* attacks the mannered femininity of Piozzi's style: 'we find in her journey all the childish feminine terms, which occur in common novels and thoughtless chat, *sweet, lovely, dear dear*, and many other pretty epithets and exclamations'.[112] Although both the *Critical* and the *Monthly* acknowledge the charm and erudition of Piozzi's work, their stylistic critique is likewise severe. The *Critical* observes that

> The style, which we might have praised in letters, is disgusting in
> the author of more collected remarks; and the inaccuracies, which
> are excusable in these unpremeditated effusions, must be
> condemned in what appears to be a more serious attempt.[113]

Similarly, the *Monthly* attacks her 'low, coarse, and vulgar phraseology', her '*ones, nows, thoughs, hows, somehows, to be sures*', and condemns her 'violations of the laws of elegant writing' in a patronizing tone: 'her style ...

---

[109] *MR*, NS 1 (1790), 194.
[110] 'Italian Journey', 2ᵛ, 11. On the manuscript 'Journeys', see below, pages 175–6.
[111] 'German Journey', 23 ᵛ, 26 ᵛ.
[112] *AR*, 4 (1789), 301.
[113] *CR*, 68 (1789), 104.

resembles a lady partly dressed from her own splendid wardrobe, and partly from the trunk, box, or bundle, of the meanest of her female servants'.[114]

The moral tone of much of this criticism – evident in terms such as 'coarse, and vulgar', 'excessive vulgarisms', 'loose negligent undress' – is bound up with the widespread public disapproval of Mrs Thrale's remarriage, aged forty-three, to the Italian singer Gabriel Piozzi.[115] As William McCarthy has demonstrated, the composition of *Observations and Reflections* was motivated at least partly by the need publicly to vindicate this marriage. 'The pleasure she represents herself as taking in Italy is her answer to the Gothic rumour of her having been "locked in a convent"', and the recorded kindness of foreigners in *Observations and Reflections* is an implicit rebuke to the cruelty and rejection of friends and family in Britain.[116] In the 'Preface' to the published travel narrative, Piozzi expresses the hope that her countrymen's 'entertainment shall serve as a vehicle for conveying expressions of particular kindness to those foreign individuals, whose tenderness softened the sorrows of absence, and who eagerly endeavoured by unmerited attentions to supply the loss of their company on whom nature and habit had given me stronger claims' (i. iv). This is quietly subversive: the entertainment of the British is no more than a means to the end of complimenting her Italian hosts. In this passage, as so often in *Observations and Reflections*, Piozzi mediates between her conflicting loyalties. That she is well aware of the conflict is evident from an entry in *Thraliana* after her return to Britain: 'I will write my Travels & publish them— why not? 'twill be difficult to content the Italians & the English but I'll try—& tis something to do'.[117] Celebrating Italy in order to vindicate her marriage, she must also be careful not to alienate the British (book-buying and otherwise) public whom she needs to convince and win over, and into whose favour she is, to an extent, anxious to return. A comparison of the published *Observations and Reflections* both with *Thraliana* and with the manuscript journals which Hester Piozzi kept during the European journeys provides a telling insight into the processes of self-fashioning which lie behind *Observations and Reflections*, and which involve complex negotiations between national loyalties.

---

[114] *MR*, NS 1 (1790), 194–5.

[115] This, and Johnson's famous denunciation of the marriage, is well documented in James L. Clifford, *Hester Lynch Piozzi (Mrs Thrale)* (1941; repr. Oxford, 1987), 202–31: 235–92 cover the period of the European journeys.

[116] William McCarthy, *Hester Thrale Piozzi: Portrait of a Literary Woman* (Chapel Hill, NC, 1985), 159: 'locked in a convent' refers to a letter from Hester Piozzi to Lysons, 20 January 1785, in which she records that while in Italy she hears from London 'that Mr. Piozzi has shut me up in a convent' (McCarthy, 39, citing *Bentley's Miscellany*, 28 [1850], 164).

[117] *Thraliana: The Diary of Mrs Hester Lynch Thrale (Later Mrs Piozzi) 1776–1809*, ed. Katharine C. Balderston (2 vols, Oxford, 1942), ii. 717 (29 May 1788).

The relationship between *Thraliana* and the journals is intricate.[118] On 3 September 1784, after six weeks of married happiness, Mrs Piozzi writes an entry in *Thraliana* on the eve of their departure for the Continent, envisaging Italy as the telos of the whole journey – 'tomorrow I set off for the finest Country in the World, in Company with the most excellent Man in it' – and describing the parting, 'coldly, not unkindly', with her unspeakable daughter Queeney (ii. 611–12). The next entry in *Thraliana* is not until 23 September, and is written from Paris, 'where I have remained a fortnight' (ii. 613). The intervening period is covered in her first travel notebook, the 'Italian Journey', which starts at Dover on 5 September 1784. This notebook, together with a second describing their travels homeward from Italy, the 'German Journey', represents the first draft of *Observations and Reflections*.[119] From 23 September 1784 until 30 March 1785, the journal runs parallel with *Thraliana*, which duplicates the journal on only three occasions during this period.[120] The accounts in *Thraliana* are more informal and gossipy than the journals, and more excited and boastful about attention paid to herself and Piozzi. 'Goldoni dined here one day, and we struck Fire vastly well ... at Turin too I was kindly treated by the Prince della Cisterna who gave Mr Piozzi the Key of his Box at the Opera for me, and I used it all the Time we were there' (ii. 614). *Thraliana* also documents personal feelings and frustrations absent from the journals – 'Susanna & Sophia have written to me very *civilly indeed*; the eldest has been either sick or Sullen for her Handwriting have I not yet seen. tomorrow we set out for Lyons where perhaps some Letters may lye in the Post Office;—mean Time I have sent Acc^{ts} to England of every thing that has past, for they shall not say that *I* am wanting in *my* Duty—whether they think proper to perform theirs or no' (ii. 614).

On 6 April 1785 the Piozzis moved on from Milan, and Mrs Piozzi left her current volume of *Thraliana* behind, so that for some sixteen months the only record of the Italian tour is that of the 'Italian Journey' manuscript. On their return to Milan on 27 June 1786, *Thraliana* is resumed alongside continuing entries in the 'Italian Journey' for the rest of their stay in Milan, until 15 September 1786, when the fourth volume of *Thraliana* was used up. The Piozzis left Milan a week later for Northern Italy, Austria and Germany, and thence home through Northern France and the Low Countries. This journey is described in the second quarto notebook of Rylands English 618, which begins at Cremona on 22 September 1786 and ends at Lille in March 1787. *Thraliana*

---

[118] Volume ii of *Thraliana* covers 1784–1809 and thus all of the Piozzis' Continental journey during 1784–7.

[119] These two quarto notebooks are now in the John Rylands Library, shelfmark Rylands English MS 618. There are 168 folios in all. The 'Italian Journey' is 115 folios of written text, the 'German Journey' merely 50. The folios are written on both sides, but the rectos only are numbered.

[120] 23 September 1784 (Paris), 3 November 1784 (Genoa), 10 February 1785 (Milan).

is resumed in a fresh, fifth volume on 29 April 1787, 'at my new House here in Hanover Square', and opens with thankful relief, 'God Almighty having graciously preserved us through a Journey of four Thousand Miles' (ii. 678).

The editor of *Thraliana* observes that the 'German Journey' is 'less carefully written, and more impersonal' than the Italian; and the *Critical Review* judges that 'we meet with nothing very interesting to record' in the corresponding section of the published *Observations and Reflections*.[121] Far fewer alterations are made to the 'German Journey' than to the 'Italian' between manuscript and publication, and the 'Italian Journey' is greatly expanded for *Observations and Reflections*. Germany, we can deduce, not only offers fewer cultural attractions for Hester Piozzi, but poses fewer ideological problems.

There is some overlap between *Thraliana* and the journals. Piozzi often refines anecdotal material from *Thraliana* into the journal manuscripts. Much material is transposed and refined between the manuscript and the published *Observations*, although the manuscripts are in fact remarkably polished; they are clearly envisaged, from their earliest stages, as the draft of a travel book rather than a casual journal. *Observations and Reflections* is more punctiliously paragraphed; and thematically organized paragraphs are frequently expanded with erudite secondary material, descriptive colouring, and additional moral reflections which can only be described as Johnsonian. Some passages in the published text, usually objective accounts of towns or cities, have no manuscript source.[122]

If Johnson is a stylistic model for *Observations and Reflections*, and indeed for the manuscript journals, his personal influence in Hester Piozzi's life is quite explicitly repudiated in the manuscript (he actually died while she was in Italy, on 13 December 1784). She writes in Paris on 18 September 1784:

> This is Dr Johnson's Birthday: may God give him many & happy returns of it; we used to spend these two Days in Mirth & Gayety at Streatham: but Pride & Prejudice hindered my longer Residence in a Place wch indeed had lost its Charms for me—I am happier at this Moment than I have been these Two & Twenty Years.[123]

And a little later she announces that:

> I shall let loose however in this Journey the Fondness for Painting which I was forced to suppress while Dr Johnson lived with me, & ridiculed my Taste of an Art his own Imperfect Sight hindered him from enjoying.[124]

---

[121] *Thraliana*, ii. 677; *CR*, 68 (1989), 111.
[122] For example, the account of Ferrara and most of the description of Bologna.
[123] 'Italian Journey', 6^v.
[124] 'Italian Journey', 8.

Not surprisingly, there is nothing this unguarded in *Observations and Reflections*. Nevertheless, the *Critical Review* for one shrewdly discerns a personal subtext to the public version of Piozzi's journey:

> We once quoted Dr. Johnson's admirable farewel letter to his 'Thralia:' it enjoined her not to quit England; not to live in Italy. We have thought, more than once, that these volumes formed a laboured answer to it. Notwithstanding heat and cold; scorpions, gnats, and beetles; the offensive smells on one side, and the parched grounds, pointed out by the lively pleasure expressed at seeing occasional verdure on the other, every thing is charming.[125]

Perhaps the most striking discrepancies between *Thraliana* and *Observations and Reflections* occur in their respective accounts of Italian religion and (im)morality. *Thraliana* contains several passages of appalled, almost hysterical reaction to Italian mores; none of these diatribes gets as far as the published version. For example:

> All I ever heard, and much more than ever I heard concerning the depraved Morals & confined Ideas of Religion reigning in this Country, are terribly true. The *Cavalieri Serventi* are indispensible, and the whole Nation adapts itself with great Composure to a settled Scheme of Vice, a System of Adultery.[126]

In *Observations and Reflections*, the remarks on cicisbeism are of a much milder cast:

> Well! we will not send people to Milan to study delicacy or very refined morality to be sure; but were the crust of British affectation lifted off many a character at home, I know not whether better, that is *honester*, hearts would be found under it ... God forbid that I should prove an advocate for vice; but let us remember, that the banishment of all hypocrisy and deceit is a vast compensation for the want of *one great virtue*. (i. 101–2)

Several more extreme passages of vitriol, including accounts of the homosexual debaucheries of the Italian clergy, disappear completely from the published account.[127] 'Could I but separate my Piozzi from these *Goats*!', she exclaims at one point;[128] but she is obviously aware that in the eyes of the British reading public, one Italian is much the same as another, and so overt criticism of Italian excess is unwise in her particular circumstances. Her

---

[125] *CR*, 68 (1768), 103.
[126] *Thraliana*, ii. 635–6. Similar sentiments are expressed at ii. 640.
[127] See, for example, *Thraliana* ii. 637–8, 640, 655–6.
[128] *Thraliana*, ii. 638.

husband is strangely absent from *Observations and Reflections*, although 'Mr Piozzi' and his opinions and activities are quite often referred to in the manuscript journals as well as in *Thraliana*. He is frequently written out of the published text; for example, we learn from the 'Italian Journey' that 'The State of Musick in Italy at present does not please Mr. Piozzi whose taste ought to regulate mine'; but in *Observations and Reflections*, anonymity prevails: 'The state of music in Italy, if one may believe those who ought to know it best, is not what it was'.[129] Anne Miller could deflect criticism of her travelling activities by stressing that she was accompanying her husband, whose judgements she quotes and defers to: but the unpatriotic light in which Hester Piozzi's second marriage was widely viewed makes such a strategy unavailable.

Most of the anti-Italian indignation of *Thraliana* is absent even from the manuscript journals, although there are brief outbursts even here – 'This is indeed a Country every way favorable to those who deserve hanging, for they enjoy a moral certainty of never being hanged.'[130] This comment does not appear in the published text. As an alternative to outright excision, Piozzi will sometimes copy an unfavourable sentiment from manuscript into published text, but will put it into the mouth of someone else (usually an Italian), as when her description of Padua as a 'very stinking nasty town' is imputed to an Italian professor of astronomy.[131] Thus, whereas *Observations and Reflections* cultivates a tolerant cultural relativity, the manuscript journals and *Thraliana* reveal an edgy sense of absolute national, and especially religious, difference, brought into sharper focus for Piozzi by the knowledge that her husband's compatriots must privately consider her a heretic.

Significantly, in both private and public accounts, Italian culture is presented most positively when its secular and sociable pleasures, rather than its religious aspect, are to the fore. The overwhelming hospitality of Venetian and Milanese society provoke an enthusiastic warmth more conventionally associated with the traveller's feelings for their native country. Returning to Milan after a lengthy tour of Italy, Piozzi pens the following rhapsody, published in *Observations and Reflections*:

> after an absence of fifteen months, we shall again see those acquaintance with whom we lived much before; a sensation always delightfully soothing, even when one returns to less amiable scenes, and less productive of innocent pleasure than these have been to me. The consciousness of having, while at a distance, seen few people more agreeable than those one left behind; the natural thankfulness of one's heart to God, for having preserved one's life

---

[129] 'Italian Journey', 35ᵛ; *Observations and Reflections*, i. 177–8.
[130] 'Italian Journey', 55ᵛ.
[131] 'Italian Journey', 29ᵛ; *Observations and Reflections*, i. 143–4.

so as to see them again, expands philanthropy; and gives
unaffected comfort in the restored society of companions long
concealed from one by accident or distance. (ii. 203)

This is the language of heartfelt homecoming, and is conspicuous by its
absence from the actual 'homecoming' at the end of the published text.
Observations and Reflections concludes with some reflections on 'the general
effect travelling has upon the human mind' (ii. 386), followed by some
doggerel verses composed in the inns at Calais and Dover. These provide a
curiously displaced and mocking version of the 'return to Dover' topos, and
conclude feebly:

> But he alone's his country's lover,
> Who, absent long, returns to Dover,
> And can by fair experience prove her
> The best he has found since last at Dover. (ii. 389)

The presentation of patriotic feeling in *Observations and Reflections* is,
then, subdued, conventional, at times parodic. In *Thraliana*, and in the
manuscript journals, the problematic and contradictory nature of Piozzi's
patriotism finds expression.[132] A passing reference in the 'Italian Journey' to
'the difference of Manners between this Nation [France] and that I left behind'
suggests a startling objectivity. Elsewhere, her feelings for England are directly
interrogated:

> Why do I not sigh to return where Liberty & Virtue hold their
> Residence? Why do I not rejoyce in the notion of kissing my
> Mother Country once again?—Yet I do not *now* as formerly, feel a
> *fondness* for England: Esteem and Preference over evry other
> Place is all that's left. I shall be half sorry in earnest to leave these
> rascally Italians—prying, pilfering, and paltry as they are—but tis
> the natural Horror of *the last*—I may perhaps not live to see them
> again.[133]

Volume iv of *Thraliana* closes just before the Piozzis are to leave Milan, and
she writes that no days since she begun *Thraliana* (in 1776) 'have been so
happily spent by me as those I have past in this beautiful Country' (ii. 676).
Nevertheless, anticipating their return to England, she admits that

---

[132] McCarthy, 162, suggests that a further complication to Piozzi's sense of national
identity is offered by her Welsh ancestry and childhood.
[133] *Thraliana*, ii. 662. C.f. *Idler*, 103 (5 April 1760), 'There are few things not purely
evil, of which we can say, without some emotion of uneasiness, "this is the last"', in
Samuel Johnson, *'The Idler' and 'The Adventurer'*, ed. W. J. Bate, John M. Bullitt and
L. F. Powell (New Haven, 1963), 314.

> I wish Mr Piozzi may like that Country to fix in, because it is *my* Country: & the Religion & Government is such as I approve. These Individuals have indeed treated me better than those at home, & I hope to be always grateful—yet I *know* that their Respect is all paid to my *Birth, Talents, & Behaviour*; while they consider & lament my Soul as forfeited to eternal Punishment:—I therefore feel a secret Uneasiness in their Company, especially that of the old bigotted Priests, whose Tears spring to their Eyes very often while they think so much Excellence forsooth devoted to Destruction—and make me obliged, afflicted, & disgusted all at once. (ii. 676–7)

Taken together or separately, *Observations and Reflections, Thraliana* and the manuscript journals present no coherent picture of national feeling or loyalty. This is partly because Hester Piozzi's own national status is complicated by her marriage, but also because her experience and literary rendering of travel problematize the very concepts of 'home' and 'happiness'. This is most explicit perhaps in the manuscript journal and *Thraliana*, where reflections on private circumstances override considerations of national belonging. At Leghorn, for example, the narrator of *Observations and Reflections* comments that 'Here we are by the sea-side once more, in a trading town too; and I should think myself in England almost, but for the difference of dresses that pass under my balcony' (i. 351). This neutral observation is very different from its original form: 'Here we are by the seaside once more, and I should think myself in England, if I did not feel happier than I had felt myself in that Island for Years before I left it'.[134]

Like the references to Johnson, this allusion to deep personal unhappiness during her marriage to Thrale is patently not suitable for public consumption. Without these admissions, however, the cultural neutrality and elevated generalizations of *Observations and Reflections* have an air of contrivance. The private complications involve conflicting national loyalties; the public version retreats into commonplace and convention. *Observations and Reflections* presents a citizen of the world, whereas *Thraliana* and the manuscript journals present a distinctively homeless narrative self, whose deracination opens up new perspectives and freedoms as well as problems. Not until Mary Wollstonecraft's Scandinavian *Letters* appeared in 1796, however, were these new and disorientating possibilities fully realized. Between Piozzi's *Observations and Reflections* and Wollstonecraft's *Letters* stand the momentous events of the French Revolution, the textual representations of which in British travel writing testify to the increasingly problematic set of relationships between nation, class and individual, in all of which gender is a complicating factor. The following chapter takes us into the Revolutionary era.

---

[134] 'Italian Journey', 47^v.

Chapter 5

Revolution and revision: the 1790s

Travellers who formerly visited France, either to investigate living manners, or explore the remains of former times; nay, even that less meditating race, who went thither in search of mere amusement; have all had their attention turned at present in that country, to the study of politics; a study which they almost find necessary, to secure their personal safety: and the same motives that have induced others, incited me also to observe the various phenomena presented by the intellectual volcano, now in eruption there.

This opening paragraph of Thomas Ford Hill's *Observations on the Politics of France*, published in 1792, captures not only the overwhelming impact of the French Revolution on British public life, but also the way in which events in France necessitated a rigorous reworking of the discourse of travel, such that 'the study of politics' replaced 'living manners', the 'remains of former times', and 'amusement' as central to the experience and the textual representation of travel in France. Political awareness was forced upon even the most uninterested of travellers ('to secure their personal safety'); and many more flocked to France to observe the 'great and sudden enterprise' of the revolutionaries.[1] Surprising numbers of Britons continued to make Continental trips during the Revolution and war, giving the lie to claims that 'intercourse with the continent, for excursions of pleasure, is almost cut off'.[2] As Hill somewhat ironically comments, 'the danger of visiting France was loudly proclaimed by popular rumour' (3). It was of course possible for British travellers during the 1790s to bypass France and explore other areas of Europe (as outlined in Chapter 1), but even evasive re-orientations would inevitably require some form of textual engagement with the situation in France, which had radically altered the cultural and ideological map of British travel.

As Hill's remarks suggest, a new seriousness becomes virtually de rigueur in travel writing after 1789. There are two main reasons for this. Firstly, the travel writer is increasingly required to function also as a journalist and political commentator, in order to cater for the intense public thirst for information on the French Revolution. The responsibility of accurate reportage may weigh heavily on travel writers, but also enables them to claim an empirical and ethical superiority to the voluminous body of Revolutionary polemic written without benefit of actually being in France. Secondly, individualism and

---

[1] *MR*, 81 (1789), 372.
[2] Robert Gray, *Letters during the Course of a Tour through Germany, Switzerland, and Italy* (1794), iv.

eccentricity become increasingly dubious, rapidly turning into qualities which radical writers would deem frivolous and reactionary writers subversive. The travel writer's nationally representative responsibilities come to the fore, and personal oddities are displaced by the requirements of intellectual and ethical reliability. This chapter will describe the aesthetic and ideological impact of this new emphasis on absolute dependability within travel writing, and some of the discernible changes in structure and narrative motif which accompanied this shift. In particular, the motif of revision is increasingly deployed by writers, allowing them to describe not only changes in authorial opinion, but also more profound reconstitutions of personal and national identity. These developments in travel writing, significant enough in their own right, are also of interest in that they provided, I shall argue, an influential paradigm for Wordsworth's use of return and revision in *The Prelude*. Related to the prominence of revision in texts describing the Revolution is a growing tendency on the part of authors and reviewers to stigmatize the kind of narrative eccentricity which travel writers had creatively deployed in previous decades: this devaluing of authorial oddity will be briefly delineated before moving on to a discussion of travelogues by women (both radical and reactionary) during the 1790s, in which the increasingly fraught implications of gender are seen powerfully to intersect with the other ideological and narrative pressures under consideration here.

'These turbulent times': from reportage to revision

In 1796 even the reactionary William Hunter (who echoes Burke's regret for the 'age of chivalry' and laments that the game on the Prince of Condé's estate has been 'totally destroyed' by the 'blind fury of the multitude'),[3] sees fit to introduce his two-volume account of a journey through Eastern Europe with over 100 pages on the present situation of France, and later explains how:

> I have purposely avoided entering into a minute account of palaces, and pictures, and public buildings, which have been already so frequently and so accurately described. On the political state of the country, I have been more ample, for it is a subject replete with novelty and wonder, and has aroused the attention and surprise of every civilized nation. (i. 124–5)

Hunter's ploy – more a means of selling copies than evidence of genuine interest in French politics – illustrates the intense thirst for information on French affairs which continued throughout the 1790s, although Britain and

---

[3]   William Hunter, *Travels in the Year 1792 through France, Turkey, and Hungary, to Vienna* (2 vols, 1796), i. 40; 27.

France were at war for many of these years. Even once war has broken out, the *Monthly Review* refers to France as 'a country, in whose concerns we are so deeply involved', and laments the 'very little communication which we have of late had' across the Channel.[4] It is worth noting at this point that the three main Reviews are liberal in their outlook on French affairs, despite a period of disappointed revulsion when it becomes clear that the Revolution is not to be bloodless. Broadly speaking, the *Monthly*, *Critical*, and *Analytical* remain pro-Revolution, and anti-war, throughout the 1790s. Hence the new *Anti-Jacobin Review* in 1798 announces its intention to '*review* the *Monthly*, *criticise* the *Critical*, and *analyse* the *Analytical*', since 'the channels of criticism have long been corrupted'.[5]

Booksellers and travel writers alike responded prolifically to the demand for material describing France, a demand fuelled by the incessantly changing state of affairs there, described by one travel writer as 'so violent and unexpected, that imagination cannot keep pace with them'.[6] One of the earliest texts to capitalize on the compelling nature of Revolutionary events was the anonymous *Six Days Tour in Normandy, from the 19th to the 25th of July, 1789; with a Short Account of Havre de Grace, Caen, and Cherbourg, the Popular Tumults at those Places* (1789). Our author claims to have set off in all innocence of the momentous events in Paris during July 1789. He presents himself as a learned and rather abstracted traveller, keenly interested in fortifications and antiquities (particularly inscriptions), who becomes caught up in the spread of disturbance and revolt. Although his title indicates the peculiarly apt timing of the expedition, the narrative insists on how accidental and indeed inconvenient was this coincidence with the French Revolution. The *Six Days Tour* describes an evocative sequence of incidents which signal the early stages of revolution: the author's ignorance of what is to follow gives the text a strange air of understatement.

The author and his companion conduct their sightseeing regardless of the public excitement and tumult, visiting naval installations and churches especially. Static details of touristic observation – for example the number of bells in the tower of the citadel at Caen – sit oddly with more dynamic moments of journalistic reportage – the ringing of the bells to announce a call '*aux armes*' (81). The travellers are slightly peeved at the inconveniences caused by the birth pangs of the Revolution: 'We could not see the *Hotel de Ville*, it being then in use for the meetings of the citizens. – On the outside of it

---

[4]   *MR*, NS 20 (1796), 62.
[5]   'Prospectus' for the *Anti-Jacobin Review*; and *Anti-Jacobin Review*, 1 (1798), 58. See Derek Roper, 'The Politics of the "Critical Review", 1756–1817', *Durham University Journal*, NS 22 (1960–61), 117–22.
[6]   James Edward Smith, *A Sketch of a Tour on the Continent in the Years 1786 and 1787* (3 vols, 1793), i. xxix.

is in *Alto Relievo* – a large equestrian figure in stone' (84). The narrator complains that their attention to such objects has been 'so distracted by the uncommonly extraordinary variety of incidents we have been witnesses to' (85), and apologizes for his incomplete account of Cherbourg, which he had to compile from memory after their visit: 'the description will proceed from recollection merely, for I did not think it prudent to make any memorandums whatsoever in writing, while on the spot, as it might have been attended with danger in these turbulent times especially' (119–20).

Few such qualms afflicted the redoubtable Arthur Young, whose *Travels in France* were published in 1792, but described journeys undertaken during 1787–9. Whereas Young's earlier 'Farmer's Tours' around the British Isles had appealed also to the general reader through offering descriptions of Claudean landscapes and 'the beauties of art and nature', such interests are replaced in the French *Travels* by 'political economy' as the main rival to Young's agricultural preoccupations. This move towards the utilitarian incorporates a rejection of the high-cultural aspects of Continental travel (and anything which might resonate of the aristocratic Grand Tour): more centrally, however, it testifies to the increasingly journalistic slant of travel writing at this time. The *Monthly Review* pronounces the work 'an extraordinary one. The *scene* of inquiry is the first in Europe; and the *time* is one of the most interesting that the world ever knew'.[7] Young himself is aware of the journalistic value of his observations:

> While I remain at Paris, I shall see people of all descriptions, from the coffee-house politicians to the leaders in the states; and the chief object of such rapid notes as I throw on paper, will be to catch the ideas of the moment; to compare them afterwards with the actual events that shall happen, will afford amusement at least. (103)

In Paris, he can follow the progress of the Revolution, which is effectively a closed book to him in the provinces, due to the almost total lack of newspapers, and the 'general ignorance of what is passing' (150).

Even despite the delay in publication until 1792 (for reasons of ill health), the *Analytical Review* values Young's documentation of the Revolution, 'at a time when every information concerning France is valuable, both on account of the actual state of the kingdom, and the probable connexion which, if established, we hope will long and happily subsist between her and Great Britain'; and the *Monthly Review* recommends the *Travels* to 'the most serious

---

[7]   *MR*, NS 10 (1793), 290. Contrast Edmund Burke's preference for the 'farmer and physician' over the 'professor of metaphysics': 'What is the use of discussing a man's abstract right to food or to medicine? The question is upon the method of procuring and administering them' (*Reflections on the Revolution in France* [1790], ed. Conor Cruise O'Brien [Harmondsworth, 1986], 151–2).

attention of the rising Republic; to whom, also, we (as citizens of the world,) think, in the same sincerity, its author might be of essential service, in assisting to establish a suitable system of *Political Economy*'.[8] As Marilyn Butler has observed, the *Travels* represent 'the rational optimism about the Revolution that was common among educated British people before the middle of 1792', and the rapid publication of second and third editions (in expensive quarto) testifies to the prestige of Young's account.[9] Just a year later, in stark contrast, Young's *The Example of France, A Warning to Britain*, published on 26 February 1793, epitomizes that moment when middle-class liberal opinion 'ceased to view the new French government benevolently once its activities threatened property'.[10] Burke wrote to congratulate Young on the pamphlet.

It was a departure for Young (one of the most prolific writers of travelogues describing the British Isles) to resort to polemical pamphleteering. That he did so underlines the sense of urgency surrounding the French Revolution and, especially, its implications for domestic stability. As Young's own career illustrates, travel writing at this time exists in implicit dialogue with other more polemical texts. Travel writers often explicitly challenge the authority of the numerous political tracts and pamphlets which responded to and fuelled the British obsession with the Revolution. Young himself emphasizes in *The Example of France* that he has previously 'resided a good deal in France during the progress of the Revolution' (2), thus reminding readers of his authoritative eye-witness status. Just as authoritative is Young's confession to having been 'for some time, a warm friend' (2) to the Revolution, which sets up a personal history of revised sympathies as a paradigm for his class and nation.

In the Reviews, lengthy accounts of Burke, Paine, and Price jostle for space with reviews of recent travelogues. The high empirical (and ethical) value of eye-witness travel accounts of France is frequently stressed, not least by the writers of such accounts, who will often draw pointed contrasts between their own texts and the numerous polemics published on the French Revolution without their authors having stirred from British shores. In 1798, Mary Wollstonecraft in the *Analytical Review* welcomes Major Tench's *Letters written in France, to a Friend in London, between the Month of November 1794, and the Month of May 1795*. These describe his experiences as a prisoner of war after being captured off the northern French coast, and somewhat clumsily capitalize on the novelty value of his predicament ('Deprived as you are in England of all communication with this country, except through the circuitous route of Switzerland and Germany, I often hear you ask me, What are the present politics and sentiments of the French?' [164], is a characteristic

---

[8]   *AR*, 14 (1792), 361; *MR*, NS 10 (1793), 290.
[9]   Marilyn Butler ed., *Burke, Paine, Godwin, and the Revolution Controversy* (1984; repr. Cambridge, 1988), 96–7.
[10] Butler ed., *Burke, Paine, Godwin, and the Revolution Controversy*, 102–3.

rhetorical gesture). Wollstonecraft nevertheless admires Tench's 'agreeable and unaffected style', and the integrity of his observations, in which he is 'for the most part, personally concerned'.[11] She observes that 'our means of information' on France 'have of late been very inadequate to our curiosity' and continues with some sarcasm (she herself had of course witnessed much of the Revolution at first hand):

> Our *regular* tour writers, shut out by the war, and the jealousy of both governments, have been unable, like Mr. Burke, to find France upon the map; and have been forced to leave the rich mine to be partially explored by interlopers, whom the fortune of war, or some other casualty, has cast upon the coast.[12]

Five years earlier, in the opening paragraphs of the anonymous *A Tour through the Theatre of War*, published in 1793, travel writing had been confidently privileged over political rhetoric in order to qualify the image of the revolutionaries which prevails in Britain:

> I had heard so much of a petty faction lording it over a mighty nation; I had heard so much of a band of ragamuffins driving before them the most powerful, and best disciplined armies in Europe; I had heard so much of all religion being destroyed, because all religions were tolerated, that I could not help feeling a wish to visit the seat of these supposed wonders, and to see if such things really were. No stranger to the manners, the language, and the customs of the French, and not totally destitute of acquaintance in the provinces that have been so lately the theatre of war, I thought I might be as good a judge of the spirit, and resources of the French nation, as many who undertake to decide upon the subject, without having ever set a foot in France. (*A Tour*, 1–2)

The ethical integrity of *A Tour* is frequently underlined in sympathetic accounts of the author's encounters with both protagonists and victims of Revolutionary events. Encountering a 'colony of French emigrants' at Dover, he insists that 'All consideration of their deserts laid aside, my heart bled for them' (3). British sympathy is here presented as bountiful and impartial; the writer's support for the revolutionaries throughout the ensuing text is therefore more powerful. A similar position of even-handed British humanity is adopted by Thomas Ford Hill, who encounters some emigrants at Coblentz, and confides that 'Though by principle, as a politician, no great friend to their cause; I could not help, as a man, feeling pity for their sufferings' (*Observations*, 19).

---

[11]   *AR*, 24 (1796), 243.
[12]   *AR*, 24 (1796), 238.

The ability to balance political and humanitarian considerations is perhaps intended, albeit subtly, as a rebuke to French extremism: the author of *A Tour* expresses regret for the 'desperate' and 'bloody' excesses of the Revolution (50) whilst finding it understandable that 'a people treated like brutes for so many centuries, should become like brutes when they break their chain' (148). More positively, he reports that, along with poverty, national prejudice has been virtually eradicated by the Revolution:

> The name of Englishman commands respect. Every body we met with at their public tables were eager to treat us with distinguished attention. It seemed as if our fellow claim to freedom, and our honourable neutrality, had made us brothers. And, indeed, I soon found myself dubbed a citizen. (13–14)

Similarly, Thomas Ford Hill observes that 'The name of Englishman has all the weight it ever possessed; or rather a great additional one, connected with the newly adopted ideas of liberty', and that recent changes in the French national character bring it closer to that of the English, as it acquires 'that freedom and dignity which was wanting to compleat it' (*Observations*, 10–11). The author of *A Tour* describes how the French 'national character of politeness' which has too often been combined with 'frivolous flippancy' is being replaced with republican 'severity', bringing the French and English national characters closer together (89–90), not least in the more intense masculinity now evident within the French army:

> The small sword, that formerly dangled at the side of the French officers and soldiers, has resigned its place to a weighty sabre. ... Their hair, for the most part cut short, is in the state nature gave it; and many of their whiskers grow unchecked by the razor. (90–91)

The innate virtue of the French, contrary to popular report of their 'disregard to all laws, human and divine' (and to what one might expect from their frightening phallic sabres), is symbolized for the author by their 'conduct in regard to our nation ... Both at Gravelines and Dunkirk, we found the English nuns excepted from the general proscription, living unmolested, and in the enjoyment of their usual revenue' (20). He criticizes the arrogance of 'us Britons', who 'have a special privilege for judging better of what passes all over the world, than all the world beside' (143), pronounces that 'the idea many people in England entertain, of a small faction domineering it over a whole nation, was totally destitute of foundation' (55), and devotes several pages to an examination of the Parisians' severe provocations to regicide. He invokes a rational, universalizing sympathy, which is both prompted and strengthened by his status as an eye-witness, and which seems an explicit challenge to Burke's stigmatization of universal philanthropy. He ends the *Tour* as he began, by stressing the integrity of journalistic travel writing; his 'own observation' is sarcastically contrasted with 'revelation' and 'men inspired' (131), and the political rhetoric of Burke and his ilk is condemned as irresponsible demonizing:

> It may, perhaps, be safer in this Christian land, for the man who rejoiced that there were prisons for the libellers of a Queen, to libel a whole nation, and to advise the cutting of his fellow creatures throats from generation to generation, than it is for another to inculcate charity to our neighbours, by a candid statement of facts, and demonstrable truth. But as my tour induced me to relate the things I saw, and as these things led me naturally to the reflections that accompany the mention of them, I defy reproach ... (148)

The author's high moral tone, here attributable to the perceived superiority of travelogue to armchair polemic, is also bound up with his long-standing knowledge of the French. To recall his opening paragraph, he insists with deliberate understatement that he is 'No stranger to the manners, the language, and the customs of the French, and not totally destitute of acquaintance in the provinces that have been so lately the theatre of war' (2). We detect here – and in other travel narratives – an implicit challenge and response to the celebrated passage in Burke's *Reflections* in which his extremely distant memory of Marie Antoinette is poetically invoked to explain the moral outrage with which he describes the assault on the French royal family: 'It is now sixteen or seventeen years since I saw the queen of France, then the dauphiness, at Versailles; and surely never lighted on this orb, which she hardly seemed to touch, a more delightful vision'.[13] As if in response to this chronologically etiolated (and indeed imprecise – 'sixteen or seventeen') nostalgia, a striking number of travel writers, conservative and radical, interleave past and present visits to France, or frame their accounts with retrospective self-criticism so as to bolster the validity of their observations.

Thomas Ford Hill informs his reader at the outset of *Observations on the Politics of France* in 1792 that he has visited France before, six years ago (3); his account gains extra force from the contrasts he draws between ancien régime and republican France. Early on, he notices the improved condition of roads, inns, building and cultivation, and the changed character of the French:

> The French, whose insipid levity had formerly disgusted me, appeared from what I had then seen, so respectable, so rationally patriotic; that, prejudiced already in favour of the Government of Liberty, I almost dared to hope the common good was really become the aim of every individual ... (10–11)

---

[13]   Burke, *Reflections*, 169.

It is instructive to compare this with an observation William Hunter records in 1792. Hunter has likewise visited France before, but his comparison flatly contradicts Hill's:

> that gaiety of heart, which had so long been the enviable characteristic of Frenchmen, was no longer apparent. A thoughtfulness, an anxiety, was visible in every countenance, and the effects which proceed from uncertainty, poverty, and distress, were openly betrayed.[14]

The difference which Hill, however, perceives, between the Paris of former times and its present state, provokes a more sober meditation on the complex and momentous nature of the revolution:

> The antient spendor of the metropolis of France, existed no more. The scenes which used to swarm with crouds of the wealthy and the gay, were become empty, or filled with people of an opposite description. ... The crouds of brilliant carriages, which used to fly and flutter through the streets of Paris, had vanished. (*Observations*, 39–40)

This nostalgic regret, and the vocabulary of sparkle and illusion, is quite Burkean, invoking with deliberately revisionist intention passages from the *Reflections* like Burke's lament for 'All the pleasing illusions, which made power gentle, and obedience liberal', or 'all the arts that beautify and polish life'.[15] In Hill's account, the palaces are emptied, the churches and convents turned into 'club rooms and theatres', and the 'absence of the rich' promotes a strange quietness. Paris 'was changed from brilliant splendor to gloomy mediocrity ... Paris had evidently sacrificed herself for the general good' (40–42). Again, there is an echo of the *Reflections*, this time more obviously dissident, as Hill reworks Burke's contention that 'France has not sacrificed her virtue to interest; but she has abandoned her interest, that she might prostitute her virtue'.[16]

---

[14] Hunter, *Travels in the Year 1792*, i. 14. In a similar vein is his description of Marie Antoinette's sadly altered appearance, which he is glad not to have witnessed at first-hand, 'since I saw her many years ago, when she was still in the zenith of beauty, when she was the admiration and delight of every beholder' (i. 39).

[15] Burke, *Reflections*, 171; 236.

[16] Burke, *Reflections*, 124. More radical still is the now notorious passage from Helen Maria Williams's *Letters from France* in which she declares that 'living in France at present, appears to me somewhat like living in a region of romance. Events the most astonishing and marvellous are here the occurrences of the day ... I sometimes think that the age of chivalry, instead of being past for ever, is just returned' (*Letters from France* [8 vols, 1792–5], ii. 4–5).

The author of *A Tour through the Theatre of War* likewise invokes Burke in order to refute the gendered nostalgia of the *Reflections*, in the following passage:

> The officers in whose company we were supping were very different from those I had been used to live with in France. Oh! What a falling off was there! When I heard how profanely vulgar was their conversation, and saw the coarseness of their manners, I could not help regretting, for a moment, with Mr. Burke, that the days of chivalry were over, that the unbought grace of life was gone. But when I reflected that they had been chosen by their comrades for their good conduct, and military qualities; when I had noticed the honourable marks of bravery many of them bore about their persons, and had listened to their relations of some well fought days, I thought that the brilliant tinsel of outward show, was well compensated by this solid merit. (36–7)

This passage, like those in which Hill registers a sense of cultural loss finally outweighed by moral gain, testifies to the radical alteration of the British experience of France, here deemed 'for the general good'.

In Hill's *Observations*, the movement of the narrative embodies these conflicting responses of excitement and loss. Early on, in the northern provincial cities, a new political utopia of classical stature seems to have emerged: 'I heard the public affairs debated with so much seeming attention to the general benefit ... that I almost conceived myself transported into the Republic of Plato' (12). This euphoria continues as Hill journeys briskly towards Paris, finding copious evidence of improvement in the French countryside. Once in Paris, however, the linear narrative of the journey is replaced by a less structured, more miscellaneous account of shifting opinions, and changes in day-to-day living. Paragraphs describing parts of the city, social groupings, buildings and politics, rumour and reportage, make up a patchwork of confused observation and hearsay. Revolution, it becomes increasingly clear, is a complex process and a mixed blessing. Hill's own early enthusiasm for the Revolution is, in fact, qualified by the retrospective nature of the narration. Having described his elation at the apparent transformation of the French national character, he adds a qualifier: 'Subsequent experience has indeed convinced me, that the warmth of a first impression had heated my imagination beyond the limits of sober truth' (11), here invoking the dichotomous frame of reference – manly common sense set against fanciful seduction – frequently applied to the Paine–Burke opposition, as in the *Analytical Review*'s assertion that Paine's 'plain, but forcible' style 'carries us away with him by the invincible energy of truth and sense', whereas 'Mr. B. delights the imagination by the splendour of his ornaments' and 'seduces us along by the charms of his

eloquence'.[17] Hill remains, however, convinced of the 'essential advantage' of
the French Revolution (11), and archly signals his own continuing radicalism
by observing that 'such is the force of our Antigallican antipathy, even liberty
itself is going out of fashion in England, because it has found favour in
France!' (65).

Less than a year after Hill's *Observations* appeared, Richard Twiss
published *A Trip to Paris, in July and August, 1792* (1793). Twiss witnessed
the Tuileries massacre of 10 August 1792, which marked a turning point in
British feeling. His account describes this pivotal moment with startling
objectivity: nevertheless, as with Hill, the traveller's own prior experience of
France provides a particularly telling insight into the cultural and psychological
effect in Britain of the French Revolution.

Although anonymous, *A Trip to Paris* was readily identified as 'the
production of the celebrated Mr. Twiss',[18] author of two respectable travel
books, on Iberia and Ireland, as well as a book on chess (alluded to in *A Trip*).[19]
The *Critical Review* pronounces the *Trip* 'a most singular melange of
dissertations upon liberty and upon chessmen; of botany and old breeches; of
dogs and cats, massacres, and two-headed boys'.[20] Twiss's declared purposes
in travelling to France are themselves miscellaneous:

> though I had been many times in Paris before, yet I had not once
> been there since the Revolution, and I was desirous of seeing how
> far a residence of a few years in France might be practicable and
> agreeable; secondly, a Counter-Revolution, or, at least, some violent
> measures were expected, and I was willing to be there at the time, if
> possible; and lastly, I wanted to examine the gardens near Paris. (1–
> 2)

In the event, most of Twiss's motives for curiosity are thwarted in some way.
Many gardens are closed, destroyed, or altered. The superintendent of the new
'Botanical National Garden' at Versailles informs him that 'We will not have
any aristocratic plants' (40). Political disturbances thoroughly scupper any
hopes of a 'residence of a few years in France', and the 'violent measures'
Twiss had anticipated are so extreme that he is forced to flee Paris, after taking
a heroic stand in the National Assembly as spokesman for the numerous

---

[17] *AR*, 9 (1791), 313. Steven Blakemore, in *Intertextual War: Edmund Burke and the
French Revolution in the Writings of Mary Wollstonecraft, Thomas Paine and James
Mackintosh* (1997), 31, observes that in the *Vindication of the Rights of Men*
Wollstonecraft represents Burke's *Reflections* as insincere, sentimental fiction.

[18] *MR*, NS 10 (1793), 65.

[19] *Travels through Portugal and Spain, in 1772 and 1773* (1775), *A Tour in Ireland in
1775* (1776), and *Chess* (2 vols, 1787–9).

[20] *CR*, NS 7 (1793), 195.

Britons stranded in Paris without valid passports.[21] The tone of the review in the *Critical* reveals more perhaps than the *Trip* itself of the dramatic change in British opinion following the events of 10 August. The reviewer observes that Twiss paints a 'disgusting' picture of Paris, 'and exhibits nothing but anarchy, licentiousness, irreligion, and immorality'.[22] The *Trip*'s engraved frontispiece displays the guillotine in action, which the reviewer describes, with rather heavy-handed irony, as 'that sublime invention of the French philosophers'.[23]

Initially, the *Trip* offers a neutral description of Revolutionary Paris, its ruins and new buildings, changed street-names and fresh coinage. Dispassionately, Twiss observes the public burning of 'volumes of heraldry, and of the registers of the nobility' (56), and notes the improved condition of the 'common people' and of the inns, and the disappearance of beggars: 'I did not see a single pair of *sabôts* (wooden-shoes) in France this time' (68). With the description of the 'Battle and Massacre at the Tuileries', however, the narrative gains pace, whilst still employing a tone of cool objectivity. Contrary to what one might expect, therefore, there is nothing shrill in Twiss's narration of the bloodbath. Much, he freely admits, is related from second-hand sources; he was 'an ear-witness' (81) rather than an eye-witness on 10 August. The accounts of the murders and mutilations which Twiss does see himself are curiously detached and objective, and draw attention to their own status as reportage:

> At six in the evening I saw a troop of national guards and *sans-culottes* kill a Swiss who was running away, by cleaving his skull with a dozen sabres at once, on the *Pont-royal*, and then cast him into the river, in less time than it takes to read this, and afterwards walk quietly on. (83)

Twiss insists that he is 'writing not as a politician, but as a spectator', since he wishes to provide a 'true and impartial narrative' (70). Implicitly, politics are associated with feeling, with partiality, even with sympathy; and all are rejected, as the Burkean association (in the *Philosophical Enquiry*) of sublime spectacle with self-realization is thoroughly dismantled.

A passage near the end of the book embodies this process of detachment with particular force. Describing the chaotic appearance of the gardens on the days following the Tuileries massacre, Twiss comments that:

> No idea of this number [of slain] could be formed by seeing the field of battle, because several bodies were there lying in heaps, and

---

[21] He is mocked in the British newspapers for his cowardice; see *A Trip to Paris*, 129–31.
[22] *CR*, NS 7 (1793), 195.
[23] *CR*, NS 7 (1793), 198.

of the others not above two or three could be seen at a time, as the streets were after the engagement filled with spectators, who walked among and over the carcases.

Of the feelings of these spectators, I judge by my own: I might perhaps have disliked seeing a single dead body, but the great number immediately reconciled me to the sight. (105)

This is a powerful moment. The language of sympathy, and the associated aesthetics of the sublime, are alike appalled and paralysed. A gap is opened up here between British spectator and French spectacle which is soon to develop into fundamental alienation.[24]

The sense of cultural loss and change to which Twiss and Hill testify is more emphatically expressed by other writers, who likewise employ the motifs of return, comparison and regret. Young's *Travels*, discussed above, describe three separate tours, made respectively in 1787, 1788, and 1789, thus providing a sense of social and political change. Moreover, within the third journey, Young visits Paris twice and is able to continue the process of comparison and evaluation. Young's use of the comparative journey is relatively neutral: other texts make more emotional and ideological capital out of the same device. A curious example is James Edward Smith, who published *A Sketch of a Tour on the Continent, in the Years 1786 and 1787* in 1793, some five or six years after the event. Smith insists that the delayed publication gave him time to compare his own observations with those of other travellers, to produce a comprehensive and reliable account. 'Linnaean Smith' generally eschews politics in favour of natural history (even his socializing takes place under the wing of eminent European botanists). Nevertheless, the *Sketch* of pre-Revolutionary France is presented as a nostalgic memorial to the many buildings and gardens that 'now exist no longer', as Smith notes wistfully in his preface – 'The tame carp at Chantilly were destroyed very early in the revolution' (i. xxx). These same carp

---

[24] Burke's earliest known comment on the Revolution (according to O'Brien; see *Reflections*, 13) is in a letter to Lord Charlemont on 9 August 1789, in which he states that 'our thoughts of every thing at home are suspended, by our astonishment at the wonderful Spectacle which is exhibited in a Neighbouring and rival Country – what Spectators and what actors!' (*The Correspondence of Edmund Burke*, ed. Thomas W. Copeland [10 vols, Cambridge, 1959–78], vi. 10. In *Reflections*, however, the theatrical metaphor is frequently used with distaste or horror, Burke for instance referring to 'the atrocious spectacle of the sixth of October 1789' (175). Frans de Bruyn observes that the metaphor of revolution as 'grand, tragic theater' is the 'most sustained ... leitmotiv running through the outpouring of letters, pamphlets, speeches, and treatises that the events in France provoked from Burke's fevered pen' (Frans de Bruyn, 'Theater and Countertheater in Burke's *Reflections on the Revolution in France*', in Steven Blakemore ed., *Burke and the French Revolution: Bicentennial Essays* (1992), 28–68; 28): and not only Burke's, one might add, since the metaphor becomes ubiquitous in accounts of the Revolution, and indeed in ironic contexts also, as when Paine describes the *Reflections* as a 'dramatic performance' (cited de Bruyn, 31).

had been admired by numerous travel writers (including Hester Piozzi) in the pre-Revolutionary years, and their disappearance is doubtless intended to resonate with powerful symbolic poignancy, similar to that invoked in William Hunter's lament for the Prince of Condé's game, 'persecuted' to extinction by the barbarous peasantry (*Travels*, i. 27).

Hunter expresses 'strong dislike' for republicanism in the first edition of his *Travels* in 1796, only to intensify this in the 1798 second edition by adding a prefatory 'Advertisement' which amounts to a call to arms addressed to all 'faithful and entire' citizens in this 'disastrous and precarious period', promising readers that 'Terrible as the French have been to the rest of Europe, they cannot injure us, if we oppose them manfully and with sincerity' (1798, i. xii–xiii). We have already observed the swing in sympathies between Young's *Travels* in 1792 and *The Example of France* in 1793: the second edition of Young's *Travels* in 1794 includes a retraction of what the *Critical Review* describes as 'certain sentiments which implied an approbation of the French revolution'.[25] Samuel Jackson Pratt's *Gleanings through Wales, Holland and Westphalia, with Views of Peace and War at Home and Abroad* (3 vols, 1795), which describe the impact of the Revolutionary wars on surrounding territories, chart various phases of personal and national sympathy. Volume i of the first edition criticizes the French Revolution but envisages some restoration of order, inspired by the British model. By Volume iii, however, once Pratt has revisited Holland and witnessed the dire changes wrought by the Dutch rebellion, all hope of international *entente* is abandoned. The Dutch rebellion demonstrates the sinister spreading flame of European anarchy and justifies Britain's declaration of war against France. France's demonization is complete, and with it British alienation. However, Pratt removes from the third edition of *Gleanings* in 1796 much of the gruesome description of the Terror to which the Reviews had objected. The *Analytical Review* commends these excisions, made out of 'compassion to the feelings of his readers, and in justice to the more manly system of government now prevailing'.[26] Here, the pendulum has swung again, from initial pro-Revolutionary enthusiasm, to revulsion from the excesses of 1793, to a renewed but cautious optimism.

In Pratt's case, personal reversal and revulsion is fully documented, and in emotional terms; we learn how he has 'wept and shuddered' at the scenes he has witnessed.[27] Moreover, the shifting sympathies between the different volumes and editions display a dynamic sensitivity to national opinion. This immediacy is not possible in the case of John Owen's *Travels into Different*

---

[25] *CR*, NS 18 (1796), 264. The expanded 1794 *Travels* occupies two volumes.

[26] *AR*, 24 (1796), 11. Pratt himself had apologized, in the 'Introduction' to the 1795 edition, for the out-of-date political remarks, and had excused himself on the grounds of a delay in publication (*Gleanings*, i. vii–x).

[27] *Gleanings* (1795), iii. 24.

Parts of Europe, in the Years 1791 and 1792. Published in 1796, the *Travels* suffer from the dramatic political changes of the intervening years. The author, identified as 'late Fellow of Corpus Christi College', refers in the 'Preface' to his new, 'grave and important' situation, which obliges him to repudiate many of the views expressed in the *Travels*, since they were 'written in the warmth of youthful impetuosity' (i. xvi–xvii). It seems that Owen has recently become a clergyman; he apologizes that his youthful text displays 'little respect for the solemnities of the Sabbath', and scant 'acknowledgement of a beneficent Providence' (i. xviii). The publication of the *Travels* has a cautionary function, dramatized in the relationship between disenchanted preface and enthusiastic text (Owen stresses in the 'Preface' that the letters have deliberately not been doctored for publication). Individual disillusionment is presented as a paradigm for national feeling. In 1794, in his new capacity as one of the 'public teachers of Christianity', Owen published a short pamphlet entitled *The Retrospect; or, Reflections on the State of Religion and Politics in France and Great Britain*, the rationale for which is explained in the 'Advertisement':

> The Author was of the number of those who admired with enthusiasm the Reformation of the French Monarchy by the events of the first Revolution.—Having had opportunities of observing the country at the very dissimilar periods of July 1790 and September 1793, he received impressions of a very opposite nature, and finds motives of abhorrence to the *later* Revolutions in the principles that led him to applaud the *first*. (*The Retrospect*, v–vi)

The text which follows is a diatribe against the 'advances of that enthusiasm which threatens to overspread the world with unexampled barbarism' (1).

If Owen avails himself of the facilities of a sceptical preface and a related polemical pamphlet, the anonymous author of *A Tour through Part of France* in 1790 makes similar use of a separately published 'Appendix' in 1793, in which he withdraws his earlier support for the Revolution. Even the relatively radical *Monthly* voices approval of this recantation, hailing it as a reaction shared by all rational Britons:

> The writer was, *then*, in common with every friend to human freedom and social happiness, a well-wisher to the French Revolution, at the time of its laudable commencement: but, *since*, in common with every friend to just government and public order, he has conceived such an abhorrence of many of the proceedings in France, that he is become a warm approver of the conduct of their opponents. For this change of sentiment he now assigns his motives and reasons; and this he has done in such a fair and manly discussion of the subject, as reflects honour on his principles and abilities, both as a politician and as a writer. It shews that candid

turn of mind, ever open to conviction, which is one of the most
honourable traits of the human character.[28]

The pervasive use of retrospective and comparative narrative structures, and the
accompanying sense that changing one's mind in the light of experience
(displaying *candour*, that peculiarly British characteristic) is somehow
inherently virtuous, coalesce in numerous 1790s travelogues.[29] This passage
from the *Monthly Review* represents a significant moment, at which strong
opinion and firmly individuated character are displaced by intellectual
flexibility as virtuous elements of national identity, in implicit or overt contrast
to the dogmatic extremism which is seen as having precipitated the ideological
violence of the French Revolution.[30] An important formulation of these newly
important virtues comes in Young's *The Example of France*: anticipating the
accusation that 'I may be reproached with changing my politics, my
"principles", as it has been expressed', Young explains that

> My principles I certainly have not changed, because if there is one
> principle predominant than another in my politics, it is the *principle
> of change*. I have been too long a farmer to be governed by any
> thing but events; I have a constitutional abhorrence of theory, of all
> trust in abstract reasoning; and consequently a reliance merely on
> experience, in other words, on events, the only principle worthy of
> an experimenter. (3–4)

The nice conjunction of individual and state in Young's use of
'constitutional', and the disingenuous understatement of 'a reliance merely on
experience' effectively naturalize Young's tone of rational common sense. But
common sense and 'a reliance merely on experience' can also be mobilized to
radical ends. We turn now to an account that makes defiantly pro-
Revolutionary use of the motifs of return, revision, and changing one's mind.
In 1793, Joshua Lucock Wilkinson published a brief eye-witness account of
Austrian atrocities and the aftermath of war in northern France and the Low
Countries, *Political Facts, Collected in a Tour, in the Months of August,
September, and October, 1793, along the Frontiers of France; with Reflexions
on the Same*. Wilkinson too has visited France before, and his response to the
new atrocities – 'these piteous scenes' (50) – gains extra force from the
experience of appalling contrast.

---

[28] *MR*, NS 11 (1793), 211.

[29] On 'candour', see Paul Langford, *Englishness Identified: Manners and Character
1650–1850* (Oxford, 2000), 85–136.

[30] On intellectual flexibility as a moral good, and as peculiarly British (as opposed to
Continental dogmatism), see David Simpson, *Romanticism, Nationalism, and the Revolt
against Theory* (1993), 40–63.

A 'Preface', couched in terms of Burkean hyperbole ('The altars of religion had been violated;—the temples of the *immaculate* Virgin had been polluted by the cockade, or the bonnet of liberty') outlines the naïve, anti-French and anti-Revolutionary views with which Wilkinson set out, 'with the most sanguine expectations of confirming my prejudices against those whom my ancestors called their natural enemies'.[31] His conversion by the end of the narrative to intensely pro-Revolutionary feeling is thus the more striking. The text closes in a radical anti-war spirit and with an exhortation to British neutrality. Two years later, Wilkinson published a travel narrative which weaves together this journey and his earlier travels on the Continent, *The Wanderer: or, a Collection of Anecdotes and Incidents, with Reflections, Political and Religious, during two Excursions in 1791 and 1793, in France, Germany and Italy* (2 vols, 1795). *The Wanderer* is a more complex and literary account of the two journeys from which the French sections were extracted into *Political Facts*. It describes at length, and interwoven into a sometimes confusing double time-scheme, his walking tours through France, Germany and Italy. In the prefatory 'To the Public', Wilkinson stresses his altruistic motives for travel, casting himself and his companion as humanitarian reporters: 'we hastened to visit the armies of the allies, and examine, with our own eyes, who were the friends of humanity and social order' (i. vi). The greatest enemy to humanity in fact turns out to be the British government, whose threatened suspension of Habeas Corpus, and prosecution of war with revolutionary France, are frequently attacked.

Wilkinson and his companion travel frugally and on foot. Anxious not to be mistaken for English 'Milords' – 'our purse was too light to preserve the reputation of our countrymen' (i. 31–2) – they pose as Polish émigrés, with the result that Wilkinson is once mistaken for the escaped Louis XVI, and briefly arrested. The narrative describes a flow of casual acquaintance, especially soldiers and merchants, of every nationality and walk of life. Indeed, Wilkinson and his companion merge into this miscellaneous cast of characters, divesting themselves of national identity and becoming universal travellers. Arriving in Turin, they are again arrested, this time on account of their shabby appearance:

> We had no appearance of better days: and the disregard of our persons had been so long habitual, that we could not lay aside the mien of *sans culottes*, nor assume the hauteur of the freeborn Englishman. (i. 101)

Frequently in *The Wanderer*, breezy invocations like this one of the discourse of English liberty are consciously ironic, and often juxtaposed with accounts of the 'illiberal' war against France which flies in the face of Wilkinson's

---

[31] 'Preface', fonts reversed, v–viii.

reiterated conviction that 'nature has made every nation friends, and brothers' (i. 167).

The structure of *The Wanderer* is curiously non-linear, and both the *Analytical* and the *Monthly* complain of its 'loose and inelegant' arrangement.[32] Chapters are thematically labelled: 'Pedestrian Ramble', 'Women', 'Superstition', 'Mountains, Lakes, and Rivers', for example. Accounts of two different journeys through Europe are interwoven, and then overlaid with anecdotal encounters with the wandering and dispossessed victims of revolution and war, with political diatribes, and with meditative 'spots of time'. Structurally, Wilkinson's account provides an important paradigm for Wordsworth's *Prelude* in this layering of memories and events, and in its thematization of wandering through a turbulent Europe. Wilkinson was a childhood acquaintance of the Wordsworths, born in Cockermouth between 1768 and 1771. He was a friend and fellow legal trainee of Wordsworth's brother Richard, and probably shared chambers with him during the early 1790s. Wordsworth writes to Richard in September 1792 that 'I look forward to the time of seeing you Wilkinson and my other friends with pleasure', and it seems likely that Wordsworth read Wilkinson's travel diaries in manuscript in late 1792, when both men had returned to London after following similar Continental itineraries.[33] Duncan Wu has noted borrowings from Wilkinson in Wordsworth's account of the desecrated Grande Chartreuse in *Descriptive Sketches* (which was widely disparaged by the Reviews, especially for its 'feeble and insipid' descriptions and the 'want of a general thread of narrative to connect the several descriptions);[34] and Chester L. Shaver has shown that Wordsworth's Vaudracour and Julia (1805 *Prelude* IX) owes something to an anecdote in Wilkinson's *The Wanderer*.[35] Wordsworth was clearly familiar with the material which went into Wilkinson's published texts: moreover, since he and Wilkinson subsequently stayed in touch, Wordsworth may well have read the published accounts as well as their manuscript sources.[36] It is

---

[32] *AR*, 21 (1795), 596–7; see also *MR*, 18 (1795), 115–16.
[33] *The Letters of William and Dorothy Wordsworth: the Early Years, 1787–1805*, ed. Ernest de Selincourt, revised Chester L. Shaver (Oxford, 1967), 81; 344. For the scant available biographical information on Joshua Wilkinson, see my entry in *New Dictionary of National Biography* (forthcoming, Oxford, 2004).
[34] *CR*, NS 8 (1793), 473; *AR*, 15 (1793), 294. See also *MR*, NS 12 (1793), 216–18.
[35] Duncan Wu, *Wordsworth's Reading, 1770–1799* (Cambridge, 1993), 148–9; Chester L. Shaver, 'Wordsworth's Vaudracour and Wilkinson's *The Wanderer*', *Review of English Studies*, NS 12 (1961), 55–7. Wordsworth himself never actually saw the Grande Chartreuse after its despoliation, but this did not prevent him from reworking the idea into an addition (1816–19) to *The Prelude* (1850), VI. 420–88. See Joseph F. Kishel, 'Wordsworth and the Grande Chartreuse', *The Wordsworth Circle*, 12 (1981), 82–8.
[36] There is a reference to Wilkinson in Dorothy's journal for 28 December 1801; *Journals of Dorothy Wordsworth*, ed. Ernest de Selincourt (2 vols, 1941), i. 97; de

unsurprising, therefore, that the reflective and revisionary structures which characterize Wilkinson's works and, as we have seen, many other 1790s travelogues, find their way into *The Prelude* and indeed into the continuing revisions of that poem.[37] Whilst Wilkinson's revisions move towards the radical, however, Wordsworth's enact conservative reaction.

James Heffernan has diagnosed the 'radically recursive form' of *The Prelude*, which enables Wordsworth simultaneously to recapture and reject 'the very past that his enthusiasm for an apocalyptic revolution had threatened to destroy'.[38] He argues that the 'traditional structures of representation' (57), which essentially amount to varieties of chronological narration, could not contain the entirety of Wordsworth's revolution experiences: hence the poem's recourse to a complex chronological scheme which interweaves layers of experience with 'spots of time'. Heffernan's analysis of the structure of *The Prelude* is shrewd, but his emphasis on innovation needs to be revised in the light of Wordsworth's evident debt to 1790s travel writing in general, and Wilkinson's accounts in particular.

In Book VI of *The Prelude*, Wordsworth strategically frames his own youthful desire of travelling to France with retrospective self-irony, thus exploiting the tropes of revision and recantation employed by many other British travel writers during the 1790s. In Wordsworth's hands, such manoeuvres situate his early interest in the Revolution firmly and patronizingly within a phase of politically ill-informed undergraduate enthusiasm, whether foolishly rebellious – 'An open slight / Of college cares and study was the scheme' (VI. 342) – or swottishly earnest – 'Led thither chiefly by a personal wish / To speak the language more familiarly' (IX. 36–7). (The unspoken justifications for his return to France in Book IX are of course further

---

Selincourt footnotes the 'Wilkinson' whom Dorothy mentions as Thomas Wilkinson, but Wu (*Wordsworth's Reading, 1770–1799*, 149) favours the identification of Joshua. Wordsworth read widely within travel literature: Brydone and Coxe, Moore, Helen Maria Williams, Mary Wollstonecraft, and possibly Beckford and George Keate. See Wu, *Wordsworth's Reading, 1770–1799*, 20; 40; 103; 148–53; 157; 174.

[37] See Nicholas Roe, *Wordsworth and Coleridge: the Radical Years* (1988; repr. Oxford 1990), 1–14 and passim, on the patterns of revision and repudiation which Wordsworth and Coleridge retrospectively apply to their lives and careers in the Revolutionary period. A nice example of the 'layering' of events and attitudes is offered by 'Tintern Abbey'; subtitled 'July 13, 1798', the poem harks back to 13 July 1790, when Wordsworth with Robert Jones (whom he and Dorothy are now visiting) landed in Calais, one optimistic year after the original Bastille day (see Roe, *Wordsworth and Coleridge*, 273). The setting of 'Tintern Abbey' is of course resolutely British, and the earlier French sympathies are thus implicitly rejected.

[38] James A. W. Heffernan, 'History and Autobiography: the French Revolution in Wordsworth's *Prelude*', in Heffernan ed., *Representing the French Revolution: Literature, Historiography and Art* (Hanover, NH, 1992), 41–62.

complicated by the Annette Vallon affair, which is beyond the scope of the current discussion.)

The heady excitements of Revolutionary Europe – 'Bliss was it in that dawn to be alive' (X. 692–3) – are presented as youthful intoxication, and Wordsworth further stresses his own remoteness from the affective power of Revolutionary events by delineating a careful dividing line between himself and the real currents of political emotion. The following passage is representative:

> We left the Swiss exulting in the fate
> Of their neighbours, and, when shortening fast
> Our pilgrimage – nor distant far from home –
> We crossed the Brabant armies on the fret
> For battle in the cause of Liberty.
> A stripling, scarcely of the household then
> Of social life, I looked upon these things
> As from a distance – heard, and saw, and felt,
> Was touched but with no intimate concern –
> I seemed to move among them as a bird
> Moves through the air, or as a fish pursues
> Its business in its proper element.
> I needed not that joy, I did not need
> Such help: the ever-living universe
> And independent spirit of pure youth
> Were with me at that season, and delight
> Was in all places spread around my steps
> As constant as the grass upon the fields. (VI. 688–705)

The emphasis here on his own youthful freedom from political fervour is, oddly, figured in images from the animal kingdom (a bird, a fish), which serve to play down any sense of political or indeed social affiliation. And the description of the Brabant armies 'on the fret' is nicely belittling.

A similar sense of isolation, though this time more introspective, is built up in the well-known account of Wordsworth's return visit to Paris in Book IX:

> Where silent zephyrs sported with the dust
> Of the Bastile I sate in the open sun
> And from the rubbish gathered up a stone,
> And pocketed the relick in the guise
> Of an enthusiast; yet, in honest truth,
> Though not without some strong incumbencies,
> And glad – could living man be otherwise? –
> I looked for something which I could not find,
> Affecting more emotion than I felt.
> For 'tis most certain that the utmost force
> Of all these various objects which may shew
> The temper of my mind as then it was

Seemed less to recompense the traveller's pains,
Less moved me, gave me less delight, than did
A single picture merely, hunted out
Among other sights, the Magdalene of le Brun,
A beauty exquisitely wrought – fair face
And rueful, with its ever-flowing tears. (IX. 63–80)

Alan Liu has observed that this image of the Magdalene was popularly (albeit incorrectly) thought to portray Louise de la Vallière, the mistress of Louis XIV, and he sees the episode as the moment at which (in retrospect) Wordsworth reaches an understanding of the Revolution as the rape of beauty by the forces of the sublime, an understanding which ironically undercuts his youthful 'glad' response.[39] Construing this passage somewhat differently, Mary Jacobus suggests that it 'puts a woman's face on the Revolution and, in doing so, makes a man of Wordsworth', thus foreshadowing the story of Vaudracour and Julia later in the same book, which likewise provides a 'means of constituting Wordsworth himself as an autobiographical subject, and specifically, as a masculine one'.[40] Within the terms of the current discussion, both these observations are pertinent: additionally, though, it is worth registering the powerful reinstatement of the ancien régime artefact over the affective value of the 'stone' (gathered, revealingly, from the 'rubbish'), and observing the curious interplay between sentimental Burkean gallantry and the eschewal of sentiment altogether in the oppositional placing of 'honest truth' and 'in the guise / Of an enthusiast'. The term 'enthusiasm' is semantically tainted with associations of fanaticism and extremism from very early on in the eighteenth century, and its use here by Wordsworth is a strikingly negative gloss on his own (and others') earlier radicalism.

The consciously dubious resonances of 'enthusiast' are symptomatic of the extent to which affective terminology (especially 'sensibility') is increasingly associated with dissidence during the 1790s.[41] Caught up in this general tide of disapproval are, inevitably, the textual and narrative strategies by which writers would previously have signalled their individuality or eccentricity. Increasingly, travellers during the 1790s construct a narrative persona which is textually and ideologically bland enough to function as a representative of the newly defensive variety of British common sense. It is possible to see Wordsworth's voice in *The Prelude* as an inheritor of this movement towards

---

[39] Alan Liu, *Wordsworth: the Sense of History* (Stanford, 1989), 366–73.

[40] Mary Jacobus, *Romanticism, Writing and Sexual Difference: Essays on 'The Prelude'* (Oxford, 1989), 194–5.

[41] On the vicissitudes of 'sensibility' see R. F. Brissenden, *Virtue in Distress: Studies in the Novel of Sentiment from Richardson to Sade* (1974), and Chris Jones, *Radical Sensibility: Literature and Ideas in the 1790s* (1993).

the position of national spokesman, the origins of which can be seen with great clarity in travelogues of the 1790s, and are worth explicating in more detail.

The eccentricity of eccentricity

As early as the 1780s, qualities such as eccentricity and individualism which had earlier functioned to demonstrate the proud superiority of British liberty became increasingly problematic. With the French Revolution, their fate was sealed, as they came to constitute a subversive sign of a writer's differentiation of him or herself from the united front of national opinion. Instead of being denoted by the varieties of 'singularity' evident in travel writing from earlier decades, British good sense and good character increasingly reside in the rehearsal of empirical evidence and the projection of a moderate, representative narrator. The *OED*'s 1794 citation for 'eccentricity' is highly suggestive in this context – 'An excursion, for the eccentricity of which I shall ... be condemned'. Seamus Deane notes that Burke's attack on Rousseau's moral hypocrisy is also an attack on the vanity which 'makes a fetish of eccentricity, valuing it to the degree that it differs from received wisdom and thereby gains attention for itself. It gives personal impulse priority over common sentiment'.[42]

The texts discussed so far in this chapter were written from a wide range of political perspectives, yet even the most radical would balk at adopting the kind of opinionated or whimsical textual persona which had been fashionable in the 1760s and 1770s. With the increasingly polemical and ideological thrust of travel writing, narrative common sense and dependability become crucial. The *Analytical Review* had ironically questioned Burke's claim to speak 'the collective sense of the great body of the people', and several travel writers express similar scepticism of Burke, even whilst tacitly pursuing the ideal of speaking with not only the 'collective sense' but the representative voice of the nation.[43]

The literary careers of Samuel Jackson Pratt ('Courtney Melmoth') and Thomas Cogan illuminate this shift. Pratt's *Travels for the Heart* (1777) and Cogan's *John Buncle, Junior, Gentleman* (1776–8) have both featured earlier in this study, by virtue of their textual playfulness, frankly sentimental style, and adventurous politics. During the 1790s, however, both writers publish travel accounts which not only cover distinctly unadventurous itineraries, but are also written in an arrestingly dull manner, Cogan's *The Rhine: or, a Journey from Utrecht to Francfort; chiefly by the Borders of the Rhine* (2 vols,

---

[42] Seamus Deane, *The French Revolution and Enlightenment in England, 1789–1832* (Cambridge, MA, 1988), 8.
[43] *AR*, 8 (1790), 414.

1794) and Pratt's *Gleanings through Wales, Holland and Westphalia* (3 vols, 1795). The comparative dreariness of these works does not seem to have troubled the reviews: the Cogan of the *Rhine* is pronounced 'an agreeable companion', and his manner is commended as lively and anecdotal.[44] Likewise, Pratt's *Gleanings* are praised for their 'light and agreeable touches', and 'light entertainment' value.[45] The *Monthly Review*, however, disapproves in *Gleanings* of 'a rambling prolixity sometimes rather conducing to swell the book than to improve the tale'.[46] This is something of an understatement: *Gleanings* weighs in at 1,384 octavo pages. Cogan's *Rhine* is well over 700 pages; each text is many times the size of the authors' earlier works. They are very different types of book also, far more learned and thorough, and eschewing the whimsicality characteristic of the 1770s. Sentiment is replaced with overt moralizing on vice and virtue, war and peace, industry and morality. Both writers stress the length of their journeys and residence abroad, as do many other travel writers during the later 1780s and the 1790s. Pratt cites John Moore's observation that 'truly to know people and places it is absolutely necessary to reside in, and amongst them, a considerable time'.[47] He even adds a new category to Sterne's 'catalogue of travellers', presenting himself as 'the *residentiary* traveller, who sets out on a plan of sojourning in the parts of the world he describes, and mixes in the societies of each long enough to observe *accurately* manners, customs, and events' (i. 9). The gleaner's observations, he emphasizes, are made with care, and attention to detail, and his journeys performed 'at a foot-pace rather than a full gallop' (i. 8).

If this insistence on residence and thoroughness is symptomatic of the move away from the impressionistic, individualistic possibilities of the 1760s and 1770s, *The Rhine* and *Gleanings* also display the discrediting of authorial anonymity and playful pseudonym. Both Cogan and Pratt had previously published either anonymously or pseudonymously; but in 1794, Cogan explains that he has put his own name on the title-page, having been informed that '*anonymous* travellers were always placed in the *suspicious class*'.[48] 'Courtney Melmoth' is for once dispensed with: *Gleanings* is dignified with the full force of 'Samuel Jackson Pratt'. Reviews of travel narrative during the 1780s and 1790s place more and more weight upon authorial respectability rather than humour, whimsy, or eccentricity. The *Analytical Review* in 1789 pronounces

---

[44] *CR*, NS 16 (1796), 31; see also *MR*, NS 14 (1794), 12–20.

[45] *CR*, NS 16 (1796), 431–45; *AR*, 23 (1796), 12–13.

[46] *MR*, NS 19 (1796), 301.

[47] *Gleanings*, ii. 385, misquoting Moore, *A View of Society and Manners in France* (2 vols, 1779), i. 411. In 1796 Mary Wollstonecraft apologizes for 'so short a residence' in Scandinavia (actually three and a half months): see 'Advertisement' to *Letters Written during a Short Residence in Sweden, Norway, and Denmark*).

[48] Cogan, *Rhine*, 'Advertisement'; an earlier edition had in fact appeared anonymously in 1793.

that 'Books of travels can only be judged of from the known credibility of the author'.[49] This drive towards the respectable and the utilitarian makes Cogan's and especially Pratt's texts extremely detailed, lengthy, and self-righteous. These qualities seem to have appealed to critics and readers of the 1790s (*Gleanings* sees a second edition within a year). Another travelogue from 1795, Charles Este's *A Journey in the Year 1793, through Flanders, Brabant, and Germany, to Switzerland*, is notable in that it replicates the exclamatory and inconsequential style which had characterized much sentimental travel writing of the 1760s and 1770s (whilst also providing a good deal of weighty information on government, history, the arts, and civic institutions). It seems odd and out of place in 1795, and the *Monthly Review* condemns Este's style – evident mainly in his copious use of exclamation marks – as 'mannerist'.[50] (One reason for Este's stylistic eccentricity may be that he hoped thereby to conceal the derivative nature of his observations, some of which are obviously plagiarized from Cogan's *Rhine*, whose route Este follows exactly.)

One of the oddest travelogues of the 1790s was, significantly, also one of the least noticed. Rowley Lascelles's *Sketch of a Descriptive Journey through Switzerland* was published in 1796. Social and political topics are conspicuously absent from this text, which instead celebrates solitary communion with nature and the beauties of the Swiss landscape. Lascelles's poetic prose is stylishly impressionistic: 'Ever-changeful dies of the lake's conscious waters; violet-purple, rosy-lilac-purple—fluid emerald—fluid sapphire' (12). The landscape shifts and pulses with the changing viewpoint of the mobile narrator, and the authorial pronoun frequently disappears beneath the active agency of the landscape and its rendering: 'Stringy cascades, whose gleam is only seen by fits, and which do not rebound from the rocks, but clinging like slime or oil, slide down them' (18). Mountains shift and rear, 'like teeth standing out of the gums' (77), and reveal sudden 'Insulated spots of verdure' (83), in a curious anticipatory conflation of *The Prelude* and 'Kubla Khan'. The observer vanishes beneath the size and extremity of the Swiss landscape. Lascelles's is an extraordinary and sometimes beautiful work, but was printed privately and anonymously, and was not noticed by the reviews.

Not surprisingly, the risqué element in travel writing, sentimental or otherwise, also falls out of favour in the 1780s and 1790s. The author of *A Tour, Sentimental and Descriptive* (1788) describes Yorick-like encounters with women in shops and on coaches – 'Talk not to me of Yorick's pulse-feeling— my whole body was pulse—' (ii. 11); but there is a new sense of propriety. A flirtation with a washerwoman is abruptly curtailed when our tourist discovers that she is married, and decides that this is

---

[49] *AR*, 3 (1789), 57.
[50] *MR*, NS 16 (1795), 553.

the moment for an honourable retreat — I conducted her to the door
not unembarrassed.

> For of the nuptial couch
> With most mysterious reverence
> I deem! — (ii. 29)

A more bizarre instance of fin-de-siècle prudery is afforded by Robert
Townson's erudite quarto with plates, *Travels in Hungary* (1797). This was
generally praised by the reviews, but they all object to 'certain libidinous
descriptions' in the *Travels*, 'which here and there present themselves, greatly
to the offence of modesty, and in no wise indicative of a rigid moral feeling in
their author'.[51] If the reader turns to the offending pages, thoughtfully listed by
the *Critical Review*,[52] they will find such offensive items as a description of
mating insects, and an account of naked peasants in the baths of Gross
Wardein, which thirty years earlier might have provoked little more than an
archly raised critical eyebrow (in 1776, both the *Monthly* and the *Critical* had
excerpted a similar passage from Wraxall's *Cursory Remarks* with interested
enthusiasm).[53] There is, however, an extraordinary passage describing the
luscious breasts ('Mammae hemisphaericae') of a 'charming girl' in the baths,
which thoroughly distract Townson from his Linnaean endeavours:

> After such a bewitching sight as this, how could I descend to the
> common affairs of life and think of—reptiles? The charming girl
> made me lose a snake I had just killed by the side of the warm
> waters which run from the baths, and which I had half examined. I
> think it was *Natrix longissima* of Laurentius ... (254–5)

Clearly, Townson's text contains its own critique of the emasculating
distractions of feminine charms, but this is not enough for the reviews. The
erotically-minded traveller is not pleasingly but intolerably eccentric. Manly
good sense and a finely judged degree of sensibility are the qualities which
entitle the travel writer of the 1790s to claim a nationally representative
function. Personal oddity will no longer do.

The 'attractions of home': domesticity and national virtue in the 1790s

The moral and political controversy so easily provoked by unconventionality at
this time mean that travel writing, and travelling itself, become increasingly

---

[51] *CR*, NS 20 (1797), 418; see also *MR*, NS 24 (1797), 175, where Townson is berated
as 'coarse and indecent'; and *AR*, 26 (1797), 35.
[52] *CR*, NS 20 (1797), 418.
[53] *MR*, 53 (1775), 15; *CR*, 40 (1775), 110.

problematic activities during the later 1790s. The strategies of virtuous and commensical self-definition outlined in preceding sections are to some extent a defensive response to the increasingly pervasive discourse of conservative insularity, which constructs a dubious ethical context for travel writing. Thomas Macdonald, for example, publishes *Thoughts on the Public Duties of Private Life; with Reference to Present Circumstances and Opinions* in 1795, outlining the threats posed by the atheistical tendencies of the French to the British 'national character' (13). Macdonald excoriates that 'general philanthropy' which would maintain that 'the heart is a citizen of the world', and which 'ranges over the universe at large, and delights in remote and distant objects of humanity, while near and familiar evils escape all observation' (19–20).[54] His tone is apocalyptic:

> the total overthrow of those laws which formed, of common consent, a code among nations; and the utter destruction of all political balance in Europe, compel us to turn our eyes inwards, in quest of that security and relief which the resources of our own character and circumstances may afford. ... Let our national attachments; our old peculiarities of sentiment; our respect for a free and manly subordination; our *honest* prejudices – let all of them be cherished and preserved, and Britain shall yet stand firm. (1–2)[55]

Natural British difference both justifies and demands a renewed alienation. This emphasis on moral insularity undoubtedly affected the status of Continental travel. While other areas of Europe such as Iberia and Northern and Eastern Europe began to be explored as alternative travel destinations (as outlined in Chapter one), even greater moral credit could be gained by realizing the aesthetic and educative potential of the British Isles, and the 1790s see the publication of many travelogues describing British itineraries, especially after war breaks out. The young Coleridge travels around Wales in the summer of 1794, for example, and the Lake District features in several published travel accounts.[56]

---

[54] Macdonald is here referring to the anti-slavery movement as well as to radical European sympathies. The two causes (in both of which the concept of human rights and liberty were central) were frequently yoked together, by both proponents and opponents.

[55] Cf. Burke, *Reflections*, 182–3, on 'liberal and manly morals': 'instead of casting away all our old prejudices, we cherish them to a very considerable degree'. Burke also reiterates the emphasis which Hume, Smith, and indeed (ironically enough) Rousseau had placed on local attachment as 'the first link in the series by which we proceed towards a love to our country and to mankind' (*Reflections*, 135).

[56] Coleridge's journey is recorded by his companion, Joseph Hucks, in *A Pedestrian Tour through North Wales, in a Series of Letters* (1793), ed. Alun R. Jones and William Tydeman (Cardiff, 1979). In 1792 had appeared *A Fortnight's Ramble to the Lakes in Westmoreland, Lancashire, and Cumberland. By a Rambler*, and Adam Walker's

The brief publishing career of Lord Gardenstone is also suggestive. He had published some unremarkable prose *Travelling Memorandums, made in a Tour upon the Continent of Europe, in the Years 1786, 87 and 88* (2 vols, 1792); but in 1796 he published some equally unremarkable verses entitled 'Peace and Home preferred to War and Travel', which celebrate the rural and homely virtues. The prospective traveller is urged not to abandon the 'lowly vale' for the dubious 'lofty mountains far away', which now signify dangerous and unpatriotic wanderlust:

> Oh, waste not then thy fleeting hours
>   In foreign climes and paths unknown;
> Return thee to the happy plains
>   That bounteous nature made thy own.[57]

In 1796, Richard Polwhele published a lumbering Spenserian hymn to the pleasures of home and Britishness, *The Influence of Local Attachment with respect to Home*. A crude version of associationism is recruited to explain the natural force of local attachment, which although common to all peoples (and indeed animals) is peculiarly strong, and morally inflected, in Britain ('Yes! British youths! The love of home inspires / Generous affections').[58] The British traveller returns thankfully from the insidious sensual pleasures with which the foreign may tempt him ('Beauty that wantons with voluptuous air', 17):

> To him more dear the oak-crown'd precipice,
> Than the deep verdure of date-crested palm,
> Where all is lap'd in ease, one languor-breathing calm. (15)

Polwhele's poem also testifies to the growth of British regionalism during the 1790s (evident also in the specific localities celebrated by Coleridge and Wordsworth): Polwhele's home county of Devon is celebrated as the moral centre of his domestic and national loyalties. *The Influence of Local Attachment* was well reviewed: the *Analytical Review* was more interested in *Local Attachment* than in Coleridge's *Poems on various Subjects* (reviewed in the

---

Remarks made in a tour from London to the Lakes of Westmoreland and Cumberland; in the Summer of MDCCXCI, both reviewed with relative prominence.

[57] *Peace and Home preferred to War and Travel. To which are added, The Volunteer, The Drum, and Scenes of my Youth* (Glasgow, 1796), 2–3 (lines unnumbered).

[58] Polwhele, *The Influence of Local Attachment with respect to Home. A Poem* (2nd edn, 1798), 34 (lines unnumbered). On the philosophical history of this idea in the eighteenth century, see Alan D. McKillop, 'Local Attachment and Cosmopolitanism – the Eighteenth-Century Pattern', in Frederick W. Hilles and Harold Bloom eds, *From Sensibility to Romanticism: Essays presented to Frederick A. Pottle* (Oxford, 1965), 191–218.

same issue),[59] and Polwhele's smug verses prompted the *Critical* to wax lyrical on the national feeling for domesticity:

> In no country can the subject be more interesting, as the very term of *home* is peculiarly English; the Englishman, from his retired and domestic disposition, requiring more, perhaps, than the inhabitant of most other countries, the comforts suggested by the term ...[60]

Just two years later, Polwhele himself published his now notorious attack on radical women writers, including Helen Maria Williams and Mary Wollstonecraft, *The Unsex'd Females*. Polwhele stigmatizes Williams in particular for entering (in her *Letters* on the French Revolution) the masculine realm of public and political discourse, thus violating the generic decorum which confines women to the safer realms of sentimental verse, figured as 'moonlight vallies' in the poem.[61] Polwhele's title-page epigraph specifically associates the violation of gender roles with involvement in French affairs – 'Our unsex'd female writers now instruct, or confuse, us and themselves, in the labyrinth of politics, or run us wild with Gallic frenzy'.[62]

Also in 1798, Coleridge's triple publication of 'France: An Ode', 'Fears in Solitude' and 'Frost at Midnight' tellingly embodied the rejection of politics and international sympathies in favour of a defensive emphasis on rural privacy, where virtue and religion depend upon patriotic feeling: 'There lives not form nor feeling in my soul / Unborrowed from my country!' – 'O native Britain! O my Mother Isle!'[63] British integrity is frequently presented in such gendered terms. In Macdonald's *Thoughts*, for example, 'a free and manly' subordination is enjoined (3), and related to 'that taste for *domestic life* which has long very honourably distinguished us as a moral people' (46). In Britain alone are 'the soft and gentle beauties' of the female sex sufficiently respected; moreover, from these 'sweet companions' are derived 'the endearing ties of society' (47–8). Coleridge strides towards his 'own lowly cottage, where my

---

[59]   *AR*, 23 (1796), 606–12.
[60]   *CR*, NS 17 (1796), 19.
[61]   Richard Polwhele, *The Unsex'd Females*, (1798), 19 (lines unnumbered). See also Vivien Jones, 'Women Writing Revolution: Narratives of History and Sexuality in Wollstonecraft and Williams', in Stephen Copley and John Whale eds, *Beyond Romanticism: New Approaches to Texts and Contexts 1780–1832* (1992), 178–99; 180.
[62]   The epigraph's source is given as '*Pursuits of Literature*, Edit. 7, p. 238'. Claudia Johnson, in *Equivocal Beings: Politics, Gender and Sentimentality in the 1790s: Wollstonecraft, Radcliffe, Burney, Austen* (Chicago, 1995), 1–19, sees Polwhele's attack as representative of an increasing tendency in reactionary writing of the 1790s to associate virtuous 'feeling' with 'the gallant ways of England' which require masculine protection rather than any female intervention.
[63]   'Fears in Solitude', 192–3; 182.

babe / And my babe's mother dwell in peace!'[64] A year later, he publishes a poem celebrating the maternal longings as much as the liberal politics which Georgiana Cavendish, Duchess of Devonshire, expressed in her poem 'The Passage of the Mountain of St Gothard. To my Children' (even though only the last four out of her 120 lines are actually concerned with said infants).[65]

British middle-class opinion in general, then, reacted to developments in France by rigorously insisting on the domestic, non-political realm of women, and equating virtue with domesticity. Linda Colley has argued that the war footing of the 1790s saw a renewed emphasis on the notion of 'separate spheres', with the masculine instincts of defence (of both hearth and realm) roused to the full.[66] Polwhele's *Local Attachment* enquires 'Doth not the patriot check the dread career / Of hostile squadrons, and with manly glow / Shielding his menac'd land, avert the fateful blow?' (35). It has also been argued, however, that the Revolution intensified a process which had in fact begun more gradually during the 1770s and 1780s, perhaps related (as Gerald Newman has suggested) to the increasing self-assertion of the middling sort – 'the native manliness of our disposition' – against the effete cosmopolitanism of the ruling élites during these decades.[67] The 1790s witnessed a rash of new and reissued conduct books which hammered home this message.[68] As the revolution rumbled on, a similar process was occurring in France itself, with strong reaction against the infamous and bloody participation of women in some of the worst Revolutionary excesses. Lynn Hunt notes that between 1793 and 1804 French 'male hostility toward women's political participation began to crystallize into a fully elaborated domestic ideology, in which women were scientifically "proven" to be suitable only for domestic occupations'.[69]

---

[64] 'Fears in Solitude', 225–6.

[65] Coleridge's poem, 'Ode to Georgiana, Duchess of Devonshire', was published in the *Morning Post* for 24 December 1799. Cavendish's poem concludes with a visionary anticipation of homecoming and the resumption of maternal duties. See Roger Lonsdale ed., *Eighteenth-Century Women Poets: an Oxford Anthology* (Oxford, 1989), 510–14.

[66] Linda Colley, *Britons: Forging the Nation, 1707–1837* (1992), 250–62.

[67] Gerald Newman, *The Rise of English Nationalism: a Cultural History 1740–1830* (1987), 123–56, citing John Andrews, *A Comparative View of the French and English Nations* (1785).

[68] For example, John Burton, *Lectures on Female Education and Manners* (2 vols, 1793), Thomas Gisborne, *An Enquiry into the Duties of the Female Sex* (1797; five editions by 1801), and Hannah More, *Strictures on the Modern System of Female Education* (2 vols, 1799).

[69] Lynn Hunt, *The Family Romance of the French Revolution* (1992), 158; see also Joan B. Landes, *Women and the Public Sphere in the Age of the French Revolution* (Ithaca, 1988). Summarizing recent feminist insights into the gender politics of the French Revolution, Adriana Craciun observes that 'revolutionary representations of Woman as Liberty, Republic, Maenad, and Mother Nature did not reflect women's power in revolutionary society, but, rather, marked its absence, and ultimately

Travel texts produced by women during the later 1790s, whose political standpoint varies from the most radical to the most conservative, provide unique insights into the relationship at this time between the private or domestic and the public or national. It is instructive to begin with a couple of anonymous travel accounts from the late 1790s, purporting at least to be written by women, which engage with the various issues of gender and virtue thrown up by the preceding years of Revolutionary turmoil.

A Residence in France, during the Years 1792, 1793, 1794, and 1795; described in a Series of Letters from an English Lady: with general and incidental Remarks on the French Character and Manners, a hefty two-volume work (912 pages), was published in 1797. It claimed to have been 'Prepared for the Press by John Gifford, Esq. Author of the History of France'.[70] The Reviews are sceptical about its authenticity. The *Critical* proclaims that:

> the publication before us appears under extremely suspicious circumstances. The name or situation of the real author is not so much as hinted at; that author is a *lady*, as if, because miss Williams has written well and successfully upon that subject, none but *a lady* could write on the French revolution.[71]

The reviewer observes, with further scepticism, that *A Residence*

> has every appearance of being, in part at least, composed after the events to which it relates. Every thing is foretold exactly as it happened; the reflections are, most of them, such as would be made at present, and in England, rather than in France, and at the moment of a revolution which has mocked all human foresight ...[72]

The *Analytical Review* disapproves of the cowardly anonymity of the work, and points out that 'When miss Williams determined to communicate to the british public the facts and observations she had collected during her residence in France, she did not scruple, though with some personal hazard, to give her narrative the authenticity of her signature'.[73] Where the *Critical*'s objections

reinscribed male sex-right and misogyny' (Adriana Craciun, 'Violence against Difference: Mary Wollstonecraft and Mary Robinson', in Greg Clingham ed., *Making History: Textuality and the Forms of Eighteenth-Century Culture* [1998], 111–41). The same might be argued of Britannia's frequent figuration in eighteenth-century visual representations of national virtue.

[70] Title-page. 'John Gifford' is the pseudonym of John Richards Green (*Dictionary of National Biography* [3rd edn, 22 vols, Oxford, 1967–8], vii. 1184), described by his biographer as a 'miscellaneous writer' and Tory hack.

[71] *CR*, NS 19 (1797), 265.

[72] *CR*, NS 19 (1797), 266–7.

[73] *AR*, 25 (1797), 71. The *Analytical*'s frequent eschewal of upper-case letters seems to have a political resonance.

are, broadly speaking, concerned with the literary aspects of authenticity and truth, the *Analytical*'s are more political: 'the writer of these letters has, through the whole, steadily pursued one single object, the indiscriminate condemnation of the principles, the agents, and the friends of the french revolution'; the reviewer remarks also on the author's 'predilection for despotism'.[74]

A Residence describes events in Paris between 1792 and 1795 as they are reported in various provincial towns where the author and her husband are resident. It is a highly reactionary text, dedicated to Burke and, so the editor claims, published as an antidote to the subversive stance of the British press. The Reviews would no doubt have been annoyed to read that 'even the pure stream of British criticism [has been] diverted from its *natural* course, and polluted by the pestilential vapours of Gallic republicanism' (i. v). Although the text makes no reference to Helen Maria Williams's *Letters from France*, it is clearly intended as both a critique of Williams's account of the Revolution, and an alternative to the image of British womanhood which her life and work presented.

The author consistently laments the disappearance of that ancien-régime culture which had provided British travel writers of a certain class with a definitive experience of European culture:

> the manners of the nation are corrupted, and its moral character
> disgraced in the eyes of all Europe. A barbarous rage has laid waste
> the fairest monuments of art—whatever could embellish society or
> contribute to soften existence has disappeared under the reign of
> these modern Goths ... (i. 297–8)

The generalizing rhetoric here is characteristic (as is the Burkean tone); the author assiduously omits any personal information and opinion. No motives or reasons for travel are sketched in: the 'Lady' functions as an embodiment of patriotic and unindividualized womanhood, and, thus, as an antidote to all that is individualistic, radical and apparently anti-patriotic:

> I make no pretensions to that sort of cosmopolytism [*sic*] which is
> without partialities, and affects to consider the Chicktaw or the
> Tartars or Thibet, with the same regard as a fellow-countryman.
> Such universal philanthropists, I have often suspected, are people of
> very cold hearts, who fancy they love the whole world, because they
> are incapable of loving any thing in it, and live in a state of '*moral
> vagabondage*', (as it is happily termed by Gregoire,) in order to be
> exempted from the ties of a settled residence. (ii. 461)

---

[74] *AR*, 25 (1797), 71; 80.

This passage is a thinly veiled personal attack on Williams (the *Monthly Review* notes that the letters which make up *A Residence* are 'probably intended as rivals to those of Miss Helen Maria Williams, and they are certainly imbued with completely opposite qualities'),[75] who had aroused the vociferous ire of conservative middle-class opinion long before. In 1793, Laetitia Matilda Hawkins had published (anonymously) *Letters on the Female Mind, its Powers and Pursuits*, a sustained and shrill attack on Williams's private and public character. Williams is presented as an unnatural monster, practising so-called 'Universal benevolence' while actually neglecting 'the interests of those with whom *natural* bonds have connected us: our kindred, our country, and our fellow-creatures'.[76] Hawkins rhetorically banishes Williams: 'if you cannot be a quiet subject of a well-regulated monarchy, you would please to remain where your republicanism may prove only one coal in a flaming furnace' (ii. 108). Her attack is extreme, and the three liberal reviews are unanimous in their disagreement, the *Analytical* dismissing it as 'rant … written with much ill temper', the *Critical* as 'feeble and contemptible'.[77] But *Letters on the Female Mind* is undoubtedly representative of a powerful body of contemporary opinion, which any writer chary of their reputation needed to take into account. The stigmatization of 'universal benevolence' relates to that of 'sensibility' at this time: John Brewer has observed that, having in the 1760s been seen as a 'patriotic assertion of sincerity against the affectation and foppery of politeness', sensibility was now associated with a dangerous, sexually deviant excess of feeling (which, given that Rousseau and Goethe were well-known enthusiasts, could also conveniently be condemned as foreign).[78]

Not surprisingly, the author of *A Residence* returns gratefully to British shores, 'wearied and disgusted with the contemplation of this despotism', and celebrating 'the blessings we enjoy in a free and happy constitution' (ii. 464). A year later, the *Analytical Review* welcomes *A Sketch of Modern France. In a Series of Letters to a Lady of Fashion. Written in the Years 1796 and 1797, during a Tour through France. By a Lady* as 'the production of a cultivated and ingenious mind, neither wedded to aristocracy and superstition, nor a blind admirer of equality and republicanism'.[79] Although, like *A Residence*, the

---

[75]   *MR*, NS 22 (1797), 282.

[76]   *Letters on the Female Mind, its Powers and Pursuits. Addressed to Miss H. M. Williams, with particular Reference to her Letters from France* (2 vols, 1793), ii. 133–4. There are clear echoes here of Burke's attack on universal philanthropy, and on Rousseau's abuse of his children.

[77]   *AR*, 15 (1793), 527; *CR*, NS 10 (1793), 313.

[78]   John Brewer, *The Pleasures of Imagination: English Culture in the Eighteenth Century* (1997), 122. See also Brissenden, *Virtue in Distress* and Jones, *Radical Sensibility*.

[79]   *AR*, 27 (1798), 21.

Sketch is anonymous, none of the reviews seems to have doubted its authenticity: its editor is C. L. Moody, himself a reviewer for the *Monthly* (and a dissenting clergyman), who explains in the 'Preface' that the 'Letters' are 'simply the Journal of an English Lady, who was lately making a tour through France, in company with her husband, a military gentleman ... They were addressed to a Lady of Fashion attached to one of the branches of the Royal Family, and have been put into my hands to prepare them for the press' (vi). Nicola Watson has argued that in the wake of Rousseau's novels and their perceived influence on Revolutionary excess, epistolarity during the 1790s and afterwards was 'widely read as an oppositional discourse – a potential disruptor of the existing social or symbolic order'.[80] Although the epistolary pedigree of travel writing as a genre to a large extent provided immunity from such dubiety, Moody's editorial sanctioning of *A Sketch* may be seen as a defensive strategy in this context.

A Sketch is elegant and open-minded, providing a lucid and detailed account of daily life, as well as more generalized political reflections. Descriptions of bustling markets and ruined churches rub shoulders with laments for the horrors of war, and anecdotes of people – of all classes – who have suffered during the Revolution (including at least two one-legged soldiers). The author's political position is hard to gauge. Emotion, whether of the radical and enthusiastic or the reactionary and horrified variety, is not only avoided but, at certain points, satirized, as in her description of arriving in Paris:

> My sensations on entering this capital of the French Republic I can but feebly describe. I trembled,—I wept;— and though I longed to see what this famous city contained, yet I was afraid that my poor nerves would be unequal to the shock which some of its scenes must unavoidably occasion. ... I shall dream of assassination and murder, and blood will be uppermost in my thoughts. (134)

The voice of sanity asserts itself, however, in a moment of ironic reversal:

> But I perceive that I am rather sketching the present state of my own mind than a picture of Paris ... Those terrific illusions which my fancy had conjured up, and which possessed my imagination, were but partly realized. If, indeed, I *sought* for traces of the revolution, I found them; but these were not marked on the countenances and in the demeanour of the inhabitants. (135–6)

The misleading nature of Gothic fearfulness is underlined here; but the imaginative faculties are not in themselves condemned, and the fanciful

---

[80] Nicola Watson, *Revolution and the Form of the British Novel 1790–1825: Intercepted Letters, Interrupted Seductions* (Oxford, 1994), 16.

'illusions' are in fact 'partly realized', in a measured reconciliation of feeling and reason characteristic of *A Sketch*.

The final letter provides the reader with some general observations on topics such as politics, religion, arts and sciences, commerce; these are designed to supplement the more hurried observations which make up the bulk of the text – written with 'what may be called a *flying-pen*' (499) – and are supplied by the author's husband:

> I have desired B., *pour faire la bonne bouche*, to assist me with some general remarks and observations, arranged under distinct heads; so that you will now have subjoined to my hasty and undigested narrative, the impression which our late view of France, and interview with the French, have made on *his* mind. (500)

Not only is feeling modified by reflection, but feminine 'impressions' are supplemented with masculine 'remarks', and domestic detail with political expansiveness. The author of *A Sketch* is frank and sensible (and acclaimed as such by the reviews); but only through stressing her dependence on a conventional relationship of subservience can she range outside the domestic realm. The same is true of Ann Radcliffe, whose influence is discernible in the *Sketch*. However, when Radcliffe herself published a travelogue in 1795, she did not do so anonymously. By putting her name to her travelogue she could of course capitalize on her significant literary reputation; but she had also to take especial care in the moral character she projected.

In 1792, the *Monthly Review* had reviewed Radcliffe's *Romance of the Forest* in facetious terms:

> The days of chivalry and romance being (ALAS! as Mr. Burke says,) for ever past, we must hear no more of enchanted forests and castles, giants, dragons, walls of fire, and other 'monstrous and prodigious things;'—yet still forests and castles remain, and it is still within the province of fiction, without overstepping the limits of nature, to make use of them for the purpose of creating surprise. By the aid of an inventive genius, much may still be done, even in this philosophical age, to fill the fancy with marvellous images, and to 'quell the soul with grateful terrors'.[81]

Three years later, in 1795, the *Monthly* reassures its readers that in *A Journey made in the Summer of 1794, through Holland and the Western Frontier of Germany, with a Return down the Rhine*, Radcliffe employs her descriptive powers appropriately to the genre, 'with the closeness of a copyist, rather than with the freedom of an original inventor', and has avoided 'every kind of

---

[81] *MR*, NS 8 (1792), 82. I have not been able to identify the quotation.

decoration which might give her narrative the air of fiction'.[82] The *Critical Review* likewise describes the Radcliffe of *A Journey* as a 'genuine copyist', and falls into rhapsodies over her descriptions of landscape – 'Language cannot do much more in a supposed state of perfection'.[83] The *Analytical* is more subdued in its praise, observing that 'From a tour written by the elegant pen of Mrs. Radcliffe, much will be expected', but adding, almost with bathos, that she has eschewed 'pathetic scenes, or wonderful events', and is 'contented if her narrative may furnish facts, which will afford some gratification of curiosity, and represent scenes, through which the good-natured reader may accompany her without lassitude'.[84] The disappointment registered by this reviewer accurately conveys the rather tedious diligence of *A Journey*, in which the celebrated passages of natural description are scattered few and far between much that is derivative and unoriginal ('Mrs. R.'s tour lay through a track which has so oft been beaten, as to leave little room for novelty of detail').[85] While Radcliffe may reign supreme in the 'province of fiction', she is but one of many travellers along the beaten track through the Low Countries and Germany, and into print.

The doyenne of Gothic fiction herself insists rather laboriously on her diffidence in entering the field of travel narrative: an untitled prefatory note to the reader explains that the journey is written in 'the plural term', since it was performed 'in the company of her nearest relative and friend', and the account is therefore a product of their 'mutual observation'. The title-page should have displayed 'the joint names of her husband and herself', had this not suggested an immodest 'design to attract attention by extraordinary novelty' (v). Specifically, she emphasizes that 'where the oeconomical and political conditions of countries are touched upon in the following work, the remarks are less her own than elsewhere' (v). (William Radcliffe was indeed a highly qualified authority, combining a career as a political journalist with the occasional translation of erudite foreign travel accounts.)[86]

A Journey is structured with some formality, divided into geographical sections and written more as essays than as letters. Radcliffe does not avail herself of the travelogue's scope for immediacy or intimacy; she does, however, supply her reader with several passages of the sublime natural description which had become the trademark of her fiction. And yet novelistic conventions and expectations are frequently confounded. The gorgeous views

---

[82]   *MR*, NS 18 (1795), 241.

[83]   *CR*, NS 14 (1795), 241–2.

[84]   *AR*, 22 (1795), 349–50.

[85]   *AR*, 22 (1795), 350.

[86]   For example, in 1790 *A Journey through Sweden, containing a detailed Account of its Population, Agriculture, Commerce, and Finances*, from the French of 'a Dutch Officer'; and also in 1790 *The Natural History of East Tartary; traced through the Three Kingdoms of Nature*, the work of an anonymous French author.

of Nimeguen, whose 'ramparts and pointed roofs' are 'just tinted by the vapour that ascended from the bay below', are spoiled by proximity: 'But Nimeguen lost much of its dignity on a nearer approach; for many of the towers, which the treachery of fancy had painted at distance, changed into forms less picturesque' (80). Gothic fancy is more explicitly rejected in a passage of ironic reversal describing their benighted and increasingly anxious journey towards Xanten: 'At length from the woods, that had concealed the town, a few lights appeared over the walls, and dissipated some gloomy fancies about a night to be passed in a forest' (89). Any horror that is present in *A Journey* is supplied by the grim reality of military atrocities and their aftermath. The text is tense with the mood of war-torn Germany, their journey is difficult and sometimes dangerous, and Radcliffe reflects sombrely on 'the unnumbered heap of the military slain' (257).

The author of the *Sketch of Modern France* makes more explicit the ways in which the Revolution has invalidated the Gothic idiom. The huge number of despoiled churches prompts a reflection on the aesthetics of age and ruin:

> I must confess, that the ruins of the castles built during the feudal system never affected me like these modern ones: I considered them as picturesque objects and, without adverting to what reduced them to neglected and mouldering ruins, I was pleased with their effect in the landscape. But not so the *ruins* that now come daily before our eyes: these are not ivy-mantled, but bearing all the naked marks of violence;—these do not relate to 'tales of other times,' but are produced by the shocks and convulsions of yesterday. (*A Sketch of Modern France*, 340–41)

The feminine realm of Gothic ruin and Gothic fiction is here invoked only to be reprimanded for its ignorance and idealism, and the reader of romance is personified and repudiated in the author's past, naïve self ('I considered them as picturesque objects').

It is significant that after *A Journey* Radcliffe wrote only one more novel, *The Italian*, and that was in large part provoked by the publication of Matthew Lewis's *The Monk* (1796).[87] Moreover, *The Italian* is set in a more remote region than the German or Swiss settings of *The Romance of the Forest* (1791), settings which Radcliffe does not use for fiction again. The Gothic romancing of near-Europe became, perhaps, impossible to sustain in the light of political developments and her own experiences. Radcliffe's examination of Catholicism in *A Journey* is likewise more politicized than her fictional use of the Catholic bugbear. Her voice is more strident; more British, indeed. A German convent is described with intense disapproval – 'Accounts of such

---

[87] See Robert Miles, *Ann Radcliffe: the Great Enchantress* (Manchester, 1995), 170–71.

horrible perversions of human reason make the blood thrill' – which modulates into a brisk, almost comic conclusion: 'The poor nuns, thus nearly entombed during their lives, are, after death, tied upon a board, in the cloaths they die in, and, with only their veils thrown over the face, are buried in the garden of the convent' (109–10). Other less extreme religious orders are treated with some sympathy, for instance the large numbers of actively charitable nuns who can be seen 'teaching children and attending the sick' in Cologne (113).

Elsewhere, the horrors of Catholicism are qualified by the political context. Returning home through Flanders, the Radcliffes encounter 'nearly an hundred' nuns evicted from their convent by the Revolutionary army:

> It might have been censured, a few years since, that mistakes, or deceptions, as to religious duties, should have driven them from the world; but it was certainly now only to be lamented, that any thing short of the gradual and peaceful progress of reason should have expelled them from their retirement. (358–9)

This more complex response (which possibly reflects also William Radcliffe's Burkean, gradualist views on political change) is, again, less unexpected within the context of 1790s travel writing than it would have been in Radcliffe's own earlier novels.[88] It is no coincidence that the later *The Italian* (1798) contains the only sympathetic portrayal of a convent community in Radcliffe's fiction. *A Journey*, moreover, includes a diatribe against travel writers who, in the time-honoured tradition of the genre, dwell minutely and satirically on Roman Catholic absurdities: 'To such writers, the probable mischief of uniting with the mention of the most divine doctrines the most ridiculous of human impositions ought to be apparent; and, as the risk is unnecessary in a Protestant country, why is it encountered?' (126). Roman Catholicism is preferable to atheism.

The voice of Protestant morality is shot through with the more consciously gendered discourse of domesticity, increasingly figured as patriotic homesickness. Radcliffe longs for the clean linen and well-stocked larders of 'every half-way house between London and Canterbury' (159), and the lively commerce of English towns, complaining at the dirt of German inns and the lassitude of their trade (161). The *Monthly Review* draws attention to her patriotism in terms which underline the close relationship between femininity and home-keeping: 'This fair writer appears to have travelled under the strong impression of attachment to her native country', the reviewer observes, and considers this 'a sentiment which, under due regulation, is both laudable and useful'. But Radcliffe, he continues, has gone too far in the direction of

---

[88] Janet Todd, *The Sign of Angellica: Women, Writing and Fiction, 1660–1800* (1989), 254–5, notes that William Radcliffe was a moderate, who by 1793 had withdrawn his earlier support for the Revolution, and become 'an upholder of national unity'.

'illiberality' by indulging her 'nationality' to excess.[89] The offending passage from *A Journey* is indeed vehemently isolationist:

> Englishmen, who feel, as they always must, the love of their own
> country much increased by the view of others, should be induced, at
> every step, to wish, that there may be as little political intercourse as
> possible, either of friendship or enmity, between the blessings of
> their Island and the wretchedness of the Continent. (108)

These sentiments may appear extreme, and yet they covertly inform *A Journey* as a whole, particularly once access to Switzerland – in many ways the motivating goal of the whole trip – has been denied to the Radcliffes by an obstreperous border patrol. At this point, the travellers' momentum is in a homeward direction, and the return journey is described with increasing excitement:

> we, in quitting the borders of Switzerland, thought only of that
> country … but, as the distance from Switzerland increased, the
> attractions of home gathered strength, and the inconveniences of
> Germany, which had been so readily felt before, could scarcely be
> noticed when we knew them to lie in the road to England. (277–8)

The grateful sense of homecoming which is conventional in eighteenth-century travel writing is developed into extended rhapsody in *A Journey*. Not only is their 'love of our own country, greatly enhanced by all that had been seen of others'; but the English landscape between Deal and London is dignified with Radcliffe's finest descriptive skills:

> The large scale, in which every division of land appeared in
> Germany, the long corn grounds, the huge stretches of hills, the vast
> plains and the wide vallies could not but be beautifully opposed by
> the varieties and undulations of English surface, with gently
> swelling slopes, rich in verdure, thick inclosures, woods, bowery
> hop-grounds, sheltered mansions, announcing the wealth, and
> substantial farms, with neat villages, the comfort of the country.
> English landscape may be compared to cabinet pictures, delicately
> beautiful and highly finished; German scenery to paintings for a
> vestibule, of bold outline and often sublime, but coarse, and to be
> viewed with advantage only from a distance. (370–71)[90]

---

[89]   *MR*, NS 18 (1795), 245.

[90]   Jonathan Bate points out that there was a longstanding (since Elizabethan times) tradition associating Kent with the especially valiant defence of England against foreign invasion and influence, to which Wordsworth's sonnet 'Composed in the Valley, near Dover' belongs. See Bate, *Romantic Regionalism, Romantic Nationalism* (Adelaide, 1994), 11–13.

A Journey is supplemented (the pagination is continuous) with *Observations during a Tour to the Lakes of Lancashire, Westmoreland, and Cumberland*, which describes a journey the Radcliffes undertook on their return from the Continent, 'as some compensation for their disappointment in not being able to visit Switzerland'.[91] Here, Britain reveals her sublime as well as beautiful character in pages of eloquent description which the *Critical Review* cites in full.[92] Radcliffe experiences the dizziness of mountain views simultaneously with the possession of England. She stands 'on a pinnacle' of Skiddaw (it is tempting to envisage Christ resisting the temptation of the Continent) 'commanding the whole dome of the sky':

> Bounding the low country to the north, the wide Solway Firth, with its indented shores, looked like a gray horizon, and the double range of Scottish mountains, seen dimly through mist beyond, like lines of dark clouds above it ... We now spanned the narrowest part of England, looking from the Irish Channel, on one side, to the German Ocean, on the other, which latter was, however, so far off as to be discernible only like a mist. (457–8)

The borders of vision coincide beautifully with desirable political boundaries. The Englishwoman has come home; and with her the sublime. This creative retreat from the Continent captures a crucial moment in the insular nationalism of the 1790s, and prefigures the relocation of the Wordsworthian sublime, following its Alpine disappointment in Book VI of *The Prelude*, to the distinctive world of British lakes and mountains.

Perhaps surprisingly, given the way Helen Maria Williams had tried to deploy an image of her own domestic femininity in her earlier works, her *Tour in Switzerland* (1798) eschews any gestures like Radcliffe's towards national attachment, and is an adventurous text. By 1798 Williams was already well known as a poet and as the author of the voluminous eye-witness account of the Revolution, *Letters from France*.[93] Gary Kelly has shown how Williams is concerned in the *Letters*, which she writes 'both as a Briton and a woman', to 'feminize' the Revolution by describing and structuring it as a romance.[94] To this end, stories such as the account of the du Fossé family are introduced (in *Letters* 1792), to provide examples of tribulation ending in joy, and to

---

[91] *CR*, NS 14 (1795), 250.
[92] *CR*, NS 14 (1795), 250–55.
[93] Wordsworth's first published poem, in 1787, was a 'Sonnet on Seeing Miss Helen Maria Williams Weep at a Tale of Distress', published anonymously in the *European Magazine*, 40 (1787), 202. The *Letters from France* were published in three instalments: series 1, vols 1 and 2 in 1792; series 1, vols 3 and 4 in 1793; and series 2, vols 1–4 in 1795.
[94] Gary Kelly, *Women, Writing, and Revolution, 1790–1827* (Oxford, 1993), 30–79; 35.

demonstrate the force of Williams's own affections for individuals caught up in the Revolution. Thus, her support for the Revolution avoids conflict with – indeed, 'arises from her feminine, domestic character and affections' (Kelly, 35–8). As Nicola Watson has observed, Williams thus makes use of the letter form to 'translate the cerebral discourse of politics into a feminized discourse of the "heart"; coaxing her fictional correspondent (and by extension the reader) into emotional, and therefore political, complicity'.[95] While the 1793 *Letters* (co-authored by Williams's lover, John Hurford Stone), express anxiety about the despotic masculinity of the Terror, Kelly argues that the 1795 *Letters* embody a revived optimism, and an extended attribution of the Revolution's feminized virtue as far as the Revolutionary army, who are, in Williams's account, motivated by protective domestic affection rather than masculine aggression (Kelly, 49–69). Williams attempts not only to naturalize the Revolution but also to protect herself against attacks such as Laetitia Matilda Hawkins's, by emphasizing characteristics of her own which might cater to the most conservative of political tastes – her femininity, her domestic affections, her love of her country. Kelly notes (39) that the 1792 *Letters* take the form of a romance journey, beginning *and* ending at home, and thus, perhaps, hoping to forestall accusations of 'moral vagabondage'.

In 1791, Williams had published, to critical acclaim, a poem entitled *A Farewell, for Two Years, to England*.[96] The poem feelingly describes her sensitivity to ties of birth and nation – 'Ah! land belov'd' – but urges also the sympathy with which her 'glowing breast / Shall hear, on any shore, of millions blest!'[97] Domestic affection is thus complicated by universal philanthropy; as, indeed, was increasingly the case with the abolitionists at this time, with whom Williams was involved.[98] *A Farewell* employs the flattering argument by which the French Revolution is inspired by England's glorious example, and the Reviews celebrate Williams's 'enthusiasm in the cause of liberty', which in 1791 is still a patriotic impulse.[99]

It becomes so again in 1798, when *A Tour in Switzerland* is published, almost coincident with the French invasion of Switzerland, which 'has been likened to the 1956 invasion of Hungary in its effect upon international opinion'.[100] Williams had travelled in and around Switzerland with Stone, who was employed as an agent for the French government, so was almost certainly aware of the planned invasion. Her defence and justification of the French

---

[95] Watson, *Revolution and the Form of the British Novel*, 30.
[96] See *AR*, 10 (1793), 188; *CR*, NS 2 (1791), 232.
[97] *A Farewell*, 2, 6; lines unnumbered.
[98] See Clare Midgley, *Women Against Slavery: the British Campaigns, 1780–1870* (1992).
[99] *CR*, 2 (1791), 232.
[100] Jones, *Radical Sensibility*, 152–3.

aggressors is at odds with most contemporary opinion: Chris Jones reminds us that for Wordsworth, for example, the subjugation of Switzerland was 'a crucial point of transition in public sympathies with the French' (153). But Williams's discussion of Swiss government and social morality, and the need for radical reform in both these areas, invoke the terms of liberty and civic virtue dear to British readers, in order to *vindicate* the French invasion. The *Critical Review*'s response to *A Tour* nicely indicates the ambiguous appeal of Williams's work, which responds to British interest in Switzerland only to prompt a deep revision of sympathies: 'now, when the fate of Switzerland is the theme of general discourse and common commiseration, this work appears to inform us rightly what those liberties are of which we are so disposed to lament the invasion'.[101] The *Analytical Review*, in contrast, explicitly opposes Williams's support for the Revolutionary army: 'what must we feel at the dissolution of a friendly nation, once the cradle, domain, and barrier of liberty, endeared to us by political alliance, religious and moral analogy, and long continued social intercourse?'[102]

In the *Tour*, Williams explodes the myth of Swiss liberty, virtue, and independence. She does this by criticizing, through irony, indirection and allusion as well as overt attack, the versions of Switzerland made available to the reading public in the travelogues of Coxe, and Moore, the fiction of Rousseau, and the stereotypes within Goldsmith's *The Traveller*.[103] Ironically, Williams herself had earlier belonged to the tribe of Swissophiles. In her verses 'An Epistle to Dr. Moore, Author of A View of Society and Manners in France, Switzerland, and Germany' (published in her 1786 collection of *Poems*), she had paid tribute to Moore's personal friendship and professional virtues, celebrating the enlivening powers of his 'various page'.[104] In reading, she treads with 'delight' the 'foreign paths you trod before', and surveys Europe through Moore, in Johnsonian moralized couplets which happily mobilize national stereotypes such as the 'ever-jocund' French (8) and the 'phlegmatic ease' of the Dutch (12). Her sketch of Switzerland is equally conventional:

> O SWITZERLAND! how oft these eyes
> Desire to view thy mountains rise;
> How fancy loves thy steeps to climb,
> So wild, so solemn, so sublime;
> And o'er thy happy vales to roam,
> Where freedom rears her humble home. (11)

---

[101] *CR*, NS 23 (1798), 10.

[102] *AR*, 27 (1798), 561.

[103] Jones makes this point (though does not mention Moore); *Radical Sensibility*, 152.

[104] *Poems* (2 vols, 1786), ii. 1–20 (lines unnumbered).

The Williams of *A Tour*, then, is not only attacking other writers' irresponsible idealization of Switzerland; she is also rejecting her own earlier acceptance of the myth.

In addition to the disjunction between past and present authorial self, the *Tour* sets up a more overt opposition between the passive, feminine reader and the active, outspoken traveller. The opening pages' enthusiasm for Switzerland recalls Ann Radcliffe's of several years earlier:

> The first view of Switzerland awakened my enthusiasm most powerfully—'At length,' thought I, 'I am going to contemplate that interesting country, of which I have never heard without emotion!—I am going to gaze upon images of nature; images of which the idea has so often swelled my imagination, but which my eyes have never yet beheld ... I shall no longer see liberty profaned and violated; here she smiles upon the hills ... and finds, in the uncorrupted simplicity of this people, a firmer barrier than in the cragginess of their rocks, or the snows of their Glaciers!' (i. 4–5)

Immediately, however, the moral state of Swiss society disappoints, as Williams relates that she 'discerned neither the love of arts, of literature, of liberty, or of any earthly good, but money' (i. 5). Williams explicitly blames 'former travellers' for her preconceived and disappointed ideas of Swiss society (i. 6). But her complaints about their idealizing are complicated by regret for a mythic era of virtue:

> All in nature is still romantic, wild, and graceful, as Rousseau has painted it; but the soothing charm associated with the moral feeling, is in some sort dissolved. The soft image of the impassioned Julia no longer hovers around the castle of Chillon; which is now converted into a Swiss Bastile, and guarded by a stern soldiery. The tear of sensibility which has so often been shed over this spot for the woes of fiction, may now fall for sorrows that have the dull reality of existence. (ii. 179–80)

Sensibility, like Radcliffe's world of romance, is edged out by political reality.

A Tour describes not only the shortcomings of Swiss politics and social morality, but also, and increasingly, the narrator's retreat from the realm of politics and society into the possibilities of transcendence offered by landscape. In Volume i, the political and the natural-descriptive are rhythmically interwoven, with a further counterpoint being provided by comparisons between Swiss 'manners and customs' and 'the present state of Paris' (i. sig. A4ʳ): these comparisons serve to illustrate the corruption of Swiss society and its ripeness for revolution. Williams is particularly repelled by the rising spirit of petty capitalism, as well as by tobacco smoke, unattractive gardens, and anti-Semitic feeling. In Volume ii, landscape increasingly dominates, and the volume is rounded off with a translation of Ramond de Carbonnière's *Observations on the Glacières and Glaciers*.

However, Williams is curiously diffident about the rhapsodic passages of sublime natural description which punctuate and come to dominate *A Tour*. 'It is the present moral situation of Switzerland that justifies the appearance of these volumes', she urges in the 'Preface' (i. sig. A3ᵛ). She elaborates on her difficulties:

> The descriptive parts of this journal were rapidly traced with the ardor of a fond imagination, eager to seize the vivid colouring of the moment ere it fled, and give permanence to the emotions of admiration, while the solemn enthusiasm beat high in my bosom; but when the sensations excited by those views of majestic grandeur had subsided, I recollected, with regret, that the paths which I had delighted to tread had been trodden before ... (i. sig. A3ʳ–A3ᵛ)

The Reviews echo Williams's own complaints in order to devalue the descriptive passages. The *Analytical* dislikes her 'elegant rhapsodies on the scenery', pointing out that 'Torrents, alps, lakes, have roared, towered, spread; forests have waved, and landscapes frowned or smiled in sudden alternatives of spring and winter, in many a page, before those of H. W., to little better purpose than to weary the reader.'[105] The *Monthly* more acutely observes that her descriptions 'display less the objects themselves, than their effects on the beholder; and ... must therefore be pronounced rather sentimental than informing'.[106]

Williams's rhapsodic transcendence is disparaged in gendered terms. The *Monthly Review* complains that 'all sound moral and practical reasoning, to which the science of politics eminently belongs, is totally incompatible with the giddy flights of an unrestrained and impassioned fancy', and links Williams's waywardness with that of Burke.[107] Unexpectedly, the usually radical *Analytical*, on the other hand, views the shortcomings of *A Tour* as explicitly and dangerously feminine:

> That common disease of female minds, of perpetually longing for something beyond or out of themselves, without appreciating the object, and of placing happiness on any other spot than where they are, did not suffer an eye, absorbed by the view of an alp, or

---

[105] *AR*, 27 (1798), 565.

[106] *MR*, NS 27 (1798), 132–3.

[107] *MR*, NS 27 (1798), 140. C.f. the terms in which the *Critical* had expressed scepticism about Burke's rhetoric in the *Reflections*: 'His tenderness, his humanity, his gallantry ... hurry him away from the path of cool argument, and lead him to substitute invective for enquiry, and the deepest lamentations instead of more sober disapprobation' (*CR*, 70 [1790], 517–18).

> fascinated by the thunders of a cataract, coolly to search for
> characters in an obscure town, or still more obscure village: we
> lament this ...[108]

Restlessness here is represented as *naturally* feminine and yet something to be
curbed at all costs. One can imagine this reviewer's disapproval of passages
like the following, in which Williams reflects on the impact of Alpine scenery:

> Upon the whole this spectacle has something in it of magic and
> supernatural, which overwhelms the mind and senses; we forget the
> mind and senses; we forget every thing, we forget ourselves, and
> have scarcely a consciousness of existence ... (ii. 8)

What Williams sees as transcendence might equally be viewed as moral danger
('we forget ourselves'), and the dubious resonances of travel for women which
inform so much eighteenth-century discourse here resurface. A similar passage
from Wilkinson's *Wanderer* in 1795 had raised no critical comment, although
its account of self-transcendence, and its sublime idiom, are very similar to
Williams's:

> If ever there was a period of my life, when my soul was abstracted
> from the world, it was at that part of this elevated passe ... from
> which the eye surveys, but knows not how to measure, the mighty
> Alps, which on every side surround it, and form the impervious
> barrier of Italy. I was lost in amazement ... (ii. 152–3)

In *A Tour* and its reception, we foresee the exclusion of women from the
'higher' and more sublime genres which will characterize 'high'
Romanticism.[109] Wandering transcendence is being appropriated as a masculine
preserve for the years which follow. Moreover, in the eclipse of Wilkinson's
Wanderer by Wordsworth's *Prelude*, for example, a Romantic hierarchy of
genres is being firmly established, which displaces prose travelogue from its
position at the heart of eighteenth-century literary culture. So profound have
been the cultural and critical implications of this displacement that much of the
material examined in this study has sunk into comparative obscurity, thus

---

[108] *AR*, 27 (1798), 566.

[109] See Kelly, *Women, Writing, and Revolution* (1993), 165–91 on the
'remasculinization of culture and literature' in the opening decades of the nineteenth
century; cf. also Lonsdale ed., *Eighteenth-Century Women Poets*, on women's edging
out of the literary mainstream by 'Romantic subjectivity and transcendence, the
"egotistical sublime"' (xli). Anne K. Mellor, *Romanticism and Gender* (1993), noting
the domination of poetry as '*the* canonical Romantic genre', recuperates an alternative
'feminine Romanticism' during the period, which rejected male definitions of public and
private spheres, advocated what Mellor describes as 'family politics' (84), and
employed a wide variety of genres, both poetry and prose.

burying the compelling evidence for vital connections between Romantic constructions of self and nation and the energetic world of eighteenth-century travelogue. In the brief Epilogue which follows, I shall offer a reading of two seminal travelogues from the late 1790s, which enact an influential move away from prose travel narrative as the most congenial form for the textual negotiation of subjecthood and national identity. Paradoxically, the genre's increasing accommodation during the Revolutionary era of complexity and contradiction – qualities likely to be cultivated in more consciously 'literary' genres – seems increasingly to disqualify it from a central role in the cultural and ideological formation of self and nation for the new literary generation.

Epilogue

If the French Revolution problematizes European travel in specifically political terms, two travelogues from the later 1790s (the itineraries of which are emphatically non-French) play out slightly different anxieties about the genre's continuing effectiveness as a textual site for the exploration of personal and national identities. The closing pages of this study will offer a reading of the travel narratives published by Mary Wollstonecraft and Robert Southey as the eighteenth century drew to a close. I will suggest that these works represent, in many ways, the vanishing point of the genre in its eighteenth-century formulation. It is a curious fact of literary history that, whilst almost every canonized writer from the eighteenth century (as well as countless lesser-known authors) turned their hand to prose travelogue at some point in their career, the Romantic period sees the dominance of poetry as the preferred medium for the literary rendering of travel: except, intriguingly, as carried out by the conscious handmaidens of the great, such as Dorothy Wordsworth in her voluminous travel journals, John Cam Hobhouse in his *A Journey through Albania* (1813) and *Historical Illustrations of the Fourth Canto of Childe Harold* (1818), and Mary Shelley in her *History of a Six Weeks' Tour through a part of France, Switzerland, Germany, and Holland* (1817), which is presented largely as a prosaic prelude to Percy's more lyrical letters, printed in the same volume which then concludes climactically with the first publication of 'Mont Blanc'.

'A particle broken off from the grand mass of mankind'

After its almost total neglect for the whole of the nineteenth century and much of the twentieth, Mary Wollstonecraft's travelogue, *Letters Written during a Short Residence in Sweden, Norway and Denmark* has enjoyed a revival of critical interest during the last twenty years or so, firmly re-establishing the central position within the literary canon which the *Letters* had in fact gained on their publication in 1796.[1] Initial critical reception insisted with notable

---

[1] Increasingly, the *Letters* came to be viewed predominantly as a significant source for more 'literary' Romantic texts. Jane Moore observes that John Livingston Lowes's identification (in *The Road to Xanadu: a Study in the Ways of the Imagination*, 1927) of debts to Wollstonecraft in Coleridge's 'Kubla Khan' 'set the agenda for much later discussion'; 'Plagiarism with a Difference: Subjectivity in 'Kubla Khan' and *Letters Written During a Short Residence in Sweden, Norway and Denmark*', in Stephen

consistency on Wollstonecraft's triumphant integration of masculine and feminine qualities: the *Monthly* commends the '*masculine* ... mind of this female philosopher', whilst *The British Critic* praises her for showing herself 'capable of joining to a *masculine* understanding, the finer sensibilities of a female', which latter qualities the reviewer attributes to her having recently become a wife and mother.[2] Unfortunately, after the publication of Godwin's misguidedly frank *Memoir* of his late wife in 1798, and the revelation of the true nature of her relationship with Gilbert Imlay, such critical generosity became impossible, and the *Letters'* descent into obscurity was rapid.

Naturally, recent critical rehabilitations of the *Letters* have highlighted the significance of their achievement from a feminist perspective. Mary Poovey has compared the *Letters* to *The Prelude*, claiming as venerable a position for Wollstonecraft as for Wordsworth within the genre of 'romantic autobiography'.[3] Mitzi Myers also argues for Wollstonecraft's position in the highest literary ranks of Romanticism, and likewise emphasizes the autobiographical element of the *Letters* over their debt to eighteenth-century travel narrative.[4] Karen Lawrence has contrasted Wollstonecraft's trenchant analysis of 'the workings of gender and class ideology as it operates throughout Scandinavian society' with the more conventional, high-political focus of previous accounts of Northern Europe (in William Coxe's ponderous two-volume *Travels into Poland, Russia, Sweden, and Denmark* of 1784, in particular).[5] Exploring Wollstonecraft's use of the epistolary form and its multivocal possibilities, Mary Favret concludes that the *Letters* 'pay off Wollstonecraft's debts both as sentimental "woman" and as "worldly" philosopher: they establish her as a successful professional woman of imagination'.[6] Examining the *Letters* in the light of revolutionary and gender

---

Copley and John Whale eds, *Beyond Romanticism: New Approaches to Texts and Contexts 1780–1832* (1992), 140–59; 140. Even Richard Holmes's 'Introduction' to the most widely available edition of Wollstonecraft's *Letters* feels obliged to bolster claims for the text's inherent interest by offering a comprehensive account of Wollstonecraft-influenced passages in the works of the early Romantic poets (Richard Holmes ed., *Mary Wollstonecraft and William Godwin, 'A Short Residence in Sweden' and 'Memoirs of the Author of "The Rights of Woman"'* [Harmondsworth, 1987]), 36–42.

[2]   *MR*, NS 20 (1796), 251; *British Critic*, 7 (1796), 607–8.

[3]   Mary Poovey, *The Proper Lady and the Woman Writer: Ideology as Style in the Works of Mary Wollstonecraft, Mary Shelley, and Jane Austen* (Chicago, 1984), 83–94.

[4]   Mitzi Myers, 'Mary Wollstonecraft's *Letters Written in Sweden*: Toward Romantic Autobiography', *Studies in Eighteenth-Century Culture*, 8 (1979), 165–85. For a critique of the more personal and sentimental tendencies in approaches to Wollstonecraft's travelogue, see Mary A. Favret, *Romantic Correspondence: Women, Politics and the Fiction of Letters* (Cambridge, 1993), 96–132.

[5]   Karen Lawrence, *Penelope Voyages: Women and Travel in the British Literary Tradition* (1994), 101.

[6]   Favret, *Romantic Correspondence*, 96–132; 119.

politics, Gary Kelly suggests that Wollstonecraft therein exploits both her established, 'public' reputation as a feminist author and her 'private' identity as a mother, to validate her vision of a 'revolutionary domesticity' which stands in moral contrast to the commercial instinct which has corrupted much of Europe as well as Gilbert Imlay.[7] Having already trespassed on the masculine territory of political history in writing her account of the French Revolution, Kelly argues, Wollstonecraft now extends Revolutionary feminism to 'another discourse not considered the cultural property of women': namely, travel writing (179). Elizabeth Bohls discusses the *Letters* within the context of eighteenth-century aesthetics and their ideological underpinning, arguing that by giving the aesthetic subject a feminine gender and a corporeal connection to her environment, Wollstonecraft subtly but audaciously redefines aesthetic pleasure, presenting herself as 'a full-fledged aesthetic subject whose feminine gender, sexuality, and motherhood are not suppressed, but rather incorporated into the specific quality of her aesthetic experience'.[8] Furthermore, Bohls argues, Wollstonecraft radically humanizes the discourse of aesthetics by putting people at the centre of the landscapes they inhabit, instead of obscuring their material connection to the land: both of these manoeuvres are undertaken in conscious opposition to Burke's relation of aesthetics to an aristocratic and masculinist ideology. Kelly and Bohls are more sensitive to the cultural significance of genre than are Wollstonecraft's other critics; yet all alike take for granted the *success* of whichever enterprise Wollstonecraft is credited with

---

[7]   Gary Kelly, *Revolutionary Feminism: the Mind and Career of Mary Wollstonecraft* (1991), 177–95; 183.

[8]   Elizabeth Bohls, *Women Travel Writers and the Language of Aesthetics* (Cambridge, 1995), 140–69; 169. Likewise exploring Wollstonecraft's subversion of aesthetic discourse, Sara Mills has observed how she reworks the generally masculine discourse of the sublime, particularly by inserting herself into the natural sublime such that she becomes simultaneously aesthetic subject and object, dispersed within nature (Sara Mills, 'Written on the Landscape: Mary Wollstonecraft's *A Short Residence in Sweden*', paper given at 'Literature and Travel: 1750 to the Present' conference, UWE Bristol, 25 April 1998). A key example of this strategy comes at the beginning of Letter VIII, when Wollstonecraft reports that 'my very soul diffused itself in the scene' of cliff and forest before her: 'I bowed before the awful throne of my Creator, whilst I rested on its footstool' (1796 edition, Letter VIII, 94). Whether the sublime, even at moments of subtle redefinition such as this, can ever be properly appropriated by the feminine subject is an ongoing topic of critical debate, the outlines of which are usefully outlined by Patricia Yaeger, 'Toward a Female Sublime', in Linda Kauffman ed., *Gender and Theory: Dialogues on Feminist Criticism* (Oxford, 1989), 191–212, and Julie Ellison, 'Redoubled Feeling: Politics, Sentiment, and the Sublime in Williams and Wollstonecraft', *Eighteenth-Century Studies*, 20 (1990), 197–215, who highlights the 'ideologically malleable' nature of the sublime during the 1790s. Jane Moore observes that instances of sublime encounter in the *Letters* are 'remarkable for the overwhelming sense of lack and loss that contemplation of nature by a woman produces' ('Plagiarism with a Difference', 149).

– subsuming travelogue beneath autobiography, writing a female *Prelude*, deconstructing gender and class ideologies, refashioning and feminizing the revolutionary travelogue, or revising the power relations inherent in the discourses of the picturesque and the sublime.

In many ways, however, it is more illuminating to explore how the *Letters* actually describe and embody failure, of a genre and of a set of cultural beliefs. This broad sense of failure contributes importantly to the peculiarly frustrated and anguished tone of the *Letters*, which is generally attributed to biographical factors alone, namely Wollstonecraft's growing estrangement from Imlay.[9] The unusual 'Appendix' which Wollstonecraft supplied to the published text draws attention simultaneously to personal circumstance and to the resulting inadequacies of the *Letters*, as she apologizes that:

> Private business and cares have frequently so absorbed me, as to prevent my obtaining all the information, during this journey, which the novelty of the scenes would have afforded, had my attention been continually awake to inquiry. This insensibility to present objects I have often had occasion to lament, since I have been preparing these letters for the press ... [10]

This 'Appendix' works curiously with the prefatory 'Advertisement', which had offered a fairly conventional apology for 'being continually the first person—"the little hero of each tale"', and excused this with the plea that 'I could not give a just description of what I saw, but by relating the effect different objects had produced on my mind and feelings, whilst the impression was still fresh'. The Johnsonian equanimity here continues – 'A person has a right, I have sometimes thought, when amused by a witty or interesting egoist, to talk of himself when he can win on our attention by acquiring our affection' ('Advertisement', pages unnumbered) – but this tone of armchair joviality in the 'Advertisement' is startlingly inappropriate to the subtle melancholia of the volume as a whole. The 'Appendix' may be seen as an acknowledgement of this failure.

Contemporary critical response, however, viewed the conflicted tone of the *Letters* more positively, the *Monthly* for example observing that:

---

[9] On the biographical background to the journey, see Per Nyström, *Mary Wollstonecraft's Scandinavian Journey* (Göteborg, 1980). Gilbert Imlay, the father of Wollstonecraft's small daughter, had sent Wollstonecraft to Scandinavia to investigate the legal ramifications of a lost ship carrying quantities of silver apparently belonging to him. While she was in Scandinavia, Imlay pursued his new affair with a London actress (probably unsuspected by Wollstonecraft, who was nevertheless aware of a crisis in their relationship).

[10] 'Appendix', page unnumbered. References are taken from the 1796 edition.

> She claims the traveller's privilege of speaking frequently of
> herself, but she uses it in a manner which always interests her
> readers: who may sometimes regret the circumstances which excite
> the writer's emotions, but will seldom see reason to censure her
> feelings, and will never be inclined to withhold their sympathy.[11]

Melancholic introspection alone, of course, does not make a travel book, and contemporary reviews also praised Wollstonecraft's assured engagement with the more rigorous and empirical aspects of the genre. The distinctive yet elusive texture of Wollstonecraft's *Letters* is produced not only by the frequent subjective interjections, but also by a series of discursive clashes within the text. More alert than most of her contemporaries to the range of discursive and ideological possibilities available to the travel writer (she had reviewed numerous travelogues for the *Analytical Review*), Wollstonecraft adopts a variety of stylistic and political positions, which contribute finally to a sense of their ultimate inadequacy to articulate the complex relationship between individual, nation and species. By exploring the main discursive clashes within the *Letters* – between the positions of anthropological observer and feminist social critic, empirical observer and subjective wanderer, and national and universalist theories of history and politics – the following pages aim to recuperate the very real strangeness, in 1796, of Wollstonecraft's text, and thus to understand its transitional potency, as the era of prose travel writing's cultural dominance begins to give way to the resurgence of lyric and epic poetry.

Some of Wollstonecraft's most significant precursors as authors of Northern European itineraries are notable for their self-conscious gallantry, or, one might more aggressively contend, their sexual imperialism. In 1786, an unlikely trio of well-heeled pranksters, Sir Henry St George Liddell, a Mr Bowes, and Matthew Consett, had travelled to Sweden for purely touristic purposes. Consett published *A Tour through Sweden, Swedish-Lapland, Finland and Denmark* in 1789, describing an elaborate wager which involved the 'importation' of 'two female Laplanders' into England, as well as five reindeer (which the *Analytical Review* judged far more useful than the girls).[12] Consett himself frankly admits that his readers will find little practical information in his book, 'for I pretend not to vie with such celebrated Travellers as Coxe or Wraxal [*sic*]' (*A Tour*, 3). The *Tour* instead describes their languid socializing in the outposts of civilization which pepper the inhospitable landscape, and their 'agreeable Scheme' of shipping home Sigree and Anea, the 'Lapland Girls', who are rewarded with fifty pounds and numerous trinkets before being rehabilitated in Lapland, having demonstrated to their English audience their

---

[11] *MR*, NS 20 (1796), 252; the review is substantial, 251–7.
[12] *AR*, 5 (1789), 17.

natural 'Modesty and Humility' (154). Wollstonecraft's encounters with Scandinavian women, not surprisingly, tell a different story, as her gender and political convictions preclude such sentimentalizing. Although she occasionally expresses concern for the state of oppression and ignorance in which Scandinavian females exist, such concern tends to function more simply as examples of women's universal condition, and the more specific portrayals of Scandinavian women (especially amongst the 'sluggish peasants', Letter XVI, 181) paint them as brutish and promiscuous, effectively the reverse of Consett's image of natural 'modesty': 'love here is merely an appetite, to fulfil the main design of nature, never enlivened by either affection or sentiment' (Letter XVI, 185).

Class in the *Letters* runs thicker than gender, such that Wollstonecraft's position as a single, middle-class woman traveller remains one of hostile isolation. The type of sentimental encounter with picturesquely needy peasants which had contributed to Nathaniel Wraxall's self-affirming projection of an aristocratic British benefactor is rigorously excluded from Wollstonecraft's account, which (as Bohls has observed) has a strongly anti-picturesque agenda in its depiction of peasant life. Similarly, in her discussion of the 'unfortunate Matilda', in whose cause Wraxall had expended so much energy, sentiment and indeed cash, Wollstonecraft rewrites Wraxall's British gallantry and his construction of a *passive* queen, presenting instead a dissident and active woman. Wollstonecraft's Matilda is destroyed by the sexual prejudices of her society, which are presented as tragically at odds with the natural instincts for maternal care (embodied in Matilda's eschewal of swaddling and her advocation of breast-feeding) and romantic affection:

> I have heard her, even after so many years have elapsed, charged with licentiousness, not only for endeavouring to render the public amusements more elegant, but for her very charities, because she erected amongst other institutions, an hospital to receive foundlings. Disgusted with many customs which pass for virtues, though they are nothing more than observances of forms, often at the expence of truth, she probably ran into an error common to innovators, in wishing to do immediately what can only be done by time. (Letter XVIII, 204)

Matilda becomes an emblem of radical femininity, and her oppressors embodiments of prejudice and tradition generally: the sense of British outrage and superiority present in Wraxall is replaced by a boldly adversarial gender politics. These are given a poignant personal twist by Wollstonecraft's evident (and curiously prophetic) identification with the unfortunate Matilda, 'hurried into an untimely grave' (206).

The same potent (yet, within the conventions of the genre, distinctly odd) integration of political analysis and intensely personal circumstance surfaces at the end of a discussion of the ill treatment of Danish servant women. Again, the analysis is of a universal rather than a nationally specific tyranny, and concludes:

> Still harping on the same subject, you will exclaim—How can I avoid it, when most of the struggles of an eventful life have been occasioned by the oppressed state of my sex: we reason deeply, when we forcibly feel.
> But to return to the straight road of observation. (Letter XIX, 214)

The use here (and in several other passages) of what we might term ironic recall – the empirical requirements of the genre reasserting themselves over emotional self-indulgence – is not of course new within travelogue, but is deployed by Wollstonecraft with particular force, to heighten the tension between empirical observation and imaginative subjectivity. A meditation on the 'venerable shadows' of 'pine and fir groves' in Norway leads her to speculate on the mysterious 'origin of many poetical fictions': 'In solitude, the imagination bodies forth its conceptions unrestrained, and stops enraptured to adore the beings of its own creation. These are moments of bliss; and the memory recalls them with delight.' However, this philosophical excursion is briskly curtailed with the recollection 'But I have almost forgotten the matters of fact I meant to relate' (Letter IX, 109–10).

In their range of 'matters of fact', the *Letters* are empirically impressive: Wollstonecraft covers a wide range of topics, from child-swaddling, wetnursing, and make-up, to crime and punishment, forms of government, theories of education, and social evolution. Her informed understanding of the relationship between politics, economics, and day-to-day existence for the people of a nation enables her to bridge the gap between the discursive fields of government and politics on the one hand, and 'manners and customs', including such essentials as food and drink, on the other. In this sense she quietly deconstructs as much as reconciles the masculine/feminine dichotomy embedded in the contrast between high politics and social detail. However, this radical achievement of the *Letters* is consciously downplayed, and the text instead highlights a peculiar apprehension of inadequacy: the empirical demands of travelogue are repeatedly invoked as an unbearable pressure, as in this passage of guilty introspection:

> I had often endeavoured to rouse myself to observation by reflecting that I was passing through scenes which I should probably never see again, and consequently ought not to omit observing; still I fell into reveries, thinking, by way of excuse, that enlargement of mind and refined feelings are of little use, but to barb the arrows of sorrow which waylay us every where, eluding

> the sagacity of wisdom, and rendering principles unavailing, if
> considered as a breast-work to secure our own hearts. (Letter
> XXII, 234)

Wollstonecraft's professed inability to work within the conventions of the genre contributes to the *Letters*' characteristic tone of frustration, and highlights the expressive impasse faced by the imaginative and dissident subject. The technique of ironic recall serves to highlight rather than play down the sense of repression and isolation.

At this point, it is pertinent to observe that her private letters home to Imlay at this time (published in 1798 by Godwin, in Volumes iii and iv of *Posthumous Works*) contain virtually no account of Wollstonecraft's travel experiences. These are documented solely in the *Letters*, which from the first were conceived of as a literary, professional project. On 18 July 1795, she informs Imlay privately that 'I have begun ——, which will, I hope, discharge all my obligations of a pecuniary kind.—I am lowered in my own eyes, on account of my not having done it sooner.'[13] The published *Letters* aspire simultaneously to commercial success and emotional recovery: the private correspondence alludes very infrequently to her physical journey, documenting instead her anguished state of mind. Repeatedly in the private correspondence, in fact, emotional anguish is figured in terms of an alienating journey: 'My friend—my friend, I am not well—a deadly weight of sorrow lies heavily on my heart. I am again tossed on the troubled billows of life ...' (300). Later, she complains that 'I am weary of travelling—yet seem to have no home—no resting place to look to.—I am strangely cast off' (311). Almost at the end of the journey, waiting at Hamburg for a ship home, she looks forward to establishing her daughter happily in the world, after which 'I shall die in peace, persuaded that the felicity which has hitherto cheated my expectation, will not always elude my grasp. No poor tempest-tossed mariner ever more earnestly longed to arrive at his port' (314).

The chilling resonances of 'port' in this passage find a parallel in the problematic signification of 'home' in the published text. The moral valency of 'home' is crucial to the projection of domestic and maternal impulses Wollstonecraft projects, yet the tragic tone of the travelogue derives largely from the sense that this moral centre has no physical or geographical grounding for her. The role of abandoned mother in which Wollstonecraft repeatedly casts herself is crucial here, enabling her to explore the tragic possibilities of solitary exile with moral impunity. She presents herself as 'destined to wander alone' (Letter XII, 142), nurturing 'the pangs arising from the discovery of estranged affection, and the lonely sadness of a deserted heart' (Letter VIII, 103), and

---

[13] Ralph Wardle ed., *Collected Letters of Mary Wollstonecraft* (Ithaca, 1979), 306.

actually envying the Swedish peasant woman who awaits the homecoming of
her labouring husband and their small children:

> My eyes followed them to the cottage, and an involuntary sigh
> whispered to my heart, that I envied the mother, much as I dislike
> cooking, who was preparing their pottage. I was returning to my
> babe, who may never experience a father's care or tenderness.
> (Letter XVI, 187–8)

The almost comic 'much as I dislike cooking' in this passage testifies to the
ambivalence with which Wollstonecraft regards conventional domesticity, such
that her own peculiar homelessness functions also as a sign of superior
sensibility, as in this passage:

> I contemplated all nature at rest; the rocks, even grown darker in
> their appearance, looked as if they partook of the general repose,
> and reclined more heavily on their foundation.—What, I
> exclaimed, is this active principle which keeps me still awake?—
> Why fly my thoughts abroad when every thing around me appears
> at home? (Letter I, 14)

This radical ambivalence – tragic but elevated isolation pulling against
domestic belonging – becomes central to the project of high Romantic poetry,
the male authors of which are less constrained by the moral dubiety of solitary
wandering than Wollstonecraft, and consequently more free to explore the
sublime possibilities of travel and exile.

If Wollstonecraft's self-dramatization as a homeless mother and abandoned
woman provides an autobiographical basis for the *Letters'* distinctive tone, the
discursive clash between travel literature's traditional dependence upon
particular national models, and Wollstonecraft's own reworking of
international culture and politics, constitutes another cause of individual
isolation. Repeatedly in the *Letters*, Wollstonecraft writes in terms of a
universal human society, within which national differences represent little more
than different stages of cultural evolution, or, at most, the differing effects of
climate and government. 'Do not forget', she urges towards the end of the
volume, 'that, in my general observations, I do not pretend to sketch a national
character; but merely to note the present state of morals and manners, as I trace
the progress of the world's improvement' (Letter XIX, 215). In general, this
project enlarges and uplifts Wollstonecraft as she expounds her 'favourite
subject of contemplation, the future improvement of the world' (Letter XXII,
245), and her essentially meliorist view of history. But this progressive vision
has a tendency to falter, either when she moves into a bleak proto-Darwinian
framework within which social progress becomes irrelevant ('it is not men, but
man, whose preservation is so necessary to the completion of the grand plan of

the universe' (Letter XXII, 241); or when the intellectual structure of universal human development intersects jarringly with the still potent discourse of national difference. This latter tension is pervasive in the *Letters*, and worth pursuing here.

Wollstonecraft's account of the Scandinavian countries is shaped by a quite conventional, Enlightenment view of the progress of human society, from barbarity through an ideal metropolitan civilization (refined but not affected) and into decadence, which is figured as an excessive and exclusively male devotion to commerce. She rejects Rousseau's version of primitivism, on the grounds that pre-civilized man is unable to commune imaginatively with nature: 'men who remain so near the brute creation, as only to exert themselves to find the food necessary to sustain life, have little or no imagination to call forth the curiosity necessary to fructify the faint glimmerings of mind which entitles them to rank as lords of the creation' (Letter I, 5–6). She herself, however, is able fully to appreciate and move between two ideal worlds, the metropolis, where 'mixing with mankind' eradicates prejudice; and rural solitude, where the cultivated soul is expanded (Letter III, 33). Wollstonecraft's vision of both these worlds is universalizing, and intersects with her theories of human development, within which national difference has minimal relevance. Thus, the Norwegians are described as 'a sensible, shrewd people, with little scientific knowledge, and still less taste for literature: but they are arriving at that epoch which precedes the introduction of the arts and sciences' (Letter VII, 78). The Germans are at a slightly different stage, 'having arrived at the period when the faculties will unfold themselves; in short, they look alive to improvement, neither congealed by indolence, nor bent down by wretchedness to servility' (Letter XXII, 185). Elsewhere, Wollstonecraft explicitly repudiates theories of national difference, 'factitious national characters', because 'they do not discriminate the natural from the acquired difference': 'It is, for example, absurd to blame a people for not having that degree of personal cleanliness and elegance of manners which only refinement of taste produces, and will produce every where in proportion as society attains a general polish' (Letter V, 58–9).

This is slightly disingenuous, because in one respect Wollstonecraft happily exploits the concept of national character. Her French maid, Marguerite, is presented as a foil to Wollstonecraft's own freedom from female or national weakness. In the first letter, we are informed that Marguerite's 'timidity always acts as a feeler before her adventuring spirit' (Letter I, 3), and we see several instances of this during the expedition: for example, her apprehensions of 'robberies, murders, or the other evil which instantly … runs foul of a woman's imagination' as they prepare to enter the cottage of a 'strange man' (Letter I, 7). Near the end of the *Letters*, once they have left Copenhagen and are travelling back towards England, Marguerite's characteristically French response to travel is delineated:

> Marguerite ... was much amused by the *costume* of the women;
> particularly by the *panier* which adorned both their heads and
> tails; and, with great glee, recounted to me the stories she had
> treasured up for her family, when once more within the barriers of
> dear Paris; not forgetting, with that arch, agreeable vanity peculiar
> to the french, which they exhibit whilst half ridiculing it, to remind
> me of the importance she should assume when she informed her
> friends of all her journeys by sea and land—shewing the pieces of
> money she had collected, and stammering out a few foreign
> phrases, which she repeated in a true parisian accent. Happy
> thoughtlessness; aye, and enviable harmless vanity, which thus
> produced a *gaité du coeur* worth all my philosophy. (Letter XXII,
> 234–5)

The '*gaité du coeur*' here perhaps consciously recalls Sterne's '*politesse de coeur*': in *A Sentimental Journey*, French national character was held up against the British, whereas in the *Letters* national character itself is set up against a supra-national progressivism which Wollstonecraft herself embodies. This manoeuvre can in part be attributed to Wollstonecraft's dissident position within British society; in part also to her Scandinavian itinerary, which frees her from having to engage with the vexed question of Anglo-French relations. As the *Letters* increasingly demonstrate, however, Wollstonecraft's position is a demanding one, particularly when hopes and expectations are disappointed: 'How frequently has melancholy and even mysanthropy [*sic*] taken possession of me, when the world has disgusted me, and friends have proved unkind. I have then considered myself as a particle broken off from the grand mass of mankind' (Letter I, 15). The reassurances as well as the limitations of national identity are unavailable to Wollstonecraft. The final letter, written from Dover, concludes with a disappointed subversion of the conventional patriotic homecoming:

> at the sight of Dover cliffs, I wondered how any body could term
> them grand; they appear so insignificant to me, after those I had
> seen in Sweden and Norway.
>   Adieu! My spirit of observation seems to be fled—and I have
> been wandering round this dirty place, literally speaking, to kill
> time ... (Letter XXV, 262)[14]

---

[14]   Compare her subversion, a little earlier, of the trope by which a foreign landscape's similarity to Britain offers solace: of Germany, she complains that 'The country resembled the most open part of England; laid out for corn, rather than grazing: it was pleasant; yet there was little in the prospects to awaken curiosity, by displaying the peculiar characteristics of a new country, which had so frequently stole me from myself in Norway' (Letter XXII, 237).

The comforting framework and moral centre of eighteenth-century British travel writing has been removed. The possibilities of homecoming and of national belonging are unavailable to the abandoned and deracinated subject. In the final letter, the fruitlessness of travel symbolizes the pointlessness of life itself, as Wollstonecraft exclaims that 'I do not feel inclined to ramble any farther this year; nay, I am weary of changing the scene, and quitting people and places the moment they begin to interest me.—This also is vanity!' (Letter XXV, 261). Perhaps intentionally, this outburst recalls Johnson's closing lines to Goldsmith's *Traveller*, 'Vain, very vain, my weary search to find / That bliss which only centres in the mind' (ll. 423–4), the echo of which serves only to underline the absence of inner certainty and tranquillity which compounds the isolation of Wollstonecraft's traveller. The subjective landscapes opened up for exploration by her Scandinavian *Letters* are to prove more congenial to poetry than to travelogue in the decades which follow; but, as I hope this study has shown, many of the key assumptions concerning subjecthood, gender and nation which Romantic poetry is to develop so fruitfully have been crucially formulated and problematized by the tradition of eighteenth-century travel writing.

Retrospective musings: from Southey to Wordsworth

The young Robert Southey, in a letter to his publisher Cottle in 1796, enquires: 'Have you ever met with Mary Wollstonecraft's letters from Sweden and Norway? She has made me in love with a cold climate, and frost and snow, with a northern moonlight.'[15] A year after her Scandinavian *Letters* had appeared, Southey himself published a travelogue (whose title seems to echo hers) which displays a similar structural and thematic dependence on frustration. Both Wollstonecraft and Southey were motivated by financial need, and the lucrative potential of travelogue. Cottle had engaged Southey in advance of his expedition to produce a published account of Spain and Portugal, on which he worked during and after the trip: but many letters, to correspondents various, make it clear that Southey himself was far more interested in his poetry, especially *Madoc*, at this point.[16]

Both writers were separated from their lovers by the expeditions their texts describe. Wollstonecraft was despatched by Imlay to Scandinavia, and Southey was whisked off to Iberia at his uncle's insistence, in a last-ditch attempt to

---

[15] *The Life and Correspondence of Robert Southey*, ed. Charles Cuthbert Southey (6 vols, 1849–50), i. 311. The first poem in Southey's own 1797 *Poems* was 'To Mary Wollstonecraft'.

[16] See Mark Storey, *Robert Southey: a Life* (Oxford, 1997), 84; and the first volume of *Life and Correspondence*.

stave off his impending marriage to Edith Fricker: in fact, unbeknownst to the uncle, a secret marriage had taken place a month before Southey's departure.[17] While Wollstonecraft's personal circumstances contribute to the mysteriously anguished tone of her published travelogue, Southey's text is more sociably framed, making periodic affectionate references to the woman he has left behind, which serve to highlight his domestic and patriotic impulses. The *Letters* from Spain and Portugal are prefaced by some verses, 'Retrospective Musings', which (as its subtitle explains) were written in January 1797, once he had returned to Britain (the expedition lasted from December 1795 to early summer 1796). 'Retrospective Musings' repudiates travel in favour of 'England, and of all my heart held dear' (xviii; ll. 19–20), and transmute the actual experience of travelling into a metaphor for the growth of a poet's mind – a sleight of hand later to be adopted by Wordsworth as the central motif of *The Prelude*, which rejects the enterprise of travel in favour of 'My last and favourite aspiration, ... some philosophic song / Of truth that cherishes our daily life' (I. 229–31). Remembering the 'pleasant scenes' of Spain, Southey briefly acknowledges pleasure before concluding the poem with a brisk forward movement:

> Often still
> I think of you, and Memory's mystic power
> Bids me re-live the past; and I have traced
> The fleeting visions ere her mystic power
> Wax weak, and on the feeble eye of Age
> The faint-form'd scenes decay. Befits me now
> Fix on Futurity the steady ken,
> And tread with steady step the onward road.
> (xx; lines unnumbered)

The most significant aspect of Southey's journey is that it is over and he has returned home; a point made with a definiteness rather striking for one so young, in the opening lines of the poem, 'Spain! still my mind delights to picture forth / Thy scenes that I shall see no more ...' (xvii; ll. 1–2). The prefatory positioning of 'Retrospective Musings' is resonant: like the early repudiation of travel in *The Prelude*, it subverts with knowing effect the conventional positioning of homecoming sentiments at the *close* of a travelogue. Hence, travel itself and its documentation are critically framed.

This negative structural framing finds an attitudinal counterpart in Southey's generally hostile account of Spain and Portugal. In a comically high-handed tone reminiscent of Samuel Sharp or Anne Miller, he presents Iberia as a superstitious and filthy land, where food is so scarce (on account of the consuming greed of the Spanish royal family plus retinue on their travels) that

---

[17]   Storey, *Robert Southey*, 81–90.

he is at one point forced to eat cat (100–101). Scarcely four pages into the *Letters* we find a Miller-esque passage of gastronomic grotesquerie: 'Our dinner was a fowl fried in oil, and served up in an attitude not unlike that of a frog, taken suddenly with a fit of the cramp' (4), and similar complaints recur throughout the volume, as Southey has to contend with the peasants' tendency to exhale 'essence of garlic hot from every pore' (186), concludes that 'The want of vegetables is a serious evil' (188), and blames everything on the 'absurdities of Popery' (72) and the 'filth and ferocity of Monks' (81), in a country where the people 'live in the same stye with their swine, and seem to have learnt their obstinacy as well as their filth' (37).

The brisk and xenophobic tone of Southey's *Letters* has an old-fashioned feel in 1797. The resolutely anti-sentimental stance he adopts towards the foreign is balanced with a carefully cultivated posture of solitary exile which again is somewhat backward-looking in its conscious invocation of Goldsmith's *Traveller*, especially in passages like the following, from some nostalgic (and rather poor) verses on 'Christmas Day, 1795': 'A weary traveller now / I journey o'er the desert mountain track / Of Leon: wilds all drear and comfortless' (76–7; lines unnumbered). Just as Goldsmith's poem addresses a home-dwelling and thoroughly domesticated brother, Southey at various points in the *Letters* occasionally makes similar rhetorical use of his wife. She is enjoined in the Christmas verses to 'Think of me, / My EDITH! Absent from thee, in a land / Of strangers!' (77), and some of the letters which make up the text of the volume are implicitly addressed to her.

Southey's cultivation of the solitary traveller in the *Letters* is tempered by accounts of energetic socializing in Lisbon, by occasional references to his manservant, and by a description towards the end of the text of the peaceful retreat enjoyed with Southey's uncle at Cintra. However, the pleasures of this arrangement are explicitly opposed to the expected contents of travelogue:

> You would not be interested by the domestic management of three men; yet these trifling circumstances so dull to others, are those that render the remembrance of Cintra pleasant to me: I shall always love to think of the lonely house, and the stream that runs beside it, whose murmurs were the last sounds I heard at night, and the first that awoke my attention in the morning. (517–18)

It is tempting to see Southey's strategies as a fairly straightforward intimation of that 'cultic valorizing of the household and of "homemaking"' which is to characterize much early nineteenth-century writing, and which Kurt Heinzelman has located specifically in the Wordsworth household at Grasmere. To this extent, *Letters* appears to deploy the rhetorical conventions of eighteenth-century travelogue to innovative (albeit politically reactionary) ends. However, although this is certainly an important strand in the *Letters*, and one which adumbrates an increasingly Romantic perspective, it would be unwise to take Southey at face value here.[18] For *Letters* is also a radical text, not in its superficial structures or its mobilization of conventionally patriotic and domestic discourses, but in its implicit privileging of poetry over prose as the genre of national consciousness: and, furthermore, in its inclusion of poetic and critical material designed to demonstrate the ideal superiority of British epic, a superiority which (in line with Whig convention) is peculiarly associated with liberty and therefore, in the 1790s, presented as peculiarly under threat.[19]

The *Letters* are permeated with an intellectual and political passion for poetry, and contain a great deal of verse, some of it Southey's own, some translated from the Spanish and Portuguese: most was weeded out for the 1799 second edition, since Southey planned to publish it separately within a projected study of epic poetry. Southey consistently denigrates Spanish and Portuguese epic poetry in favour of the British tradition: 'there is more genius in one of our old metrical Romances than can be found in all the Epic Poems of Portugal' (482). The *Letters* contain a short 'Essay on the Poetry of Spain and Portugal' (121–30), in which the 'slow and continued' decline of Iberian literature since medieval times is blamed entirely on the 'double tyranny of their Kings and Priests' (125), such that 'the human mind has been fettered by their accursed government and their accursed hierarchy' (127).

The resonances of such remarks in 1796 are at least potentially subversive. And more overtly politicized than Southey's literary theories of epic are the various 'inscriptions' published within the *Letters*. These exemplify a genre which he had begun to make his own, and the value of which he expounds as follows:

> the book of history is placed on the shelf of the student, and he is left to make those inferences in his study which should be forced upon the eyes of the public. Every spot that has been consecrated by a good action, or rendered notorious by being the scene of villainy should be marked out, that the traveller reflecting on the past, might learn a lesson for the future. (223–4)

---

[18] I am indebted to a talk given by Lynda Pratt for this suspicious reading of Southey's *Letters*: 'Home Thoughts from Abroad? Literature, Politics and the Nation in Southey's *Letters Written during a Short Residence in Spain and Portugal*', 'Literature and Travel: 1750 to the Present' conference, UWE Bristol, 25 April 1998.

[19] The *Critical Review* observes that 'Mr. Southey, already known to the literary world by the early brilliancy of his poetic genius, in this volume appears in the character of a tourist, not however quitting entirely that of a poet, since his letters are interspersed with many translations from the Spanish and Portuguese, and prefaced by a pleasing copy of verses' (*CR*, NS 20 [1797], 378–84). In 1796–8, Southey contributed a series of essays 'Of the Poetry of Spain and Portugal' to *The Monthly Magazine* (2 [1796], 451–3; 697–700; 3 [1797], 270–72; 4 [1797], 26–9; 5 [1798], 11–12; 275–6).

Such 'lessons' are offered within the *Letters* by inscriptions celebrating the martyred defender of Spanish 'liberties', Juan de Padilla (95), and excoriating the murderous energies of Pizarro, who 'slaughtered thousands' and 'subdued a rich / And ample realm' (225).

Imaginatively inscribed on sites of special historic significance, the inscriptions embody Southey's growing (and at this stage still resolutely radical) conviction that poetry should be the 'portrait of a public mind, and the characteristic traits of every age and of every people may be read in their poetry' (130). This phrase, ambivalently suggestive both of national consensus and of the nationally representative nature of the poet's 'mind', adumbrates the more reactionary trajectory of *The Prelude*, and the appropriation of literary travel to the project of Romantic self-fashioning. Indeed, *The Prelude* itself may be seen as an attempt not only to valorize domestic British loyalties over errant European sympathies, but also (not unlike the project of *Lyrical Ballads*, especially 'Tintern Abbey') consciously to appropriate discussion of such issues for the middle-class and masculine poet, whose interior self as articulated in poetry is projected as the repository of national virtue. In the framing books of *The Prelude*, revealingly, travel is relegated to a metaphorical function, serving 'the story of my life', of which 'The road lies plain before me. 'Tis a theme / Single and of determined bounds' (I. 667–9). By the time we reach Book III, the message is clearer still, in the assertion that 'A traveller I am, / And all my tale is of myself' (III. 196–7). Heffernan has described how Wordsworth is centrally concerned, in *The Prelude*, to convert the chaotic events of the French Revolution into 'an intelligible and meaningful shape ... that could take its place in what he conceived as the providential design of a life destined to make him a poet'.[20] The sublime egotism of this strategy (whereby international history serves the British poet's destiny) is ideologically grounded in Grasmere, such that the promised but false paradise offered by the Revolution ('Bliss was it in that dawn to be alive, / But to be young was very heaven', X. 692–3) is regained within a setting which is emphatically British, locally specific, the domestic. These pincer movements – towards the eminence of poetry as a medium for the articulation of Romantic selfhood, and towards the domestic – together invalidate the structures and assumptions of eighteenth-century prose travelogue.

Furthermore, for all its much-vaunted celebration of individualism, the Wordsworthian self is arguably anodyne in comparison to the varied world of humour, wit, and creative controversy which had characterized eighteenth-century travel writers' self-constructions. In that world, the lively variables of gender, class, political affiliation and (sometimes) region had been articulated

---

[20] James A. W. Heffernan, 'History and Autobiography: the French Revolution in Wordsworth's *Prelude*, in Heffernan ed., *Representing the French Revolution: Literature, Historiography and Art* (Hanover, NH, 1992), 41–62; 42.

by amateur and professional writers alike, and popularized by a reviewing arena whose judgements and tastes were less exclusive, and less consciously 'literary', than the critical dispensation of the early nineteenth century.[21] I hope in this study to have gone some way towards redrawing the map of eighteenth-century travel literature, and highlighted its crucial role in developing notions of British identity – notions more protean and unexpected than the monolithic sense of Britishness which is too often assumed to characterize national identity during these formative and energetic years would have us believe. By excavating the largely buried life of a genre, it becomes possible to rethink the cultural and political landscape of an era.

---

[21] See Marilyn Butler, 'Culture's Medium: the Role of the Review', in Stuart Curran ed., *The Cambridge Companion to British Romanticism* (Cambridge, 1993), 120–47.

Bibliography

Place of publication is London unless otherwise stated.

Primary sources

Adams, John, ed., *The Flowers of Modern Travels: being ... Extracts, Selected from the Works of the most Celebrated Travellers; ... Intended Chiefly for Young People of Both Sexes* (2 vols, 1788).

Addison, Joseph, *Remarks on Several Parts of Italy, &c. In the Years 1701, 1702, 1703* (1705).

Addison, Joseph, *The Miscellaneous Works of Joseph Addison*, ed. A. C. Guthkelch (2 vols, 1914).

Addison, Joseph, and Steele, Richard, *The Spectator* (1711–12), ed. Donald F. Bond (5 vols, Oxford, 1965).

Addison, Joseph, and Steele, Richard, *The Guardian* (1713), ed. John Calhoun Stephens (Lexington, KY, 1982).

An Additional Volume to the Letters of the Right Honourable Lady M—y W—y M—e: written, during her Travels in Europe, Asia and Africa, to Persons of Distinction, Men of Letters, &c. in different Parts of Europe (1767).

Alexander, William, *The History of Women, from the Earliest Antiquity, to the Present Time; giving Some Account of almost every interesting Particular concerning that Sex, among all Nations, ancient and modern* (2 vols, 1779).

Amory, Thomas, *The Life of John Buncle, Esq; Containing Various Observations and Reflections, Made in several Parts of the World; and Many extraordinary Relations* (2 vols, 1756, 1766).

Andrews, John, *Account of the Character and Manners of the French; with occasional Observations on the English* (1770).

Andrews, John, *A Review of the Characters of the Principal Nations in Europe* (2 vols, 1770).

Andrews, John, *Remarks on the French and English Ladies, in a Series of Letters; interspersed with various Anecdotes, and additional Matter arising from the Subject* (1783).

Andrews, John, *A Comparative View of the French and English Nations, in their Manners, Politics, and Literature* (1785).

An Appendix to a Tour through Part of France (1793).

Armstrong, John, as 'Lancelot Temple', *A Short Ramble through some Parts of France and Italy* (1771).

Ayscough, Samuel, *A General Index to the Monthly Review* (2 vols, 1786, 1796).

Baillie, Grisell, Lady, *The Household Book of Lady Grisell Baillie, 1692–1733*, ed. Robert Scott Moncrieff (Edinburgh, 1911).

Baltimore, Frederick Calvert, 7th Baron (Lord Baltimore), *A Tour to the East, in the Years 1763 and 1764. With Remarks on the City of Constantinople and the Turks. Also Select Pieces of Oriental Wit, Poetry, and Wisdom* (1767).

Banister, J., 'Verses supposed to have been written in the Isle of Cyprus', *GM*, 63 (1793), 358–9.

Baretti, Joseph, *An Account of the Manners and Customs of Italy; with Observations on the Mistakes of some Travellers, with Regard to that Country* (2 vols, 1768).

Baretti, Joseph, *An Appendix to the Account of Italy, in Answer to Samuel Sharp, Esq.* (1768).

Baretti, Joseph, *A Journey from London to Genoa, through England, Portugal, Spain, and France* (4 vols, 1770).

Becket, Andrew, *A Trip to Holland. Containing Sketches of Characters: Together with Cursory Observations on the Manners and Customs of the Dutch* (2 vols, 1786).

Beckford, William, *Dreams, Waking Thoughts and Incidents: in a Series of Letters, from Various Parts of Europe* (1783); in Guy Chapman ed., *The Travel-Diaries of William Beckford of Fonthill* (2 vols, Cambridge, UK, 1928).

Beckford, William, *Dreams, Waking Thoughts and Incidents*, ed. Robert J. Gemmett (Cranbury, NJ, 1971).

Bell, John, *Travels from St. Petersburgh in Russia to Divers Parts of Asia* (2 vols, Glasgow, 1763).

Bennett, John, *Strictures on Female Education; chiefly as it relates to the Culture of the Heart. In four Essays. By a Clergyman of the Church of England* (1787).

Berchtold, Leopold, *An Essay to Direct and Extend the Inquiries of Patriotic Travellers; with further Observations on the Means of Preserving the Life, Health, and Property of the Unexperienced, in their Journies by Land and Sea* (2 vols, 1789).

Boswell, James, *An Account of Corsica; the Journal of a Tour to that Island, and Memoirs of Pascal Paoli* (Glasgow, 1768).

Boswell, James, *Boswell in Holland, 1763–1764*, ed. Frederick A. Pottle (1928; repr. New Haven, CT, 1952).

Boswell, James, *Boswell on the Grand Tour: Germany and Switzerland, 1764*, ed. Frederick A. Pottle (1928; repr. New Haven, CT, 1953).

Boswell, James, *Boswell on the Grand Tour: Italy, Corsica, and France, 1765–1766*, ed. Frank Brady and Frederick A. Pottle (1928; repr. New Haven, CT, 1955).

Boswell, James, *Life of Johnson* (1791), ed. G. B. Hill and L. F. Powell (6 vols, Oxford, 1934–64).

Broadley, A. M., and Melville, Lewis, *The Beautiful Lady Craven: The Original Memoirs of Elizabeth Baroness Craven afterwards Margravine of Anspach and Bayreuth and Princess Berkeley of the Holy Roman Empire (1750–1828). Edited with Notes and Historical Introduction containing much unpublished matter* (2 vols, 1914).

Brydone, Patrick, *A Tour through Sicily and Malta. In a Series of Letters to William Beckford, Esq. of Somerly, in Suffolk* (2 vols, 1773).

Budworth, Joseph, *A Fortnight's Ramble to the Lakes in Westmoreland, Lancashire, and Cumberland* (1792).

Burke, Edmund, *A Philosophical Enquiry into the Origin of our Ideas of the Sublime and Beautiful* (1757), ed. Adam Philips (Oxford, 1990).

Burke, Edmund, *Reflections on the Revolution in France* (1790), ed. Conor Cruise O'Brien (1968; repr. Harmondsworth, 1986).

Burke, Edmund, *The Correspondence of Edmund Burke*, ed. Thomas W. Copeland (10 vols, Cambridge, 1958–78).

Burney, Charles, *Dr. Burney's Musical Tours in Europe*, ed. Percy A. Scholes (2 vols, 1959).

Burney, Charles, *The Present State of Music in France and Italy; or, the Journal of a Tour through those Countries* (2 vols, 1771).

Burney, Charles, *The Present State of Music in Germany, the Netherlands, and United Provinces* (2 vols, 1773).

Burton, John, *Lectures on Female Education and Manners* (2 vols, 1793).

Calderwood, Margaret, *Letters and Journals of Mrs. Calderwood of Polton from England Holland and the Low Countries in 1756*, ed. Alexander Fergusson (Edinburgh, 1884).

Carver, Jonathan, ed., *The New Universal Traveller. Containing a Full and Distinct Account of all the Empires, Kingdoms, and States, in the Known World* (1779).

Cayley, Cornelius, *A Tour thorough Holland, Flanders, and Part of France. In the Year, 1772* (Leeds, 1773).

Chandler, Richard, *Travels in Asia Minor: or an Account of a Tour made at the Expence of the Society of Dilettanti* (1775).

Chesterfield, Lord, see Stanhope.

Clarke, Edward, *Letters concerning the Spanish Nation: Written at Madrid during the Years 1760 and 1761* (1763).

Cogan, Thomas, *John Buncle, Junior, Gentleman* (2 vols, 1776, 1778).

Cogan, Thomas, *The Rhine: or, a Journey from Utrecht to Francfort; chiefly by the Borders of the Rhine, and the Passage down the River, from Mentz to Bonn: described in a Series of Letters, written from Holland, to a Friend in England, in the Years 1791 and 1792* (2 vols, 1794).

Coleman, Deirdre, ed., *Maiden Voyages and Infant Colonies: Two Women's Travel Narratives of the 1790s* (1999).

Coleridge, Samuel Taylor, *The Complete Poetical Works of Samuel Taylor Coleridge*, ed. Ernest Hartley Coleridge (1912; repr. 2 vols, Oxford, 1975).

A Collection of Poems, by Several Hands (4 vols, 1748–9).

A Comparative Sketch of England and Italy, with Disquisitions on National Advantages (2 vols, 1793).

A Compendium of the Most Approved Modern Travels. Containing a distinct Account of the Religion, Government, Commerce, Manners, and Natural History, of Several Nations (4 vols, 1757).

Consett, Matthew, *A Tour through Sweden, Swedish-Lapland, Finland and Denmark. In a Series of Letters, illustrated with Engravings* (1789).

Continuation of Yorick's Sentimental Journey (1788).

Cook, John, *Voyages and Travels through the Russian Empire, Tartary and Persia* (2 vols, Edinburgh, 1770).

Correspondence between Frances, Countess of Hartford (afterwards Duchess of Somerset) and Henrietta Louisa, Countess of Pomfret between the years 1738 and 1741 (3 vols, 1805).

Coryat, Thomas, *Coryat's Crudities. Hastily gobled up in five Moneths travells* (1611; repr. 2 vols, Glasgow, 1905).

Coxe, William, *Sketches of the Natural, Civil, and Political State of Swisserland; in a Series of Letters to William Melmoth, Esq* (1779; repr. 1780).

Coxe, William, *Travels in Switzerland. In a Series of Letters to William Melmoth, Esq.* (3 vols, 1789).

Coxe, William, *Travels into Poland, Russia, Sweden, and Denmark. Interspersed with Historical Relations and Political Inquiries. Illustrated with Charts and Engravings* (2 vols, 1784).

Craven, Elizabeth, Lady, *A Journey through the Crimea to Constantinople. In a Series of Letters from the Right Hon. Elizabeth Lady Craven, to his Serene Highness the Margrave of Brandebourg, Anspach, and Bareith. Written in the Year MDCCLXXXVI* (1789).

Craven, Elizabeth, Lady, Margravine of Anspach, *Letters from the Right Honorable Lady Craven, to His Serene Highness the Margrave of Anspach, during her Travels through France, Germany, and Russia in 1785 and 1786* (1814).

Craven, Elizabeth, Lady, Margravine of Anspach, *Memoirs of the Margravine of Anspach, Written by Herself* (2 vols, 1826).

Defoe, Daniel, *The True-Born Englishman: A Satyr* (1701), in *The Shortest Way with the Dissenters and Other Pamphlets* (Oxford, 1927), 21–71.

Defoe, Daniel, *A Tour Thro' the whole Island of Great Britain, Divided into Circuits or Journies* (3 vols, 1724, 1725, 1726).

Dillon, John Talbot, Sir (trans.), *Travels through Spain, with a View to illustrate the Natural History and Physical Geography of that Kingdom, in a Series of Letters ... Written in the Course of a late Tour through that Kingdom by John Talbot Dillon, Knight and Baron of the Sacred Roman Empire* (1780).

Dillon, John Talbot, Sir, *Letters from an English Traveller in Spain, in 1778, on the Origin and Progress of Poetry in that Kingdom; with occasional Reflections on Manners and Customs; and Illustrations of the Romance of Don Quixote. Adorned with Portraits of the most eminent Poets* (1781).

Drummond, Alexander, *Travels through Different Cities of Germany, Italy, Greece, and Several Parts of Asia, as far as the Banks of the Euphrates; in a Series of Letters* (1754).

Dryden, John, *On Dramatic Poesy, and Other Critical Essays*, ed. George Watson (2 vols, 1962).

Erskine, Henry, *The Travels and Adventures of Mademoiselle de Richelieu ... Who made the Tour of Europe, dressed in Men's Cloaths, attended by her Maid Lucy as her Valet de Chambre* (3 vols, 1740).

Este, Charles, *A Journey in the Year 1793, through Flanders, Brabant, and Germany, to Switzerland* (1795).

Falconbridge, Anna Maria, *Two Voyages to Sierra Leone, during the Years 1791, 1792, 1793, in a Series of Letters* (1794).

Fanshawe, Ann, Lady, *The Memoirs of Ann, Lady Fanshawe, 1600–72*, ed. H.C. Fanshawe (1907).

Fitz-Henry, James, *Observations on several Passages extracted from Mr. Baretti's Journey from London to Genoa* (1770).

The Flowers of Modern Travel (2 vols, 1788).

Fordyce, James, *Sermons to Young Women* (2 vols, 1766).

Fordyce, James, *The Character and Conduct of the Female Sex, and the Advantages to be derived by Young Men from the Society of Virtuous Women* (1776).

Garden, Francis, Lord Gardenstone, *Travelling Memorandums, made in a Tour upon the Continent of Europe, in the Years 1786, 1787 and 1788* (2 vols, Edinburgh, 1792).

Garden, Francis, Lord Gardenstone, *Peace and Home preferred to War and Travel. To which are added, The Volunteer, The Drum, and Scenes of my Youth* (Glasgow, 1796).

The Gentleman's Guide in his Tour through France. By an Officer in the Royal Navy (1766).

Gibbon, Edward, *Memoirs of my Life and Writings*, ed. A. O. J. Cockshut (Keele, 1994).

Gibbon, Edward, *The History of the Decline and Fall of the Roman Empire* (6 vols, 1776–88).

Gilpin, William, *Observations on the River Wye, and Several Parts of South Wales, etc. relative chiefly to Picturesque Beauty; made in the Summer of the Year 1770* (1782).

Gilpin, William, *Observations relative chiefly to Picturesque Beauty, made in the Year 1776, on Several Parts of Great Britain; particularly the Mountains, and Lakes of Cumberland, and Westmoreland* (1786).

Gilpin, William, *Observations, relative chiefly to Picturesque Beauty, made in the Year 1776, on Several Parts of Great Britain; particularly the High-Lands of Scotland* (1789).

Gisborne, Thomas, *An Enquiry into the Duties of the Female Sex* (1797).

Godwin, William, *Memoirs of the Author of 'A Vindication of the Rights of Woman'* (1798), ed. W. Clark Durant (1927).

Godwin, William, *Memoirs of the Author of 'A Vindication of the Rights of Woman'*, ed. Richard Holmes, with Mary Wollstonecraft, *A Short Residence in Sweden, Norway and Denmark* (Harmondsworth, 1987).

Goldsmith, Oliver, *The Collected Works of Oliver Goldsmith*, ed. Arthur Friedman (5 vols, Oxford, 1966).

Goldsmith, Oliver, *Gray, Collins and Goldsmith: The Complete Poems*, ed. Roger Lonsdale (1969).

Gray, Robert, *Letters during the course of a Tour through Germany, Switzerland, and Italy, in the Years MDCCXCI, and MDCCXCII. With Reflections on the Manners, Literature, and Religion of those Countries* (1794).

Guthrie, Maria, *A Tour, Performed in the Years 1795-6, through the Taurida, or Crimea, The Antient Kingdom of Bosphorus ... and all the other countries on the North Shore of the Euxine ... Described in a series of Letters to her Husband, the Editor* (1802).

Hanway, Mary Ann, *A Journey to the Highlands of Scotland. With Occasional Remarks on Dr Johnson's Tour. By a Lady* (no date; probably 1777).

Harvey, Jane, *A Sentimental Tour through Newcastle; by a Young Lady* (Newcastle, 1794).

An Hasty Sketch of a Tour through Part of the Austrian Netherlands, and Great Part of Holland, made in the Year 1785. With an Account of the Internal Policy, Government, &c. of the Cities of Brussels and Amsterdam. By an English Gentleman (1787).

Hawkesworth, John, *An Account of the Voyages Undertaken ... for Making Discoveries in the Southern Hemisphere ... by Commodore Byron, Captain Wallis, Captain Carteret, and Captain Cook* (3 vols, 1773).

Hawkins, Laetitia Matilda, *Letters on the Female Mind, its Powers and Pursuits. Addressed to Miss H. M. Williams, with particular reference to her Letters from France* (2 vols, 1793).

Hill, Brian, *Observations and Remarks in a Journey through Sicily and Calabria, in the Year 1791* (1792).

Hill, Thomas Ford, *Observations on the Politics of France, and their Progress since the last Summer: made in a Journey from Spa to Paris during the Autumn of 1791* (1792).

A History of the Political Connection between England and Ireland, from the Reign of Henry II to the Present Time (1780).

Hobhouse, John Cam, *A Journey through Albania* (1813).

Hobhouse, John Cam, *Historical Illustrations of the Fourth Canto of Childe Harold* (1818).

Hodgson, H., Revd, *Letters to Mrs Kindersley* (1778).

Howard, John, *An Account of the Principal Lazarettos in Europe; with Various Papers relative to the Plague* (Warrington, 1789).

Howard, John, *The State of the Prisons in England and Wales, with Preliminary Observations, and an Account of some Foreign Prisons and Hospitals* (Warrington, 1777).

Hucks, Joseph, *A Pedestrian Tour through North Wales, in a Series of Letters* (1793), ed. Alun R. Jones and William Tydeman (Cardiff, 1979).

Hume, David, *A Treatise of Human Nature* (1739–40), ed. P.H. Nidditch and L.A. Selby-Bigge (2nd edn, Oxford, 1978; repr. 1990).

Hume, David, *Essays, Moral and Political* (1748).

Hunter, William, *Travels in the Year 1792 through France, Turkey, and Hungary, to Vienna: concluding with an Account of that City. In a Series of Familiar Letters to a Lady in England* (1796).

Hurd, Richard, *Dialogues on the Uses of Foreign Travel; Considered as a Part of an English Gentleman's Education: Between Lord Shaftesbury and Mr. Locke* (1764).

Instructions for the Conduct of Females, from Infancy to old Age, Collected from Speculation, Observation, and Practice; by Way of Familiar Letters to a Friend (1789).

Ireland, Samuel, *A Picturesque Tour through Holland, Brabant, and Part of France; made in the Autumn of 1789. Illustrated with Copper-Plates in Aquatinta from Drawings made on the Spot* (2 vols, 1790).

Irwin, Eyles, *Eastern Eclogues: written during a Tour through Arabia, Egypt, and other Parts of Asia and Africa, in the Year 1777* (1780).

Irwin, Eyles, *Occasional Epistles. Written during a Journey from London to Busrah, in the Gulf of Persia, in the Years 1780 and 1781. To William Hayley* (1783).

Johnson, Samuel *'The Idler' and 'The Adventurer'* (1753; 1759–60), ed. W. J. Bate, John M. Bullitt and L. F. Powell (New Haven, CT, 1963).

Jones, William, *Observations in a Journey to Paris, by Way of Flanders, in the Month of August, 1776* (2 vols, 1777).

'Journal of a Tour from Rotterdam through Austrian Brabant, and Flanders, in an Epistle to a Friend in England', *GM*, 35 (1765), 286–7; 333–4; 381–2.

Justice, Elizabeth, *A Voyage to Russia ... The Second Edition. To which is added, Four Letters, wrote by the Author when at Russia to a Gentleman in London* (1746).

Justice, Elizabeth, *A Voyage to Russia: Describing The Laws, Manners, and Customs, of that Great Empire, as govern'd, at this present, by that Excellent Princess, the Czarina. Shewing the Beauty of Her Palace, the Grandeur of Her Courtiers, the Forms of Building at Petersburgh, and other Places: With several Entertaining Adventures, that happened in the Passage by Sea, and Land* (York, 1739).

Justice, Elizabeth, *Amelia, or, The Distress'd Wife: a History founded on Real Circumstances. By a Private Gentlewoman* (1751).

Kant, Emmanuel, *Anthropology from a Pragmatic Point of View* (1798), trans. Mary J. Gregor (The Hague, 1974).

Keate, George, *A Short Account of the Ancient History, Present Government, and Laws of the Republic of Geneva* (1761).

Keate, George, *Ancient and Modern Rome* (1755).

Kenrick, William, *The Whole Duty of Woman* (1753).

Kindersley, Jemima, *An Essay on the Character, the Manners, and the Understanding of Women, in Different Ages. With Two Original Essays* (trans. from the French of Antoine Léonard Thomas [Paris, 1772], 1781).

Kindersley, Jemima, *Letters from the Island of Teneriffe, Brazil, the Cape of Good Hope, and the East Indies* (1777).

Knight, Phillipina, Lady, *Lady Knight's Letters from France and Italy, 1776–1795*, ed. Lady Eliott-Drake (1905).

Lascelles, Rowley, *Sketch of a Descriptive Journey through Switzerland* (1796).

Lassels, Richard, *The Voyage of Italy ... With Instructions concerning Travel* (1670).

The Laws respecting Women, as they regard their natural Rights, or their Connections and Conduct (1778).

A Letter to a Young Nobleman Setting out on his Travels (1776).

Letters from an Officer in the Guards to his Friend in England. Containing some Accounts of France and Italy (1778).

Letters from Paris during the Summer of 1791 (1792).

Letters from Scandinavia, on the past and present State of the Northern Nations of Europe (1796).

Macdonald, John, *Memoirs of an Eighteenth-Century Footman*, ed. Peter Quennell (1985).

Macdonald, John, *Travels in various Parts of Europe, Asia, and Africa, during a Series of thirty Years and upwards* (1790).

Macdonald, Thomas, *Thoughts on the Public Duties of Private Life; with Reference to Present Circumstances and Opinions* (1795).

MacNally, Leonard, *Sentimental Excursions to Windsor, and other Places* (1781).

Martyn, Thomas, *Sketch of a tour through Swisserland* (1787).

Martyn, Thomas, *The Gentleman's Guide in his tour through France* (1787).

Martyn, Thomas, *The Gentleman's Guide in his tour through Italy* (1787).

Melmoth, Courtney, see Pratt, Samuel Jackson.

Miller, Anne, *Letters from Italy, describing the Manners, Customs, Antiquities, Paintings, &c. of that Country, in the Years MDCCLXX and MDCCLXXI, to a Friend residing in France, by an English Woman* (3 vols, 1776).

The Modern Traveller: Being a Collection of useful and entertaining Travels, lately made into various Countries; the Whole carefully abridged (6 vols, 1776–7).

Moir, John, *Female Tuition: or an Address to Mothers, on the Education of Daughters* (1784; repr. 1786).

Montagu, Mary Wortley, Lady, *Letters of the Right Honourable Lady M—y W—y M—e: Written, during her Travels in Europe, Asia, and Africa, to Persons of Distinction, Men of Letters, &c. in different Parts of Europe. Which contain, among other curious Relations, Accounts of the Policy and Manners of the Turks; drawn from Sources that have been inaccessible to other Travellers* (3 vols, 1763).

Montagu, Mary Wortley, Lady, *The Complete Letters of Lady Mary Wortley Montagu*, ed. Robert Halsband (3 vols, Oxford, 1965–7).

Montagu, Mary Wortley, Lady, *Letters*, ed. Clare Brant (1992).

Moore, John, *A View of Society and Manners in Italy: with Anecdotes relating to some Eminent Characters* (2 vols, 1781).

Moore, John, *A View of Society and Manners in France, Switzerland, and Germany: with Anecdotes relating to some Eminent Characters. By a Gentleman, who resided several Years in those Countries* (2 vols, 1779).

More, Hannah, *Essays on Various Subjects, Principally designed for Young Ladies* (1777).

More, Hannah, *Strictures on the Modern System of Female Education. With a View of the Principles and Conduct Prevalent among Women of Rank and Fortune* (2 vols, 1799).

Morgan, Mrs, *A Tour to Milford Haven, in the Year 1791* (1795).

Morris, Corbyn, *Essay towards Fixing the True Standards of Wit, Humour, Raillery, Satire, and Ridicule* (1744).

Murphy, James, *Travels in Portugal; through the Provinces of Entre Douro e Minho, Beira, Estremadura, and Alem-tejo, in the Years 1789, and 1790. Consisting of Observations on the Manners, Customs, Trade, Public Buildings, Arts, Antiquities, &c. of that Kingdom* (1795).

Newbery, John, ed., *The World Displayed: or, a Curious Collection of Voyages and Travels, selected from the Writers of all Nations* (20 vols, 1759–61).

Nichols, John, *Literary Anecdotes of the Eighteenth Century* (9 vols, 1812–15).

Nugent, Thomas, *The Grand Tour. Containing an Exact Description of most of the Cities, Towns, and Remarkable Places of Europe. Together with a distinct Account of the Post-Roads and Stages* (4 vols, 1749).

Observations on the Present State of Denmark, Russia, and Switzerland. In a Series of Letters (1784).

'Ode on a Distant Prospect of Rome', *European Magazine*, 10 (1786), 211–13.

Orrery, John, Earl of, *Letters from Italy, in the Years 1754 and 1755, by the late right hon. John Earl of Corke and Orrery. Published from the Originals, with explanatory Notes, by John Duncombe* (1773).

Owen, John, *The Retrospect: or, Reflections on the State of Religion and Politics in France and Great Britain* (1794).

Owen, John, *Travels into Different Parts of Europe, in the Years 1791 and 1792: with familiar Remarks on Places – Men – and Manners* (2 vols, 1796).

Palmer, Joseph, *A Four Months Tour through France* (2 vols, 1776).

Parker, Mary Ann, *A Voyage round the World, in the Gorgon Man of War, Captain John Parker; Performed and Written by his Widow; for the Advantage of a Numerous Family* (1795).

Paterson, Samuel, as 'Coriat Junior', *Another Traveller! Or Cursory Remarks and Tritical Observations Made upon a Journey through Part of the Netherlands in the latter End of the Year 1766* (2 vols, 1768–9).

Paterson, Samuel, as 'Coriat Junior', *An Appeal to the candid and spirited Authors of the Critical Review, against Ignorance, Malevolence and Detraction* (1769).

Paterson, Samuel, *An Entertaining Journey to the Netherlands* (3 vols, 1782).

Peckham, Harry, *The Tour of Holland, Dutch Brabant, the Austrian Netherlands, and Part of France; in which is included a Description of Paris and its Environs* (1772).

Pennant, Thomas, *A Tour in Scotland and Voyage to the Hebrides* (1774).

Pennant, Thomas, *A Tour in Wales, 1770* (1778).

Percy, Elizabeth, Duchess of Northumberland, *A Short Tour made in the Year One Thousand Seven Hundred and Seventy One* (1775).

Piozzi, Hester Lynch, 'Italian and German Journals', John Rylands Library, Rylands English MS 618.

Piozzi, Hester Lynch, *Observations and Reflections Made in the Course of a Journey Through France, Italy, and Germany* (2 vols, 1789).

Piozzi, Hester Lynch, *Thraliana: The Diary of Mrs Hester Lynch Thrale (Later Mrs Piozzi), 1776–1809*, ed. Katharine C. Balderston (2 vols, Oxford, 1942).

Polwhele, Richard, *The Influence of Local Attachment with Respect to Home. A Poem* (1796; repr. 1798).

Polwhele, Richard, *The Unsex'd Females* (1798).

Pope, Alexander, *The Correspondence of Alexander Pope*, ed. George Sherburn (5 vols, Oxford, 1956).

Pope, Alexander, *The Twickenham Edition of the Poems of Alexander Pope*, ed. John Butt (11 vols, 1961–9).

Pratt, Samuel Jackson, as 'Courtney Melmoth', *Travels for the Heart. Written in France* (2 vols, 1777).

Pratt, Samuel Jackson, *Sympathy; or a Sketch of the Social Passion. A Poem* (1781).

Pratt, Samuel Jackson, *Gleanings through Wales, Holland and Westphalia, with Views of Peace and War at Home and Abroad. To which is added, Humanity; or the Rights of Nature. A Poem, revised and corrected* (3 vols, 1795).

Priestley, Joseph, *Lectures on History and General Policy* (Birmingham, 1788).

Radcliffe, Ann, *The Romance of the Forest* (1791), ed. Chloe Chard (Oxford, 1986).

Radcliffe, Ann, *A Journey made in the Summer of 1794, through Holland and the Western Frontier of Germany, with a Return down the Rhine. To which are added, Observations during a Tour to the Lakes of Lancashire, Westmoreland, and Cumberland* (1795).

Radcliffe, Ann, *The Italian* (1797), ed. Frederick Garber (Oxford, 1968).

Ray, John, *A Collection of English Proverbs* (1670).

Remarkable Views of the Mountains of Switzerland, drawn and coloured from Nature (1786).

Remarks on the Character and Manners of the French. In a Series of Letters, written during a Residence of Twelve Months at Paris and its Environs (2 vols, 1769).

A Residence in France, during the Years 1792, 1793, 1794, and 1795; described in a Series of Letters from an English Lady: with general and incidental Remarks on the French Character and Manners. Prepared for the Press by John Gifford, Esq. (2 vols, 1797).

Richard, John, *A Tour from London to Petersburgh* (1781).

Richardson, Jonathan, *An Account of Some of the Statues, Bas-reliefs, Drawings and Pictures in Italy* (1722).

Richardson, 'Mr', *Anecdotes of the Russian Empire. In a Series of Letters* (1784).

Riddell, Maria, *Voyages to the Madeira and Leeward Caribbean Islands; with Sketches of the Natural History of those Islands* (Edinburgh, 1792).

Rogers, Samuel, *Italy* (1822).

Rousseau, Jean-Jacques, *Eloisa; or, a Series of Original Letters* (from the French *La Nouvelle Héloïse* of 1760), trans. William Kenrick, 4 vols, 1761).

Rousseau, Jean-Jacques, *Emilius and Sophia: or, An Essay on Education* (from the French of 1761), trans. Thomas Nugent (2 vols, 1763).

Russell, Francis, 5th Duke of Bedford, *A Descriptive Journey through the Interior Parts of Germany and France, Including Paris: with Interesting and Amusing Anecdotes* (1786).

Sage, Mrs, *A Letter, addressed to a Female Friend. By Mrs Sage, the first English Female Aerial Traveller; describing the General Appearance and Effects of her Expedition with Mr. Lunardi's Balloon; which ascended from St George's Fields on Wednesday, 29th June, 1785, accompanied by George Biggin, Esq.* (1785).

Schaw, Janet, *Journal of a Lady of Quality; Being the Narrative of a Journey from Scotland to the West Indies, North Carolina, and Portugal, in the years 1774 to 1776*, ed. Evangeline Walker Andrews and Charles McLean Andrews (New Haven, CT, 1921; enlarged edn 1939).

A Sentimental Journey to Bath, Bristol, and its Environs (1778).

A Sentimental Journey. Intended as a Sequel to Mr. Sterne's. Through Italy, Switzerland, and France (2 vols, 1793).

A Series of Letters between Mrs. Elizabeth Carter and Miss Catherine Talbot, from the Year 1741 to 1770. To which are Added, Letters from Mrs. Elizabeth Carter to Mrs. Vesey, between the Years 1763 and 1787 (4 vols, 1809).

Sharp, Samuel, *Letters from Italy, Describing the Customs and Manners of that Country, in the Years 1765, and 1766. To which is Annexed, an Admonition to Gentlemen who pass the Alps, in their Tour through Italy* (1766).

Sharp, Samuel, *A View of the Customs, Manners, Drama, &c. of Italy, as they are described in The Frusta Letteraria; and in The Account of Italy in English, Written by Mr. Baretti: compared with The Letters from Italy, Written by Mr. Sharp* (1768).

Shelley, Mary, *History of a Six Weeks' Tour through a part of France, Switzerland, Germany, and Holland* (1817).

Sherlock, Martin, *Letters from an English Traveller* (1779).

Sherlock, Martin, *New Letters from an English Traveller. Written originally in French. By the Rev. Martin Sherlock, M.A. Chaplain to the Earl of Bristol: and now first translated into English by the Author* (1781).

Six Days Tour in Normandy, from the 19th to the 25th of July, 1789; with a Short Account of Havre de Grace, Caen, and Cherbourg, the Popular Tumults at those Places (1789).

A Sketch of Modern France. In a Series of Letters to a Lady of Fashion. Written in the Years 1796 and 1797, during a Tour through France. By a Lady (1798).

Sketches and Observations, made on a Tour through various Parts of Europe, in the Years 1792, 1793, and 1794 (1797).

Smith, Adam, *A Theory of Moral Sentiments* (1757), ed. D. D. Raphael and A. L. Macfie (Oxford, 1976).

Smith, James Edward, *A Sketch of a Tour on the Continent, in the Years 1786 and 1787* (3 vols, 1793).

Smollett, Tobias, *A Compendium of Authentic and Entertaining Voyages, Digested in a Chronological Series. The Whole exhibiting a Clear View of the Customs, Manners, Religion, Government, Commerce, and Natural History of Most Nations in the Known World* (7 vols, 1756).

Smollett, Tobias, *Travels through France and Italy, containing Observations on Character, Customs, Religion, Government, Police, Commerce, Arts, and Antiquities, with a particular Description of the Town, Territory, and Climate of Nice: to which is added, a Register of the Weather, kept during a Residence of Eighteen Months in that City* (2 vols, 1766), ed. Frank Felsenstein (Oxford, 1979).

Smollett, Tobias, *The Present State of All Nations* (8 vols, 1768–9).

Smollett, Tobias, *The Expedition of Humphry Clinker* (1771), ed. Lewis M. Knapp (Oxford, 1966).

Snell, Hannah, *The Female Soldier: or, The Surprising Life and Adventures of Hannah Snell* (1750), ed. Dianne Dugaw (1989, Los Angeles).

Southey, Robert, *Letters Written during a Short Residence in Spain and Portugal, by Robert Southey. With some Account of Spanish and Portugueze Poetry* (Bristol, 1797).

Southey, Robert, *Poems* (1797).

Southey, Robert, *Poems of Robert Southey*, ed. Maurice H. Fitzgerald (1909).

Stanhope, Philip Dormer, 4th Earl of Chesterfield, *Letters to His Son and Others*, ed. R.K. Root (1929; repr. 1986).

Stanyan, Temple, *An Account of Switzerland. Written in the Year 1714* (1714).

Starke, Mariana, *Travels in Italy, between the Years 1792 and 1798; containing a View of the Revolutions in that Country ... likewise pointing out the Matchless Works of Art which still embellish Pisa, Florence, Siena, Rome, Naples, Bologna, Venice &c. With Instructions for the Use of Invalids and Families who May not choose to Incur the Expence attendant upon Travelling with a Courier* (2 vols, 1800).

Sterne, Laurence, *A Sentimental Journey through France and Italy by Mr. Yorick* (1768), ed. Gardner D. Stout, Jr (Berkeley and Los Angeles, 1967).

Sterne, Laurence, *The Letters of Laurence Sterne*, ed. Lewis Perry Curtis (1935; repr. Oxford, 1965).

Sterne, Laurence, *The Life and Opinions of Tristram Shandy, Gentleman* (9 vols, 1760–1767), ed. Ian Campbell Ross (Oxford, 1983).

Sterne, Laurence, *The Sermons of Mr Yorick* (1760, 1766, 1769; repr. 2 vols, Oxford, 1927).

Swinburne, Henry, *Travels in the Two Sicilies in the Years 1777, 1778, 1779, and 1780* (2 vols, 1783–5).

Swinburne, Henry, *Travels through Spain, in the Years 1775 and 1776. In which several Monuments of Roman and Moorish Architecture are Illustrated by Accurate Drawings taken on the Spot* (1779).

Swinton, Andrew, *Travels into Norway, Denmark, and Russia, in the Years 1788, 1789, 1790, and 1791* (1792).

'Temple, Lancelot', see Armstrong.

Temple, Sir William, 'Of Poetry', (1690), in Samuel Holt Monk ed., *Five Miscellaneous Essays by Sir William Temple* (Ann Arbor, 1963).

Tench, Major, *Letters written in France, to a Friend in London, between the Month of November 1794, and the Month of May 1795* (1796).

Thicknesse, Philip, *A Narrative of what passed between General Sir Harry Erskine and Philip Thicknesse, Esq; in consequence of a Letter written by the Latter to the Earl of B—, Relative to the Publication of some Original Letters and Poetry of Lady Mary Wortley Montague's, then in Mr. Thicknesse's Possession* (1766).

Thicknesse, Philip, *Observations on the Customs and Manners of the French Nation, in a Series of Letters, in which that Nation is vindicated from the Misrepresentations of some Late Writers* (1766).

Thicknesse, Philip, *Useful Hints to those who make the Tour of France, in a Series of Letters, written from that Kingdom* (1768).

Thicknesse, Philip, *A Year's Journey through France, and Part of Spain* (2 vols, 1777).

Thicknesse, Philip, *Useful Hints to those who travel into France or Flanders, by the way of Dover, Margate, and Ostend* (1782).

Tonkin, Mary, *Facts. The Female Spy: or Mrs Tonkin's Account of her Journey through France, at the order of Charles James Fox* (1783).

Topographical, Picturesque, Philosophical, Historical, Moral, Political, and Literary Descriptions of Switzerland (2 vols, 1780).

A Tour, Sentimental and Descriptive, through the United Provinces, Austrian Netherlands, and France: Interspersed with Parisian, and other Anecdotes: with some Observations on the Howardian System (2 vols, 1788).

A Tour through Part of France (1790).

A Tour through Ireland (1780).

A Tour through Part of France and Flanders. The whole intended as a Guide to the curious Traveller, and an instructive Amusement to those who have no Opportunity of visiting the Places mentioned in this Work (1768).

A Tour through the Theatre of War, in the Months of November and December, 1792, and January, 1793. Interspersed with a Variety of Curious, Entertaining, and Military Anecdotes. To which are subjoined, Interesting Particulars of the Death of Louis XVI. By an Eye-witness of the Fact (1793).

Townsend, Joseph, *A Journey through Spain in the Years 1786 and 1787, with particular Attention to the Agriculture, Manufactures, Commerce, Population, Taxes, and Revenue of that Country; and Remarks in passing through a Part of France* (3 vols, 1791).

Townson, Robert, *Travels in Hungary, with a Short Account of Vienna in the Year 1793* (1797).

The Traveller's Companion and Guide through France, Flanders, Brabant, and Holland (1753).

Travelling Anecdotes through various Parts of Europe (2 vols, 1782).

Travels into France and Italy. In a Series of Letters to a Lady (2 vols, 1771).

Twiss, Richard, *Travels through Portugal and Spain, in 1772 and 1773* (1775).

Twiss, Richard, *A Tour in Ireland in 1775. With a Map, and a View of the Salmon-leap at Ballyshannon* (1776).

Twiss, Richard, *A Trip to Paris, in July and August 1792* (1793).

'Verses On a Journey from Rome to Leghorn', *Universal Magazine*, 93 (1793), 68.

Vigor, Jane ('Mrs'), *Letters from a Lady, who resided some Years in Russia, to her Friend in England. With historical notes* (1775).

Vigor, Jane ('Mrs'), *Eleven Additional Letters from Russia, in the Reign of Peter II. By the Late Mrs Vigor. Never before published. With a Preface and Notes* (1785).

Walpole, Horace, *The Correspondence of Horace Walpole*, ed. W. S. Lewis (48 vols, New Haven, CT, and Oxford, 1937–83).

Wilkinson, Joshua Lucock, *Political Facts, Collected in a Tour, in the Months of August, September, and October, 1793, along the Frontiers of France; with Reflexions on the Same* (1793).

Wilkinson, Joshua Lucock, *The Wanderer: or, a Collection of Anecdotes and Incidents, with Reflections, political and religious, during two Excursions in 1791 and 1793, in France, Germany and Italy* (2 vols, 1795).

Williams, Helen Maria, *Poems* (2 vols, 1786).

Williams, Helen Maria, *A Farewell, for Two Years, to England. A Poem* (1791).

Williams, Helen Maria, *Letters from France* (8 vols, 1792–5: series 1, vols 1 and 2 in 1792; series 1, vols 3 and 4 in 1793; series 2, vols 1–4 in 1795).

Williams, Helen Maria, *A Tour in Switzerland: or, a View of the Present State of the Government and Manners of those Cantons: with Comparative Sketches of the Present State of Paris* (2 vols, 1798).

Wollstonecraft, Mary, *Vindication of the Rights of Woman* (1792), ed. Miriam Brody (1975; repr. Harmondsworth, 1983).

Wollstonecraft, Mary, *Letters Written During a Short Residence in Sweden, Norway and Denmark* (1796).

Wollstonecraft, Mary, *Posthumous Works of the Author of 'A Vindication of the Rights of Woman'*, ed. William Godwin (4 vols, 1798).

Wollstonecraft, Mary, *Collected Letters of Mary Wollstonecraft*, ed. Ralph M. Wardle (Ithaca, 1979).

Wollstonecraft, Mary, *A Short Residence in Sweden, Norway and Denmark*, ed. Richard Holmes (Harmondsworth, 1987), with William Godwin, *Memoirs of the Author of 'A Vindication of the Rights of Woman'*.

Wollstonecraft, Mary, *The Works of Mary Wollstonecraft*, ed. Marilyn Butler and Janet Todd (7 vols, 1989).

Woman. Sketches of the History, Genius, Disposition, Accomplishments, Employments, Customs, and Importance of the Fair Sex, in all Parts of the World (1790).

Wordsworth, Dorothy, *Journals of Dorothy Wordsworth*, ed. Ernest de Selincourt (2 vols, 1941).

Wordsworth, Dorothy and William, *The Letters of William and Dorothy Wordsworth: The Early Years, 1787–1805*, ed. Ernest de Selincourt, revd Chester L. Shaver (Oxford, 1967).

Wordsworth, William, *Descriptive Sketches. In Verse. Taken during a Pedestrian Tour in the Italian, Grison, Swiss, and Savoyard Alps* (1793).

Wordsworth, William, *The Prelude (1799, 1805, 1850)*, ed. Jonathan Wordsworth, M. H. Abrams, and Stephen Gill (New York, 1979).

Wraxall, Nathaniel, *Cursory Remarks made in a Tour through Some of the Northern Parts of Europe, Particularly Copenhagen, Stockholm, and Petersburgh* (1775).

Wraxall, Nathaniel, *Memoirs of the Kings of France of the Race of Valois* (1776).

Wraxall, Nathaniel, *A Tour through the Western, Southern, and Interior Provinces in France* (1784).

Wraxall, Nathaniel, *Historical Memoirs of my own Time, from 1772 to 1784* (2 vols, 1815).

Wraxall, Nathaniel, *Posthumous Memoirs* (3 vols, 1836).

Young, Arthur, *A Six Weeks' Tour through the Southern Counties of England and Wales* (1768).

Young, Arthur, *A Six Months' Tour through the North of England* (1770).

Young, Arthur, *The Farmer's Tour through the East of England* (1771).

Young, Arthur, *A Tour in Ireland: with General Observations on the Present State of that Kingdom: Made in the Years 1776, 1777 and 1778, and brought down to the end of 1779* (1780).

Young, Arthur, *Travels, during the Years 1787, 1788 and 1789. Undertaken more particularly with a View of ascertaining the Cultivation, Wealth, Resources, and National Prosperity of the Kingdom of France* (Bury St Edmunds, 1792).

Young, Arthur, *The Example of France, A Warning to Britain* (1793).

Young, Arthur, *Travels in France and Italy* (1915; repr. 1927 and 1934).

Young, Edward, *Conjectures on Original Composition* (1759).

Secondary sources

Abbott, John Lawrence, *John Hawkesworth, Eighteenth-Century Man of Letters* (Madison, WI, 1982).

Adams, Percy, *Travelers and Travel Liars, 1660–1800* (1962; repr. New York, 1980).

Adams, Percy, *Travel Literature and the Evolution of the Novel* (Lexington, KY,1983).

Anderson, Benedict, *Imagined Communities: Reflections on the Origin and Spread of Nationalism* (1983; rev. edn 1991).

Andrews, Malcolm, *The Search for the Picturesque: Landscape Aesthetics and Tourism in Britain, 1760-1800* (1989; repr. Aldershot, 1990).

Armstrong, Isobel, and Blain, Virginia, eds, *Women's Poetry in the Enlightenment: the Making of a Canon, 1730–1820* (1999).

Aubin, Robert Arnold, *Topographical Poetry in XVIII-Century England* (New York, 1936).

Barker-Benfield, G.J., *The Culture of Sensibility: Sex and Society in Eighteenth-Century Britain* (Chicago, IL, 1992).

Barrell, John, 'Blame it on the French', *London Review of Books*, 14/19, 8 October 1992, 6–8.

Basker, James G., *Tobias Smollett: Critic and Journalist* (Newark, NJ, 1988).

Bate, Jonathan, *Romantic Regionalism, Romantic Nationalism* (Adelaide, 1994).

Batten, Charles L., *Pleasurable Instruction: Form and Convention in Eighteenth-Century Travel Literature* (Berkeley and Los Angeles, CA, 1978).

Beaglehole, J. C., *The Exploration of the Pacific* (1934; repr. Stanford, CA, 1968).

Bennett, Andrew J., '"Devious Feet": Wordsworth and the Scandal of Narrative Form', *English Literary History*, 59 (1992), 145–73.

Bermingham, Ann and Brewer, John, eds, *The Consumption of Culture 1600–1800: Image, Object, Text* (1995).

Black, Jeremy, *The British and the Grand Tour* (1985).

Black, Jeremy, *Natural and Necessary Enemies: Anglo-French Relations in the Eighteenth Century* (1986).

Black, Jeremy, 'Tourism and Cultural Challenge: the Changing Scene of the Eighteenth Century', in McVeagh ed. (1989), *All Before Them*, 185–202.

Black, Jeremy, *The British Abroad: the Grand Tour in the Eighteenth Century* (Stroud, 1992).

Blakemore, Steven, ed., *Burke and the French Revolution: Bicentennial Essays* (1992).

Blakemore, Steven, *Intertextual War: Edmund Burke and the French Revolution in the Writings of Mary Wollstonecraft, Thomas Paine, and James Mackintosh* (1997).

Bloch, Jean H., 'Women and the Reform of the Nation', in Jacobs et al eds (1979), *Woman and Society in Eighteenth-Century France*, 3–18.

Blunt, Alison, *Travel, Gender and Imperialism: Mary Kingsley in West Africa* (New York, 1993).

Bodek, Evelyn Gordon, 'Salonières and Bluestockings: Educated Obsolescence and Germinating Feminism', *Feminist Studies*, 3 (1976), 185–99.

Bohls, Elizabeth A., 'The Aesthetics of Colonialism: Janet Schaw in the West Indies, 1774–1775', *Eighteenth Century Studies*, 27 (1994), 363–90.

Bohls, Elizabeth, *Women Travel Writers and the Language of Aesthetics 1716–1818* (Cambridge, UK, 1995).

Brewer, John, *Party Ideology and Popular Politics at the Accession of George III* (Cambridge, UK, 1976).

Brewer, John, 'The Wilkites and the Law', in John Brewer and John Styles eds, *An Ungovernable People: the English and their Law in the Seventeenth and Eighteenth Centuries* (1980).

Brewer, John, 'The Binding of the Free: Creating Great Britain and its Other', *Times Literary Supplement*, 4672, 16 October 1992, 5–6.

Brewer, John, *The Pleasures of Imagination: English Culture in the Eighteenth Century* (1997).

Brinkley, Robert, and Hanley, Keith, eds, *Romantic Revisions* (Cambridge, UK, 1992).

Brissenden, R. F., *Virtue in Distress: Studies in the Novel of Sentiment from Richardson to Sade* (1974).

Brown, Laura and Nussbaum, Felicity, eds, *The New Eighteenth Century: Theory, Politics, English Literature* (New York, 1987).

Burg, B. R., *Sodomy and the Pirate Tradition: English Sea Rovers in the Seventeenth-Century Caribbean* (1984).

Butler, Marilyn, *Romantics, Rebels and Reactionaries: English Literature and its Background 1760–1830* (1981; repr. Oxford, 1992).

Butler, Marilyn, ed., *Burke, Paine, Godwin, and the Revolution Controversy* (1984; repr. Cambridge, 1988).

Butler, Marilyn, 'Culture's Medium: the Role of the Review', in Stuart Curran ed., *The Cambridge Companion to British Romanticism* (Cambridge, UK, 1993), 120–47.

Buzard, James T., *The Beaten Track: European Tourism, Literature, and the Ways to 'Culture', 1800–1918* (Oxford, 1993).

Campbell, Jill, 'Lady Mary Wortley Montagu and the Historical Machinery of Female Identity', in Tobin ed. (1994), *History, Gender and Eighteenth-Century Literature*, 64–85.

Campbell, Mary M., *The Witness and the Other World: Exotic European Travel Writing* (Ithaca, NY, 1988).

Carter, Philip, 'Mollies, Fops and Men of Feeling: Aspects of Male Effeminacy and Masculinity in Britain, c.1700–1780' (DPhil thesis, University of Oxford, 1995).

Cash, Arthur H., *Laurence Sterne: the Early and Middle Years* (1975; repr. 1992).

Cash, Arthur H., *Laurence Sterne: the Later Years* (1986; repr. 1992).

Castronovo, David, *The English Gentleman: Images and Ideals in Literature and Society* (New York, 1987).

Chambers, Douglas, *The Reinvention of the World: English Writers 1650–1750* (1996).

Chaney, Edward, *The Evolution of the Grand Tour: Anglo-Italian Cultural Relations since the Renaissance* (1998).

Chard, Chloe, and Langdon, Helen, eds, *Transports: Travel, Pleasure, and Imaginative Geography, 1600–1830* (1996).

Chard, Chloe, *Pleasure and Guilt on the Grand Tour: Travel Writing and Imaginative Geography 1600–1830* (Manchester, 1999).

Christie, Ian, review of Gerald Newman, *The Rise of English Nationalism*, *English Historical Review*, 104 (1989), 134–6.

Churchill, Kenneth, *Italy and English Literature 1764–1930* (1980).

Clark, Steve, ed., *Travel Writing and Empire: Postcolonial Theory in Transit* (1999).

Clifford, James L., *Hester Lynch Piozzi (Mrs Thrale)* (1941; repr. Oxford, 1987).

Clifford, James, 'No innocent eyes', *Times Literary Supplement*, 4667, 11 September 1992, 3–4.

Clingham, Greg, ed., *New Light on Boswell: Critical and Historical Essays on the Occasion of the Bicentenary of 'The Life of Johnson'* (Cambridge, 1991).

Clingham, Greg, ed., *Making History: Textuality and the Forms of Eighteenth-Century Culture* (1998).

Coats, A. W., 'The Relief of Poverty: Attitudes to Labour, and Economic Change in England, 1660–1782', *International Review of Social History*, 21 (1976), 98–115.

Coe, Charles Norton, 'Did Wordsworth read Coxe's *Travels in Switzerland* before making the Tour of 1790?', *Notes and Queries*, 195 (1950), 145.

Coe, Charles Norton, *Wordsworth and the Literature of Travel* (New York, 1953).

Cohen, Erik, 'A Phenomenology of Tourist Experiences', *Sociology*, 13 (1979), 179–201.

Colley, Linda, 'Whose Nation? Class and National Consciousness in Britain, 1750-1830', *Past and Present*, 113 (1986), 97–117.

Colley, Linda, *Britons: Forging the Nation, 1707–1837* (1992).

Collins, A. S., *Authorship in the Days of Johnson, 1726–1780* (1927).

Collins, A. S., *The Profession of Letters: a Study of the Relation of Authors to Patron, Publisher, and Public, 1780-1832* (1928).

Constantine, David, *Early Greek Travellers and the Hellenic Ideal* (Cambridge, 1984).

Copley, Stephen, and Whale, John, eds, *Beyond Romanticism: New Approaches to Texts and Contexts 1780–1832* (1992).

Coulson, Mavis, *Southwards to Geneva: 200 Years of English Travellers* (Gloucester, 1988).

Craciun, Adriana, 'Violence against Difference: Mary Wollstonecraft and Mary Robinson', in Clingham ed. (1998), *Making History*, 111–41.

Curley, Thomas M., *Samuel Johnson and the Age of Travel* (Athens, GA, 1976).

Curley, Thomas M., 'Sterne's *Sentimental Journey* and the Tradition of Travel Literature', in McVeagh ed. (1989), *All Before Them*, 203–16.

Curley, Thomas M., 'Boswell's Liberty-Loving *Account of Corsica* and the Art of Travel Literature', in Clingham ed., *New Light on Boswell* (1991), 89–103.

Curley, Thomas M., 'William Beckford and the Romantic Tradition of Travel Literature', *Studies in Voltaire and the Eighteenth Century*, 305 (1992), 1819–23.

Davidoff, Leonore, and Hall, Catherine, *Family Fortunes: Men and Women of the English Middle Class, 1780–1850* (Chicago, IL, 1987).

Davie, Donald, 'Notes on Goldsmith's Politics', in Andrew Swarbrick ed., *The Art of Oliver Goldsmith* (1994), 79–89.

Deane, Seamus, *The French Revolution and Enlightenment in England, 1789–1832* (Cambridge, MA, 1988).

De Bruyn, Frans, 'Theater and Countertheater in Burke's *Reflections on the Revolution in France*', in Blakemore ed., *Burke and the French Revolution* (1992), 28–68.

Dictionary of National Biography (3rd edn, 22 vols, Oxford, 1967–8).

Duffy, Edward, *Rousseau in England: the Context for Shelley's Critique of the Enlightenment* (Berkeley and Los Angeles, CA, 1979).

Duffy, Michael, *The Englishman and the Foreigner* (Cambridge, UK, 1986).

Eagleton, Terry, *The Function of Criticism: from 'The Spectator' to Post-Structuralism* (1984; repr. 1991).

Earle, Peter, review of James Raven's *Judging New Wealth* in *Times Literary Supplement*, 4659, 17 July 1992, 22.

Edmond, Rod, *Representing the South Pacific: Colonial Discourse from Cook to Gauguin* (Cambridge, UK, 1997).

Edwards, Philip, *The Story of the Voyage: Sea-Narratives in Eighteenth-Century England* (Cambridge, UK, 1994).

Eisenstein, Elizabeth, *The Printing Press as an Agent of Change* (2 vols, Cambridge, UK, 1979).

Ellis, Kate Ferguson, *The Contested Castle: Gothic Novels and the Subversion of Domestic Ideology* (Chicago, IL, 1989).

Ellis, Markman, *The Politics of Sensibility: Race, Gender and Commerce in the Sentimental Novel* (Cambridge, UK, 1996).

Ellison, Julie, 'Redoubled Feeling: Politics, Sentiment, and the Sublime in Williams and Wollstonecraft', *Eighteenth Century Studies*, 20 (1990), 197–215.

Evans, Eric, 'Englishness and Britishness: National Identities *c.*1790–1870', in Alexander Grant and Keith J. Stringer eds, *Uniting the Kingdom? the Making of British History* (1995), 223–43.

Everest, Kelvin, and Yarrington, Alison, eds, *Reflections of Revolution: Images of Romanticism* (1993).

Ezell, Margaret, *Writing Women's Literary History* (Baltimore, MD, 1993).

Fabricant, Carole, 'The Aesthetics and Politics of Landscape in the Eighteenth Century', in Ralph Cohen ed., *Studies in Eighteenth-Century British Art and Aesthetics* (Berkeley and Los Angeles, CA, 1985), 49–81.

Fabricant, Carole, 'The Literature of Domestic Tourism and the Public Consumption of Private Property', in Brown and Nussbaum eds (1987), *The New Eighteenth Century*, 254–75.

Fairer, David, ed., *Pope: New Contexts* (Hemel Hempstead, 1990).

Favret, Mary A., *Romantic Correspondence: Women, Politics and the Fiction of Letters* (Cambridge, UK, 1993).

Fletcher, Pauline, and Murphy, John, eds, *Wordsworth in Context* (1992).

Forster, Antonia, 'From "Tasters to the Public" to "Beadles of Parnassus": Reviewers, Authors, and the Reading Public 1749–1774' (PhD diss., University of Melbourne, 1986).

Forster, Antonia, *Index to Book Reviews in England, 1749–1774* (Carbondale, IL, 1990).

Foster, Shirley, *Across New Worlds: Nineteenth-Century Women Travellers and their Writings* (Hemel Hempstead, 1990).

Fothergill, Brian, *Beckford of Fonthill* (1979).

Foucault, Michel, *The Order of Things: an Archaeology of the Human Sciences* (first published as *Les Mots et les Choses*, Paris, 1966) (1970; repr. New York, 1973).

Frank, Judith, '"A Man who Laughs is never Dangerous": Character and Class in Sterne's *A Sentimental Journey*', *English Literary History*, 56 (1989), 97–124.

Frawley, Maria H., *A Wider Range: Travel Writing by Women in Victorian England* (1994).

Fritz, Paul, and Morton, Richard, eds, *Woman in the 18th Century and Other Essays* (Toronto, 1976).

Fulford, Tim, *Romanticism and Masculinity: Gender, Politics and Poetics in the Writings of Burke, Coleridge, Cobbett, Wordsworth, De Quincey and Hazlitt* (1999).

Fussell, Paul, 'Patrick Brydone: the Eighteenth-Century Traveler as Representative Man', *Bulletin of the New York Public Library*, 66 (1962), 349–63.

Fussell, Paul, *Abroad: British Literary Travelling Between the Wars* (Oxford, 1980).

Gallagher, Catherine, *Nobody's Story: Women's Vanishing Acts in the Marketplace* (Berkeley and Los Angeles, CA, 1992).

Gill, Stephen, *William Wordsworth: a Life* (1989; repr. Oxford, 1990).

Gilmore, David D., *Manhood in the Making: Cultural Concepts of Masculinity* (1990).

Gilmour, Ian, *Riots, Risings and Revolution: Governance and Violence in 18th Century England* (1992).

Golden, Morris, 'Travel Writing in the *Monthly Review* and *Critical Review*, 1756–1775', *Papers on Language and Literature*, 13 (1977), 213-23.

Goodman, Dena, 'Public Sphere and Private Life: toward a Synthesis of Current Historiographical Approaches to the Old Regime', *History and Theory*, 31 (1992), 2–20.

Gosse, Philip, *Dr Viper: the Querulous Life of Philip Thicknesse* (1952).

Grewal, Inderpal, *Home and Harem: Nation, Gender, Empire, and the Cultures of Travel* (Durham, NC, 1996).

Grundy, Isobel, '"The barbarous character we give them": White Women Travellers Report on Other Races', *Studies in Eighteenth Century Culture*, 22 (1992), 73–86.

Grundy, Isobel; Blain, Virginia; and Clements, Patricia, eds, *The Feminist Companion to Literature in English: Women Writers from the Middle Ages to the Present* (1990).

Guerrero, Ana Clara, 'British Travellers in Eighteenth-Century Spain', *Studies in Voltaire and the Eighteenth Century*, 305 (1992), 1632–5.

Gutwirth, Madelyn, *The Twilight of the Goddesses: Women and Representation in the French Revolutionary Era* (New Brunswick, NJ, 1992).

Habermas, Jürgen, *The Structural Transformation of the Public Sphere: an Inquiry into a Category of Bourgeois Society*, trans. Thomas Burger (Cambridge, MA, 1989).

Halsband, Robert, 'Women and Literature in 18th Century England', in Fritz and Morton eds (1976), *Woman in the 18th Century*, 55–71.

Halsband, Robert, *The Life of Lady Mary Wortley Montagu* (Oxford, 1956).

Hartley, Lodwick, 'Sterne's Eugenius as Indiscreet Author: the Literary Career of John Hall-Stevenson', *Proceedings of the Modern Languages Association*, 86 (1971), 428–45.

Hartley, Lodwick, 'Yorick's Sentimental Journey Continued: a Reconsideration of the Authorship', *South Atlantic Quarterly*, 70 (1971), 180–90.

Hayman, John G., 'Notions of National Characters in the Eighteenth Century', *Huntington Library Quarterly*, 35 (1971–2), 1–17.

Hazen, Allen T., *Samuel Johnson's Prefaces and Dedications* (New Haven, CT, 1937).

Heffernan, James A. W., ed., *Representing the French Revolution: Literature, Historiography and Art* (Hanover, NH, 1992).

Heffernan, James A. W., 'History and Autobiography: the French Revolution in Wordsworth's *Prelude*', in Heffernan ed. (1992), *Representing the French Revolution*, 41–62.

Heinzelman, Kurt, 'The Cult of Domesticity: Dorothy and William Wordsworth at Grasmere', in Mellor ed. (1988), *Romanticism and Feminism*, 52–78.

Hibbert, Christopher, *The Grand Tour* (1987).

Hilles, Frederick W., and Bloom, Harold, eds, *From Sensibility to Romanticism: Essays presented to Frederick A. Pottle* (Oxford, 1965).

Himmelfarb, Gertrude, *The Idea of Poverty: England in the Early Industrial Age* (1984).

Hitchcock, Tim, *English Sexualities, 1700–1800* (1997).

Hobby, Elaine, *Virtue of Necessity: English Women's Writing, 1649–88* (1988).

Howes, Alan B., *Yorick and the Critics: Sterne's Reputation in England, 1760–1868* (New Haven, CT, 1958).

Howes, Alan B., ed., *Sterne: the Critical Heritage* (1974).

Hulme, Peter, *Colonial Encounters: Europe and the Native Caribbean 1492–1797* (1986).

Hunt, Lynn, *The Family Romance of the French Revolution* (1992).

Hunt, Margaret, 'Racism, Imperialism, and the Traveler's Gaze in Eighteenth-Century England', *Journal of British Studies*, 32 (1993), 333–57.

Hunt, Margaret, *The Middling Sort: Commerce, Gender, and the Family in England, 1680–1780* (Berkeley and Los Angeles, CA, 1996).

Jackson, J. R. de J., *Romantic Poetry by Women: a Bibliography, 1770–1835* (Oxford, 1993).

Jacobs, Eva, Barber, W. H., Bloch, Jean H., Leakey, F. W., and Le Breton, Eileen, eds, *Woman and Society in Eighteenth-Century France: Essays in Honor of John Stephenson Spink* (1979).

Jacobus, Mary, *Romanticism, Writing and Sexual Difference: Essays on 'The Prelude'* (Oxford, 1989).

Jarvis, Robin, *Romantic Writing and Pedestrian Travel* (1997).

Jimack, P. D., 'The Paradox of Sophie and Julie: Contemporary Response to Rousseau's Ideal Wife and Ideal Mother', in Jacobs et al. eds (1979), *Woman and Society in Eighteenth-Century France*, 152–65.

Johnson, Claudia, *Equivocal Beings: Politics, Gender and Sentimentality in the 1790s: Wollstonecraft, Radcliffe, Burney, Austen* (Chicago, IL, 1995).

Jones, Chris, *Radical Sensibility: Literature and Ideas in the 1790s* (1993).

Jones, Vivien, 'Women Writing Revolution: Narratives of History and Sexuality in Wollstonecraft and Williams', in Copley and Whale eds (1992), *Beyond Romanticism* (1992), 178–99.

Kabbani, Rana, *Imperial Fictions: Europe's Myths of Orient* (1986; rev. edn 1994).

Kahrl, G. M., *Tobias Smollett: Traveler-Novelist* (Chicago, IL, 1945).

Kaufman, Paul, *Borrowings from the Bristol Library, 1773-1784* (Charlottesville, VA, 1960).

Kaufman, Paul, *Libraries and their Users: Collected Papers in Library History* (1969).

Kay, Carol, *Political Constructions: Defoe, Richardson, and Sterne in Relation to Hobbes, Hume, and Burke* (Ithaca, NY, 1988).

Kelly, Gary, *Revolutionary Feminism: the Mind and Career of Mary Wollstonecraft* (1991).

Kelly, Gary, *Women, Writing, and Revolution 1790–1827* (Oxford, 1993).

Kernan, Alvin, *Samuel Johnson and the Impact of Print* (Princeton, NJ, 1989).

Kishel, Joseph F., 'Wordsworth and the Grande Chartreuse', *The Wordsworth Circle*, 12, (1981), 82–8.

Knapp, Lewis Mansfield, *Tobias Smollett: Doctor of Men and Manners* (Princeton, NJ, 1949).

Kraft, Elizabeth, 'The Two Amelias: Henry Fielding and Elizabeth Justice', *English Literary History*, 62 (1995), 313–28.

Landes, Joan B., *Women and the Public Sphere in the Age of the French Revolution* (Ithaca, NY, 1988).

Langan, Celeste, *Romantic Vagrancy: Wordsworth and the Simulation of Freedom* (Cambridge, UK, 1995).

Langford, Paul, *A Polite and Commercial People: England 1727–1783* (Oxford, 1989).

Langford, Paul, *Englishness Identified: Manners and Character 1650–1850* (Oxford, 2000).

Lawrence, Karen R., *Penelope Voyages: Women and Travel in the British Literary Tradition* (1994).

Leask, Nigel, *British Romantic Writers and the East: Anxieties of Empire* (Cambridge, UK, 1992).

LeGates, Marlene, 'The Cult of Womanhood in Eighteenth-Century Thought', *Eighteenth Century Studies*, 10 (1976), 21–39.

Lew, Joseph W., 'Lady Mary's Portable Seraglio', *Eighteenth Century Studies*, 24 (1991), 432–50.

Lewis, Barnard, *Islam and the West* (Oxford, 1993).

Liu, Alan, *Wordsworth: the Sense of History* (Stanford, CA, 1989).

Loewenstein, Joseph, 'The Script in the Marketplace', in Stephen Greenblatt ed., *Representing the English Renaissance* (Berkeley and Los Angeles, CA, 1988), 265–78.

Lonsdale, Roger, ed., *Eighteenth Century Women Poets: an Oxford Anthology* (Oxford, 1989).

Lough, John, 'John Howard's Account of French Prisons and Hospitals', *Studies in Voltaire and the Eighteenth Century*, 284 (1991), 385–99.

Loveridge, Mark, *A History of Augustan Fable* (Cambridge, UK, 1998).

Lowenthal, Cynthia, 'The Veil of Romance: Lady Mary's Embassy Letters', *Eighteenth Century Life*, 14 (1990), 66–82.

Lowes, John Livingston, *The Road to Xanadu: a Study in the Ways of the Imagination* (1927; repr. 1951).

Lubbers-van der Brugge, Catharina Johanna Maria, *Johnson and Baretti: some Aspects of Eighteenth-Century Literary Life in England and Italy* (Groningen, Netherlands, 1951).

Markley, Robert, 'Sentimentality as Performance: Shaftesbury, Sterne, and the Theatrics of Virtue', in Brown and Nussbaum eds (1987), *The New Eighteenth Century*, 210–30.

Marshall, P. J., and Williams, Glyndwr, *The Great Map of Mankind: British Perceptions of the World in the Age of Enlightenment* (1982).

Martin, Philip, and Jarvis, Robin, eds, *Reviewing Romanticism* (1992).

Martz, Louis L., *The Later Career of Tobias Smollett* (New Haven, CT, 1942).

Maurer, Shawn Lisa, *Proposing Men: Dialectics of Gender and Class in the Eighteenth-Century English Periodical* (Stanford, CA, 1998).

Mavor, Elizabeth, *The Grand Tour of William Beckford* (Harmondsworth, 1986).

McCarthy, William, *Hester Thrale Piozzi: Portrait of a Literary Woman* (Chapel Hill, NC, 1985).

McKeon, Michael, *The Origins of the English Novel, 1600–1740* (Baltimore, MD, 1987).

McKillop, Alan D., 'Local Attachment and Cosmopolitanism – The Eighteenth-Century Pattern', in Hilles and Bloom eds (1965), *From Sensibility to Romanticism*, 191–218.

McLuhan, Marshall, *The Gutenberg Galaxy: the Making of Typographic Man* (1962).

McVeagh, John, ed., *All Before Them, 1660–1780* (1989).

Meehan, Michael, *Liberty and Poetics in Eighteenth-Century England* (1986).

Mellor, Anne K., ed., *Romanticism and Feminism* (Bloomington, IN, 1988).

Mellor, Anne K., *Romanticism and Gender* (1993).

Melman, Billie, *Women's Orients: English Women and the Middle East, 1718–1918* (1991).

Midgley, Clare, *Women Against Slavery: the British Campaigns, 1780–1870* (1992).

Miles, Robert, *Ann Radcliffe: the Great Enchantress* (Manchester, 1995).

Mills, Sara, *Discourses of Difference: an Analysis of Women's Travel Writing and Colonialism* (1991).

Mills, Sara, 'Written on the Landscape: Mary Wollstonecraft's *A Short Residence in Sweden*', discussion paper, 'Literature and Travel: 1750 to the Present' conference, UWE Bristol, 25 April 1998.

Moore, Jane, 'Plagiarism with a Difference: Subjectivity in 'Kubla Khan' and *Letters Written During a Short Residence in Sweden, Norway and Denmark*', in Copley and Whale eds (1992), *Beyond Romanticism*, 140–59.

Moorehead, Alan, *The Fatal Impact: an Account of the Invasion of the South Pacific, 1767–1840* (1966).

Mullan, John, *Sentiment and Sociability: the Language of Feeling in the Eighteenth Century* (1988; repr. Oxford, 1990).

Müllenbrock, Heinz-Joachim, 'The political implications of the *Grand Tour*: Aspects of a specifically English contribution to the European travel literature of the age of the Enlightenment', *Trema*, 9 (1984), 7–21.

Myers, Mitzi, 'Mary Wollstonecraft's *Letters Written ... in Sweden*: Toward Romantic Auto-biography', *Studies in Eighteenth Century Culture*, 8 (1979), 165–85.

Myers, Sylvia Harcstark, *The Bluestocking Circle: Women, Friendship, and the Life of the Mind in Eighteenth-Century England* (Oxford, 1990).

Nangle, Benjamin, *The Monthly Review, First Series, 1749–1789: Indexes of Contributors and Articles* (Oxford, n.d.).

Nangle, Benjamin, *The Monthly Review, Second Series, 1790–1815: Indexes of Contributors and Articles* (Oxford, 1955).

New Dictionary of National Biography (forthcoming, Oxford, 2004).

Newman, Gerald, *The Rise of English Nationalism: a Cultural History 1740–1830* (1987: repr. 1997).

Nussbaum, Felicity, 'Eighteenth-Century Women's Autobiographical Commonplaces', in Shari Benstock ed., *The Private Self: Theory and Practice of Women's Autobiographical Writings* (1988), 147–71.

Nussbaum, Felicity, *The Autobiographical Subject: Gender and Identity in Eighteenth-Century England* (Baltimore, MD, 1989).

Nyström, Per, *Mary Wollstonecraft's Scandinavian Journey* (Göteborg, Sweden, 1980).

O'Gorman, Francis, '"The Mightiest Evangel of the Alpine Club": Masculinity and Agnosticism in the Alpine Writing of John Tyndall', in Andrew Bradstock, Sean Gill, Anne Hogan and Sue Morgan eds., *Masculinity and Spirituality in Victorian Culture* (2000), 134–48.

Oates, J. C. T., *Shandyism and Sentiment, 1760–1800* (Cambridge, UK, 1968).

Ogée, Frédéric, 'Channelling Emotions: Travel and Literary Creation in Smollett and Sterne', *Studies in Voltaire and the Eighteenth Century*, 292 (1991), 27–42.

Owen, David, *English Philanthropy, 1660–1960* (Cambridge, MA, 1965).

Perry, Gill, and Rossington, Michael, eds, *Femininity and Masculinity in Eighteenth-Century Art and Culture* (Manchester, 1994).

Poovey, Mary, *The Proper Lady and the Woman Writer: Ideology as Style in the Works of Mary Wollstonecraft, Mary Shelley, and Jane Austen* (Chicago, IL, 1984).

Porter, Dennis, *Haunted Journeys: Desire and Transgression in European Travel Writing* (Princeton, NJ, 1991).

Porter, Roy, and Rousseau, George, eds, *Exoticism in the Enlightenment* (Manchester, 1990).

Pratt, Lynda, 'Home Thoughts from Abroad? Literature, Politics and the Nation in Southey's *Letters Written during a Short Residence in Spain and Portugal*, discussion paper, 'Literature and Travel: 1750 to the Present' conference, UWE Bristol, 25 April 1998.

Pratt, Mary Louise, *Imperial Eyes: Travel Writing and Transculturation* (1992).

Redford, Bruce, *The Converse of the Pen: Acts of Intimacy in the Eighteenth-Century Familiar Letter* (Chicago, IL, 1986).

Redford, Bruce, *Venice and the Grand Tour* (1996).

Reimann, K. A., '"Great as he is in his own good opinion": the Bounty Mutiny and Lieutenant Bligh's Construction of Self', in Alvaro Ribeiro and James G. Basker eds, *Tradition in Transition: Women Writers, Marginal Texts, and the Eighteenth-Century Canon* (Oxford, 1996), 198–218.

Rennie, Neil, *Far-Fetched Facts: the Literature of Travel and the Idea of the South Seas* (Oxford, 1995).

Retzleff, Garry, 'Ancient and Modern Romans Compared: the Transformation of Stereotypes in British Travel Literature', *Studies in Voltaire and the Eighteenth Century*, 305 (1992), 1640–44.

Robinson, Jane, *Wayward Women: a Guide to Women Travellers* (Oxford, 1990).

Roe, Nicholas, *Wordsworth and Coleridge: the Radical Years* (1988; repr. Oxford, 1990).

Roe, Nicholas, 'Revising the Revolution: History and Imagination in *The Prelude*, 1799, 1805, 1850', in Brinkley and Hanley eds (1992), *Romantic Revisions*, 87–102.

Roper, Derek, 'The Politics of the *Critical Review*, 1756–1817', *Durham University Journal*, NS 22 (1960–1), 117–22.

Roper, Derek, *Reviewing before the Edinburgh, 1788–1802* (1978).

Roper, Michael, and Tosh, John, eds, *Manful Assertions: Masculinities in Britain since 1800* (1991).

Ross, Marlon B., 'Romantic Quest and Conquest: Troping Masculine Power in the Crisis of Poetic Identity', in Anne Mellor ed. (1988), *Romanticism and Feminism*, 26–51.

Sahlins, Peter, *Boundaries: the Making of France and Spain in the Pyrenees* (Berkeley and Los Angeles, CA, 1989).

Said, Edward, *Orientalism* (1978).

Samuel, Raphael, ed., *Patriotism: the Making and Unmaking of British National Identity* (3 vols, 1989).

Schama, Simon, *Patriots and Liberators: Revolution in the Netherlands 1780–1813* (1977).

Scott, Joan Wallach, 'Gender: a Useful Category of Historical Analysis', in Joan Wallach Scott ed., *Feminism and History* (Oxford, 1996), 152–80.

Sekora, John, *Luxury: the Concept in Western Thought, Eden to Smollett* (Baltimore, MD, 1977).

Shaver, Chester L., 'Wordsworth's Vaudracour and Wilkinson's *The Wanderer*', *Review of English Studies*, NS 12 (1961), 55–7.

Shaw, Stanford, *History of the Ottoman Empire and Modern Turkey* (2 vols, Cambridge, UK, 1976).

Shevelow, Kathryn, *Women and Print Culture: the Construction of Femininity in the Early Periodical* (1989).

Shoemaker, Robert B., *Gender in English Society, 1650–1850: the Emergence of Separate Spheres?* (1998).

Simpson, David, *Romanticism, Nationalism, and the Revolt against Theory* (Chicago, IL, 1993).

Smith, Christopher, *A Quest for Home: Reading Robert Southey* (Liverpool, 1997).

Smith, K. E., 'Ordering Things in France: the Travels of Sterne, Tristram and Yorick', *Studies in Voltaire and the Eighteenth Century*, 292 (1991), 15–25.

'The South Pacific in the Eighteenth Century: Narratives and Myths', special issue of *Eighteenth Century Studies*, 18 (1994).

Spencer, Jane, *The Rise of the Woman Novelist: from Aphra Behn to Jane Austen* (Oxford, 1986).

Spender, Dale, *Mothers of the Novel: 100 Good Women Writers before Jane Austen* (1986; repr. 1987).

Stanlis, Peter J., 'Burke, Rousseau, and the French Revolution', in Blakemore ed., *Burke and the French Revolution* (1992), 97–119.

Storey, Mark, *Robert Southey: a Life* (Oxford, 1997).

Storm, Leo, 'Conventional Ethics in Goldsmith's *The Traveller*', *Studies in English Literature*, 17 (1977), 463–76.

Strachan, Michael, *The Life and Adventures of Thomas Coryate* (1962).

Suleri, Sara, *The Rhetoric of English India* (Chicago, IL, 1992).

Swarbrick, Andrew, ed., *The Art of Oliver Goldsmith* (1984).

Tave, Stuart M., *The Amiable Humorist: a Study in the Comic Theory and Criticism of the Eighteenth and Early Nineteenth Centuries* (Chicago, IL, 1960).

Taylor, Richard C., 'The Politics of Goldsmith's Journalism', *Philological Quarterly*, 69 (1990), 71–89.

Tobin, Beth Fowkes, ed., *History, Gender, and Eighteenth-Century Literature* (1994).

Tobin, Beth Fowkes, 'Arthur Young, Agriculture, and the Construction of the New Economic Man', in Tobin ed. (1994), *History, Gender, and Eighteenth-Century Literature*, 179–97.

Todd, Janet, ed., *A Dictionary of British and American Women Writers, 1660–1800* (1987).

Todd, Janet, *The Sign of Angellica: Women, Writing and Fiction, 1660–1800* (1989).

Tomalin, Claire, *The Life and Death of Mary Wollstonecraft* (1974; repr. Harmondsworth, 1992).

Towner, John, 'The Grand Tour: a Key Phase in the History of Tourism', *Annals of Tourism Research*, 12 (1985), 297–333.

Turner, Cheryl, *Living by the Pen: Women Writers in the Eighteenth Century* (1992).

Turner, Katherine, 'From Classical to Imperial: Changing Visions of Turkey in the Eighteenth Century', in Clark ed. (1999), *Travel Writing and Empire*, 113–27.

Uphaus, Robert W., 'Sentiment and Spleen: Travels with Sterne and Smollett', *Centennial Review*, 15 (1971), 406–21.

Vickery, Amanda, 'Golden Age to Separate Spheres? A Review of the Categories and Chronology of English Women's History', *Historical Journal*, 36 (1993), 383–414.

Vrooman, Alan H., 'The Origin and Development of the *Sentimental Journey* as a Work of Travel Literature and of Sensibility' (PhD diss., Princeton University, 1940).

Wallace, Anne D., *Walking, Literature, and English Culture: the Origins and Uses of Peripatetic in the Nineteenth Century* (Oxford, 1993).

Watson, Nicola J., *Revolution and the Form of the British Novel 1790–1825: Intercepted Letters, Interrupted Seductions* (Oxford, 1994).

Watt, Ian, *The Rise of the Novel* (Berkeley and Los Angeles, CA, 1957).

Weinbrot, Howard D., *Britannia's Issue: the Rise of British Literature from Dryden to Ossian* (Cambridge, UK, 1993).

Wiley, Michael, *Romantic Geography: Wordsworth and Anglo-European Spaces* (1998).

Williams, Glyndwr, *The Expansion of Europe in the Eighteenth Century: Overseas Rivalry, Discovery and Exploration* (1966).

Wilson, Arthur M., '"Treated Like Imbecile Children" (Diderot): the Enlightenment and the Status of Women', in Fritz and Morton eds (1976), *Woman in the 18th Century*, 89–104.

Wilson, Kathleen, 'Empire of Virtue: the Imperial Project and Hanoverian Culture *c.*1720–1785', in Lawrence Stone ed., *An Imperial State at War: Britain from 1689 to 1815* (1994), 128–64.

Wilson, Kathleen, *The Sense of the People: Politics, Culture and Imperialism in England, 1715–1785* (1995; repr. Cambridge, UK, 1998).

Withey, Lynne, *Voyages of Discovery: Captain Cook and the Exploration of the Pacific* (1987).

Woodman, Thomas, *Early Romantics: Perspectives in British Poetry from Pope to Wordsworth* (1998).

Wraight, John, *The Swiss and the British* (Salisbury, 1987).

Wu, Duncan, *Wordsworth's Reading, 1770–1799* (Cambridge, UK, 1993).

Yaeger, Patricia, 'Toward a Female Sublime', in Linda Kauffman ed., *Gender and Theory: Dialogues on Feminist Criticism* (Oxford, 1989), 191–212.

Youngs, Tim, *Travellers in Africa: British Travelogues, 1850–1900* (Manchester, 1994).

Index

NOTE: page numbers in **bold** type refer to main sections. In book titles the initial definite or indefinite article is ignored for alphabetization.

notebooks 3
La Nouvelle Héloïse (Rousseau) 33–4, 136, 138
novel *see* fiction
Nussbaum, Felicity 131

Oates, J.C.T. 100
Observations on the Customs and Manners of the French Nation (Thicknesse) 68, 70–1
Observations during a Tour to the Lakes of Lancashire, Westmoreland and Cumberland (Radcliffe) 219
Observations (Gilpin) 30–1
Observations on a Journey to Paris (Jones) 30
Observations made in the Course of a Journey through France, Italy and Germany (Piozzi) 172–80
Observations on the Politics of France (Hill) 181, 188–9, 190–1
Observations on the Religion, Law, Government and Manners of the Turks (Porter) 153
Orrery *see* Cork and Orrery, John, Earl of
'Other': British reaction to the 6–7
Owen, John 131, 194–5

Pacific world accounts 5–6n11
pamphleteering, polemical 185
Parker, Mary Ann 144
Paterson, Samuel 61, **101–9**, 121, 122
   see also individual titles
patriotism *see* character (British), patriotism
Pennant, Thomas 31
Percy, Elizabeth (Duchess of Northumberland) 142
Percy, Thomas 31
periodicals 10
Philosophical Enquiry (Burke) 28
Picturesque Tour through Holland, Brabant and Part of France (Ireland) 35
Piozzi (formerly Thrale), Hester 132, 145, **172–80**, 194
   contrasting narrative styles 173–4, 176
   relationship between *Thraliana* and journals 175–8
Piozzi, Gabriel 174
plagiarism 72

Pleasure and Guilt on the Grand Tour (Chard) 9
poetry, travel 13–14, 28
Political Facts Collected in a Tour (Wilkinson) 196–7
politics
   of charity 88, 91–2, 108–9, 114, 121–3
   geography and 21
   and landscape 219
   sexual politics in travelogues 121
   see also French Revolution, impact on travel writing
Polwhele, Richard 207, 209
Pomfret, Lady Henrietta 133
Poovey, Mary 227
Pope, Alexander 118, 160–1, 162, 163
Porter, Dennis 17
Porter, James 153
Portugal 83, 135, 239
poverty 50, 69, 71, 122–3, 171
   see also charity, politics of
Pratt, Mary Louise 6
Pratt, Samuel Jackson 14, 36, 105, 124, 194, 202–4
The Prelude (Wordsworth) 198–202, 224
The Present State of All Nations (Smollett) 44
Priestley, Joseph 41
print culture 2, 6–7, 25n13
print-capitalism 9–10
public sphere 9
publishing 3–4, 29–30, 58n5, 63, 75–6, 117
   during French Revolution 183
   of women writers 135, 144, 146, 154

racism 6
Radcliffe, Ann 3, 35, 37, 144, 214–19, 222
Radcliffe, William 215, 217
readership 11, 12, 25, 86–7, 117
   expansion of reading public 28, 135
   for Hester Piozzi 174
Redford, Bruce 17, 58
regionalism, growth of British 207–8
religion
   attitudes to practice of 148, 169
   see also Roman Catholic Church, attitudes to
Remarks on the French and English Ladies (Andrews) 143, 150